Praise for *Mothers of Invention*

"This gathering of outstanding film and media scholars and makers demonstrates how becoming and recognizing mothers—quite literally the oldest job in the world—has changed and challenged their work. Here the fusion of their personal experience, art-making, and scholarship breathes new life into disciplinary methods."

—Amelie Hastie, author of *Cupboards of Curiosity: Women, Recollection, and Film History*

"What a timely collection on parenting, caregiving—and especially mothering—in film and media cultures. Contributors examine not just representations of motherhood and maternity onscreen but working conditions for mothers and caregivers in media industries, mothering as a form of media labor and media consumption, and the radical possibilities of feminized caregiving on set, in the classroom, and at home."

—Shelley Stamp, author of *Movie-Struck Girls* and *Lois Weber in Early Hollywood*

"Never has the media industry been in greater need of attention. In *Mothers of Invention*, Mayer and Columpar approach this challenge—with care. They propose a refocused media scholarship that turns the spotlight from longstanding discourses of innovation to reveal the foundational underpinnings of the industry: labours of caregiving. This wide-ranging collection of essays effortlessly models what it means to care, and the manifold benefits of caring about care, carers, and caregiving in global audiovisual industries."

—Deb Verhoeven, Canada 150 Research Chair, University of Alberta

Mothers of Invention

Contemporary Approaches to Film and Media Series

A complete listing of the books in this series can
be found online at wsupress.wayne.edu.

Mothers of Invention

FILM, MEDIA, AND CAREGIVING LABOR

Edited by
SO MAYER *and*
CORINN COLUMPAR

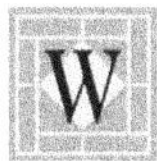

WAYNE STATE UNIVERSITY PRESS
DETROIT

ISBN (paperback): 978-0-8143-4852-9
ISBN (hardcover): 978-0-8143-4853-6
ISBN (e-book): 978-0-8143-4854-3

Library of Congress Control Number: 2021943124

On cover: Agnès and Rosalie Varda on the set of *Cléo from 5 to 7* (1961), a film by Agnès Varda. Photograph by Liliane de Kermadec. © Ciné-Tamaris. Cover design by Will Brown.

Wayne State University Press rests on Waawiyaataanong, also referred to as Detroit, the ancestral and contemporary homeland of the Three Fires Confederacy. These sovereign lands were granted by the Ojibwe, Odawa, Potawatomi, and Wyandot nations, in 1807, through the Treaty of Detroit. Wayne State University Press affirms Indigenous sovereignty and honors all tribes with a connection to Detroit. With our Native neighbors, the press works to advance educational equity and promote a better future for the earth and all people.

Wayne State University Press
Leonard N. Simons Building
4809 Woodward Avenue
Detroit, Michigan 48201-1309

Visit us online at wsupress.wayne.edu.

For the beloveds who are helping us learn about caregiving:
Freddie, Issy, and Mollie on one side of the pond,
and Daniel and Harper on the other

Contents

II.
Aesthetics of Maternity

III.
Forms of Collectivity

IV.
Alternate Genealogies

Acknowledgments

We would like to thank the following people: our acquisitions editor, Marie Sweetman, and series editor, Barry Keith Grant, both of whom supported this project enthusiastically and recognized its historical urgency; all the other people at Wayne State University Press, especially Carrie Downes Teefey, Robin DuBlanc, Emily Nowak, and Kristina Stonehill, who were not only proficient and attentive but a joy to work with; our two anonymous peer reviewers, who agreed to read our manuscript in the midst of a pandemic and their own working practices, and whose endorsement stoked our belief in the project and our excitement in reaching an audience; the Raising Films family, including its many research contributors, crowdfunders, collaborators, and community, and the faculty, staff, and students at the University of Toronto's Cinema Studies Institute, all of whom provided institutional and moral support; Cine-Tamaris, whose lead archivist, Sherine El Sayed Taih, dug deep in the archives for our stunning cover image; and finally, our contributors, whose insightful, innovative, and careful work has been a source of ongoing inspiration.

Introduction

So Mayer and Corinn Columpar

Pandemic as Preface

As we complete this introduction to *Mothers of Invention: Film, Media, and Caregiving Labor*, the world is navigating the COVID-19 pandemic, and both of us live in countries—the United Kingdom for So and Canada for Corinn—that are in the fourth month of a quarantine conditioned by stay-at-home orders and social-distancing protocols. We begin our work with this expository note as a way of acknowledging both the magnitude and the uncertainty of our current historical moment and, by extension, the radically shifting ground on which we suddenly find ourselves as feminist critics and as editors of a book that is midway through a multiyear production process. Yet as much as things change, they also stay the same when it comes to a key topic in *Mothers of Invention*: the demands of caregiving, particularly parenting. Indeed, multiple realities that this volume explicitly addresses not only persist right now but are being thrown into starkly fresh relief as parents and other caregivers dedicate themselves to acts of care during a quarantine. As a result, even though most of the essays that comprise *Mothers of Invention* were written in the era before COVID-19, they add up to an anthology that in both content and spirit speaks volumes to our present moment—and likely far beyond.

The unprecedented workload of COVID-19 caring, including the supervision of remote learning, and the toll it is taking led pediatrician Robin C. Williams and child psychologist Jean Clinton to title their recent opinion piece in the *Globe and Mail* "The Parents Are Not Okay."[1] Yet that headline is misleading: many studies highlight the ways that the pandemic has further entrenched the highly significant gender gap in caregiving labor. Its systemic nature is visible both in sharply rising unemployment rates among women, especially women of color, leading some researchers to describe the economic fallout of COVID-19 as a "shecession" disproportionately affecting Black working mothers; and in the finding that women who continue to work are experiencing a much more severe decrease in their productivity and/or increase in their precarity than men.[2] One of the primary reasons for this trend among working women is the fact that they typically take on more caregiving activity in individual family units still dominated by Euro-Western heteronormative models, making for a situation in which mothers, especially, are not okay.

More than three decades after sociologist Arlie Hochschild, with Anne Machung, famously identified working women's "second shift," the inequitable division of domestic labor that term names, along with the ideological forces undergirding it, has changed very little: as Moira Donegan writes in the midst of the pandemic, "Everyone has a public health obligation to stay home, but only women have a socially enforced responsibility to take on disproportionate domestic work while they are there."[3] What has changed, however, is the documentation of this double standard and its myriad effects: both UNESCO and the Canadian-based organization ALIGN have created online archives that are collating articles on COVID-19 and gender, many of which are dedicated to the disproportionate care burden that women tend to shoulder.[4] Brimming with anecdotal and empirical evidence, these materials detail the extent to which women's "second shift" has become even more taxing than usual—in all parts of the world and by workers in "essential" and "nonessential" sectors alike. A large-scale study of thirty-five hundred families with two opposite-gender parents in England undertaken between April 29 and May 15, 2020 by the United Kingdom's Institute for Fiscal Studies offered two startling and significant findings.[5] First, while fathers are currently spending roughly twice the amount of time on childcare and housework than they did in 2014–15, working mothers are still spending significantly more time on such unpaid domestic labor. Second, on average, working women are completing one hour of uninterrupted paid work for every three completed by their male partners. Taken together, these statistics reveal a sizeable gender gap in terms of how working parents are dividing their time among competing demands in the time of COVID-19. We cannot yet know what the full effect of this gap will be once things return to relative normalcy, but given the extent to which future prospects typically depend on past performance in professional contexts, it is likely that women will be severely disadvantaged in the coming years.[6] For this reason Donegan concludes: "[The post-pandemic world] could mean the loss of what feminists have been fighting for: women's freedom from the domestic sphere, freedom from financial dependence on men and freedom to access public life."[7]

As worrying as this speculation is, Donegan's use of the word *could* is significant, for it suggests that an alternate future is not foreclosed. After all, there is arguably more public discussion of caregiving labor—its value, demands, rewards, and gendered nature—in the midst of the COVID-19 pandemic than there ever has been previously, and as a result many aspects of it are being laid bare. As Tithi Bhattacharya notes, "The coronavirus crisis . . . has clarified what social reproduction feminists have been saying for a while, which is that care work and life-making work are the essential work of society."[8] The question now is what to do in light of such clarification. How can we parlay a renewed, or even newfound, awareness into critique and, in turn, change? Ironically, this difficult period is an ideal time to contemplate such questions since it is, in the words of Kim Stanley Robinson, allowing us to "[learn] our way into a new structure of feeling."[9] Insofar as this structure of feeling holds in tension paradoxical phenomena—alienation and solidarity, dread and hope, grief and reinvention—it allows us to imagine the previously unimaginable, to think an alternative to our all-too-familiar status quo. In other words, it allows us to enter into a project that is central not only to the genre of science fiction, as Robinson notes, but also to that of feminist criticism.

With *Mothers of Invention* we both build on and extend that genre, specifically within the context of film and media studies, in order to think carefully, critically, and creatively about both the "new normal" taking shape and the old normal in its various forms. In considering the role that parenting, as both a theme and a diversified practice, plays in film and media cultures, the volume brings together film and media studies with parenting studies in order to stake out a field, or at least a conversation, that is thick with historical and theoretical dimension and invested in cultural and methodological plurality. In the process it acknowledges a wide variety of caregiving acts and practices, but with particular emphasis on the labor of mothers, since those who identify as female have historically been and, as the pandemic has made abundantly clear, continue to be disproportionately responsible for matters both domestic and familial. It simultaneously acknowledges that it is among mothers that the process of rethinking "life-making work," foregrounded by the current crisis, has already begun.

From Crisis to Critique

In 2019 Jennifer Lee, co-director of *Frozen* (2013) and *Frozen 2* (2019) as well as chief creative officer of Walt Disney Animation Studios, discussed her status as a working mother during a Q&A at the London premiere of *Frozen 2*. After her directing partner, Chris Buck, praised her impressive "juggling" skills, she noted, "That's what mothers do," and then thanked her daughter for "teaching her how to handle multiple things at once."[10] With this comment, Lee joined a small chorus of women in the film and television industries, including Jocelyn Moorhouse, Marielle Heller, and Greta Gerwig, who have recently talked about their status as working mothers, thus drawing attention to the challenges that bely the liberal feminist aspiration of "having it all." At the same time, Lee's comment also normalizes those challenges and, moreover, invokes a model of "Lean In" motherhood, in which parenting is valuable primarily for the workplace skills it confers, thereby suggesting that even if the taboo on being simultaneously a primary caregiver and A-list filmmaker has been broken, capitalist and patriarchal assumptions about the relative value of those two forms of labor remain.[11] The net effect is a sense of Lee as, paradoxically, both an ordinary mother and an exceptional woman who has managed to achieve tremendous power and prominence in an industry that is not cut to the measure of her desire—or her needs.

As important as individual testimonies and isolated success stories are for making visible the experience of women, or any caregivers, who are regularly working "second shifts," it is a handful of grassroots organizations that are collating the experiences of caregivers in the film and media industries—those in both above- and below-the-line positions—in order to analyze and attempt to redress the structural and systemic inequalities that determine those experiences. The most well-established and active of those organizations is Raising Films, founded in the United Kingdom in 2015 by five film industry workers, four mothers and one non-parent, which has subsequently formed branches in Australia and Ireland. (Branches in Canada and New Zealand are currently under consideration.) Drawing on the community knowledge and needs of parents and carers both in, and excluded from, the screen sector, Raising Films campaigns to change working practices across that field. This work has multiple implications for film and media scholars as well as practitioners: not only does the data produced by Raising Films include scholars as both researchers and subjects facing similar pressures and exclusions, it also highlights what film and media studies has to gain from attending to labor practices in production and exhibition. Indeed, it amplifies something that the reportage around Harvey Weinstein's criminal abuse of women workers has shown: researching and bearing witness to the unequal conditions in which mainstream film and television are made, exhibited, and distributed must inform our work as feminist scholars. In light of this imperative, Raising Films plays a significant role in this volume. One co-editor (So) is a co-founder of the organization, and the first two essays in the volume discuss its research findings and ongoing work, thereby setting the stage for a volume that foregrounds the relationship between parenting and participation in film and media culture, be it through the lens of industry analysis, ethnographic research, production histories, and/or personal reflection.

Insofar as *Mothers of Invention* pursues this line of discussion, it does so in order to inform and form relations with issues that are far more central to existing work on motherhood in film and media studies: namely, representation and spectatorship. In other words, Raising Films' advocacy work matters because it connects to and contextualizes the important foundations laid by key scholars in the field. The most notable of those are E. Ann Kaplan, who published *Motherhood and Representation: The Mother in Popular Culture and Melodrama* in 1992, and Lucy Fischer, whose *Cinematernity: Film, Motherhood, Genre* appeared four years later.[12] Both analyzed popular cinema in order to discuss, as Fischer puts it, "the mother's status as a figure" in various kinds of film and media.[13] While one could imagine this pair of texts laying the foundation for a veritable subfield in film and media studies, the lines of inquiry they initiated have instead been taken up in fits and starts and within the context of other subfields. One such subfield is the study of certain genre traditions, especially melodrama, science fiction, and horror, to which psychoanalytically inclined scholars such as Christine Gledhill, Mary Ann Doane, Constance Penley, Barbara Creed and, most recently, Sarah Arnold have contributed.[14] Another is the study of certain national cinemas, including those of Poland, Mexico,

Italy, and the United States, where the figure of the mother is read as and/or against the nation-state.[15]

The work invoked above is instructive in the way it recognizes motherhood and its representation as historically and socially contingent within generic or national frameworks. *Mothers of Invention* is similarly concerned with motherhood, and caregiving more broadly, as a variegated practice—one that, moreover, takes shape within the politics of class, race, and sexuality that perpetuate social asymmetries. As a result, it takes on the topic of parenting in a broad range of film and media texts with global reach. Yet despite this diversity, the volume is nonetheless an incomplete representation of the inequalities attendant on caregiving labor and its devaluation. Aware of this, we intend this selective collection to be the entrance to a larger conversation about caregiving labor in audiovisual media and its scholarship that takes into account questions that it begs but does not necessarily answer—questions related, for example, to certain types of caregiving, such as disabled, elder, and foster care; to certain radical parenting theories and practices, including some that have long emerged from communities of color; or to the whole industry of professional caregiving and it attendant politics of race, class, and gender. Moreover, we intend to help frame that larger conversation in a manner that recognizes how very political the intersection between media and parenting can be, something that Hepi Mita captures in such resonant terms when describing the work of his mother, Māori filmmaker Merata Mita. In the concluding voice-over of his documentary *Merata: How Mum Decolonised the Screen* (2018), he states unequivocally, "Only a mother could have done the things she did. . . . It wasn't money or power or war that decolonised the screen. It was a mother's love."

Technologies and Transformations

Following the lead of Lisa Baraitser, a key scholar of mothering and/as creative labor, *Mothers of Invention* employs a capacious understanding of the term *mother*: "anyone who both identifies as female and performs primary maternal work, with a 'child' being understood as the other whom such a 'mother' elects, names and claims as her child."[16] As a result, the collection takes into consideration a wide array of mothers and parents—biological and adopted, cisgendered and trans, literal and symbolic—in pointed refusal of an essentialist understanding of motherhood or the conservative politics that such an understanding often undergirds. This breadth is a direct result of the many nationalities, racializations, classes, sexualities, and gender identities of not only the volume's subjects but also its contributors, who hail from multiple continents, have varying levels of seniority, and occupy different positions within the academy and/or the creative industries.

With so many writers coming to the topic of caregiving in the context of film and media studies, each from their own intellectual and professional vantage, each with their own sense of personal and political stakes, *Mothers of Invention* frames its object of study in a manner that is dynamic, engaging, and relevant to a wide array of audiences—not just to those readers who readily identify as mothers. In *Revolutionary Mothering: Love on the Front Lines*, Alexis Pauline Gumbs asks: "What would it mean for us to take the word 'mother' . . . as a possible action, a technology of transformation?"[17] Our contributors highlight the necessary ways in which mothering, as radical caring labor, can actualize what is often obscured or suppressed: the transformative potential of audiovisual technologies.

The first section of the volume, titled "Working Parents," examines the work lives of parents in the film and media industries, paying particular attention to the systemic inequalities that working mothers face by virtue of their dual status as caretakers and women. Both the Raising Films Research Collective's and Susan Berridge's essays use as a jumping-off point *Making It Possible*, a report published in 2016 by Raising Films that examines labor conditions for parents and caregivers in the UK film and television industries. In "Messy Play: Privileging Anec-Data and Messy Research Practice to Understand Creative Working Lives," the collective analyzes the impetus and process for grassroots campaigners undertaking qualitative and quantitative research around caregiving workers in the screen sector, framed through the shared "messiness" of feminist scholarship and lived experience. The chapter unpacks Raising Films' participatory research strategies and excerpts *Making It Possible*'s key points alongside those of *Raising Our Game* (2017), a review of employment practices and legislation in the UK context, and *We Need to Talk about Caring* (2019), the first-ever report on carers in the UK screen sector. Berridge, in turn, fleshes out the specific challenges that working parents in the UK creative industries face, especially in relation to work/life balance, in "Managing Feelings: Raising Films' Testimonials and the Impact of Caring Responsibilities on the Emotional Well-being of Mothers Who Work in the UK Film and Television Sector." Analyzing the testimonials collected in and around the Raising Films reports, Berridge contrasts them with institutional, often statistically based, discourses that omit the affective aspects of caring labor in order to identify why and how those absences matter.

Recentering the affective within film culture via mothering, the second pair of essays in this section feature filmmakers and film and media scholars reflecting on the ways their parenting activities and their vocations influence each other. In the co-authored dialogue "How to Do Everything: A Conversation between Filmmakers," Kristy Guevara-Flanagan and Irene Lusztig, two American mother-filmmaker-scholars discuss the ways the role of parent that they both occupy shapes their respective creative practices, from the production of their documentary work to the circumstances of its distribution and exhibition. Highlighting the centrality of improvisation, in the dual sense of expedience and camaraderie, they demonstrate how the practical and theoretical requirements of parenting on the one hand and feminist film production on the other necessarily inform each other as both ethics and aesthetics. In "Watching while a Mother: Parenting, Spectatorship, Criticism," Claire Perkins uses—and fuses—critical parenting studies, queer theory, and film theory to frame her ethnographic research with film and media scholars and to reflect on the ways parenting affects one's identity as a viewing subject and one's output as a professional critic. Among the topics that she and her subjects discuss are the cascading effects of lived experiences and daily exigencies on one's cultural tastes, spectatorial position, affective engagement, communal affiliations, and scholarly endeavors.

Picking up where Perkins's work leaves off, the volume's second section, "Aesthetics of Maternity," begins with an essay that makes clear that parenting can radically change the way one sees: in "Visualizing with New Comprehension: Mothering and Autoethnography," Rashna Wadia Richards takes as her point of departure Margaret Mead's proposition that motherhood endows women with the capacity to see "with new comprehension." Examining the ways that the work of mothering is akin to that of a cultural anthropologist, she proposes an emergent maternal anthropology that includes not only a conventional documentary, *The Anthropologist* (Seth Kramer, Daniel A. Miller, and Jeremy Newberger, 2015), but also parenting blogs and social media platforms that engage practices of participant observation.

The vantage of the participant observer as well as its capacity to engage the viewer-scholar are also central to the remaining three essays in this section, all of which foreground the highly personal and self-reflexive work of certain international auteures working on the margins of commercial film and media industries. In "'You Have Absolutely No Control over Your Mind and Body Anymore': Pregnancy, Autonomy, and Prepartum Anxiety in Alice Lowe's *Prevenge*," Alice Haylett Bryan foregrounds questions of maternal mental health as she entwines a close reading of Lowe's British horror-comedy from 2016 with an account of her own pregnancy and postpartum anxiety. Her discussion culminates in a considered address of the Kristevan abject as a figure that can be mobilized to explore *Prevenge*'s representation of an extreme experience of pregnancy-related depression, one that has the potential to refract the experience of filmmaker and viewer alike. In "Pregnant Situations in Agnès Varda's and Anne Claire Poirier's Film Creations," Tessa Ashlin Nunn uses feminist phenomenology and affect theory to discuss the way pregnancy is made palpably material in two Francophone proto-feminist films, Varda's *L'Opéra-Mouffe* (1958) and Poirier's *De mère en fille* (1968). Insofar as both Varda and Poirier strategically incorporate their own pregnant bodies and experiences into their work, they shed light on the phenomenology of pregnancy and prompt Nunn to theorize links between the acts of creating cinema and creating life, as well as the ways film can engage viewers to think through their own relationship to acts of (re)production. Last, in a discussion that looks across a range of nonstandard reproductive representations, including surrogacy, adoption, phantom pregnancies, and teen pregnancies, Missy Molloy turns her attention to Jane Campion's recent foray into television in "Fetal Imagery and Alternative Maternities in Jane Campion's *Top of the Lake*." Specifically, she reads the series' second season, "China Girl" (2017), as a culmination of two of Campion's career-long foci: masochism and the passionately ambivalent mother-daughter bond as one of its most haunting permutations.

While the first two sections of *Mothers of Invention* are centrally concerned with literal mothers (factual or fictional) and the material realities of their individual experiences, the last two sections broaden the volume's discussion of motherhood to encompass the figurative, symbolic, and collective possibilities of motherhood as well. In the third section, "Forms of Collectivity," these possibilities involve, among other things, the extension of caregiving practices beyond the family unit. For Sara Saljoughi and

Corinn Columpar, it is a particular text that charts this course. In "Crow, Child, Stranger: Radical Mothering in *Bashu*," Saljoughi examines *Bashu, Gharib-e Kuchak / Bashu, the Little Stranger* (Bahram Beyzai, 1986), one of the most significant films of the Iran-Iraq war, in order to explore its representation of not only an adoptive mother and son but also a larger community bound by reciprocal and negotiated care. Arguing for a politically potent extension of maternity beyond the dyadic, Saljoughi posits a recuperative scenario that both disentangles caring labor from biological essentialisms and offers a radical form of ethics running counter to capitalist productivity and nationalist/militarist histories. Columpar, in contrast, turns her attention to a televisual text in "Confessions of an Aca-Fan-Mom: *Jane the Virgin*, Motherhood, and Community." Therein she discusses *Jane the Virgin* (2014–19), Jennie Snyder Urman's American adaptation of a Venezuelan telenovela, in order to posit a conjunction between Henry Jenkins's notion of the aca-fan (that is, a hybrid of scholar and fan) and the maternal spectator. Paying particular attention to the viewing practices and fan cultures that this transnational televisual text represents and in turn produces, Columpar argues that *Jane the Virgin* creates a maternal community that is defined by difference and resistance to the isolating logic of neoliberalism, which shapes the lives of so many contemporary mothers.

Collective practices of care are at the center of the remaining essays in this section. Elissa Rashkin's "Obstetric Violence and the Creative Exploration of Alternatives in Guadalupe Sánchez Sosa's *La primera sonrisa*" takes as its focus an approach to maternal care and obstetrics that is rooted in Indigenous culture. In considering both the innovative formal strategies of Sosa's 2014 documentary about that approach and the film's distribution in grassroots, health, and educational spaces within its national context of Mexico, Rashkin offers a complete account of the film as extending the affective and effective languages of transnational feminist cinema aesthetically and politically. In "'We Insist on This Project of Life': A Conversation with Loira Limbal," film programmer Maria Cabrera interviews filmmaker and organizer Limbal, whose feature-length documentary *Through the Night* (2020) focuses on a twenty-four-hour daycare in New Rochelle, New York. Reflecting on the daycare's, and the film's, various acts of community building, Cabrera and Limbal take up issues raised by the rise of "extreme daycare": the lack of structural support for caregiving, particularly among Black, brown, immigrant, and working-class communities in the United States; the transformative possibilities of vulnerability as an aesthetics located in the mutual impact of filmmaking and caregiving on each other; and the challenges for both artists and caregivers in the midst of COVID-19.

Like "Forms of Collectivity," the volume's fourth and final section, "Alternate Genealogies," is also interested in formulating mothering as radical resistance to isolation through the extension of caregiving practices beyond the family unit, but what is of particular interest in this section is the way this creates connections to dislocated pasts and, in turn, affirms the possibility of feminist futures. In "From (An)other Mother: Maternal Genealogies and Experimental Film History," Elinor Cleghorn situates her personal history as a scholar and mother in relation to her wide array of "symbolic mothers," in Teresa de Lauretis's phrase—including feminist filmmakers, critics, theorists, historians, and programmers—in order to propose a maternal genealogy of experimental film culture. With this new way of engendering film history, she makes central the mothers of experimental cinema, their various film practices, and the intergenerational exchange they inspire. In "Mother-Storyteller," Jules Arita Koostachin suggests that such a historiographical strategy is necessary for a truly intersectional feminism that also decolonizes film histories when she places her work as a MoshKeKo AsKi Cree documentary filmmaker and mother in a historical context peopled by other Indigenous "mother-storytellers." Koostachin proposes that mother-storytellers—"experts in [their] own lives"—are leading an Indigenous resurgence by addressing intersectional oppression and erasure through an endeavor that shapes both form and function in filmmaking toward a truly transformative technology.

In this section's third essay, "Becoming A(p)parent: New (and Old) Ways of Making *A Deal with the Universe*," So Mayer proposes a parental cinema of radical anti-visibility practices that challenge Euro-Western rationalisms and realisms from within the body via *A Deal with the Universe* (2018), Jason Barker's first-person account of trans parenting. Drawing on Eliza Steinbock's theory of trans cinematic "shimmering images," Mayer connects the film's representation of pregnancy to a tradition of queer film and video practice that foregrounds performance, spirituality, and community as a form of giving care and a means of creating alternate family. Finally, rounding out this section, and the volume as a whole, is Kristi McKim's "On Sharing Films, Learning Care, Keeping Watch, and Finding," an essay that is equal parts lyrical autobiography and critical meditation on pedagogy. In particular, McKim examines the way that the study of film, in the context of both the university classroom and the familial home, constitutes an exercise in shared care, one that has the capacity to engender a mode of attentive engagement with the world and one another that "moves us through generations and histories."

Final Feelings

In *Motherhood and Representation*, Kaplan notes that prior to 1982, when she first conceived of her book, "few scholars had been interested in understanding [the mother's] positioning or her social role from *inside* the mother's discourse."[18] In addition to Kaplan, several other writers from both within and beyond academia have partially remedied this situation with personal and/or polemical work about mothering. Some of these writers—among them, Julia Kristeva, Iris Marion Young, Lee Edelman, Maggie Nelson, and Jacqueline Rose—are touchstones for our contributors: even when they are not present in citation, they are palpable in the volume's approach. The intimacy and complexity of parenting relations, and the slow emergence of an Anglophone literary, cinematic, and critical vocabulary for addressing them, are highlighted by how many of the essays, and the texts they address, take up a subjective analysis "from *inside*" parenting as a scholar and/or filmmaker, in strategies both reflective and rigorous.

In light of this, it is perhaps unsurprising that the most frequently cited author of all is Vivian Sobchack. While her work on film and phenomenology, particularly *Carnal Thoughts: Embodiment and Moving Image Culture*, may not be about motherhood or parenting per se, its ongoing play at, and with, the boundary between the subjective and the scholarly sets the tone for *Mothers of Invention*.[19] Insofar as Sobchack's work serves as precedent, *Mothers of Invention* shares ground with those texts that have precipitated the "affective turn" in cinema studies. Yet while many such works foreground processes that are variously described as unconscious, preconscious, or nonconscious, and account for those processes with reference to an abstracted ideal, be it that of a generic spectatorial body or a film's form, the contributors to this volume are more interested in feelings, in all of their embodied particularity. As Berridge's analysis of Raising Films' interviews and testimonials shows, feeling is exactly what is excluded from the screen sector and academic workplaces, which makes the ways that parent and carer professionals and scholars analyze their experience "from *inside*" all the more acute and significant. Their determination—sometimes at great cost—to articulate that which has been silenced as unacceptably messy and to represent, in various ways, acts of caregiving that have been invisibilized serves to extend feeling into film and media studies as a critical and political act, and even as a form of labor politics. In sum, *Mothers of Invention* attends to precarious forms of productive and reproductive labor that subtend larger ecological questions—those related to what Nancy Fraser called, in 2016, "capitalism's crisis of care"—and in so doing demonstrates that the discourse of parenting and caring is an intervention that challenges film and media studies to expand its discursive frameworks to address and redress current theoretical, political, and social debates about the interlinked futures of work and of the world.[20]

Much like the volume's vision of caregiving labor, the intended audience for this act of intervention is "broadly conceived." Whether acknowledged or not, caregiving labor enables every act of film and media making, and thus its characterization, examination, and recognition are potentially relevant to all creators, viewers, and scholars of screen media, including those who experience enmeshment in communities of care as well as those who do not—or do not do so knowingly. In offering a new lens for understanding the labor inherent in the production of film, video, television, new media, *and* their scholarship, *Mothers of Invention* not only contributes to labor studies, wherein creative industries are increasingly represented, but also offers insights to readers looking for parallels, precursors, and parent-pals. Indeed, during the time of writing and editing, this project has mapped a growing community, not only of parent-scholars and parent-filmmakers, of aca-fan-moms and caregiving curators, but also of scholars, makers, teachers, students, and audiences keen to engage with a breadth of rigorous interdisciplinary approaches that are centered by, and on, underexamined lived experiences. Just as mothering and caregiving are not niche skill sets or isolated practices, writing about mothering and caregiving models a form of scholarship that is collective in a dual sense: on the one hand collaborative, citational, and community building; and on the other ethically collating multiple approaches, histories, and practices within a robust framework that is accountable to the community from which it emerges. In "broadly conceiving" (of) our project and readership, we are working to make space for even more collective engagements to come and to ensure that the significance of caregiving in screen media, as well as the stakes of the crisis of care invoked above, do not disappear from view yet again.

Notes

1 Robin C. William and Jean Clinton, "The Parents Are Not Okay," *Globe and Mail*, May 13, 2020, www.theglobeandmail.com/opinion/article-the-parents-are-not-okay/.

2 Alisha Haridasani Gupta, "Why Some Women Call This Recession a Shecession," *New York Times*, updated May 13, 2020, www.nytimes.com/2020/05/09/us/unemployment-coronavirus-women.html; Elaine He and Nicole Torres, "Women Are Bearing the Brunt of the Covid-19 Economic Pain," *Bloomberg*, May 8, 2020, www.bloomberg.com/graphics/2020-opinion-coronavirus-gender-economic-impact-job-numbers/; Armine Yalnizyan, "COVID-19's Impact: Not Recession, but a Completely Different Economics," *Toronto Star*, April 9, 2020, www.thestar.com/opinion/contributors/2020/04/09/covid-19s-impact-not-recession-but-a-completely-different-economics.html; Christine Michel Carter, "New Research Shows How the Coronavirus Recession Is Disproportionately Affecting Black Working Mothers," *Forbes*, May 19, 2020, www.forbes.com/sites/christinecarter/2020/05/19/new-research-shows-how-the-coronavirus-recession-is-disproportionately-affecting-black-working-mothers/; Pregnant Then Screwed's survey of twenty thousand UK working mothers, "Childcare, Covid and Career: The True Scale of the Crisis Facing Working Mums," July 24, 2020, pregnantthenscrewed.com/childcare-covid-and-career/.

3 Arlie Hochschild with Anne Machung, *The Second Shift: Working Families and the Revolution at Home* (New York: Penguin Books, 2012); Moira Donegan, "This Pandemic Threatens to Undo What Generations of Feminists Have Fought For," *Guardian*, May 21, 2020, www.theguardian.com/commentisfree/2020/may/21/this-pandemic-threatens-to-undo-what-generations-of-feminists-have-fought-for.

4 UNESCO, Mapping of Online Articles on Covid-19 and Gender, April 21, 2020, en.unesco.org/news/mapping-online-articles-covid-19-and-gender; ALIGN, "Gender Norms and the Coronavirus," accessed June 29, 2020, www.alignplatform.org/gender-norms-and-coronavirus.

5 See Alison Andrew et al., *How Are Mothers and Fathers Balancing Work and Family under Lockdown?* (London: Institute for Fiscal Studies, 2020); Alexandra Topping, "Working Mothers Interrupted More Often Than Fathers in Lock-Down Study," *Guardian*, May 27, 2020, www.theguardian.com/world/2020/may/27/working-mothers-interrupted-more-often-than-fathers-in-lockdown-study.

6 In the time between drafting this introduction and sending it to press, multiple indicators have suggested that it is not just likely, but in fact certain. One such indicator is the World Economic Forum's *Global Gender Gap Report 2021*, which draws the following conclusion: "As the impact of the COVID-19 pandemic continues to be felt, closing the global gender gap has increased by a generation from 99.5 years to 135.6 years." World Economic Forum, "Pandemic Pushes Back Gender Parity by a Generation, Report Finds," March 31, 2021, www.weforum.org/press/2021/03/pandemic-pushes-back-gender-parity-by-a-generation-report-finds/.

7 Donegan, "This Pandemic Threatens."

8 Sarah Jaffe, "Social Reproduction and the Pandemic, with Tithi Bhattacharya," *Dissent*, April 2, 2020, www.dissentmagazine.org/online_articles/social-reproduction-and-the-pandemic-with-tithi-bhattacharya.

9 Kim Stanley Robinson, "The Coronavirus Is Rewriting Our Imaginations," *New Yorker*, May 1, 2020, www.newyorker.com/culture/annals-of-inquiry/the-coronavirus-and-our-future.

10 BFI, *"Frozen 2" Directors Jennifer Lee and Chris Buck/BFI Q&A*, YouTube video, November 27, 2019, youtu.be/8_wFFpMTx2o?t=1245.

11 Sheryl Sandberg, *Lean In: Women, Work, and the Will to Lead* (New York: Knopf, 2013).

12 E. Ann Kaplan, *Motherhood and Representation: The Mother in Popular Culture and Melodrama* (New York: Routledge, 1992); Lucy Fischer, *Cinematernity: Film, Motherhood, Genre* (Princeton, NJ: Princeton University Press, 1996).

13 Fischer, *Cinematernity*, 4.

14 Christine Gledhill, ed., *Home Is Where the Heart Is* (London: BFI, 1987); Mary Ann Doane, *The Desire to Desire: The Woman's Films of the 1940s* (Bloomington: Indiana University Press, 1987); Constance Penley, ed., *Close Encounters: Film, Feminism and Science Fiction* (Minneapolis:

Minnesota University Press, 1991); Barbara Creed, *The Monstrous-Feminine: Film, Feminism, Psychoanalysis* (London: Routledge, 1993); Sarah Arnold, *Maternal Horror Film: Melodrama and Motherhood* (London: Palgrave, 2013).

15 Ewa Mazierska and Elzbieta Ostrowska, *Women in Polish Cinema* (New York: Berghahn, 2006); Isabel Arredondo, *Motherhood in Mexican Cinema, 1941–1991: The Transformation of Femininity on Screen* (Jefferson NC: McFarland, 2014); Giovanna Faleschini Lerner and Maria Elena D'Amelio, eds., *Italian Motherhood on Screen* (London: Palgrave, 2017); Heather Addison, Mary-Kate Goodwin-Kelly, and Elaine Roth, eds., *Motherhood Misconceived: Representing the Maternal in US Films* (New York: State University of New York Press, 2009); Asma Sayed, ed., *Screening Motherhood in Contemporary World Cinema* (Bradford, ON: Demeter, 2016).

16 Lisa Baraitser, "Mothers Who Make Things Public," *Feminist Review* 93 (2009): 10.

17 Alexis Pauline Gumbs, "M/other Ourselves: A Black Queer Feminist Genealogy for Radical Mothering," in *Revolutionary Mothering: Love on the Front Lines*, ed. Alexis Pauline Gumbs, China Martens, and Mai'a Williams (Oakland, CA: PM, 2016), 23.

18 Kaplan, *Motherhood and Representation*, 3.

19 Vivian Sobchack, *Carnal Thoughts: Embodiment and Moving Image Culture* (Berkeley: University of California Press, 2004).

20 Sarah Leonard and Nancy Fraser, "Capitalism's Crisis of Care," *Dissent*, Fall 2016, www.dissentmagazine.org/article/nancy-fraser-interview-capitalism-crisis-of-care.

I

Working Parents

1

Messy Play

Privileging Anec-Data and Messy Research Practice to Understand Creative Working Lives

Raising Films Research Collective

Stories matter. Many stories matter. Stories have been used to dispossess and to malign, but stories can also be used to empower and to humanize. Stories can break the dignity of a people, but stories can also repair the broken dignity. . . . When we reject the single story, when we realize that there is never a single story about any place, we regain a kind of paradise.

—Chimamanda Ngozi Adichie, "The Danger of a Single Story," *TEDGlobal*, July 2009

British sociologist Bev Skeggs makes a claim for "messy" research in her book on feminist cultural theory. She highlights that although research is a "difficult, messy, fraught, emotional [and] tiring" process that is rarely shared, what we celebrate is the final clean project, the crisp findings clearly and objectively set out. And yet, much of feminist research practice comes from the personal, the emotional, the fraught, and the unjust. It is a place of discomfort.[1] In her recent book *Stigma: The Machinery of Inequality*, Imogen Tyler includes a story from "Stephanie," a single mother, educated teacher, and parent-carer, whose experience of the systematic abuse she had lived through in the British social care system had led her to carve words associated with stigma into her body using a razor blade. Tyler writes, "When I arrived home after my conversation with Stephanie, I lay down on my bed and wept for a long time."[2]

There is a history of pain and emotion related to feminist research practice. Theorist bell hooks writes in *Teaching to Transgress*, "I came to theory because I was hurting—the pain within me was so intense that I could not go on living. I came to theory desperate, wanting to comprehend—to grasp what was happening around and within me. Most importantly, I wanted to make the hurt go away. I saw in theory then a location for healing."[3] In feminist research practice we want to privilege the power that is present in the anecdotal story, but gathering testimonies and anecdotes of pain and injustice in order to present them in a way that they can be valued as objective research findings takes a certain amount of skill. The image of the lone researcher is not a healthy one for this model. Collective research practice enables a community to collaborate and share the responsibility of working with and from anecdotal data. This is not to prioritize the pain of the researchers over that of their participants, but to acknowledge that the power of listening to and documenting painful experiences enables researchers to reflect on their own messy narratives. It is to recognize and implement Chimamanda Ngozi Adichie's refusal of the single story as a feminist ethic, working "to empower and to humanize" the research process by thinking relationally and reflexively about how it is framed, especially when addressing painful experiences that have broken participants' dignity. The process of reflection makes us accountable for creating a space that can hold messy research practice in which plural narratives are held to "matter" *because* they reflect messy lived experience.

This chapter provides an insight into one particular messy research practice and how it stemmed from the value of anecdotal data, abbreviated as anec-data. Herein, we summarize the process of developing a series of research publications for the campaign and community organization Raising Films. Raising Films was founded in the United Kingdom in 2015 by a group of Britain-based screen sector workers who wanted to start a conversation about being a parent, a carer, and a filmmaker.[4] Informal conversations developed into a movement of voices all frustrated with the structural challenges and the absence of a collaborative, collective framework that sufficiently addressed their views. The network emerged at a time when scholarly research on the experiences and position of carers as creative workers was evolving in the United Kingdom from industry-led or academic sources, which contributed to an awareness of work-based inequality within academic circles and at gatekeeping levels of the industry but did not necessarily reach mainstream workers within the industry.[5]

Despite the growing body of evidence concerning the inequalities that shape the creative workforce, there was a crucial lack of satisfactory response that provided a roadmap for structural change. As the Raising Films founders state in their afterword to the first research publication, *Making It Possible*, "It became clear that to effect change, we needed to show how widespread and thoroughgoing the challenges are. And to do that, we needed data."[6] In response to this understanding, Raising Films created a network that brings together creative workers from across the UK screen sectors, academics interested in creative and cultural work, and activists engaged in raising awareness of the need for structural change to increase the opportunity for participation in the creative sector in a grassroots, solidarity-based collective. In this chapter we refer to the three research reports published by Raising Films and provide commentary on the process by which they were produced in order to make visible the network and its relationship with messy research practice.

Excerpts from the original research documents are included to illustrate the visual representation of the findings and the commitment to sharing positive, accessible data.[7] This chapter is credited to all who contributed to the research process, highlighting the collective labor required for messy research practice and also the positive and playful support network that collaboration fosters. It is our intention that the transparency of our approach can be adapted and reproduced by others, empowering them to create their own messy research collaborations, so we can foster and learn from the narratives that arise when stories are heard in all their multiplicity.

Making It Possible

Making It Possible was the first survey of parents in the UK film and television industries; unlike in surveys created by gatekeepers, its questions were developed through community dialogue.[8] Raising Films was founded from a conversation, and its research practice developed conversationally. The organization initially launched as Family Friendly Filmmaking, which led to some surprising responses from the United States; the founders changed the name to Raising Films in order to clarify that its campaigns and community

Afterword

We started Raising Films to have a conversation about being parent filmmakers. We soon heard that many of our colleagues were frustrated with the structural challenges they face, not least due to the high number of freelance contracts and the prevalent long hours culture in our industry. It became clear that to effect change, we needed to show how widespread and thoroughgoing the challenges are. And to do that, we needed data.

The data speaks to the actions the film and TV industry must take to serve its parent members better, and to increase their number. We will keep working with our partner organisations to address the equality, diversity and inclusion issues raised by their recent studies, in order to shape sustainable careers. Many are making it possible, despite challenges: respondents told us that these role models are a crucial inspiration, so Raising Films will continue to share their stories.

We know our greatest challenge is the wider context: a society that doesn't value the caring work that it relies upon. As filmmakers we make work within this society, but also have the power to change society through our work. It is essential, therefore, that the film industry aspires to the best possible practice, to make it possible for all our voices to be heard.

—— Nicky Bentham, Hope Dickson Leach, Laura Giles, Line Langebek, Jessica Levick, Sophie Mayer, Erin McElhinney, and Samantha Ward, Raising Films.

Call to Action

"There is an assumption that the industry can't change, and that parents need to find ways of participating full-time or not at all. Wanting to divide time between creative/work and parenting does not show lack of interest in or commitment to the industry." —— Female, freelance and part time development, Scotland, 45-64

We believe the industry can change, by committing to the following actions:

- **Enable financial assistance for child and elder care**
- **Encourage industry-wide adoption of flexible working and access to child and/or elder care**
- **Formalise a way to combat discrimination**
- **Normalise conversations around caring commitments with employers**

From our Partners

"This year has seen the publication of three key reports on the shocking lack of gender equality in our industry, from Directors UK, the European Women's Audiovisual Network, and the University of Southampton. There is no doubt that, in an increasingly casualised industry, having children is a career killer for women much more than for men. This timely report drills down into the practical problems faced by women and provides some excellent recommendations for the way ahead. This is essential reading for everyone interested in maximising the talent pool in our creative industries." —— *Kate Kinninmont MBE, CEO, Women in Film & Television (UK)*

"This important and timely piece of research makes it clear that financial provisions, whilst desperately needed, are not going to solve inequality in the film industry. Working practices must also change. Those who cannot or do not want to work excessive hours or full time must be understood as no less committed or capable. In 2016 the film industry can no longer expect workers to have someone else at home who can do the childcare, but must make it possible for parents, particularly mothers, to be involved in all aspects of filmmaking." —— *Dr Natalie Wreyford, "Calling the Shots", University of Southampton*

"Raising Film's report offers statistics to back up the anecdotes. It's the kind of crucial information that makes the issue that much harder to ignore. Yes, this is definitely happening, here and now. And not only the workers/carers lose out – so does the industry, on their skills, intelligence and life experience. The Raising Films report give us the hard and unpalatable facts in easy-to-digest form, but also practical and tenable suggestions as to how the situation could be improved." —— *Olivia Hetreed, President, Writers' Guild of Great Britain*

"Raising Films' Making it Possible Report makes an important and timely contribution to continuing research into gender inequalities in the film industry. It identifies not only the many challenges of care in this sector, but also several potential solutions, by gathering detailed responses directly from industry professionals across a range of roles, including those working in UK film production, exhibition and distribution." —— *Dr. Susan Berridge, Lecturer in Film and Media, Centre for Gender and Feminist Studies, University of Stirling*

"This research is proof that the future of the British film industry depends on our ability to embrace new ways of working. We must take the lead from other sectors that have identified workforce development as key to success, and find our own creative solutions. Imagine the diverse wealth of talent and experience if these barriers to work were removed?" —— *Cassie Raine, Parents in Performing Arts*

The closing page of the *Making It Possible* campaign report, designed by Samantha Ward, featuring the afterword and "Call to Action" by Raising Films' founders and endorsements from UK guilds and researchers.

would be focused on labor practices rather than censorship (although it took until 2019 to be able to change the Twitter handle from @FFFilmaking to @RaisingFilms). The website launched in May 2015 with testimonials from TV producer Naomi Wright; actor and screenwriter Tracy Brabin, who subsequently became Labour MP for Batley and Spen and is now the first woman to be a United Kingdom metro mayor, and a crucial advocate for working parents and the creative industries; and three founders: writer/director Hope Dickson Leach, writer Line Langebek, and producer Jessica Levick.[9]

Community engagement was driven on social media via the regular publication of testimonials by and interviews with parents working in film and television, including established practitioners such as filmmaker Susanne Bier, filmmaker Marie-Hélène Cousineau, actor Romola Garai, and actor and screenwriter Sarah Solemani. Solemani's affective blog post detailed continuing gendered inequality in parenting and went on record about the impact of motherhood on the creative self in the context of combining care with screen industry labor: "I have the perfect baby, with a freshly-baked biscuity smell, radiating joy and All That Is Good. When my arms become her cradle she sparks endorphins that buoy me beyond ecstasy. She is the most blessed of blessings, most miraculous of miracles. Only, why must I die because I have given her life? Why must I self-destroy so that she may grow?"[10] Her story inspired others to reach out, including filmmaker Beeban Kidron, who was awarded a life peerage in the United Kingdom's House of Lords as a result of creative work and activism.

In her interview, Baroness Kidron told a story that exemplified the culture of silence around parenting that Raising Films was formed to combat, saying she encountered "so-many-sexist-fucked-up-unacceptable-things-explicit-implicit and on occasion positively illegal. The most evocative of which is that I went into labor with my second child the day before the Director's Cut screening [of *Too Wong Foo, Thanks for Everything! Julie Newmar* (1995)]. My assistant asked the studio to delay for a couple of days—but they refused. At 4am I gave birth. At 11am I was at the screening. By 2pm I was back in hospital with my baby."

The founders were struck by what these transnational and intergenerational dialogues revealed: that while new articulations of work/life balance had apparently become possible in relation to changing rights legislation, any surface gains were being erased by austerity politics—while the underlying structural and systemic exclusions remained the same.[11] It was from this informal, impassioned anec-data that the impetus and structure of the survey arose.

In summer 2015, the founders' team ran a crowdfunder in order to create a paid project manager position to administrate the survey and develop a training program in relation to the findings; it then hired experienced project manager Laura Giles. From the outset, Raising Films' research processes reflected parent- and carer-friendly working practices: with a team dispersed from Glasgow in Scotland to Cornwall in the southwest of England, remote working, file sharing, and meetings via video call were used from the start, with built-in flexibility around caring needs. Planning and research tools included Skype and Dropbox, which featured Raisings Films on the Dropbox Business Blog on International Women's Day 2017 as an example of its #BeBoldForChange campaign for working practices toward a gender-inclusive world.[12]

Like the working practices, our research strategy was positioned as community- and solutions-oriented; for every frustration they noted, parent-filmmakers also shared creative responses and ideas for activism. The survey design was developed in response to issues and ideas that arose repeatedly across the testimonials and interviews, as well as those that emerged from community responses on social media, including asynchronously and informally to Facebook posts and in a number of planned, themed "post-bathtime and bedtime" Twitter hashtag chats. By meeting the parent-filmmaking community where they were—often already informally sharing everyday information about both parenting and work practices—Raising Films developed a form of informal participatory research that also enabled a wide reach for the survey distribution.[13]

The survey reached 640 participants over six weeks in spring 2016. Its headline figure revealed the stark truth: 79 percent—that is, 77 percent of female respondents and 50 percent of male respondents—reported that their caring role had a negative impact on their industry role. As the data analysts, Danielle Porter, Leah McCabe, and Kylie Grant from the Centre for Gender and Feminist Studies, University of Stirling, reported in their executive summary to the full report, "This survey reveals very clear barriers for parents and carers who work within film and TV, which do not only affect women, but continue to affect them disproportionately."[14] The survey was published in two forms: a compact four-page executive summary, distributed in print

MAKING IT POSSIBLE

THE PAID CHILDCARE LANDSCAPE

In addition to the suggested types of childcare, many parents report using paid pre- and post- school childcare (e.g. breakfast club, after school).

> "I am **sinking under the stress** of juggling childcare. I only see my children for one hour a day. This year I have worked one, if not two, weekend days every week, there is **no choice** not to.
>
> Female, 24-44, freelance/self-employed, producer, Greater London

The majority of respondents find it impossible or difficult to access flexible or adhoc childcare, with freelancers more likely to find this impossible (this may be suggestive of a greater need among freelancers for flexible childcare).

For those working as directors, all of those who reported it impossible to flex their childcare arrangements (14%) were freelance or self-employed, while simultaneously it was only freelance or self-employed directors who were who found it easy (14%). This supports what has been seen elsewhere, that freelancers may undertake more flexible work patterns, thus making it impossible to find childcare to match, or they have managed to source suitable childcare which suits their needs.

THE IMPACT OF CARING ON CAREER DEVELOPMENT

79% of respondents say their caring role has had a negative impact on their role within the industry.

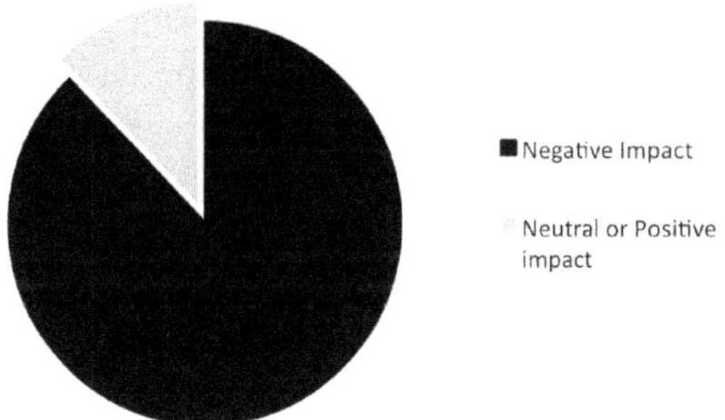

- Those who were employed part time were slightly more likely to report a strongly negative impact.
- Women (77%) were one-and-a-half times as likely to report a negative impact as men (50%)

40% of respondents said financial or in-kind assistance is **absolutely crucial** to performing their role in the industry, while 35% of respondents said it was somewhat important. Women were more likely than men to find assistance crucial or important.

This page from the full report of *Making It Possible*, designed by Samantha Ward and written by Laura Giles, shows the headline graphic of 79 percent of respondents reporting the negative impact of parenting and/or caring on their career in the screen sector.

at launch events, that included short texts by the data team, by filmmakers Jeanie Finlay and Steve Sheil (married parents of a teenager), by the founders, and by supporters; and a longer full report that presented all the data analysis undertaken by the Stirling team, with analysis written by Giles. Both included anonymous quotations from respondents taken from qualitative responses to survey questions, offering "thick descriptions" of the day-to-day experience of exclusion.

Late 2015 saw rising conversations in the United Kingdom about "unconscious bias" training as a cure-all for improving representation after The Geena Davis Institute on Gender in Media's symposium at that year's London Film Festival.[15] Yet *Making It Possible* demonstrated that, while embedded cultural narratives such as those around risk and reputation do play roles in hiring, systemic exclusion is in fact an issue of the labor practices that underpin perceptions of who is able to work consistently. For parents and carers, this included factors such as long working hours and weeks when shooting away from home; short-notice meetings, castings, and deadlines; and financial concerns around short-term freelance work. All of these concerns applied to workers across the sector, with the below-the-line union Bectu, the United Kingdom's Broadcasting Entertainment Communications and Theatre Union, campaigning concurrently to decrease on-set hours for all to increase safety and work/life balance, but they have been exacerbated for parents by a Conservative austerity politics that has eviscerated childcare provision.[16]

While legislative and sociopolitical change is needed, Porter, McCabe, and Grant did note that the survey reflected "a strong desire for cultural change within the industry to support these structural changes towards a more equal workplace."[17] In response to the survey, funder Creative Scotland redesigned its application for film funding to include additional support for accessibility and/or caring needs. This change represented the transformative potential of reframing the conversation by providing data that demonstrated that exclusion was endemic. Creative Scotland, along with Directors UK, funded the first round of Making It Possible training, which took place along with the report launch at the Edinburgh International Film Festival 2016 Screen Summit. The survey had launched earlier in the year at the Glasgow Film Festival, testament to the strength of festivals in the Scottish screen sector.

This became a key part of Raising Films' identity as an organization representing the entire United Kingdom, across all four nations (England,

Northern Ireland, Scotland, and Wales) and their regions, concerned with support for regional filmmaking and filmmakers. CLOSR, a training program and network designed to enable regional filmmakers to work closer to home, emerged responsively from the findings of our survey, which emphasized the ways in which London-centricity contributed to the exclusion of parents and carers from the sector. Both the festival events and the training programs, along with informal regular local meet-ups organized via Facebook, indicated the significance of face-to-face connection and information sharing alongside remote and digital working, and the need for a balance of both for work within the screen sector and research.

Making It Possible and CLOSR both became informal sites where anecdata was shared among participants, alongside invited speakers from our community, mentors, and experts; some participants subsequently went on to contribute testimonials to the website and/or to become mentors themselves, in a demonstration of Raising Films' communitarian, nonhierarchical practices.[18] As experienced filmmakers and life coaches, as well as legal and financial consultants, spoke and listened during the trainings, it became apparent that there was a pattern of poor employment practice that resonated with reports from the theater-based organization Parents and Carers in Performing Arts (PiPA), formed at the same time as both Raising Films and legal advisory service and campaigners Pregnant Then Screwed, founded by Joeli Brearley.[19] *Making It Possible*, both as a survey and the training it inspired, enabled the formulation of the next stage of research: a literature review looking at how employment legislation was being implemented across the sector, where cultural change might already be taking place within the industry, and what positive results could be demonstrated through case studies.

Raising Our Game

Following the results of the *Making It Possible* collaboration came a desire to involve participants in creating the research output. To develop the next research project, the organization decided to hold a one-day conference involving involving academics; industry organizations including the major broadcasters, distribution networks, studios, and unions; and independent industry professionals to produce the language and research that would inform the next publication. The aim was to bring participants and stakeholders from across the industry together and to co-produce questions and solutions from the community. This form of participatory research, established in health and social care studies, is a growing method within cultural and creative sociology, where the value of research participants in establishing the research questions is understood.[20] Recognizing the value of the participants within the research design, however, is an established practice within feminist and intersectional research.[21]

The "Raising Our Game" conference was hosted in February 2017 at Soho House in central London, funded by a grant received via the British Film Institute's (BFI) Diversity Fund.[22] The conference was attended by representatives from all major broadcasters—the British Broadcasting Corporation (BBC), Channel 4, ITV, and Sky—and from the sector's unions and guilds: Bectu, Equity, Directors' UK, Writers' Guild of Great Britain (WGGB), and Pact (the producers' guild). It also involved representatives from many major national organizations, including the government Department for Culture, Media and Sport (DCMS), the BFI, the British Council, BAFTA, ScreenSkills, Women in Film and Television (WFTV), Film London, the Independent Cinema Office, the Film and Television Charity (FTC), and Into Film, as well as production companies Pinewood, Film4, Bandit Television, Eon Films, FilmBath, and Dark Pictures.

The purpose was to bring people together to "engage industry influencers in discussing and developing practical solutions that could improve access, career development and employment sustainability for parents and carers in the film and TV industries."[23] We wanted to encourage sector-specific discussions of the advantages and disadvantages to increasing diversity and inclusion in the industry and of the barriers to achieving that increase. Attendees were divided into four breakout groups, and each group discussion was chaired by a Raising Films founder and attended by an independent academic researcher who took notes in order to reflect those findings back at the closing plenary. The four groups were divided across areas of engagement in the industry: support organizations, including unions, guilds, agents, charities, campaigning organizations, and individual talent; production companies and financiers across film and TV; representatives from guilds, standards, and schemes; and representatives from film exhibition and distribution. Delegates were invited to speak freely under the Chatham House Rule on anonymity and were reassured that their names would not be associated with the research findings.[24] Collaborative group discussions were transcribed, analyzed, and reflected on

To create change we needed to work out what the barriers to inclusion were. The first step in creating this report was a conference held at Soho House, 7 February 2017. We shared this worksheet with industry personnel and the responses to these key questions informed the development of this report and its industry checklists (see Section 7).

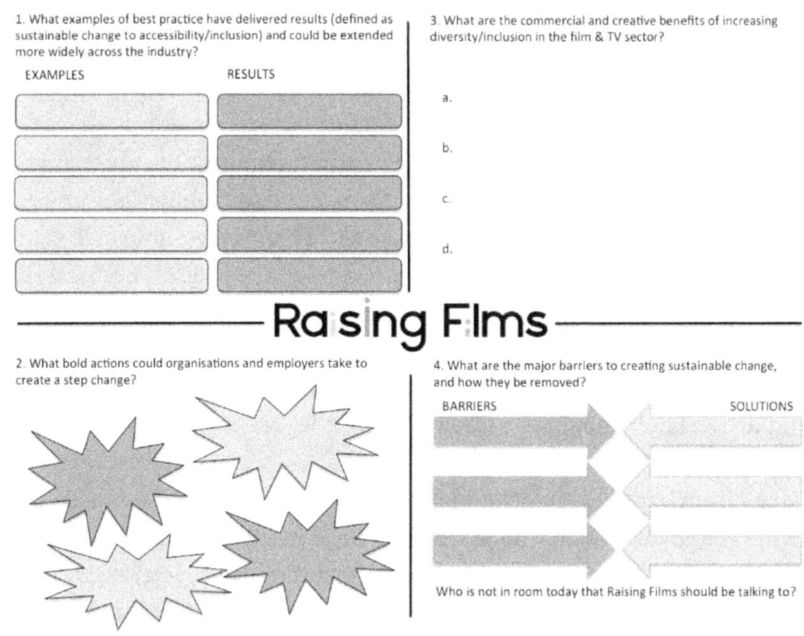

Raising Our Game conference worksheet, February 7, 2017

"Raising Our Game" conference worksheet, designed by Laura Giles, on the inside front cover of *Raising Our Game.*

by the independent researcher, and no material was attributed to a single individual.

Following the conference, the academic findings from the transcripts were shared, and that process of documentation and reflection resulted in a report titled *Raising Our Game*, written by Tamsyn Dent and So Mayer with contributions from the founders and Giles. We included a review of the literature on labor in the creative industries in the United Kingdom in order to establish a shared body of knowledge between the industry and researchers. In particular, we were motivated by learning of one particular piece of highly significant research that had been neglected and uncited. As the founders wrote in their foreword, "Our report builds on wide-ranging research into the causes and contributing factors to inequality and exclusion in the industry, including Reena Bhavnani's comprehensive 2007 review *Barriers to Diversity in Film*, commissioned by the UK Film Council and concluding with clear, actionable recommendations based on in-depth data. Bhavnani's decade-old review is still pressing today, and we dedicate our report to her work and memory."[25] To remedy the lack of a shared library, we created a public Dropbox folder containing the academic articles and reports cited in the research in order to democratize access.[26]

This enabled us to use these studies as a framework for summarizing the themes that emerged from the conference and to highlight the unusual status of good practices that challenged some of the themes. A notable theme that emerged from the conference discussion was that "there is a critical lack of HR (Human Resources) support and knowledge of the wider support legislation across the industry."[27] This was a key finding. We had assumed that as part of the skills-focused discussion there would be a level of engagement and understanding of basic UK employment legislation. The findings from the conference suggested that this was not the case, and that even representatives from large institutions and organizations had critical misconceptions of the employment framework. This finding was linked to a further reflection on language and discourse indicating that certain characteristics related to race or ethnicity were conflated with concepts of "risk," or that unlawful, discriminatory practices were conflated with "under-representation."[28]

The absence of knowledge about employment legislation and the income taxation system related to employment status is a widespread issue across the screen sector, affecting both individual workers and the institutions and corporations that engage their labor power. This finding enabled us to create a series of targeted recommendations as "checklists" that provided information at the individual and the institutional level, which we made available as printable single-page PDF files on the Raising Films website.[29] In order to incentivize the adoption of best practice, we used the report to showcase organizations whose understanding of good HR ensures that they provide a framework of employment that is lawfully fair, even when engaging with project-based laborers who have caregiving responsibilities. Interviews with such employers illustrated that it was possible to provide creative workers with adequate contracts and sufficient, fair pay, and to engage in an open, caring employment partnership that valued individual workers, not just for their economic impact but for the knowledge and skills they bring to their work. Highlighting good practice

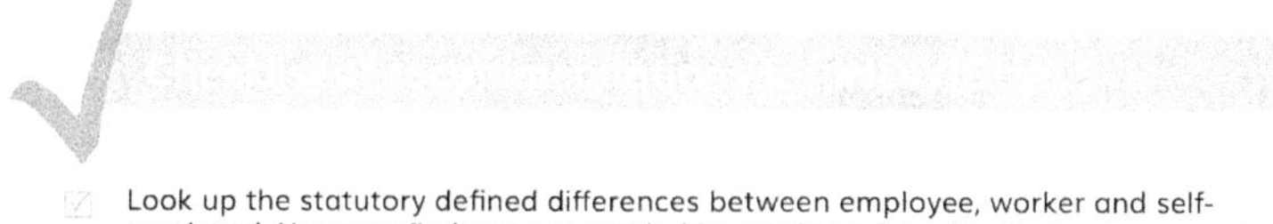

- Look up the statutory defined differences between employee, worker and self-employed. You may find you are entitled to employee benefits that you were not aware of: https://www.gov.uk/employment-status
- Join your union! If you do have an employment grievance and decide to make an independent claim to an employment tribunal (see below), your union can provide legal and financial support.
- If you feel you have been treated unfairly in the workplace or subjected to discrimination you can make an independent formal complaint to an employment tribunal. You must make this within three months of the incident taking place. The Citizens Advice Bureau provides a step-by-step guide including a link to the ET1 form needed to make a claim: https://www.citizensadvice.org.uk/work/problems-at-work/employment-tribunals/starting-an-employment-tribunal-claim/
- As well as through the unions and the Citizens Advice Bureau, individuals can seek guidance through the Acas helpline: http://www.acas.org.uk/index.aspx?articleid=2042
- Join support groups, guilds and networks including Raising Films and Women in Film and Television.
- Workers/employees: find out what financial support you can get for childcare through either the Child Tax Credit or a Childcare voucher scheme: https://www.gov.uk/help-with-childcare-costs.
- Self-employed workers can apply for tax-free childcare vouchers directly via HMRC. This currently applies to children who are aged under four on 31st August 2017 or who are disabled and under 17 years old. There are issues with this policy and, following wider criticism of the legislative framework (TUC 2017; Taylor 2017), we call for a review of this measure. However, if you are eligible you can apply to this scheme here: https://childcare-support.tax.service.gov.uk/
- Pregnant employees or on short term PAYE contracts have the right to ask their employer to act to protect their health and safety in the workplace and the right to reasonable, paid time off for antenatal care. They are also protected by the Equality Act against unfair treatment and unfair dismissal because of pregnancy.
- In recruitment, employers should not ask an individual if they are pregnant, if they are planning to have children or, if they have children, what their childcare arrangements are.

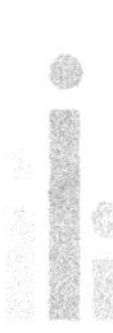

31

Checklist for individuals in *Raising Our Game*, designed by Samantha Ward.

provided an opportunity to showcase and illustrate how problematic languages and discourses within the screen sector labor market provide a smokescreen for the absence of knowledge and for discriminatory practices that have been able to thrive within the sector.

This was particularly apparent in a second theme that emerged from the conference: "training schemes and education have not effectively increased diversity."[30] This indicative finding correlates with wider contemporary criticism of the diversity and inclusion agenda within creative and cultural institutional spaces. Sociologists Sara Ahmed and Elaine Swan have argued that "doing diversity" has evolved into a performative term that invisibilizes the sexism, classism, and racism that have created the need for diversity.[31] Within this literature is the articulation of a distinction between "empowering" and "transforming" policy interventions into the diversity agenda in creative/cultural work, with the former referring to empowering "diverse" marginalized individuals to self-improve, and the latter referring to "transforming" interventions that actually tackle systemic exclusionary practices through targeted, challenging interventions.[32] There is a growing awareness in the academic community that empowering interventions such as training and mentoring schemes do not effect structural change and can in fact exacerbate inequality.

The failure of training schemes to challenge inequality effectively was recognized anecdotally at the conference. Our response was to highlight proactive "transforming" interventions that embed women within the labor force. Film London's pathbreaking returnship scheme, created by Nahrein Kemp, was a rare example of an embedded method that provided those with caring responsibilities the opportunity to work within the sector at their paid rate, rather than offering an unpaid or underpaid internship, shadowing or probationary experience, or even an expensive training scheme that could be accessed only by those with means.[33] The report also highlighted other transformative approaches, including the job-sharing platforms Further&More and Media Parents, two organizations designed to challenge and transform concepts around individualized working practices within the screen sector.[34]

Raising Our Game concluded with a series of recommendations targeted at each level of engagement: individuals, employers, institutions, and funding schemes. We wanted to create a space that would bring together our knowledge of employment law, including the available rights for caregivers,

They have worked in the financial sector, professional services, engineering, education, NGOs, and the legal profession; workforces with similarly demanding and dynamic working patterns and cultures to film and television. According to Allen:

"I haven't found anywhere yet where it doesn't work. The only line that we draw is that we don't do junior roles." Sara Allen

Their organisation is committed to matching up complementary job-sharing candidates, and we believe that – on this model – the industry can draw from their example and apply it to develop key creative job-sharing partnerships within the film and television sector.

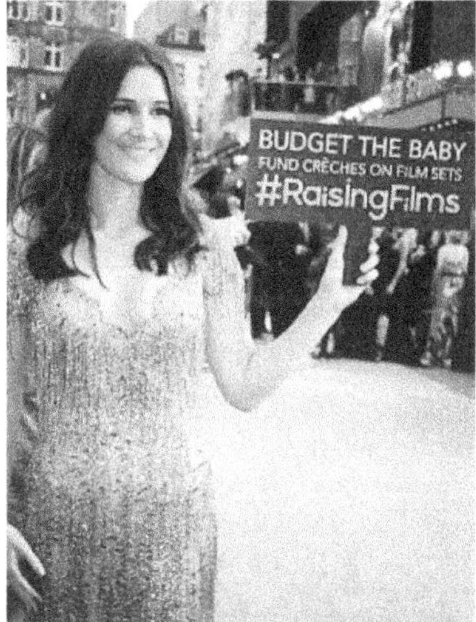

Sarah Solemani on the red carpet for the London premiere of *Bridget Jones' Baby* (2016), with a sign designed by Amy Merry. Photograph © Anna Solemani

As part of our research into good employment practice we want to showcase three female leaders, all of whom run their own companies within the film and television sector, and who have used their leadership to adopt lawful employment practice.

Kharmel Cochrane, Casting Director

Casting director Kharmel Cochrane set up her own company in 2012.[39] The company works across a range of creative content including film, television, advertising and music promos. Cochrane spoke of her commitment to good employment practice: her team are on fixed PAYE contracts; she ensures they work regular hours; and if there is a requirement to work overtime offers them time-off-in-lieu (TOIL).

"[Everyone] in the office is on PAYE which is a nightmare and it costs me a fortune but, you know, I can go to bed at night knowing that I'm not breaking the law." Kharmel Cochrane

As a casting director, she works with acting talent and recognises the hidden costs of finding work as an actor and how those costs act as a barrier to many who come from lower-income backgrounds. In recognition of this obstacle, her company often reimburses talent for their travel fees, and is open to parents bringing children to auditions if they cannot secure childcare. As Cochrane observed:

27 [39] http://kharmelcochrane.com/

Good employment practice in *Raising Our Game*, designed by Samantha Ward. The page includes a photograph of Sarah Solemani on the red carpet for the London premiere of *Bridget Jones' Baby* (Sharon Maguire, 2016) holding a sign, designed by Amy Merry, reading, "Budget the Baby: Fund Crèches on Film Sets. #RaisingFilms." (Photograph © Anna Solemani, 2016.)

in order to challenge some of the systemic myths and unjust working patterns that have evolved in the highly individualized, deregulated, profit-driven creative sector. We wanted to embed the value of the creative worker within the creative sector through a process of discussion, collaboration, attentive listening, and highlighting tangible examples of "good" employment practice. Creating the checklists showed the inadequacies of current employment legislation provision for both employees and freelancers, particularly when it comes to the complex lived needs of parents and carers. *Raising Our Game* became a motivation to ourselves to undertake more critical, challenging research that could lead to transformative interventions.

We Need to Talk about Caring

We Need to Talk about Caring emerged as a research project following communication from the Raising Films community that the measures put in place to support parents in the sector did not offer support for carers, who face distinctive barriers. To address that gap, the survey and hashtag #WeNeedToTalkAboutCaring were launched in March 2019. This project was a collaboration between Raising Films and the British national charity Carers UK. Carers UK provided consultation on the survey design and language as well as support with marketing and dissemination. The survey design was aimed at gathering detailed information on the relationship between care and screen labor. Two surveys were launched, one targeted at those who defined themselves as "carers" working in the industry, and another targeted at those creative screen workers who require care.

The definition of *carer* for the purpose of the two surveys was taken from the Carers UK framework—the term relates to anyone, including a child, who cares (unpaid) for a family member or a friend who, due to illness, disability, a mental health problem, or an addiction, cannot cope without their support.[35] In keeping with our messy agenda, we acknowledge that the current British concept of the term is not directly translatable to other historical moments, geographical contexts, or languages, but the increased demand for unpaid caring support as a result of financial pressures on central economies, coupled with a growing elderly population, is a global issue.

It is estimated that unpaid carers contribute £132 billion per year to the UK economy, which is more than the gross value of the entire creative industry.[36] Yet, as emerged from the Raising Films community, care and care labor are consistently misunderstood, unsupported, unrecognized, and undervalued, both as economic contributors and as activities more broadly. In the United Kingdom, state, social, and community care provision has been subject to a range of funding cuts and forced privatization.[37] This has left many paid care workers in a particularly precarious labor market and many local councils without sufficient funding to meet growing care needs. Lydia Hayes coined the term "institutionalized humiliation" to define the devaluation of paid carers within the United Kingdom.[38] As such, a focus on the distinctive relationship between care and creative work was a necessary research need.

Accessing data was a complicated process. As discussed, being an officially defined "carer" is distinct from being a parent, although Carers UK applies the term "sandwich carer" to define those who have both parenting and caring responsibilities. Actor and writer/director Kate Hardie wrote about being a sandwich carer for a teenager and an aging parent in her Raising Films testimonial in August 2015, describing a scenario that the Raising Films community reports as increasingly common: "Just as my son got his place at university my 83 year old mother had a fall. . . . Overnight she went from being a pretty able-bodied, active, independent woman to not being able to walk unaided. Her whole life turned upside down."[39] In the same month, also as part of an inaugural round of testimonials used by Raising Films to drive their first crowdfunder, producer Stevie Lee wrote a testimonial about being a parent with additional caring responsibilities due to a child's disability. Writing that "my children, especially my son, who can't be cared for by many people at all, simply don't stick to a schedule firmly enough to allow me to be at work in an office every day of the week," Lee drew attention to the additional impact of a lack of flexible and remote working on parents of disabled children.[40] Raising Films had thus included and represented sandwich carers and parent-carers within their community from its inception, and it was their voices, which offered grounds for solidarity between parents and carers, that shaped the research project.

We wanted to gather both a breadth and depth of data to identify situated experiences of care and creative work and to thematically examine patterns and emergent findings from within the data. The survey had a total of fifty-eight questions, including detailed demographic information in relation to age, ethnicity, country of origin, regional location, sexuality,

Survey Profile

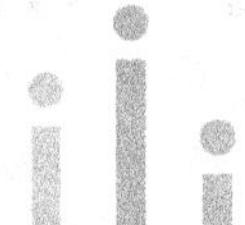

Sexuality

17% of respondents within our survey identified their sexuality as lesbian, gay, bisexual or other. 12% of women identified as lesbian or bisexual, and 29% of men identified as gay. Of those stating their gender as other, 1 stated they were heterosexual, 2 bisexual and 1 other.

Creative Skillset (2014) found that 7% of the creative media workforce identify as LGBTQ+, a slightly higher proportion than within the UK population of between 5-7% (based on estimates by the UK charity Stonewall).

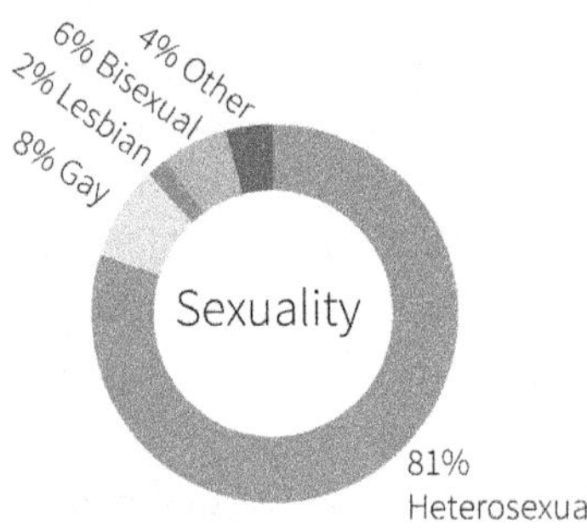

There is little information on or for Lesbian, Gay, Bisexual, Transgender and Queer or Questioning carers. The Carers UK policy briefing (2015) estimates that there are around 390,000 LGBTQ+ carers in Britain. Carers UK Wales have produced a report highlighting some of the particular issues and challenges faced by LGBTQ+ carers (2017). Research conducted by Stonewall revealed that one in twenty (5%) staff in the social care profession have witnessed other colleagues discriminate against, or provide poorer service to, a patient or service user because they are lesbian, gay or bisexual (Stonewall 2015).

Our survey corresponds with industry-wide data that there is a significant representation of LGBTQ+ individuals within the screen sector who have caring responsibilities, and we recommend further research into the relationship between sexuality and care.

Region

92% of our respondents reside in England, 1% Northern Ireland, 5% in Scotland and 2% in Wales.

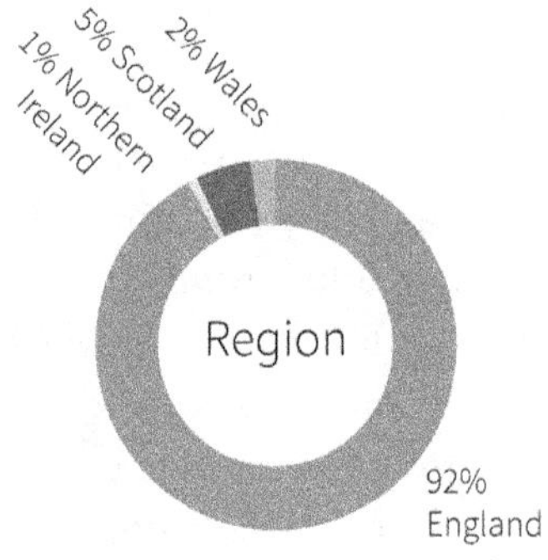

The regional data we collected is similar to that of the 2015 Creative Media Industries Employment Survey, both in terms of breakdown for each nation and for specific regions within it (Creative Skillset 2015). Data yielded from our survey illustrates that 39% of our respondents resided in Greater London, 28% resided in the South East, 12% resided in the South West, 7% resided in the North West, 6% resided in the West Midlands, 5% resided in Yorkshire, 2% resided in the North East and 1% resided in the East Midlands.

Survey data showing granular information on respondents' sexuality and region in *We Need to Talk about Caring*, which led to research on LGBTQ+ carers. Report and graphics designed by Eilidh Walker.

job role, job sector, pay, financial situation (including existing levels of debt and access to external forms of financial support, including private wealth and welfare), level of education, usual contract type, and additional forms of employment. We also asked about dependents, marital status, religion, and physical and mental health. In addition to the demographic information, participants were invited to write about their experiences of and attitudes toward care, their experiences of creative work, how they spoke about their caring responsibilities in their work environments, and how colleagues and employers reacted or responded to their situation. We received 135 responses from the "carers" survey and 11 from the "cared for." Due to the absence of substantive data, the final report focused primarily on the responses from the carers survey, but it highlighted the need for more research on the relationship between disability and screen labor. As this was a scoping study, we wanted to gather as much demographic information as possible within the confines of anonymity to be able to analyze and present fine-grained evidence.

To manage the analysis and write-up of the survey data in its granularity, a team of three doctoral students—Herval Almenoar-Webster, Cat Forward, and Sarah Louise Smyth—were employed to support Dent as lead researcher alongside Raising Films' new project manager, Mounira Almenoar. Using a combination of communication methods, including WhatsApp, Dropbox, and Zoom, we developed a thematic coding system and divided the analysis across the five members of the research team. We played to the strengths and interests of each independent researcher, separating out themes that emerged from the data, in particular the relationship between race, gender, sexuality, class, and age and the impact of caring responsibilities. Each researcher took on a body of literature that they then shared with the rest of the group so we could collaboratively apply it to the data. As the coding developed, so did the shared bibliography, creating conditions and opportunities for learning and development across the collaboration.

The findings included in the Raising Films report are merely a snapshot of the empirical evidence we uncovered—the project has created the opportunity for future analysis and publication opportunities for all involved. Together with the commitment to making visible the experiences of carers in the UK screen sector was a commitment to supporting emerging academic researchers: each contributor was paid and encouraged to develop further research outputs from the study. We are co-producers of this research

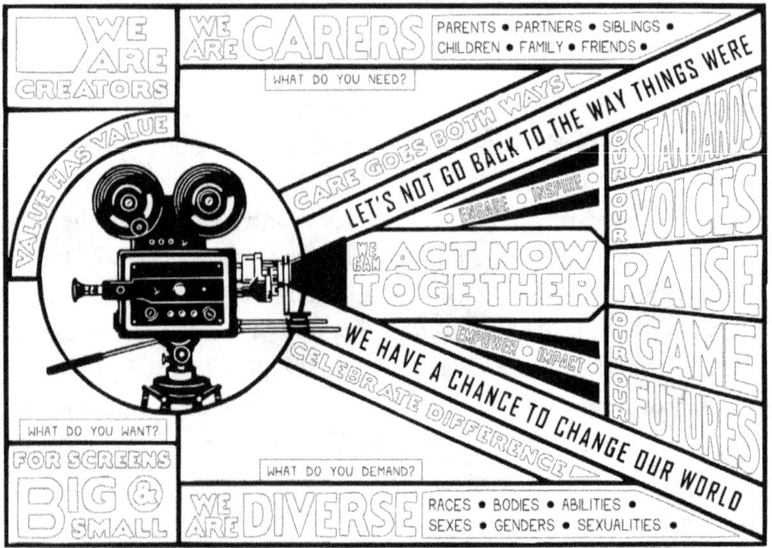

Visual response to *Raising Our Futures* provocations (2020) by Alex J. Gardner. Digital composition from linocut.

with the research participants, and the knowledge developed is an evolutionary process that includes many voices.

Conclusion

The Raising Films' messy research process was collaborative and supportive. It was also enjoyable and created a sense of community across the research team. Illustrating messy research makes visible the multiple participants that contribute to knowledge production. It also highlights the ongoing nature of research, with further publication opportunities emerging from the research data and collaborations that have been created through the Raising Films community.[41] Raising Films has a commitment to pay fairly, acknowledge the labor of all who contribute to its research agenda, and recognize the value of the work produced. All reports include detailed appendices, reference lists, and suggestions for future research.

Raising Films' approach has been applied in two further geographical contexts: in both cases, the UK research collective shared all details of its methodology on data collection and analysis, fund-raising, and report publication and distribution when the grassroots international collectives in Australia and Ireland reached out. Raising Films Australia was launched in 2018 and soon thereafter published its first research report, *Honey, I Hid the Kids*, produced in partnership with feminist data expert Deb Verhoeven, who was then associate dean of engagement and innovation at the University of Technology in Sydney and is currently research chair in gender and cultural informatics at the University of Alberta, Canada.[42] Raising Films Ireland was announced in August 2020, in collaboration with Susan Liddy from Mary Immaculate College, part of the University of Limerick, through an online conversation between Dr. Liddy and Raising Films founder member, writer/director Hope Dickson Leach. In spring 2021, it launched its first survey, *The Pursuit of Change*, led by Liddy.[43]

During the COVID-19 lockdown and subsequent effects on employment, it has become clear that Raising Films' interventions are ever more necessary. Recognizing the imperative to address the crisis from a carers' perspective, the founders' team published a series of provocations by leading agitators in our community in July 2020. Entitled *Raising Our Futures*, these challenging statements will shape our future research, as set out in Alex J. Gardner's visualization, available as a color print and in a black-and-white version for coloring in at home, with space to add your own demands.[44] It seems clear that there is a need for our messy model of anec-datal activism, which combines grassroots organizing, participatory-led engagement, and change-based activism in solidarity with social research into creative working lives. There are ways other than top-down research to make visible the reality of caring responsibilities within the creative workforce. Creating an open collaboration built on concepts of equal participation while engaging with other stakeholders with a commitment to care-driven research that attentively responds to issues that emerge from the community is a model that we hope can be adopted and practiced by others.[45] At the confluence of screen sector creative practice, academic and participatory research, and activism, our commitment remains to making it possible.

Acknowledgments

The Raising Films Research Collective thanks the funders of our research, especially the Raising Films community members who contributed to our crowdfunders in 2015 and 2018, making it possible for us to pay our team. *Making It Possible* was funded by the 2015 crowdfunder and Creative Scotland, with in-kind support from the University of Stirling. *Raising Our Game* was funded by the BFI's Diversity Fund. *We Need To Talk about Caring* was funded by the #RaisingRaisingFilms 2018 crowdfunder and made possible by Carers UK. We also wish to thank Holly Aylett, Susan Berridge, Clive Nwonka, and Natalie Wreyford for their research contributions to *Raising Our Game*. Thanks also to our designers, Samantha Ward and Eilidh Walker, and to Maria Cabrera, Sophie Mair, and Sally Hodgson, Raising Films' communications managers, for making it possible for us to share our research with the community members who generate it.

Notes

When citing this essay, please attribute it to Herval Almenoar-Webster, Mounira Almenoar, Tamsyn Dent, Cat Forward, Laura Giles, So Mayer, and Sarah-Louise Smythe (Raising Films Research Collective).

1 Bev Skeggs, *Feminist Cultural Theory: Process and Production* (Manchester: Manchester University Press, 1995), 2.
2 Imogen Tyler, *Stigma: The Machinery of Inequality* (London: Zed Books, 2020), 7.
3 bell hooks, *Teaching to Transgress: Education as Practice of Freedom* (New York: Routledge, 1994), 59.
4 The founders of Raising Films are producer Nicky Bentham, screenwriter and director Hope Dickson Leach, screenwriter Line Langebek, producer Jessica Levick, and film critic and independent scholar So Mayer.
5 Creative Skillset, "Women in the Creative Media Industries," *ScreenSkills*, September 2010, https://www.screenskills.com/media/1507/women_in_the_creative_media_industries_report_-_sept_2010.pdf; Rosalind Gill, "Unspeakable Inequalities: Post Feminism, Entrepreneurial Subjectivity, and the Repudiation of Sexism among Cultural Workers," *Social Politics: International Studies in Gender, State & Society* 21, no. 4 (2014): 509–28; Natalie Wreyford, *Gender Inequality in Screenwriting Work* (Cham: Springer International, 2018); Tamsyn Dent, "Feeling Devalued: The Creative Industries, Motherhood, Gender and Class Inequality" (PhD diss.,

Bournemouth University, 2016), eprints.bournemouth.ac.uk/29424/1/DENT%2C%20Tamsyn_Ph.D._2017.pdf.

6 Raising Films, *Making it Possible: Voices of Parents & Carers in the UK Film and TV Industry: Campaign Report* (London and Edinburgh: Raising Films, 2016), 4, https://www.raisingfilms.com/portfolio-items/making-it-possible/.

7 *Making It Possible* and its data visualizations were designed by Samantha Ward, as was *Raising Our Game* and the social media cards for Raising Films' 2018 crowdfunding campaign. Ward was able to work with Raising Films through an internship program at Michigan State University, thanks to MSU professor, parent-filmmaker, and Raising Films testimonial contributor Alexandra Hidalgo, part of our collaborative feminist network.

8 See the research page at www.raisingfilms.com/portfolio-items/making-it-possible/.

9 The first testimonials are all available on the final page of the "Stories" section: www.raisingfilms.com/stories/page/8/.

10 Sarah Solemani, "Testimonial," *Raising Films*, May 2015, www.raisingfilms.com/testimonial-sarah-solemani/.

11 See Berridge's chapter 2 in this volume for a discourse analysis of the shared language of affect across the testimonials and interviews.

12 "International Women's Day: The Band of Mothers Bringing Women Back into Filmmaking," *Dropbox Business Blog*, March 8, 2017, dropboxbusinessblog.co.uk/international-womens-day-band-mothers-bringing-women-back-filmmaking/.

13 For more on social media as a form of parental autoethnography, see Richards's chapter 5 in this volume.

14 Danielle Porter, Leah McCabe, and Kylie Grant, executive summary, in Raising Films, *Making It Possible*, 1, www.raisingfilms.com/wp-content/uploads/2018/12/Making-It-Possible-Full-Report-Results.pdf.

15 See Leo Barraclough, "London Film Festival Turns Spotlight on Gender Equality," *Variety*, October 2, 2015, variety.com/2015/film/festivals/london-film-festival-geena-davis-institute-symposium-1201603843/.

16 For Bectu campaigning, see bectu.org.uk/get-involved/eyes-half-shut/.

17 Porter, McCabe, and Grant, executive summary, 1.

18 This anec-data is not recorded or transcribed; any material recorded during digital iterations of Making It Possible and CLOSR are for

participant use only and are not available as material to researchers to protect privacy.

19 See www.pipacampaign.com/; pregnantthenscrewed.com/covid-19/.

20 Ian Hargreaves and John Hartley, eds., *The Creative Citizen Unbound: How Social Media and DIY Culture Contribute to Democracy, Communities and the Creative Economy* (Bristol: Policy, 2016); Sarah Banks, Angie Hart, Kate Pahl, and Paul Ward, *Co-producing Research: A Community Development Approach* (Bristol: Policy, 2018).

21 Mary Margaret Fonow and Judith A. Cook, eds., *Beyond Methodology: Feminist Scholarship as Lived Research* (Bloomington: Indiana University Press, 1991); Sumi Cho, Kimberlé Williams Crenshaw, and Leslie McCall, "Toward a Field of Intersectionality Studies: Theory, Applications, and Praxis," *Signs: Journal of Women in Culture and Society* 38, no. 4 (2013): 785–810.

22 Shortly after the event, the BFI's open Diversity Fund was closed in favor of a more dispersed commitment to embedding diversity standards as a measure for accessing its Film Fund. A recent report by Clive Nwonka has exposed the ineffectiveness of this approach on ethnic and racial diversity, and there is no available data to show the impact of this approach on caregivers. See Nwonka, *Race and Ethnicity in the UK Film Industry: An Analysis of the BFI Diversity Standards* (London: LSE, 2020), eprints.lse.ac.uk/105675/1/Race_and_Ethnicity_in_the_UK_Film_Industry_An_Analysis_of_the_BFI_Diversiy_Standards_Report_SPREAD_PRINT_VERSION.pdf.

23 Raising Films, *Raising Our Game: Next Steps for the UK Film & Television Industry* (London: Raising Films, 2017), 18, www.raisingfilms.com/portfolio-items/raising-our-game/.

24 See www.chathamhouse.org/chatham-house-rule.

25 Raising Films, *Raising Our Game*, 3, citing Reena Bhavnani, *Barriers to Diversity in Film: A Research Review* (London: UK Film Council, 2007), www.bfi.org.uk/sites/bfi.org.uk/files/downloads/uk-film-council-barriers-to-diversity-in-film-2007-08-20.pdf.

26 Available at bit.ly/2XffRPI (accessed August 1, 2020).

27 Raising Films, *Raising Our Game*, 19.

28 Raising Films, *Raising Our Game*, 21–22.

29 See www.raisingfilms.com/portfolio-items/raising-our-game/.

30 Raising Films, *Raising Our Game*, 20.

31 Sara Ahmed and Elaine Swan, "Doing Diversity," *Policy Futures in Education* 4, no. 2 (2006): 96–100.
32 Jack Newsinger and Doris Eikhof, "Explicit and Implicit Diversity Policy in the UK Film and Television Industries," *Journal of British Cinema and Television* 17, no. 1 (2020): 47–69.
33 Raising Films, *Raising Our Game*, 24–25.
34 See www.furtherandmore.com/; www.mediaparents.co.uk/.
35 See www.carersuk.org/home.
36 Carers UK, *State of Caring 2018* (London: Carers UK, 2018), www.carersuk.org/for-professionals/policy/policy-library/state-of-caring-2018-2.
37 Lydia Hayes, *Stories of Care, a Labour of Law: Gender and Class at Work* (London: Palgrave, 2017).
38 Hayes, *Stories of Care*, passim.
39 Kate Hardie, "Testimonial," *Raising Films*, August 2015, www.raisingfilms.com/testimonial-kate-hardie/.
40 Stevie Lee, "Testimonial," *Raising Films*, August 2015, www.raisingfilms.com/testimonial-stevie-lee/.
41 See Berridge's chapter 2 in this volume.
42 Raising Films Australia, *Honey, I Hid the Kids: Experiences of Parents and Carers in the Australian Film Industry* (Sydney: Raising Films Australia, 2018), www.raisingfilms.com/wp-content/uploads/2019/05/HoneyIHidtheKids_FullSurveyReportFinal.pdf.
43 See www.raisingfilmsireland.com/news/the-pursuit-of-change-raising-films-ireland-survey-is-live.
44 Gardner's visual response was created in linocut and printed in sections before being scanned and composited using digital design tools. The black-and-white version is available as a downloadable PDF, and the color version available to view and to order on the Raising Films website: www.raisingfilms.com/visual-response-to-raising-our-futures/.
45 Joan Tronto, *Moral Boundaries: A Political Argument for an Ethic of Care* (New York: Routledge, 1993).

2

Managing Feelings

Raising Films' Testimonials and the Impact of Caring Responsibilities on the Emotional Well-being of Mothers Who Work in the UK Film and Television Sector

Susan Berridge

This chapter explores the impact of caring responsibilities on the emotional well-being of mothers who work in the UK film and television industries. Childcare responsibilities are often identified as a significant reason behind gender imbalances in the sector, with a 2010 Skillset report concluding that many women aged thirty-five and older were leaving the media industries due to difficulties reconciling work with family life.[1] Although this chapter argues that care is not essentially gendered, women remain disproportionately affected by caring responsibilities.[2] In recent years, there has been a growing body of feminist scholarship on gender inequalities in the film and television industries, with care often identified as a key issue.[3] Despite this awareness of the significant impact that caring responsibilities have on women's experiences of creative work, several feminist scholars have argued that challenges posed by childcare, along with wider gender inequalities, remain silenced in competitive neoliberal and postfeminist working cultures that privilege self-regulation above all else.[4] In 2016 three key industry reports and initiatives emerged that challenged this silencing and explored these inequalities in more depth, looking at various gendered barriers to access.[5] The official discourses of care that have emerged in this context are significant in highlighting the scale of the issue and the number of parents and carers impacted. However, the focus of these reports, mirroring wider scholarship on this issue, has predominantly been on practical challenges posed by caring responsibilities. In comparison, there has been little research into how these challenges are experienced and felt by women on an emotional level.

This chapter aims to expand upon official discourses of care by examining also the unofficial discourses that emerge in online spaces, specifically the testimonials of parents who work in the film and television industries collected and published on the website of activist organization Raising Films. Raising Films was founded in 2015 by independent scholar So Mayer, producers Nicky Bentham and Jessica Levick, writer Line Langebek, and director Hope Dickson Leach to explore the challenges of balancing work in the film and television industries with caring responsibilities.[6] I argue that these testimonials offer different and valuable insights into the challenges women face, moving beyond a focus on practicalities to highlight the significant detrimental impact that negotiations involving work/life balance can have on women's emotional well-being. The findings presented here expose just what is at stake when women are expected to suppress or deny their lived—and felt—experiences of balancing caring responsibilities with creative work. In turn, they point to the value and necessity of centering the emotional dimensions of these experiences in order to effectively challenge the sector's normative masculine working cultures that produce and reinforce wider gender inequalities in the first place.

Scholarship on Creative Working Cultures and Inequalities

Traditionally, there has been a lack of scholarship on the experiential reality of the work lives of creative workers in favor of a focus on the more celebratory aspects of this labor. However, in recent decades, there has been a shift toward challenging the notion of the wider cultural industries as "cool, creative and egalitarian," with many scholars seeking to expose the more punishing nature of contemporary creative working cultures and the potentially poor quality of work life.[7] Mark Banks calls for more attention to be paid to contemporary labor conditions, noting that the economic imperatives underpinning the creative industries have resulted in cultural workers' "material conditions of existence, and their meaningful lives and ambitions becoming increasingly undermined."[8] Similarly, in a U.S. context, Andrew Ross argues that while there are many statistics about the cultural industries from a policy perspective, "by contrast, there has been precious little attention to the quality of work life with which creative livelihoods are associated. Job gratification, for creatives, has always come at a heavy sacrificial cost."[9] The tension between pleasure and pain in creative work has been interrogated by a number of creative labor scholars who seek to understand the reasons given by cultural workers for continuing to work in conditions that potentially offer such a poor work/life balance.[10]

David Hesmondhalgh and Sarah Baker interrogate this tension further in their research on the quality of working life in three cultural industries: independent television production, magazine publishing, and music. They are centrally concerned with the relationship of work to well-being, defined as "whether the relationships between the different parts of our selves operate in a healthy way, whether they allow us to flourish over time." They argue that while celebrations of creative labor frequently ignore negative aspects of this work, even critical accounts often fail "to scrutinise the normative implications of their critiques." This absence of scrutiny, in turn, results in a lack of clarity regarding how to make effective interventions into these working cultures. To address this lack, they devise models of good and bad work. Good work is characterized by "good wages, working hours, high levels of safety, autonomy, interest, involvement, sociality, self-esteem, self-realisation, work-life balance, security." Bad work, in contrast, is marked by "poor wages, working hours and levels of safety, powerlessness, boredom, isolation, low self-esteem and shame, frustrated development, overwork, risk."[11] The creative industries are marked by ambivalence: on the one hand, they provide workers with high levels of self-fulfillment, but on the other hand, the working cultures can be highly punishing, falling into the category of "bad work." For example, the increasing deregulation and casualization of the film and television industries has led to precarious working conditions and, in turn, greater degrees of risk being displaced onto individual workers. In a competitive climate, long hours, feast/famine patterns of work, an eradication of work/life boundaries, and financial insecurity are common.

Hesmondhalgh and Baker, motivated by a commitment to "equality, social justice, well-being and democratization of creativity," recognize the way in which other identities shape experiences of the quality of working life.[12] However, they are not centrally concerned with the impact of gender or caring responsibilities on these experiences. Despite this, many of the aspects of "bad work" that they outline have been similarly identified by feminist scholars as key factors in, as well as outcomes of, the persistence of gendered inequalities in the film and television industries and the wider creative sector.[13] For example, the notion of "powerlessness" is reflected strongly in Leung Wing-Fai et al.'s interviews with women working in the UK film and television industries, who commonly expressed that they felt a profound lack of choice in terms of their decisions about returning to work after having children.[14] "Frustrated development" is evident in Natalie Wreyford's research into the gendered impact of informal recruitment practices on screenwriters; many women with caring responsibilities are unable to progress in their careers due to not being able to attend the necessary evening and weekend networking events.[15] High levels of personal "risk" are also identified by several feminist scholars as endemic in a predominantly freelance working culture, where there are few workplace benefits and no maternity pay.[16] As Rosalind Gill identifies, inequalities are produced by the working cultures themselves.[17]

Official Discourses on Care in the UK Film and TV Industries

In 2016 three key industry reports were published that sought to explore further the relationship between these working cultures and broader inequalities to uncover precisely what barriers exist: Creative Scotland's *Screen Equalities, Diversity and Inclusion* report, the Directors UK *Cut out of the Picture* report, and Raising Films' *Making It Possible* report. A concern with gender inequalities is key to each report, but only that of Raising Films places a consideration of caring responsibilities at the center. All three reports draw on quantitative methodologies to expose the scale of inequalities in the sector, documenting the numbers and percentages of workers impacted by particular barriers. In doing so, they have proved vital in challenging common myths that these industries are egalitarian.

Cut out of the Picture focuses exclusively on gender inequalities among directors in the UK film industry. It argues that the sector's "permanent short-termism" precludes long-term thinking, planning, and positive HR practices, "best exemplified by the un-family-friendly nature of the industry."[18] Because recruitment occurs in very tight time frames, the tendency is to hire people who are already known. As the report explains, "The sporadic employment, long hours, and unpredictable and constantly changing nature of the work make it nearly impossible to effectively progress in the industry whilst also being the primary care-giver in a family, a role which is disproportionately held by women."[19]

Creative Scotland's *Equalities, Diversity and Inclusion* report, published in May 2016, more directly focuses on care. This report, based on a survey of over five hundred people working in the Scottish screen industries, addresses wider barriers to equality, inclusion, and diversity, including geography, socioeconomic status, and ability. It includes a section devoted to gender and parental responsibilities, highlighting that 39 percent of women cited gender as a key barrier to participation in the screen industries (compared with just 7 percent of men). Further, women with children were 75 percent more likely to cite parental responsibilities as a barrier to work than their male counterparts, despite more men identifying as parents across the survey as a whole.[20]

This section on parenting is followed by one on gender and work/life balance, exclusively associating this balance with childcare.[21] As one open response explains, "The fact remains that from commissioning downward, this remains a fatally family-unfriendly business. Unless you are willing to have your entire life consumed by work, a meaningful career is hard to maintain."[22] Another response similarly comments on the "enormous impact" that the sector's working cultures have on the family (and wider social) lives of employees, "particularly those with children or caring responsibilities."[23] In the open responses, respondents identify specific challenges in reconciling caring responsibilities with career progression, including "limited parental leave" and long, erratic hours of work that make childcare difficult to schedule. As the report notes, "Women are still perceived culturally as the primary child-carers," with several respondents noting the commonality of women with children leaving the industry due to the lack of provision for and understanding of new parents.[24]

These are important and urgent issues yet the brevity of the open responses means that the emphasis remains on practical challenges rather than on how these barriers might be felt or experienced by women, and how they might impact their emotional well-being. The question of well-being is addressed later in the report in a separate section unrelated to gender, the only section where the psychological and emotional impact of the film and television sector's working cultures is raised. Many of the open responses here refer to the effects of pressurized working conditions on mental health and well-being.[25] One respondent recalls having had "serious concerns about the health and safety" of colleagues due to long, unpredictable working hours. A five-day working week is identified by another as having a positive impact upon the mental health of crew members. However, again these responses are relatively brief and broad, giving little insight into the complexities of the experiences of working in the sector. Further, despite long hours being similarly identified as a key challenge in the section on parental responsibilities, no connections are drawn. Because well-being is addressed in a separate section, the specific gendered dimensions of the impact of caring responsibilities on well-being remain invisible.

Raising Films' *Making It Possible*, based on an online survey of 640 film and television practitioners across the United Kingdom, explores various barriers that caring responsibilities pose for career development and retention. It found that 79 percent of respondents view caring responsibilities as having a negative impact on their role in the industry, with women one and a half times more likely than men to report this.[26] The report focuses in particular on practical barriers to parents and carers posed by the industries' working cultures, such as location shooting, long hours, financial insecurity, lack of industry infrastructure, and lack of long-term stable employment.[27] Indeed, 63 percent of respondents identified as freelance. The report also identifies key issues around discrimination, such as being asked at interviews about childcare arrangements, having contracts pulled when pregnant, and ceasing to get work after disclosing caring responsibilities.

While the focus is on pragmatic challenges posed by care, the report includes short quotes from open responses that speak to the way in which these challenges are felt by practitioners. A freelance female discloses, "I am sinking under the stress of juggling childcare," adding that "there is no choice" not to work long hours and weekends.[28] The term *frustration* is used by several other respondents to describe various limitations, such as the lack of understanding in the industry around issues of care, the rarity of acting roles for pregnant women, and the broader impact of exclusion.[29] In the section "Further Responses" toward the end of the report, a female freelancer notes, "As a BAME [Black, Asian, and minority ethnic] female parent in this industry, I feel like I'm drowning sometimes."[30]

These brief snapshots of the emotional challenges of negotiating caring responsibilities and work in the industries provide further important insights into how practical limitations are felt and experienced by women working in the sector. I turn now to the testimonials of mothers gathered and published on Raising Films' website to gain a deeper understanding of the emotional challenges of balancing caring responsibilities with a career in film and television.

Unofficial Discourses of Care in Raising Films' Testimonials

Raising Films' website includes a section entitled "Stories" that typically features testimonials written by industry practitioners on their experiences of negotiating a balance between caring responsibilities and their careers.[31] At the time of writing, there are sixty testimonials published on the site, spanning an almost three-year period from May 2015 to March 2018. The majority of these testimonials are written by mothers (forty-five), with a smaller number written by fathers (six) or by childfree practitioners who were raised by parents who worked in the creative sector (three). Three are jointly written by co-parents, and one by two mothers who work together. An additional two are written by family-friendly companies. The majority of contributors are freelancers based in the United Kingdom. These testimonials are gathered by Raising Films or solicited from practitioners at events the group runs. Raising Films primarily view its site as a platform for these accounts, and therefore, any editing of the testimonials is done with a very light touch. There are no specific guidelines on tone and content, although potential questions to address are identified. In a context in which the challenges of care are often silenced, it is notable that the majority of authors provide names and often accompanying images. I focus exclusively in this chapter on mothers' accounts, the majority of the testimonials.

The testimonials offer rare and valuable insights into lived experiences. They are typically addressed to other practitioners (and often implicitly other mothers), and as such they are commonly written with humor and warmth, enhancing their relatability.[32] There is frequently a slight uneasiness about seeming to complain. For example, Stevie Lee, a development producer and script editor, notes after outlining some of the challenges posed by care, "Sorry this sounds very woe-is-me! When actually I feel lucky every day to have my kids and, like many of the people who have written testimonials for the site, I know that they have brought me bags of pragmatism and common sense and a much readier sense of humour—all of which informs my work in a really positive way." Lee's unease is reflective of the "antipathy to whinging" that Leung Wing-Fai et al. identify as a key feature of creative industries, which expect workers to suppress challenges around care in favor of a can-do entrepreneurial mindset.[33]

A common argument in creative labor scholarship is that creative workers typically accept their working conditions as "unremarkable," seeing changes in their work cultures as "the new normal."[34] Further, several scholars have argued that passionate engagement with creative work often makes for a conducive context for the justification of self-exploitation or exploitation by others.[35] Reflecting this notion of creative labor as "passionate work," many of the women begin their testimonials by stating their deep love of their jobs, frequently mentioning how "lucky" they are to be able to work in a sector they feel invested in.[36] However, rather than uncritically accepting their working cultures, the writers are often highly self-reflexive, open, and critical about the difficulties of negotiating the industries' intense and unrelenting laboring conditions. For example, many of the mothers refer to frustrations, feeling like their work is a hobby due to the lack of adequate respect and payment.

Like the official discourses of care in the industry reports and initiatives mentioned above, the testimonials frequently draw attention to the practical challenges emerging from the incompatibility of caring responsibilities with the industries' intense working cultures. For example, Deborah Sathe comments on the lack of job security, while several other mothers mention the difficulties of scheduling regular childcare when hours are long and erratic, and finances are irregular. Significantly, the testimonials also provide an insight into how these practical challenges are experienced and felt. Frustration is one of the most common emotions expressed. An anonymous mother notes that the common expectation that people will work for free in order to gain a commission is "difficult and frustrating," adding that while she would have accepted this in the past, "now that I'm paying out a fortune each month for childcare, I just can't be hanging around waiting 6 months to be paid a meagre amount or not paid at all." Fear is another commonly expressed emotion, often related to financial insecurity and what this means for accessing regular and reliable childcare. Freelance film editor and screenwriter Olivia Hetreed describes it as "scary" to schedule expensive childcare without the security of regular work.

Fear and anxiety around the potential impact of caring responsibilities on women's careers are evident even before pregnancy. Producer Nicky Bentham explains, "I was terrified of everything that lay ahead of me and although I had a really strong desire to forge ahead in my career, I was pretty sure that the best advice would be to bow out for a bit." Alexis Strum, actor and screenwriter, describes being "terrified, literally terrified about how motherhood would affect my productivity," adding, "How sad is that?" Laura Scrivano similarly reveals, "When I found out I was pregnant, I was terrified that my career was over." This fear resonates with Gill's argument around new laboring subjectivities and the way in which "power and compulsion operate psychosocially, through a remade worker subjectivity that is . . . profoundly anxious, and fearful of being displaced."[37]

Anxieties around displacement due to the competitive nature of the sector manifest again in an explicit frustration caused by the apparent lack of choice in women's decisions regarding work and childcare. Assistant director Mel Heseltine writes, "I find it so frustrating that there isn't a balance to have their career and be a Mum. What if I were to call one morning and say I couldn't come in as one of my boys wasn't well? I can't imagine being employed again and word would soon get out that I was unreliable and uncommitted." Another woman, who left the industries after having children, notes her frustration at not being able to find a way to reconcile her career with caring responsibilities, despite having invested several years in the sector before having children. Lee similarly mentions feeling frustrated by having to work in the evenings when her children are asleep in order to accommodate caring responsibilities.

The industries' expectation that workers should be committed to their job above all else results in a relentless "always on" culture. As MP, writer, and actor Tracy Brabin argues, "There are never *any* concessions that you might have family commitments when you get notes on a Friday afternoon for a Monday morning delivery." This culture is reflected in a sense of temporal urgency in the testimonials—it is difficult for mothers to fully live in the present due to always needing to look ahead to find the next job, but the future is also a space of fear and uncertainty. In their study of conceptualizations of the future by people on precarious contracts, Barbara Read and Carole Leathwood note that "the effects of precarisation have a strong temporal element," which manifests in a sense of "being 'stuck' in the present."[38] They draw on Carmen Leccardi's notion of "presentification," defined as a "reduction of ability to plan for the future in any confident sense."[39] This inability to plan ahead comes through strongly in the testimonials, with many women speaking of finding it difficult to schedule family holidays even in the short term for fear of missing out on potential work. There is an inherent tension here: working conditions leave women stuck in the present on a practical level, but nevertheless they are always looking to the future on a more affective level. A number of testimonies end with reflections on the future and a longing for a time when life will be more stable and less pressurized, usually in relation to young children starting school and childcare becoming cheaper and potentially less difficult to manage. For example, producer/director Naomi Wright concludes, "I try to be patient and remember that my children are only small for a very short time. I am hoping to store up all the inspiration that life brings now and see it flower in the future. The near future, I hope."

Hesmondhalgh and Baker argue that, in the creative industries, "the lure of self-realisation brings about an over-identification of the self with work."[40] The result of this intimate connection, combined with the industries' relentless working cultures, is articulated by many women as creating a profound rupture in their identity once caring responsibilities are added in. Several of the testimonials make a clear distinction between their work life before and after having children, noting that the advent of caring responsibilities resulted in a loss of their former identity. Actress, writer, and activist Sarah Solemani questions, "Why must I die because I have given her life?" Writer Joy Wilkinson similarly articulates a loss of identity: "With each kid, it seemed to take the first two years to get through the firefighting stage and find time to really get myself back in focus again." Kate Hardie notes that "so much of this is about me trying to juggle, feeling guilty, losing myself, unsure if I wanted to be a good mum or have a successful career, and nearly always feeling I was failing at both." Similarly, Pippa Best recalls, "My career had provided both my sense of identity and my self-worth and now I had neither. . . . I had absolutely no idea who I was anymore. The only thing I was sure of was that I was a failure." The central conflict for women—expected to be wholly committed to work above all else, but also disproportionately responsible for caring responsibilities—results in them being pulled in two different directions, with a highly detrimental impact on their well-being.

This identity split is further reinforced by the way in which the industry often expects women to suppress or silence the emotional and practical challenges of care. In the neoliberal climate, the ideal cultural worker is characterized as vigilant, self-regulating, individualistic, flexible, passionate, driven to perfection, entrepreneurial, autonomous, and possessed of a "can-do" attitude—characteristics that are seen to have strong economic value.[41] Feminist scholars have acknowledged the paradox in the kind of skills valued by contemporary neoliberal working cultures that are typically feminine—for example, the ability to multitask and be adaptable—and the way that these same cultures create and reinforce barriers for women.[42] The firm emphasis on individual resilience leaves little room to critique the quality of work life or to raise challenges of caring responsibilities.

Notably, however, rather than internalize the challenges posed by balancing caring responsibilities with creative work as their own personal problems, women frequently do draw attention to and critique the way in which the film and television industries expect them to deny or suppress these difficulties. Some mothers reflect back on this previously internalized denial, now with the benefit of hindsight and a more critical perspective. Scrivano, for example, speaks of having been determined to "buck the trend" of women whose careers dry up after having children, adding, "I was still on set at 38 weeks pregnant. I was going to be a working-mama-director and it would all be fine." She then goes on to detail the challenging realities of complications in the late stages of pregnancy, childbirth, issues with feeding, and exhaustion. Becca Ellson, development producer and script editor, recalls being in denial that her life had changed "rather profoundly" after having a child: "I had it all. Except for my sanity."

This notion of the denial resonates with Arlie Russell Hochschild's conception of care as emotional labor in her influential work *The Managed Heart*. In her analysis of U.S. flight attendants in the 1980s, Hochschild defined emotional labor as "the management of feeling to create a publicly observable facial and bodily display."[43] There is a parallel here with the way in which the film and television industries expect certain feelings or emotions to be managed by workers, and further, the way in which these expectations then become internalized by workers themselves. Cinematographer Laura Bellingham recounts feeling guarded when a former colleague asked after her children, explaining, "My daughter appears to have fallen in with the unmentionables: pregnancy, children and childcare, motherhood, a healthy romantic partnership . . . in fact any passion or commitment that could be perceived as preceding your passion and commitment to the job at hand. It seems someone would have us believe that in order to excel in this industry you need to keep these parts of your life quiet, if they are to be indulged at all."

The mothers' testimonials often argue instead for the benefits of bringing emotion *to* work in terms of enhancing creativity. Lorna Martin, for example, argues that "being a mother opens up a range of emotional experiences that I couldn't have imagined and that are invaluable for writing drama or comedy." Similarly, Kerry Fox notes, "I found acting an awful lot easier as a mother, because I had more emotional range," adding that she also required fewer takes and had more self-confidence in her own ability. Scrivano also describes an enhanced ability to "access deep emotions" after having a child. All three, then, challenge the idea that suppressing or denying motherhood on set is necessary for producing strong creative work.

Both Kate Hardie and Sunshine Jackson identify writer/director Joey Soloway as being particularly inspirational in recognizing the value of emotion on set. Hardie argues, "For the most part women are told if they want to be working in the film industry they must be really strong and not lose their tempers or cry at work. They need to do everything they can to prove wrong the cliched idea that women are too emotional and cannot separate their feelings from their day jobs." These gendered stereotypes set all women—not just those who have caring responsibilities—up for a fall. Hardie continues, "The industry is not a huge forgiver of emotions at work, however intermittent or, in fact, justified," arguing in line with Soloway that we should instead celebrate displays of emotion at work as beneficial for enabling emotionally complex creative outputs. Jackson echoes this admiration for Soloway, highlighting that Soloway's "daily emotional check-in" with their on-set crew has "enormous" implications: "imagine a creative workplace where you can bring your whole self? Where it is explicitly encouraged that you share what is going on for you outside of the narrow confines of the workplace."

Conclusion

The testimonials reveal the significant impact that caring responsibilities have on the emotional well-being of women working in the film and television industries, a sector that has intense working cultures and expects women to suppress the challenges of caring responsibilities in favor of presenting a neoliberal resilient and can-do attitude. The women's experiences indicate that in order to create a more egalitarian and inclusive sector for all parents—both mothers and fathers—one where their well-being can flourish, the working cultures need to change. We need collective action. I share Angela McRobbie's call for the reclamation of the term "welfare-in-work."[44] She argues that "being expected to work without workplace entitlements severs a connection with past generations who not only had such protection (in the form of sick pay, pensions, maternity leave etc.) but also fought hard to get them."[45] She continues that it is difficult to conceive of such entitlements being reinstated due to the intense struggle it took to win them in the first place.

Over the past few years, important work has been undertaken to challenge the traditional silencing around the difficulties of reconciling caring responsibilities with normative working cultures in the film and television industries and the way in which these challenges disproportionately impact women. However, the focus has predominantly been on the practical rather than emotional challenges or how these challenges make primary caregivers who work in the industry—predominantly women—feel. If we overlook the emotional dimensions of these issues, any potential solutions to addressing barriers posed by caring responsibilities will only ever be partial. We need to take a holistic approach to understanding the issue. Examining the testimonials gathered and published on the Raising Films website offers a way to begin to think about this, providing rare and valuable insights into the experiential realities of balancing caring responsibilities with work in the sector.

Notes

1 Creative Skillset, "Women in the Creative Media Industries," *ScreenSkills*, September 2010, www.screenskills.com/media/1507/women_in_the_creative_media_industries_report_-_sept_2010.pdf.

2 Creative Scotland, *Equalities, Diversity and Inclusion in the Scottish Screen Sector: A Report on the Findings of the Screen Equality Survey by Creative Scotland* (Edinburgh: Creative Scotland, 2016), www.creativescotland.com/__data/assets/pdf_file/0010/35020/ScreenEqualitiesSurveyMay2016.pdf; Raising Films, "*Making It Possible: Voices of Parents & Carers in the UK Film and TV Industry*" (London and Edinburgh: Raising Films, 2016), www.raisingfilms.com/wp-content/uploads/2018/12/Making-It-Possible-Full-Report-Results.pdf.

3 Natalie Wreyford, "Birds of a Feather: Informal Recruitment Practices and Gendered Outcomes for Screenwriting Work in the UK Film Industry," *Sociological Review* 63, no. 1 (2015): 84–96; Tamsyn Dent, "Feeling Devalued: The Creative Industries, Motherhood, Gender and Class Inequality" (PhD diss., Bournemouth University, 2016), eprints .bournemouth.ac.uk/29424/1/DENT%2C%20Tamsyn_Ph.D._2017.pdf; Leung Wing-Fai, Rosalind Gill, and Keith Randle, "Getting In, Getting On, Getting Out? Women as Career Scramblers in the UK Film and Television Industries," *Sociological Review* 63, no. 1 (2015): 50–65; Anne O'Brien, "Producing Television and Reproducing Gender," *Television and New Media* 16, no. 3 (2015): 259–74.

4 Gill, "Unspeakable Inequalities: Postfeminism, Entrepreneurial Subjectivity and the Repudiation of Sexism among Cultural Workers," *Social Politics* 21, no. 4 (2014): 509–28; Wing-Fai, Gill, and Randle, "Getting In, Getting On, Getting Out?"

5 Creative Scotland, *Equalities, Diversity and Inclusion*; Raising Films, *Making It Possible*; Stephen Follows and Alexis Kreager with Eleanor Gomes, *Cut out of the Picture: A Study of Gender Inequality amongst Film Directors in the UK Film Industry, Directors UK*, 2016, https://d3gujhbyl1boep .cloudfront.net/uploads%2F1462302197658-3hv8831pb1bagm48 -b4e5c367ebd7882e3502f05bc451aea6%2FDirectors+UK+PRESS+PACK +-+Cut+Out+of+The+Picture+-+Research+Report+%5B2016%5D.pdf.

6 See Raising Films Research Collective's chapter 1 in this volume.

7 Gill, "Cool, Creative and Egalitarian? Exploring Gender in Project-Based New Media Work in Europe," *Information, Communication and Society* 5, no. 1 (2002): 70–89.

8 Mark Banks, "Moral Economy and Cultural Work," *Sociology* 40, no. 3 (2006): 40.

9 Andrew Ross, *Nice Work if You Can Get It: Life and Labor in Precarious Times* (New York: NYU Press, 2009), 18.

10 Angela McRobbie, "Clubs to Companies: Notes on the Decline of Political Culture in the Speeded Up Creative Worlds," *Cultural Studies* 16, no. 4 (2002): 516–31; David Hesmondhalgh and Sarah Baker, *Creative Labour: Media Work in Three Cultural Industries* (London: Routledge, 2011); David Lee, *Independent Television Production in the UK: From Cottage Industry to Big Business*. (Oxford: Palgrave Macmillan, 2018).

11 Hesmondhalgh and Baker, *Creative Labour*, 30, 7–8, 39, 2.

12 Hesmondhalgh and Baker, *Creative Labour*, 2.

13 Wreyford, "Birds of a Feather"; Wreyford, *Gender Inequality in Screenwriting Work* (Oxford: Palgrave Macmillan, 2018); Gill, "Unspeakable Inequalities"; Wing-Fai, Gill, and Randle, "Getting In, Getting On, Getting Out?"

14 Wing-Fai, Gill, and Randle, "Getting In, Getting On, Getting Out?"

15 Wreyford, "Birds of a Feather."

16 George Morgan and Pariece Nelligan, "Labile Labour—Gender, Flexibility and Creative Work," *Sociological Review* 63, no. 1 (2015): 66–83; Wreyford, "Birds of a Feather."

17 Gill, "Unspeakable Inequalities," 514.

18 Follows, Kreager, and Gomes, *Cut out of the Picture*, 9.

19 Follows, Kreager, and Gomes, *Cut out of the Picture*, 9.

20 Creative Scotland, *Equalities, Diversity and Inclusion*, 21.

21 Creative Scotland, *Equalities, Diversity and Inclusion*, 18–19.

22 Creative Scotland, *Equalities, Diversity and Inclusion*, 19.

23 Creative Scotland, *Equalities, Diversity and Inclusion*, 19.

24 Creative Scotland, *Equalities, Diversity and Inclusion*, 19.

25 Creative Scotland, *Equalities, Diversity and Inclusion*, 21.

26 Raising Films, *Making It Possible*, 9.

27 Raising Films, *Making It Possible*, 11.

28 Raising Films, *Making It Possible*, 9.

29 Raising Films, *Making It Possible*, 11.

30 Raising Films, *Making It Possible*, 18.

31 See www.raisingfilms.com/stories/.

32 Akane Kanai, "On Not Taking the Self Seriously: Resilience, Relatability, and Humour in Young Women's Tumblr Blogs," *European Journal of Cultural Studies* 22, no. 1 (2019): 60–77.

33 Wing-Fai, Gill, and Randle, "Getting In, Getting On, Getting Out?" 50–51.

34 Susan Luckman and Stephanie Taylor, *The New Normal of Working Lives: Critical Studies in Contemporary Work and Employment* (Oxford: Palgrave Macmillan, 2018), 5.

35 O'Brien, "Producing Television"; David Lee, "The Ethics of Insecurity: Risk, Individualization and Value in British Independent Television Production," *Television and New Media* 13, no. 6 (2012): 480–97.

36 McRobbie, *Be Creative: Making a Living in the New Culture Industries.* (Cambridge: Polity, 2016).

37 Gill, "Unspeakable Inequalities," 516.
38 Barbara Read and Carole Leathwood, "Tomorrow's a Mystery: Constructions of the Future and 'Un/Becoming' amongst 'Early' and 'Late' Career Academics," *International Studies in Sociology of Education* 27, no. 4 (2018): 8–9.
39 Read and Leathwood, "Tomorrow's a Mystery," 8.
40 Hesmondhalgh and Baker, *Creative Labour*, 19–20.
41 Banks, "Moral Economy"; Ross, *Nice Work*; Lee, "The Ethics of Insecurity."
42 Rosalind Gill and Christina Scharff, introduction to *New Femininities: Postfeminism, Neoliberalism and Subjectivity*, ed. Rosalind Gill and Christina Scharff (London: Palgrave Macmillan, 2013), 7.
43 Arlie Russell Hochschild, *The Managed Heart: Commercialisation of Human Feeling* (1983; repr., Berkeley: University of California Press, 2012), 7.
44 McRobbie, *Be Creative*, 13.
45 McRobbie, *Be Creative*, 13.

3

How to Do Everything

A Conversation between Filmmakers

Kristy Guevara-Flanagan and Irene Lusztig

> *My due date is in nine days and that feels like many things. It feels very close. I just stopped working about a week ago, and I just move around my house . . . I'm spending a lot of time at home thinking about this . . . what's to come. It just feels like this big precipice. In a way that—I don't know—you can't even really think about and understand. People keep asking me if I'm ready, and I just keep saying no. I don't think there's a way that you can be ready. What would that look like?*

Our first conversation about motherhood happened on camera in the summer of 2012—Irene behind the camera and Kristy in front. Since that time, we've both released films that center on maternal subjects, discourses, and bodies, and we've collaborated on curating a touring microcinema program, "Mothering Every Day." We are mothers, feminist filmmakers, and educators, and in our respective recent practices we've both reckoned with the deeply entrenched ways that motherhood is devalued and rendered invisible in the culture industries and academic institutions where we circulate and produce our work.

The following conversation was pieced together via a shared Google document over several months in 2018, patch-worked between syllabus writing, grant writing, grading, film shoots, festival submissions, school drop-offs and pickups, sound mixes, sick days, dinnertime, bedtime, and school holidays. We asked each other questions, elaborated on each other's answers, and generated more questions for each other as we passed our document back and forth. As our own film work shifts away from explicitly foregrounding maternity and our children grow older, how does the ongoing care labor of parenting continue to structure and inform our art practices and the subjects we choose?

Our conversation began in the aftermath of the #MeToo and #TimesUp movements and during the age of Trump; it is framed by a moment in the United States (and beyond) when women are speaking up and out, and feminism and women's rights are being centered again after a long relegation to the sidelines. At the same time, our exchange is shaped by our awareness of a growing counterwave of legitimized attacks on our bodies and rights that are sanctioned at the highest levels of state power. We take up this space to reimagine what being working artist mothers can look like and how doing everything isn't all it's cracked up to be.

IL: The day we first met, you were pregnant with your daughter Zora and nine days away from your due date—I filmed an interview with you reflecting on being at the threshold of new motherhood that became the ending of my 2013 film *The Motherhood Archives*. Obviously, a lot has changed in your life since then! How has your creative practice changed? What kinds of creative and material conditions make it possible for you to keep making work as a single parent to a young child?

KGF: I remember that day so well. That was such a pivotal moment in my pregnancy, when things started to get really real! I remember so vividly feeling on the precipice of motherhood, to the point where I began to feel I was in a liminal place. Frightened is probably an understatement. When I did become a parent, I was struggling to keep up with the launch and distribution of my feature documentary, *Wonder Women! The Untold Story of American Superheroines* (2012/2013). There was a lot of work that needed to be done on that, and it was terribly hard to access that part of my brain right after my daughter's birth. Opening up the computer felt so foreign. A couple months later I was selected for a residency, and by that point I was ready to venture forth and see how I was going to be an artist and single mother. The organization, the Bay Area Video

Coalition, was very supportive: I needed a lactation room, a fridge, and a system whereby people would know not to accidentally use my stored pumped milk, and a childcare provider who was willing to take care of my daughter on the premises of a nonprofit arts organization. When that all came together, I started to feel more confident. But every step of the way trying to navigate being a single parent, a teacher, and a working artist has felt like reinventing the wheel.

The work I've made since my daughter was born has been dictated by the limitations of parenting and also fueled by them. The first project was a short archival piece, *What Happened to Her* (2016), which I had been mulling over for years. I wanted to do something immediate and for which I needed no crew and no funding, and—equally important—no pressure. I have always been fascinated and repulsed by the volume of dead women seen in popular film and television. I gathered hundreds of clips of dead women and paired these clips with the voice of a woman who had played the role of a corpse on-screen. Practically speaking, a voice-only interview is much easier and quicker to conduct than one filmed on camera and that requires lighting. And editing and archival research were things I could do from home during naps and after bedtime in the cracks of the limited time

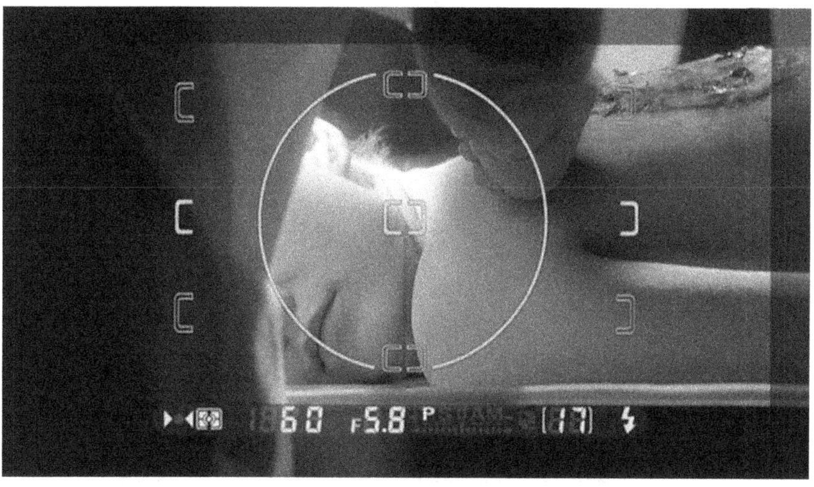

Film still from *What Happened to Her* (Kristy Guevara-Flanagan, 2016).

I had. It is ironic that while I was in the midst of bonding with my daughter, something so physical and emotionally intimate, I was spending all my free time looking at images of extreme violence against women. After having my daughter I felt a wave of emotions that were often on the surface in a way that they hadn't been before I had her. I wanted to make a piece from this emotional space or that harnessed it in some way.

I made that piece very much from a place of anger, from being pissed off. I felt very sensitized to the world and its injustices after having my daughter. In making the film, I felt protective of the women's images on-screen. I wanted to hold these images of dead women, bear witness to them, and possibly even honor them in some way. That instinct drove my editing process. Or perhaps it allowed me to keep coming back to such gruesome imagery. Of course, I became aware all over again of how our visual and gendered culture damages girls from a very young age. How everyone commented on the way my daughter looked from the moment she was out of the womb! The intense emphasis on girls' appearances above all else is so upsetting and damaging. And our girls internalize that so quickly.

Practically speaking, I took a semester off teaching. When I went back to a full teaching load after five months, I took a deep breath, packed up my breast pump, signed up for a billion daycare waiting lists, and stitched it together with various—and I do mean various—childcare situations. I had babysitters, nanny shares, in-home daycares, and childcare swaps. It sometimes felt like a full-time job securing childcare because after a few months, the childcare situation always seemed to change. Eventually, I found a three-way, nearly full-time nanny share with two of my neighbors, which finally made teaching and making art doable. My childcare provider, Maria, was incredible—patient, supportive, even instructive. I learned so much about this underappreciated and very critical population of the labor market.

IL: I remember how hard it was to negotiate all of those things—teaching, filmmaking, and being a new mother. I started my first full-time film teaching job with a four-month-old. My first day of work, every time I met a new colleague, I was in the process of moving between the public bathroom, where I needed to wash my breast pump, and my office, where I was pumping. Over and over again, I had to shake hands with new work colleagues who ran into me in the hallway while holding dripping-wet breast pump parts and unruly tubes behind my back. Everything felt so hard and there was no roadmap for how to do it.

KGF: What ridiculous situations working mothers find themselves in! I pumped in a huge community college parking lot because we only had shared offices and my classes were all across campus. I pumped in a classroom filled with students with nothing more than a curtain separating us!

What about you—what was the practical and artistic process like for you in making your first film after having a baby?

IL: Like you and for similar reasons, my first film after having a baby—*The Motherhood Archives*—was also an archival project. I

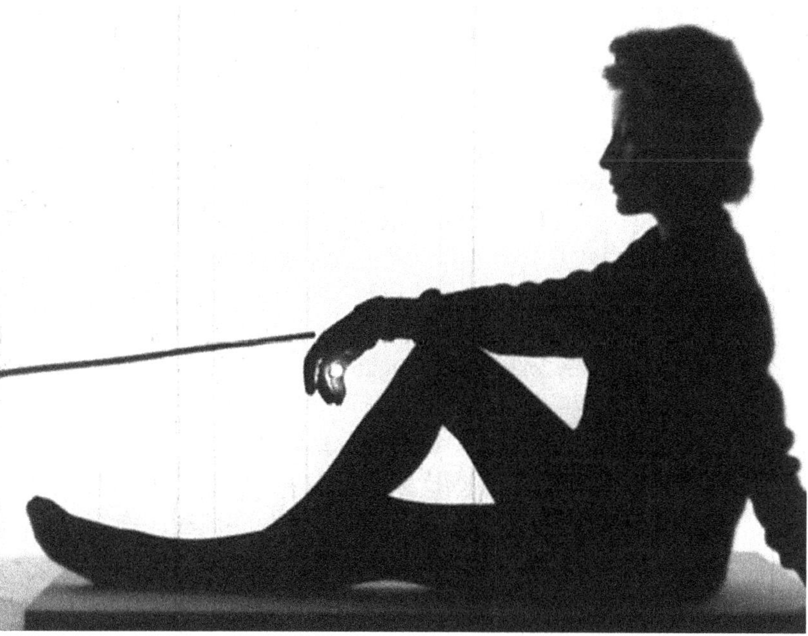

Film still from *The Motherhood Archives* (Irene Lusztig, 2013).

started buying discarded prenatal education films on eBay early in my pregnancy in 2006. I have a long-standing interest in thinking about visual cultures of propaganda, so the self-help section of pregnancy books in my local bookstore immediately made me feel suspicious and full of questions. The pregnant (and breastfeeding) body is a space of intense public scrutiny, policing, and surveillance—from anti-abortion rhetoric at the policy/state level down to the minutiae of exactly which foods and chemicals you should and should not ingest while you are pregnant. During pregnancy and beyond, early parenting is a profoundly judgmental space: Did you get an epidural? Are you breastfeeding? Are your kids vaccinated? Do you co-sleep? Whenever I am trying to puzzle through an issue that feels complex, I try to figure out if there's an archive or set of histories that can help me think about it. I was curious to understand why these spaces of talking about mothering, childbirth, and labor pain felt so ideological and fraught.

I also hated my prenatal education class. I was definitely aware that it felt weird and wrong to try to prepare for an event that would pretty much be out of my control—the experience of childbirth seems fundamentally incommensurate with the promise of order offered by these spaces of rehearsal and training. And I hated giving birth. I had read a lot of childbirth books that promised that I would feel empowered and fantastic while giving birth—if I went into the experience with the right feminist attitude about unmedicated "natural" birth—so I was shocked in the moment to realize how abject and disempowering the pain felt to me. So, after giving birth to my son, I continued to have a lot of questions about childbirth that I wanted to unpack, and I continued my archival viewing project. Over time, I amassed a substantial collection of nearly one hundred films from 1919 to the present, and I began constructing the archival essay film that became *The Motherhood Archives*. So, on one level, the project started from my efforts to dig into the ideological histories of prenatal education in order to answer very personal questions that felt pressing and urgent to me. I wanted to make the kind of critical, historically complex, and thoughtful prenatal education film that I wish had existed for me when I was pregnant.

But, like you, this project also emerged from practical concerns. When I found out I was pregnant in 2006, I was a week into my first-ever artist residency; within a week of my positive pregnancy test I was overcome with nausea so intense that I spent my residency days curled up in a fetal position in my artist cabin and finally had to go home early. The fact that my pregnancy literally coincided with the beginning and end of my artist residency career definitely made me panic about how I would be able to maintain my creative life as a new mom, and I think I've been reckoning and negotiating with those constraints ever since. Actually, the very first project I finished after having my son was a web-based interactive project, *The Worry Box Project*: I invited strangers to share their waking and dreaming anxieties about motherhood, and I committed to hand-transcribing each worry on paper and uploading a video that showed the transcription process. The project is about care, attention, the time and labor of handwriting, and the idea of spending time with people's worries. But also, for many months, this project, which was repetitive, durational, and process-focused—unlike anything I had made before—was literally the only way I could figure out how to feel like I was making something. It was very hard to find the kind of expansive time and space I needed to write the voice-over for

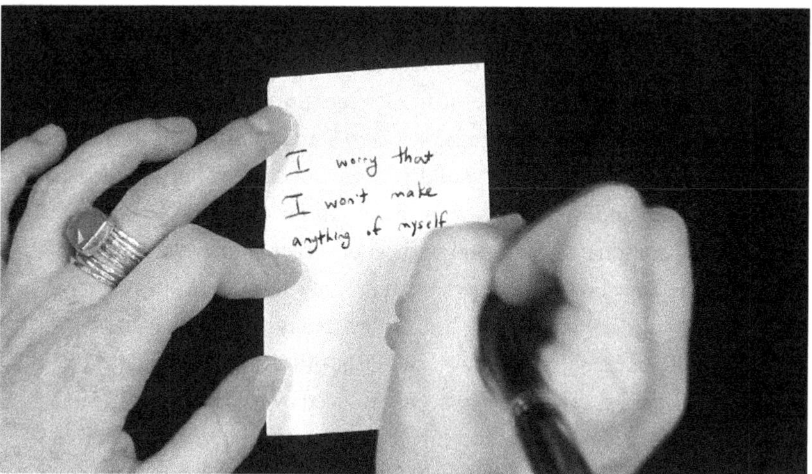

The Worry Box Project (Irene Lusztig, 2011).

The Motherhood Archives or to do more intellectually challenging research and editing. For a long time I just gathered archival films (work I could do from my living room) and hand-transcribed people's maternal worries. My weekly handwriting ritual was the only thing that kept me feeling connected to any kind of creative process. Making work about and from inside motherhood was definitely a creative survival strategy.

You must have been working through many of these same constraints when you started the GoPro shooting practice that has become *Mothertime* (2017). I love the way this film foregrounds the isolation, claustrophobia, repetition, and boredom of early parenting. These feelings are a huge part of the experience, but they are rarely the subject of creative work; there is something both very loving and politically important about foregrounding these everyday moments of care labor and maintenance work that all of us take on as new parents. Can you talk about how you worked through the form of the film in shooting, in your collaboration with Zora, and in editing?

KGF: When I went back to teaching and while I was working piecemeal on *What Happened to Her*, I decided I had to start filming. This was when my daughter was about a year old and I wanted to flex those muscles, to see what I was capable of on the other side of parenthood. Again, I came up with a simple concept and some constraints: I decided to film both of us using those small, portable cameras generally used in extreme sports. At first I sometimes strapped the camera to myself, and sometimes I tried to strap it on her. Eventually, I would just set the camera out on various ledges and surfaces as we went about our day. I was looking for a durational and textural portrait of early parenthood. I also was curious about how my daughter would respond to the camera, not understanding what the camera really does. To her the camera was an object like any toy and she did not understand that the images I showed her had been produced by the camera. It became clear soon after I began this "experiment" that the only kind of filming I could take on would be during early mornings and on the weekends. And so, as I collected material and reviewed it, the piece became more about our homebound routines, our relationship in bloom, and her linguistic development. I realized early on that my filming didn't and couldn't show the totality of our existence: there was nothing about the other people and community in our lives or activities like my work or her play with other children. I found myself instead focusing on the mundane, the everyday, and the various labors of my life. But the result is true in a close-up way to the texture of this particular period of our relationship. I think I gravitated toward documentation because I was lonely and isolated and wanted to feel myself an artist! A lens provides another eye and vantage of one's life. Something about that felt right for exploring this new life of mine as a parent. And, of course, it was practical and doable.

It was funny how Zora began to mimic how I used the camera—putting it on ledges, bringing it from room to room, turning it toward where the "action" might be even when I don't think she understood its relationship to image gathering.

I stopped filming when I got a new job and we moved across the state. It seemed a fitting conclusion to this particular time period. I put the material away for a few months, and then I received a small grant, just enough to hire an up-and-coming editor, Esther Shubinski. She was a new mom and pregnant with her second child, so it felt very intuitive, and even exciting, to work together. We paid a lot of attention to the material that she responded to most strongly from her own perspective as a mom. I wanted to move back and forth between three perspectives: when I wore the camera, when Zora wore or carried the camera, and when the camera was on the ledge filming the two of us from a wider POV. I also wanted each scene to have a strong real-time temporality, so keeping a durational perspective was important. And finally, we wanted Zora's development arc in terms of language acquisition to be made subtly apparent.

IL: Has Zora seen *Mothertime*?

KGF: Zora has seen *Mothertime* and she loves watching herself at that age act "silly" and make pre-linguistic sounds. She thinks the

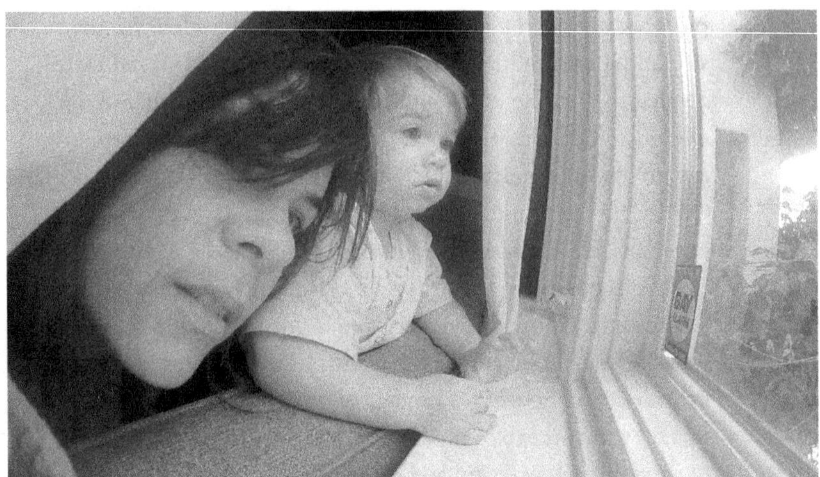

Film still from *Mothertime* (Kristy Guevara-Flanagan, 2017).

parts with me alone are utterly boring. Recently when Zora watched it with an audience, she thought her baby self hilarious and was talking to the screen the entire time. But at five years old, with a growing self-consciousness, she has also had reservations about sharing the film with an audience.

I do wonder what Zora will think about it when she is older, and I have had many conversations with friends who are parents about consent. Obviously, my daughter did not give consent to participate in this film and often balked when I asked her to wear the camera. I did push her at times to wear it (and that is in the film) but I also tried to incorporate the filming into our lives without taking away from our interactions. My initial take on this is that, at that particular age, she felt like an extension of myself. In fact, that was one of the main aspects that interested me in making the film in the first place. Also, I feel confident that it will not be broadcast to the public widely in any way that could cause her harm. The smaller scale of both the production and distribution have seemed appropriate: these are images that I would like to retain some control over in terms of where and how people view them.

IL: Those questions about consent are really interesting and complicated (and I think we are barely aware of what it might mean in the future that we have saturated our social media networks with images of our children). Many mother-artists I know—Courtney Kessel, Natalie Loveless, Jill Miller, and others—make collaborative performance work with their children, which makes complete sense given both the histories of feminist performance art and the incredible logistical constraints of raising a young child. When I invited a few of those artists to the University of California, Santa Cruz, where I teach, one of my students told me that the work felt incredibly exploitative to her, that she felt uncomfortable with the idea of artists "using" their children in their art. While I think that position is extreme, I personally haven't wanted to make work that uses images of my son for some of the reasons that you've brought up. Even when children consent to or enjoy being filmed, they can't possibly fully understand how digital images circulate in the world or how they might feel about those images in ten or twenty years. But I do think there are interesting models for how to have an ongoing negotiation with your children about collaborating that is attuned to their desires at different developmental stages. Artist Courtney Kessel does an iterative performance piece, *In Balance With*, where she and her daughter Chloe sit on opposite ends of a seesaw in a gallery space. Once the seesaw is balanced, they sit together "in balance" and in silence until Chloe indicates (nonverbally) that she wants to end the performance. I've seen them perform this piece in person, and there's something incredibly moving and powerful about watching them silently negotiate how and when to end their collaborative performance. The act of negotiating consent feels palpable and intimate.

KGF: We've talked a lot in the past about how little space maternity and motherhood take up in the art and film worlds as subjects worthy of attention. How was your film received? How and when did you discover who your true audience would be?

IL: The film was incredibly hard to screen! It got rejected by forty film festivals in a row during the first year of sending it out, including many places that had shown my previous films. Even though in the end a couple of really wonderful festivals with feminist programmers did show the film, it never had a big film world life. I heard over and over again from programmers that childbirth is an uninteresting topic, and that feminism, women's issues, and women's bodies are "niche" concerns for "academic feminists" or something their "wife might find interesting." People were really not shy about sharing these opinions! I know from other artist and writer friends working on childbirth- and maternity-focused creative work that this kind of discrimination is pervasive. Maternity (and maybe aging as well) is still among the least visible, least acceptable, and most marginalized of feminist work—maybe it does have to do with visibility, that when you are home with an infant it's hard to advocate for that work out in the world. But also there's this widespread perception that work about motherhood is sentimental, indulgent, narrow, narcissistic, domestic, and boring; that it's not an experience worth considering or thinking about, and that it therefore could only possibly be interesting to other new mothers.

I also found initially that a lot of women didn't like the film either. It has a critical take on histories and ideologies of childbirth that is very different from more familiar and comfortable "miracle of childbirth" films like *The Business of Being Born* (Abby Epstein, 2008). The film doesn't shy away from talking about pain, and something about combining a complex analytical discourse with a subject that makes people uncomfortable is hard for some viewers. Some people have told me that it's a very negative film. However, people also get in touch regularly to tell me that it means a lot to them to see a film that thinks critically about these experiences. And not showing in the film world forced me to look for other kinds of spaces for the film—feminist groups and medical schools and midwifery conferences and academic settings. The film has been very well received outside of the film world, and I'm grateful that I was pushed to look for those other kinds of viewers.

KGF: Can I respond to this? Mothers, in particular, are the subject of so much judgment. I feel this acutely with my film. I have definitely had audiences, including women and even mothers, who were very critical of the material. Is she a stay-at-home mother? Doesn't she work? This is so old-fashioned! Because I did not focus on my outside work but instead only highlighted my relationship with my daughter and parenting, that seems to be very confusing and even embarrassing to audiences. This makes sense because as a culture, we are confused about what a mother should and can be. I can only imagine what audiences think hearing the sounds of parenting, of that mother's sing-song tone of voice before the child is conversant. That voice is even hard for me to hear, in some kind of internalized self-loathing. How critical were audiences of the mothers in your film? What was it like trying to get feedback on the film as you were finishing?

IL: The work-in-progress feedback was brutal and unbelievably judgmental. It felt personal, and very different from the usual kind of criticism that is about form, structure, and pacing. People asked me reproachful questions about whether I was trying to "work through" my own negative experience with childbirth, or they wondered why I wasn't depicting "the joy of childbirth." And they definitely also felt very comfortable judging the mothers who speak in the direct-address sections of the film. One of the women in my film talks about being afraid of childbirth, wanting a C-section, and feeling relieved to have a very medically managed birth. She happened to be in the audience the first time I showed a work-in-progress version of the film, to a group of academic colleagues in a fellowship, and the audience basically turned on her. People asked her incredibly rude questions—if she regretted becoming a mother, why she became a mother when her attitude about childbirth was so bad—it was a kind of conversation I have never heard before or since in an academic setting! It's still unbelievable to me that these very educated people somehow conflated enjoying pregnancy and birth with being a fit or loving parent.

What kinds of responses have you gotten to *Mothertime*? I know you've experienced similar difficulties with getting screenings.

KGF: Like you, I have been rejected by dozens of film festivals—in fact, I never got into any with this film. I understand that as a very experimental, personal documentary feature there are already limited opportunities for the work. But I have been shocked. I attend festivals and see other experimental documentary works and I have to ask myself why these communities, my communities, reject this piece and deem it utterly unworthy of intellectual or artistic exploration. I think the experimental documentary world, in particular, is not open to feminist films. And maybe the trend in those communities right now, with the interest in works from places like the Harvard Sensory Ethnography Lab, is more outward looking in a way that my film and *The Motherhood Archives* are not. I hope that this moment is changing, and it seems like your new piece, *Yours in Sisterhood* (2018), is striking a chord and providing a compelling feminist context for the #MeToo and #TimesUp conversations, among other things.

I feel like I am just starting to reach my real audience. Film professors are screening this work in their feminist film classes, and students seem to be responding to it. There is not a lot of new work out there that speaks on the subject of motherhood, especially from a personal perspective. Through you, Irene, I connected with Deirdre Donoghue, who screened the film at her space, m/other voices in Rotterdam. The foundation has a monthly event called a "field trip" where it informally invites a guest, and kids are welcome. It was a great experience and fun to screen to a group where children were responding to the film.

IL: The most empowering thing that came out of my depressing year of festival rejections is that it made me realize that I had to find and activate my own networks for feminist maternal art—that if no one in the film or art world is having the conversation you want to have, you can either give up or go out and make your own space for that conversation. There's a politics to making space where there isn't any space, to putting on your own events and screening programs and art shows, to finding other people who want to collaborate, to building new networks. I started "Complicated Labors," an interdisciplinary research network on maternity and creative practice at my university. I tried to figure out who else was making and showing work about motherhood and sent cold emails to people. I organized a symposium and gallery show at the University of California, Santa Cruz on intergenerational feminist maternal art and writing. Over time and through this kind of work, I've become part of an incredible international network of mother-artists. Finding and building these robust networks over time has been rewarding and important work for me.

You approached me with the idea of co-curating "Mothering Every Day," a full-length screening program of films about maternity that we've been touring around to microcinemas and alternative screening spaces. That project feels very much part of this kind of DIY programming and network building that I've been talking about. It's a way of making space together, of supporting each other's work, of starting a conversation.

What are you working on now? Do you want to keep making work that centers on maternity? Or is your maternal experience shaping your new work in other, less explicit ways?

KGF: I would love to do a piece on nannies in the future. Something performative. I would love to work with caregivers and have them reenact their daily scenarios and speak about their children and hopes for the future. But for the time being I am making *Body Parts*, another film on gender and representation that looks at how nudity is performed on-screen and all the behind-the-scenes machinations deployed to make this happen. I am talking to a wide range of people including A-list and lesser-known actresses, body doubles, rape stunt coordinators, make-up artists, CGI artists, editors, SAG representatives, and lawyers who specialize in nudity clauses. It feels scary and ambitious. And timely. I think the piece is shaped by my constraints as a parent: I can't film extensively away from where I live, I can't follow in verité style or spontaneously film events unfolding in real time. I have to construct my argument and make my film within a containable production schedule that unfolds in fits and starts over a long arc.

What about you? How did *The Motherhood Archives* lead to *Yours in Sisterhood*?

IL: I'm still thinking about a kind of maternal ethics and still thinking about the kinds of questions around care labor that really came into focus for me when I became a parent. But I'm trying to think more expansively about these ideas—to untether my thinking about things like care and listening from embodied/biological maternity. I think the long take, very open-ended eleven-minute 16 mm film "conversations" that I was filming with women for *The Motherhood Archives*—like the one I filmed with you the day we first met—very directly informed the methods I've developed for *Yours in Sisterhood*, my recently finished film where women perform and respond to letters sent to *Ms.* magazine in the '70s. While the new film looks and feels very different from *The Motherhood Archives*, it definitely started as an evolution of some of the core questions I had when I was making the more explicitly maternity-focused work: what kinds of spaces do we have for feminist conversation, and how can we make new kinds of spaces for feminist speaking and listening?

I barely knew any other mother-artists before I made *The Motherhood Archives* and went looking for that community. In my MFA program very few female faculty members had kids. I didn't really see many models for people who had both kids and an art career. Did you have role models or influences who were mother-artists or filmmakers? Models of work that made you believe that making a film about mothering was a viable thing to do?

KGF: The short answer is no! Similarly, in my MFA program where I studied, there were no visible faculty with children. Where I teach now there are some men with older children (something tells me they were not primary care providers) and no women who are practitioners with children. None. There are so few models and there is so much silence and invisibility. I can't tell you how much that visibility—that is, me visibly and outwardly juggling parenthood and career—is noticed and remarked on by my students. I've had many female students quite interested in talking about this aspect of my life. And so, I want to be visible. I want to bring my baby to film festivals and onstage when I speak. I want to bring my daughter to the faculty meetings that are scheduled after school hours. I want to bring my child to classes when she has the day off or is sick. Or to the edit session. Well, I have to. I want audiences, students, and my faculty to see this, to have to deal with it.

IL: Yes, there is a lot of invisibility around early motherhood (and the hidden corporate pumping room seems like the wrong kind of neoliberal solution—why not nursing out in the open at the board meeting?). There is definitely a visibility politics around mothering in public and at work. I was just at a film festival where the festival organizers told me they used to have a kindergarten, but they canceled it. How do you go to film festivals as a single parent? So much of building a film career—as in most male-dominated careers—seems to happen through participating in social spaces (festival parties, drinks, and so on) that are not child or parent friendly.

KGF: What a concept, a kindergarten at a festival! The festivals are probably the hardest part. Attending festivals was easier when Zora was not in school, didn't need a plane ticket, and I could simply wear or hold her. And I just can't attend the parties—I'm lucky if I make it to the festivals themselves! Sometimes I can finagle to bring someone with me to the festival to help, but that is usually beyond my budget. Or I might have friends in cities where festivals occur who can help out. I have been impressed by artists and filmmakers who do manage to bring their children to festivals. Kirsten Johnson brought her twins around the world when *Cameraperson* (2016) came out. She really was on the stomping grounds with that film. It is so incredibly hard, though. When I finish my next feature in a couple years, I will have to, once again, reinvent the wheel and figure this out all over again. Conferences are easier. A few of them do have organized caregiving, which is brilliant. I make it a point to ask every conference about childcare so they get used to that request. Maybe I should follow suit with festivals!

IL: I was going through old pages of notes in my project notebook recently and found a page with a heading that said "HOW TO DO EVERYTHING," followed by several pages of densely spaced bullet points that basically broke down a strategy for how to do everything (at the time this included finishing a feature-length film, raising $20,000 to finish the film, and stuff like making sure my kid finished his science fair project). The weird mix of high-level filmmaking and quotidian domestic tasks on the list made me laugh. But also it made me think about how we are very much stuck in this broken power feminism "having it all/doing it all" paradigm that we inherited from the Reagan era. How can we possibly do it all? And what might it look like not to have to do it all? What are ways we can build different kinds of support structures for making and screening work that are more distributed or collective?

KGF: This is such an excellent point. I am involved in this very active social media group for single mothers in academia. I love the unedited conversations of these spaces. And no, we can't possibly do it all. As a joke in one of these spaces when one mom was looking for creative ways to keep all the balls she juggles in the air, I said to look for the life "slacks" rather than the "hacks." I have started to rebel against the word *hack* as emblematic of this unattainable goal of women trying to do it all. What we really need are more "slacks" and to celebrate them. More meals of just crackers and cheese or hummus and carrots. Bare minimum packed lunches. Dishes in the sink, fewer showers. No enrichment classes for the kiddos on the weekend that I really don't want to attend anyway. It's much harder to celebrate the slacks in the workspace, I recognize. I am still working on how to sell this!

I feel my young women students experiencing this same pressure to be everything all the time—perfectly composed, perfectly in shape, the perfect student—and they haven't even come to the parenting and career world yet. Something has got to give.

I have recently started to participate more in women-centered media-making spaces. This collectivity is incredibly efficient and emotionally buoyant. Pooling our resources together, demanding a seat at the table, and sharing our knowledge, skills, and personal connections form the basis of what these groups have to offer. I just went to one of these meetings last night, and there was a deep recognition that now is our moment to occupy and seize the spaces that have traditionally been so elusive. Take up that space, I say!

Filmography

Maternity Test. Directed by Irene Lusztig. Komsomol Films, 2014.

The Motherhood Archives. Directed by Irene Lusztig. Women Make Movies, 2013.

Mothertime. Directed by Kristy Guevara-Flanagan. Women Make Movies, 2017.

What Happened to Her. Directed by Kristy Guevara-Flanagan. Women Make Movies, 2016.

Wonder Women! The Untold Story of American Superheroines. Directed by Kristy Guevara-Flanagan. Women Make Movies, 2012/2013.

The Worry Box Project. Created by Irene Lusztig. Komsomol Films, 2011, www.worryboxproject.net/.

Yours in Sisterhood. Directed by Irene Lusztig. Women Make Movies, 2018.

4

Watching while a Mother

Parenting, Spectatorship, Criticism

Claire Perkins

In part 6 of *Twin Peaks: The Return* (2017), there is a scene where a young, unnamed boy is run down and killed by a raging character speeding through a pedestrian crossing on the wrong side of the road. The scene is bluntly and deliberately shocking, lingering on both the mother's anguish and the physical aftermath of the crime. Watching as the mother of a nearly two-year-old son, though, my reaction veered far beyond shock. The scene literally sickened me in the moment of viewing, and kept me in a state of consistent acute anxiety for more than a week after as I involuntarily replayed it over and over in my head. The scene is quite tangential to the main narratives of the series and is explicitly referred to only once more over the show's entire run. It was, however, my defining experience of watching this series and without doubt the most tangible and intense reaction I've had to any film or television work—ever. As I am someone who makes a living watching, writing about, and teaching screen media, this reaction both bothered and compelled me. It continued to gnaw at me for months after I saw the scene, even as the affective charge faded. I can draw readily on numerous theories, histories, and knowledges to explain (if not justify) the function of the scene in the context of David Lynch's dark and obscure revival of his series. I know, intimately, how the event is not "real." But my primeval reaction stubbornly governed my experience of the scene in a way that I'm convinced it would not have before I became a mother. The Child, to draw on Lee Edelman, became the "perpetual horizon" of my spectatorship.[1]

Taking this experience as a cue, this chapter investigates how parenting impacts upon the act and labor of screen criticism by shaping one's identity as a viewing subject. Mobilizing screen scholarship as a specific strand of media practice, it seeks to understand if and how parenthood centers spectatorship for screen scholars, and to comprehend both the challenges and inventions this gives rise to. In addition to exploring the affective charge described above as an altered mode of viewing subjectivity, I am also interested in how the practical dimensions of caring labor impact the work of screen criticism. How, for instance, do inevitable limitations on time and mental space manifest in the texts we consume and reflect upon? How do cultural tastes and patterns of identification change? The investigative work of this chapter is grounded in my own personal experience as a screen scholar and a mother. And, to a certain degree, my experience with *Twin Peaks: The Return* is wholly obvious and unsurprising. The entire field of media reception studies is founded upon the understanding that media consumers will draw different meanings from the same text based on their individual social situations. Here, then, my response can be understood as a relatively straightforward example of a "negotiated" reading where the scene's shocking impact is amplified by my identity as a mother, an identity defined by attachments, experiences, and memories that bring intensified meaning to the screen moment. This understanding of the phenomenon is endorsed by the contemporary moment, when the notion of "trigger" warnings in media and education culture is being rapidly mainstreamed, premised upon the understanding that certain material may cause predisposed individuals to have a strong emotional response.[2] In my case, the "trauma" that was triggered by this scene is not a historical event but the driving anxiety that attends the overwhelming love and responsibility for one's child(ren)—the relentless fear for their well-being that has been documented in works on parenthood as diverse as *Stepmom* (Chris Columbus, 1998) and Karen Russell's story "Orange World."[3] Finally, to react to screen content "as if real" is not so surprising either. In the phenomenological terms of Vivian Sobchack, my response is carnal—it springs from the relation between the scene and my sensate body, with its particular, reflexive intelligibility an example of my body "making sense" in its own right.[4] As Sobchack shows, for much seminal film theory this ability to stimulate us physiologically and sensually *is* cinema; it is the medium's unique ability to "directly stimulate the *material layers* of the human being: his nerves, his senses, his entire *physiological substance*."[5]

Beyond these rationalizations, though, my response continued to preoccupy me. I feel my experience as a limit, insofar as I was (and still am) loath to return to the *Twin Peaks* scene to look carefully at its arrangement and evaluate my reaction. I am fascinated by my response, but violently opposed to experiencing it again—it feels like a type of illness I would have to endure and slowly recover from once more. Further, this fear has actively shaped my avoidance (for the moment) of screen narratives where children suffer. It has got in the way of my seeing, studying, or teaching content that I would otherwise like to, as well as returning to texts that I enjoyed before becoming a parent where this theme is prominent or striking. It is both the extreme and expansive nature of this response and—more compellingly—the way it seems to function as a *limit*, that made me keen to explore the experience further.

In order to begin to theorize this phenomenon, I wanted to gain insight into the experience of other screen scholars. This approach was not primarily devised as a way of combating the charges of subjectivism that can attend phenomenological description. Indeed, it was precisely this type of description that I hoped to elicit from my participants and—as will become clear below—that I understand to be central to the phenomenon I'm investigating. The decision to speak with other parents was motivated by a desire to understand whether others who are already unique viewing subjects—that is to say, individuals with a comprehensive understanding of film theory, media effects, and the complex ways in which cinema's carnal address is part of its very ontology—could or could not mobilize this expertise to "short-circuit" the kind of emotional response I experienced. As such, my primary method for the study was a series of seven semi-structured one-on-one interviews with screen scholars who are also parents. The interviewees were all tenured academics working in screen and media studies departments across seven universities in Australia and the United States. Five were mothers and two were fathers, ranging in age from forty-one to fifty-one and in positions from senior lecturer to professor. They had between one and five children each, the ages ranging from six months to twenty-five years. Six were white and one Asian-Australian, and two identified as queer women. Three were currently living with the other parent of their child(ren). The interviews ran for between thirty-five minutes to one hour, with three of the four Melbourne interviews conducted on weekdays at the interviewee's university office, and one in my own university office. The interstate and international interviews were conducted via Skype outside of office hours when childcare could be secured. All interviews were audio recorded with the interviewees' consent.

The participants were all colleagues that I have known for at least two years and with whom I worked in various (primarily research) capacities before requesting the interview. I regard all as friends, but part of the motivation for my methodology came from observing how the majority of these friendships have developed out of purely professional connections since I became a parent. As soon as I became pregnant I noticed this shift in rapport with almost all colleagues who are also parents, and for this project I selected interviewees with whom I'd had particularly interesting or intriguing interactions based on this shared experience, interactions that signaled a high level of self-awareness around the parent-scholar identity. These were people who offered to me advice and support but, more immediately, they were and remain genuinely interested in my child and my experience as a parent. These connections demonstrate a great deal to me about the experience of being a parent in academia. They highlight the place of challenges that are instantly recognizable, but largely invisible to non-parents, such as the heightened difficulty of international travel and of attending events outside of work (and daycare) hours. They are sites for the shared understanding of how one's research career is changed and limited in both practical and affective ways by having a child.

Perhaps most significantly, they emphasize the expansive and demanding identity of academic labor, and of how the pressures of a job that is already routinely characterized as "too much" are amplified by being a parent. I aimed to touch on these themes in the interviews by developing questions that focused on professional identity, practical arrangements for managing the labor of viewing and writing, perceived differences in the affective quality of screen media since becoming a parent, memories of using screen media at different stages of parenthood, and experiences of interacting with children in media contexts (including both shared viewing and regulation). In what follows, I draw on ideas from embodied film theory, cine-ethics, and parenting culture studies to contextualize some key themes that emerged in these interviews regarding how one's identity as a screen scholar is impacted by parenthood. The key themes I will discuss are the differing affective charge of screen material involving children, and different approaches to viewing and working. Some interesting issues also arose around the experience of watching *with* children, but I won't have the space to cover this topic here.

Affective Charge

> That film kicked me in the guts emotionally from the very, very beginning, and it was a kind of embodied visceral connection to the mother's experience and to that sense of overwhelming grief, or of even thinking about the premature death of your child, a child predeceasing the mother, just kind of blew it apart for me emotionally.

This quote is from Jillian, an interviewee with a twenty-three-year-old daughter, describing her reaction to the film *Arrival* (Denis Villeneuve, 2016).[6] The description encapsulates many of the compelling aspects that all interviewees reported experiencing as a type of "heightened sensitivity" or "altered perspective" toward screen content involving an emotionally charged situation concerning a child when watching as a parent. The death of the teenage daughter in *Arrival* is not central to its narrative, which concerns a linguistics professor's attempt to communicate with extraterrestrial life-forms that suddenly appear on Earth. As a result, it was not promoted or even revealed in the film's marketing, and Jillian went to see the film because she was interested in Villeneuve as a director and likes science fiction. Nonetheless, it was this dimension of the protagonist's (Amy Adams) backstory that became the defining point of engagement for this mother, that ultimately, in her revealing words, "blew it apart for me emotionally." This pattern proved to be common among all interviewees. All volunteered instances of screen texts where an acentral plot point or detail regarding the child-parent relationship became—in diverse ways—an emotional anchor for their viewing, in examples from *Under the Skin* (Jonathan Glazer, 2013) to *The Good Dinosaur* (Peter Sohn, 2015), *Lion* (Garth Davis, 2016) to *Battleship Potemkin* (Sergei Eisenstein, 1925), *Nocturnal Animals* (Tom Ford, 2016) to *The Walking Dead* (2010–).

Many also described how this response was augmented when there was a match in age, gender, name, or personality between the onscreen character and their own child(ren): "I had that watching *Lion* when the little boy was left on the train. . . . It's that match, it's the identification—that is what causes a trauma for me. So older kids, much younger girls, I don't have that, but it's seeing a child of around the same age as mine" (Audrey, mother of a seven-year-old boy). David, a father of five, including a nine-year-old son, said of the ending of *The Boy in the Striped Pyjamas* (Mark Herman, 2008), "It's quite beautifully done in the film, but it's just impossibly tragic, and I've got mischievous kids . . . and I could just see [my youngest son] doing that, you know how you translate, it is literally memorial."

Interestingly, one father reported the opposite tendency, describing how he now watches coming-of-age texts as a parent:

> The strangest thing that I've found is that, once [my older son] turned two or three, when I watch coming-of-age films I think about—I anticipate and am anxious about—his first experiences as a teen or late teen. So I kind of project fifteen years ahead. And that's not impacted by the sex of the protagonist, so it's as much *The Edge of Seventeen* [Kelly Fremon Davis, 2016] [or] *Lady Bird* [Greta Gerwig, 2017]. . . . But maybe first I look ahead to those kinds of experiences that he will hopefully get to have, and wanting him to go through those but also hoping that they're not . . . they don't feel soul destroying. (Gabriel, father of two sons, aged four years and six months)

The most consistent theme across all interviews was the subjects' conviction that they wouldn't have had these heightened reactions before becoming a parent. This was clearest, unsurprisingly, for those with younger children, who could readily contrast their modes of viewing before and after becoming a mother or father. What became obvious through the discussions, then, was that this identity represents a wholly different type of emotional engagement with narrative content. In some cases, this registered as a renewed perspective on entire genres:

> So I really enjoy suspense thrillers, psychological thrillers, murder mysteries. And particularly as a mother of a daughter, you're just immediately hit in the face with how many media texts in popular culture are predicated on the rape, abuse, and murder of young women. . . . And it's not that I wasn't aware of this before, but I think it's just different when you start positioning that girl, that fictional

> girl—you're projecting your child onto that, and it completely changes the dynamic of these stories. And particular genres—it's all about essentially the abuse of children, and you're like, wow, that is just so sick—why didn't I realize this before? (Megan, mother of a two-year-old daughter)

Jillian, mother of a twenty-three-year-old daughter, noted, "I became much more sensitive to violence on-screen when I was a young mother. Hadn't really bothered me very much prior to that, doesn't bother me at all now, but as a young mother I was very sensitive to and attuned to screen violence, particularly violence against women and children. *Cape Fear* [Martin Scorsese, 1991] was a huge one for me, really rattled me."

For others, the altered emotional engagement was focused on specific types of characters or representations, particularly the absent parent. Audrey recalled going to see *The Boxcar Children: Surprise Island* (Anna Chi, 2018) with her son: "I'm quite traumatized by films and TV shows where there are absent parents. I'm constantly worried about the children. . . . You are thinking, why are these children left there to fend for themselves? So when [my son] watched it he thought it was a great adventure, that they're having all this fun on their own and I was just kind of traumatized that they had been left there to their own devices." Gabriel reported a different type of response to the absent parent while reflecting on another children's film, *The Good Dinosaur*: "I'm really sensitive to fathers dying in films. . . . I think that I find that difficult, more difficult than when there's a bumbling dad or a selfish dad. I find the absenting of the father more affecting . . . perhaps because of how I think about myself as a dad."

Naturally, but importantly, the reported reactions were also shaped by the individual circumstances of the interviewee, demonstrating how the "parent perspective" is far from a singular or universal position. David, who lives in a different country than his three youngest children, described his overwhelming response to the moment in *Under the Skin* where the young baby is left on the beach alone, presumably to die: "It's corporeal, it's sensorial, it seems to be unspeakable, and you don't want to go back—it's like a form of existential nausea . . . when language fails you and you're trying to hold onto terra firma to find a root, an anchor, a branch so you don't die in despair in an emotional sense, but you can't—there's nothing you can do. . . . And I think it's heightened for me too because they are not all with me. . . . I can't control my kids' fate because I am not in their spaces, not in their everyday life."

The Parental Cinesthetic Subject

Together, these repeated descriptions of bodily, traumatic, and highly emotive experiences of screen content involving children and parents begin to suggest that the parent-viewer is an automatic, or at least privileged, type of cinesthetic subject. Sobchack coined this term to describe the mode of "sensual being" at the movies that no viewer—including film theorists—can evade: "As 'lived bodies' (to use a phenomenological term that insists on 'the' objective body as always also lived subjectively as 'my' body, diacritically invested and active in making sense and meaning in and of the world), our vision is always already 'fleshed out.'"[7] By pointedly contextualizing this experiential reality as a problem or embarrassment for film theory as an approach that has (historically) been distinguished by detached, critical reflection, Sobchack's concept is situated right at the core of my concern with the unique viewing subjectivity of the parent-critic. In these terms, it is clearly *not* possible, or desirable, for theoretical expertise to "short-circuit" the type of amplified affective engagements described above; indeed, these responses should be taken as evidence of how "the film experience is meaningful *not to the side of our bodies but because of our bodies*."[8] They demonstrate heightened, consistent, and remarkably pure examples of how human bodies are "touched" and "moved" by screen content, reinstating the experience as something highly intimate. As Jennifer Barker writes, "To say that we are touched by cinema indicates that it has significance for us, that it comes close to us, and that it literally occupies our sphere."[9] Part of the amplification I see with these particular experiences, though, derives from the way they are not restricted to cinema or being "at the movies." They can be sparked by watching films at home on a TV or computer (as parents often have to), well outside of the experience, and logic, of the cinematic apparatus.

Being a parent, then, seems to cast our experience of screen material as unusually sensate; it remakes certain content in terms of a cinema of sensation. Resting upon a wholly altered emotional engagement, the experience is most readily explicable in terms of empathy which, as Jane Stadler explains, "is not an emotion in its own right but is closely associated with the role of emotion as an index of value."[10] Empathy is central to both aesthetics and hermeneutics as operational schema and, at a more specific level, to narrative arts, insofar as it governs how the reader or viewer projects or attunes to the artwork as a way of producing meaning. Indeed, as Robert Sinnerbrink shows, the core meaning of *Einfühlung*—the German word from which "empathy" derives—is to "feel one's way into."[11] The manner in which this embodied production of meaning occurs can differ substantially between media. Every narrative representation operates according to a principle of intersubjectivity whereby attention and emotion are shared between text and consumer. As Stadler argues, though, whereas a narrative format such as literature will primarily facilitate *cognitive* empathy in the form of appraisal and taking on others' perspectives, film and television fictions also centrally elicit *affective* empathy through strategies of embodied simulation and imagination.

This "affective transfer" describes "the ways in which stylistic techniques may facilitate corporeal empathy by directing the audience's attention to screen characters' affective experience."[12] Sinnerbrink theorizes this specifically audiovisual transfer within a framework of empathic ethics that he terms "cinempathy," claiming that "film provides a powerful means of enacting the affective temporal dynamic between empathy and sympathy, emotional engagement, and multiple perspective-taking."[13] Sinnerbrink's premise here rests upon a phenomenological understanding of the relationship between empathy and sympathy as poles between which we are moved: "poles marking two distinct yet related kinds of subjective perspective-taking having different but related emotional dynamics and evaluative valences (more immediate, immersive, and affective in the case of empathy, more mediated, reflective, and normative in the case of sympathy)."[14] A useful way to understand the distinction, he suggests, is to describe empathy as *feeling with* and sympathy as *feeling for*, or—drawing on Murray Smith—*central* versus *acentral imagining*. In both cases, the terms describe the imaginative adoption of another's perspective from either a first-person or an observer point of view, whereas the latter term describes a situation where one imagines the emotional response without *experiencing* the emotion as such.

Interestingly, an example that Sinnerbrink mobilizes to illustrate this distinction is the moment in *The Tree of Life* (Terrence Malick, 2011) when the mother (Jessica Chastain) is struck by grief over the death of her son. His choice demonstrates the relatability, even the ubiquity, of this scenario as an emotionally charged plot point for any viewer. As he writes, "I can imaginatively participate in her emotional experience despite knowing she is fictional, and despite being neither a mother nor having experienced this type of devastating loss."[15] Sinnerbrink's primary interest, then, is in how his emotional participation in this moment is enabled by the film's stylistic language, in how he is moved, depending on the mode of cinematic presentation, between a central and peripheral perspective on the experience of grief. This concern fits precisely with his book's overarching inquiry into cinema as a conduit for ethical experience, and chimes with the textual approach that many other theorists who work on cinema and empathy also take.[16]

My focus is different, insofar as I'm interested in how this phenomenological movement between empathy and sympathy is driven by the *extratextual* condition of being a parent. My own experience and those reported by my interviewees suggest that this condition substantially alters how the oscillation between the two poles occurs. Many commented on being aware of taking a different emotional point of view on screen material since becoming a parent in terms that can quite clearly be understood as an observant (sympathetic) perspective versus an affective (empathic) one. This is Megan, reflecting upon her different response to violence against young women in psychological thrillers: "I mean, it's not that I wasn't aware of how often that's a plot point in films . . . it's not that it didn't bother me, but it just didn't hit me at a gut level like it does now." Jillian reflected, "You know, [*Arrival*] very well could have been an emotional film for anybody else, but having a daughter of that particular age related to the death . . . certainly augmented the emotional response." And Gabriel commented, "I just think that . . . there's a new aspect in which I self-identify that shapes how I watch. . . . So it just feels like I'm more aware of my identity, that part of my identity when I watch, than I am for other parts. . . . As a parent, it just makes us much more aware of how we watch through our bodies and through our lived experience."

Intensive Parenting

Here, then, the movement toward a form of central imagining is controlled not (or not only) by audiovisual presentation but by the "paradigm scenario" of being a parent. Sinnerbrink draws on this concept of Ronald de Sousa's to illustrate one of the most salient constitutive elements of emotions as phenomena: they are intimately related to narratives. Acquired paradigm scenarios are, in Sinnerbrink's terms, "characteristic patterns of feelings, actions, and reactions, organized in narrative terms, that occur in specific situations leading to a 'learned' emotional response."[17] It is at once a commonsense truism and a point of much discussion in the baby industrial complex that becoming a parent very often leads to fundamental changes in one's feelings, actions, and reactions. Indeed, the very premise of maternal ambivalence as both the symptom of a diagnosable phenomenon (such as postnatal depression) and a cultural trope (from Naomi Wolf's *Misconceptions* [2001] to the Australian Broadcasting Corporation/Netflix series *The Letdown* [2017–]) is a perceived change in selfhood, which is often theorized or dramatized as a *loss* of self. While my interview questions did not ask directly about experiences of ambivalence in this sense, many of the interviewees' responses, in concert with the cultural reality of their lives as "thinkers," did indicate that their lived experience of parenthood is highly *intensive* at both an emotional and practical level. And it is this reality, I believe, that can be understood as the core of the paradigm scenario that shapes both the empathic reactions I have been exploring and—as I will explore next—the everyday labor of being a screen scholar.

The concept of "intensive parenting" is a core ideology in contemporary parenting culture studies, with most scholars orienting their diverse inquiries in the terms of seminal work from the 1990s and early 2000s by Sharon Hays as well as Susan Douglas and Meredith Michaels on the gendered practices and models of motherhood in modern middle-class America.[18] Hays theorizes intensity as the manner in which modern mothers do much more than simple physical care: the "more" is the intensity, which is structured by child-centered, expert-guided, emotionally absorbing, labor-intensive, and financially expensive methods. The logic of child rearing, she summarizes, "involves lavishing copious amounts of time, energy and material resources on a child whose needs are put above the mother's own."[19] Douglas and Michaels coin the term the *new momism* to describe the romanticized, demanding, and ultimately impossible conditions of this style of mothering, which rest upon the premise that "to be a remotely decent mother, a woman has to devote her entire physical, psychological, emotional and intellectual being, 24/7, to her children."[20] Many of the interviewees I spoke with demonstrated the impact of this perfectionist model when describing their efforts to be fully present when with their child(ren), not distracted by the demands of work or technology. Beyond this imperative, though, I also perceived evidence of a specifically *existential* dimension of intensity with this group, whereby the condition of parenthood provoked a certain awareness and reflection upon both their own and their child(ren)'s being in the world. This is Gabriel, responding to a question on what the concept of "watching as a parent" meant to him: "It goes to my—to all of our—anxieties about our capacity to ensure their welfare and well-being far into adulthood . . . it's kind of unending. . . . So it's about that anxiety about our capacity, which we can never fulfill, we can never ensure, to protect them."

Again, there is an entirely unremarkable dimension to this structure of feeling, insofar as having a child is often put in terms of how the "miracle"—and mystery—of life gives parents a privileged, renewed perspective on the "big picture" or what "really matters." Hays touches on this, I believe, when she describes how a critical element of intensive mothering is the logic of the sacred child, whereby children are naturally valued for their innocence and lovingness rather than their potential material gains. In this way, Hays writes, "not only are children understood as distinct from participants in the larger corrupt world, but child rearing also stands in opposition to the self-interested, competitive pursuit of personal gain."[21]

For scholars and thinkers such as my group of interviewees, this logic is taken up more readily than it would be by others, perhaps, to lead to a—not necessarily conscious—conception of their child as *the Child*, the emblem of futurity that is theorized, in notably diverse ways, by writers including Edelman, Kathryn Bond Stockton, and Rebekah Sheldon.[22] In all these works, the child—and by extension the experience of having a child—becomes a figural site for understanding human anxiety toward the future of life on Earth or, as Sheldon puts it, "the way the child-figure comes to inform the rhetorical figuration of future catastrophe; and the effect of that rhetorical form on the epistemological and cultural fabrications of nature, matter and life-itself."[23] It is an intuitive grasp, I believe, of this child-future relationship that constitutes an important part of the paradigm scenario that primes the parent-critic to have a particular "learned" emotion—a viscerally empathic response—to screen material such as that discussed above, and to simultaneously observe themselves *having* that emotion; as Gabriel put it, "Yeah, it's a weird distancing moment; it's like 3D [*laughs*]. It kind of takes me out of the film and then also connects me to the film."

Through these interviews, it became clear how the experience of parenting as a new mode of selfhood also impacts in very pragmatic ways the everyday labor of screen scholarship. Here, the logic of intensive parenting manifested in two dominant themes: the challenges presented by the personal and cultural imperative to put one's child first, and the manner in which child-centeredness comes to shape the actual content of one's work and intellectual focus. Much of what was conveyed around the former theme is part of the familiar plight of all working parents, with interviewees describing the challenges of being limited to restricted work hours and the practical and intellectual difficulties of having to continually switch headspaces between work and parenting. A number mentioned making a conscious decision not to work weekends, as they had before becoming a parent, and revealed that they found themselves too tired to work at night. What was striking in these responses was the intensity of the commitment to being *present* with one's child(ren): "I try to be a very hands-on mum, to help at [my daughter's] school and also to try to be completely 100 percent present when I'm with her" (Megan). "I can work once my responsibilities and obligations as a father and a partner are done. Not the other way around. . . . So I'm even quite conscious when I'm with [my older son] of trying not to check my email or my phone, like I need to be fully present. . . . So those are quite precious moments where we talk an awful lot, and kind of talk about his experience in the world" (Gabriel).

An issue specific to the labor of academic screen scholarship that was frequently mentioned was the difficulty of keeping up with new film and television material. While an unquestioned prerogative of the job before becoming a parent, afterward it is mentally relegated to a sphere of pleasure or entertainment that there isn't time for; according to Megan, "I don't have time to go to the movies anymore. I feel like it's this really special, rare thing that I get to do, and I almost feel guilty when I do it now because I feel like that's two hours of time that I should be spending doing something else. Which is silly, because it is my research—it's work, right?" The blurred function of viewing for screen scholars as both labor and leisure was starkly shown up in responses that described the compromises that get made with one's partner over viewing material. As a parent, of young children especially, shared viewing in the evening is a common way to spend time together. For parent-scholars with partners, then, this tends to be where the bulk of their viewing occurs, and is necessarily subject to their partner's tastes and preferences.

Here, numerous interviewees described prioritizing (if unconsciously) this hour or so of viewing in the evening as a way of spending time with their partner, rather than watching for work: "Luckily our tastes do align in a lot of ways, but there are certain things that I'm interested in that he's not that interested in, so I just don't end up having time to watch them."

In all of these responses, the (perceived) needs of the child(ren) are put above the needs and desires of the parent. In a second theme, this child-centeredness was shown to shape the parent-scholar's work itself. At one level, this occurs as a shift in the *mode* of work:

> I think maybe my mode of writing might have shifted away from much more conceptual and theoretical forms of thinking—the ones where you do need time to think and build these ideas. . . . But you find yourself just writing in different modes that allows you to get the work out . . . the kind of work that you can do in between things that you need to do as a parent. So I suppose the flip side of intensive parenting is less intensive forms of thinking and writing. (Audrey, mother of a seven-year-old son)

Megan echoes this: "It's true, I don't really find that I have time to sit and ponder big ideas most of the time."

From another angle, parenthood was shown to shape the material that is watched and written about, with interviewees describing both a renewed attention to screen media for children and a drive to understand the effects of this for their child(ren). Audrey related, "I started a project on children's animation in order to be able to watch some of those things with my son, and I'm watching more animation than I ever have; it's not something that I've ever really enjoyed doing before."

> I started being interested in media effects research. I had never prior to that, prior to having a child, had any interest in empirical research. I considered my work to be more about screen aesthetics and textual analysis and qualitative research and I was a bit suspicious of the quantitative stuff, but it really did make me want to know more about how the media was affecting my child. So I started reading a lot more widely as a result as she went through different developmental phases. (Jillian)

These type of responses reflect a different attunement to screen media that, like the affective charge discussed above, also suggest how one's viewing subjectivity shifts as a parent. This is a different empathic attunement, not to screen material so much as to one's child(ren) themselves, as we intuitively feel into what will impact them and how. Jillian reflected on this interestingly when she recounted her daughter's fear of the flying monkeys in *The Wizard of Oz* (Victor Fleming, 1939), when she was five or six: "I felt *so* guilty for that, because my empathic attunement to what would frighten a child had just not kicked in, I had just not realized what was going to scare them at that age." Both modes of attunement reflect a distinctive awareness of how we are interpellated by screen media as parents—we are called and spoken to differently, through different registers of the text. We are made over as different viewers. Not only, then, do we change a text, or access it differently, as a parent; the text *changes us*: it consolidates our subject position through the playing out of these changed empathic connections, and by forcing a different perspective on the material, revealing different logics and affects. As David put it, "At the level of embodiment and feeling . . . yes, I sometimes deeply feel myself as a father of five children, and whatever's happening [on-screen]—it produces triggers, a series of memories or issues or feelings about what might happen, or what's happening."

This dual relationship chimes closely with the discourses around personal criticism, or the logic of "watching *while*," a touchstone for which remains Robin Wood's argument that "there will always be a close connection between critical theory, critical practice, and personal life; and it seems important that the critic should be aware of the personal bias that must inevitably affect his choice of theoretical position, and prepared to foreground it in his work."[24] Wood's call is especially relevant in the contemporary "woke" environment, where the demand for more diverse perspectives in criticism speaks directly to the value that one's personal life has on the interpretation and discursive construction of a text.[25] It is hardly the case that parents are underrepresented as screen scholars. But what is clear is that this identity, this "personal bias," is rarely, if ever, mobilized or even revealed in the practice of screen scholarship. Indeed, as the second part of my study demonstrates, it registers largely as an obstacle or challenge that one works *in spite of*. What this chapter has attempted to demonstrate is that being a parent-scholar also enables a renewed perspective and a site of invention; it is a position so powerful that it remakes both the emotional dynamic and the effects-based logic that underpin and determine our screen media encounters: "I can tell you that some of the strongest screen reactions I've had in my life have been because I'm a mother" (Jillian).

Notes

1 Lee Edelman, *No Future: Queer Theory and the Death Drive* (Durham, NC: Duke University Press, 2004), 3.
2 See, for instance, Greg Lukianoff and Jonathan Haidt, "The Coddling of the American Mind," *Atlantic*, September 2015, www.theatlantic.com/magazine/archive/2015/09/the-coddling-of-the-american-mind/399356/.
3 Karen Russell, "Orange World," *New Yorker*, June 4 and June 11, 2018, www.newyorker.com/magazine/2018/06/04/orange-world.
4 Vivian Sobchack, *Carnal Thoughts: Embodiment and Moving Image Culture* (Berkeley: University of California Press, 2004), 58.
5 Siegfried Kracauer, quoted in Sobchack, *Carnal Thoughts*, 55.
6 Names have been changed throughout.
7 Sobchack, *Carnal Thoughts*, 60.
8 Sobchack, *Carnal Thoughts*, 60.
9 Jennifer Barker, *The Tactile Eye: Touch and the Cinematic Experience* (Berkeley: University of California Press, 2009), 2.
10 Jane Stadler, "The Empath and the Psychopath: Ethics, Imagination, and Intercorporeality in Bryan Fuller's *Hannibal*," *Film-Philosophy* 21, no. 3 (2017): 412.
11 Robert Sinnerbrink, *Cinematic Ethics: Exploring Ethical Experience Through Film* (New York: Routledge, 2016), 91.
12 Stadler, "The Empath and the Psychopath," 414.
13 Sinnerbrink, *Cinematic Ethics*, 80.
14 Sinnerbrink, *Cinematic Ethics*, 92–93.
15 Sinnerbrink, *Cinematic Ethics*, 93.
16 See, for instance, Carl Plantinga, *Moving Viewers: American Film and the Spectator's Experience* (Berkeley: University of California Press, 2009); Shohini Chaudhuri, *Cinema's Dark Side: Atrocity and the Ethics of Film Spectatorship* (Edinburgh: Edinburgh University Press, 2014); Sarah Kozloff, "Empathy and the Cinema of Engagement: Reevaluating the Politics of Film," *Projections* 7, no. 2 (2013): 1–40.
17 Sinnerbrink, *Cinematic Ethics*, 87–88.

18 Sharon Hays, *The Cultural Contradictions of Motherhood* (New Haven, CT: Yale University Press, 1996); Susan Douglas and Meredith Michaels, *The Mommy Myth: The Idealization of Motherhood and How It Has Undermined Women* (New York: Free Press, 2004). For scholarly investigations of these works, see, for instance, Julie A. Wilson and Emily Chivers Yochim, *Mothering through Precarity: Women's Work and Digital Media* (Durham, NC: Duke University Press, 2017); Frank Furedi, *Paranoid Parenting* (London: Continuum, 2008); Judith Warner, *Perfect Madness: Motherhood in the Age of Anxiety* (New York: Riverhead Books, 2006).

19 Hays, *Cultural Contradictions*, 8.

20 Douglas and Michaels, *The Mommy Myth*, 4.

21 Hays, *Cultural Contradictions*, 125.

22 Kathryn Bond Stockton, *The Queer Child; or, Growing Sideways in the Twentieth Century* (Durham, NC: Duke University Press, 2009); Rebekah Sheldon, *The Child to Come: Life After the Human Catastrophe* (Minneapolis: University of Minnesota Press, 2016).

23 Sheldon, *The Child to Come*, 6.

24 Robin Wood, "Responsibilities of a Gay Film Critic," *Film Comment* 14, no. 1 (1978): 13.

25 In recent years, one of the places this debate surfaced was following a speech made by Brie Larson at the Crystal + Lucy Awards in June 2018, in which she called out the lack of diversity in film criticism. The hottest quote from her speech is "I do not need a 40-year-old white dude to tell me what didn't work for him about *A Wrinkle in Time*. It wasn't made for him," quoted in Patrick Lenton, "Brie Larson Would Very Much Like to Hear From Film Critics Who Aren't Just White Dudes," *Junkee*, June 15, 2018, junkee.com/brie-larson-film-critics/163504. Larson's speech referenced a recent study on film criticism undertaken at Stacy Smith's USC's Annenberg Inclusion Initiative: Marc Choueiti, Stacy L. Smith, and Katherine Pieper, "Critic's Choice? Gender and Race/Ethnicity of Film Reviewers across 100 Top Films of 2017," June 2018, assets.uscannenberg.org/docs/cricits-choice-2018.pdf.

II

Aesthetics of Maternity

5

Visualizing with New Comprehension

Mothering and Autoethnography

Rashna Wadia Richards

While testing an app that would collect data on her infant son's diaper changes, Anna Prushinskaya notes, "always I feel like I am gathering data, observing, making decisions about how to properly record our interactions."[1] Observation and documentation are fundamental to the work that mothers do. In the beginning, it is about keeping track of feedings and diaper changes and naps. This then turns to keeping track of milestones, like rolling over and sitting up and crawling and walking. Even when an infant turns into a kid, the observation and recording—of actual growth in terms of height and weight but also of more significant developmental milestones—changes but never ceases. Digital technology enhances the work of documenting that mothers regularly do, like taking and sharing photos and videos or posting on blogs. But many mothers move beyond data gathering to contemplate the impact of childbearing and mothering. What kind of observers can mothers be? Do their observations yield new ways of comprehending their children, themselves, or their worlds? Can their observations blend testimony and analysis in order to offer larger cultural reflections? These are the questions that animate this essay, which focuses on the work of maternal observers. My central argument is that the work of maternal observation is similar to autoethnography. The essay is divided into two parts: the first half explores maternal observation in relation to cultural anthropology, and the second extends that view to include nonprofessional maternal observers. I begin with Seth Kramer, Daniel A. Miller, and Jeremy Newberger's *The Anthropologist* (2015), in order to trace the connection between mothering and autoethnography. I then expand the essay's focus by turning to mothering in the digital mediasphere and interrogating whether the work of mothers in social media can also be seen as autoethnographic. Ultimately, this essay argues that maternal observing is an autoethnographic practice, and it examines the insights gained by maternal observers who reflect on themselves and their children.

Discussing the key concerns of anthropology, Matthew Engelke has recently argued that the discipline "has been driven by a curiosity with humankind's cultural expressions, institutions, and commitments" over the past one hundred and fifty years or so.[2] Whether they are studying the foodways of the Zuni or electronic trading in London, cultural anthropologists in particular are interested in the following question: "What is it that makes us human?"[3] This question lies at the convoluted intersection of nature and culture, and it prompts cultural anthropologists to use an ethnographic methodology to observe, record, and understand their subjects' social lives. Ethnographers tend to rely on participant observation, a process of intimately observing their subjects. Autoethnography is a form of anthropology in which the self becomes the subject of observation. Though it is self-reflexive, autoethnography explores how the radically personal lived experience is situated historically, thereby undermining traditional disciplinary divisions between anthropology, history, autobiography, and fiction. That is why Deborah E. Reed-Danahay calls autoethnography a postmodern construct, for it destabilizes "the realist conventions and objective observer position" of conventional ethnography as well as "the notion of the coherent, individual self" of conventional autobiography.[4] While some distinguish between evocative and analytical autoethnography—the former foregrounds storytelling to evoke emotional responses and the latter emphasizes a theoretical engagement with broad social phenomena—there is usually a blending of the two approaches. As Carolyn Ellis points out, autoethnographers may begin with "an ethnographic wide angle lens, focusing outward on social and cultural aspects of their personal experience; then, they look inward, exposing a vulnerable self that is moved by and may move through, refract, and resist cultural interpretations."[5] Autoethnographers tend to move dialectically between the personal and the cultural, a move that enhances both self-interrogation and cultural critique.

The Anthropologist weaves this double perspective together beautifully. The documentary offers two parallel narratives. It chronicles cultural anthropologist Susie Crate's fieldwork in Siberia, Kiribati, and Peru, where she examines different cultures' capacity for adjusting to change. Crate travels to these places with her teenage daughter Katie Yegorov-Crate, whom we see grow over five years from a teenager into a young woman heading to college. This mother-daughter duo's journeys are framed with commentary by anthropologist Mary Catherine Bateson, daughter of the legendary Margaret Mead. Bateson remarks on the discipline of anthropology as well as the pioneering role her mother played in defining and advancing it. As Crate does with the impact of climate change on humans, Mead studied the impact of unprecedented changes, like modernity and war, affecting people in previously isolated locations. The documentary thus evolves into a portrait of empathetic women anthropologists. It also hints at a connection between their professional and personal work.

Following Davis Guggenheim's *An Inconvenient Truth* (2006), in which former U.S. vice president Al Gore educates citizens about global warming, many documentaries have depicted climate change as the geopolitical crisis of the twenty-first century. Gore frames his presentation as a "planetary emergency," and films such as Mark Terry's *The Antarctica Challenge* (2009), Jeff Orlowski's *Chasing Ice* (2012), and Fisher Stevens's *Before the Flood* (2016) have followed suit, zooming in on places affected most acutely by melting glaciers, rising sea levels, escalating temperatures, changing vegetation, and diminishing populations of animals and aquatic life. *Before the Flood*, for instance, follows Leonardo DiCaprio in his role as UN messenger of peace as he travels to the Greenland ice sheet; flies over Sumatran forests being cleared for palm oil plantations; and interviews environmentalists, presidents, and the pope. In the Pacific Ocean, he visits Kiribati and Palau, island nations that represent "paradise in peril" because destroyed ecosystems have been "reversing half a billion years of evolution." Though DiCaprio gets closer to the locations of impending disaster than Gore, his is still an overhead view of the situation. These documentaries tend to use situations like the ones in the Pacific as quick examples to illustrate a larger problem and emphasize what we might do to reverse the effects of climate change.

But there is no examination of the people who are directly impacted. That is where Kramer, Miller, and Newberger's documentary differs dramatically.

The Anthropologist begins with Bateson echoing Engelke, claiming that the fundamental question all cultural anthropologists ask is: "What is it to be human?" This implies that anthropology is a way of seeing the world, of seeing how people make their lives in their worlds—and, in this particular documentary, how they adjust to climate change. The film then cuts to photographs of Mead's field trip to Samoa in 1925. Mead was only twenty-four years old then and, Bateson tells us, "she spent most of her time talking with young girls" and learning that "there was a lot less anxiety about sex" among them. In the following scene, Crate travels to Kiribati to learn about climate change, but her daughter prompts her to ask about the significance of tiny piglets used for ceremonial purposes. Their guide, Claire Anterea, a local climate change activist, explains that piglets are raised and then slaughtered for birthdays, Christmas, and also when young girls begin menstruating, which is "a very big celebration to mark the womanhood." Both anthropologists are shown being curious about cultural beliefs that specifically pertain to young women. As we know, Mead's fieldwork in Samoa led her to publish *Coming of Age in Samoa* (1928), which wasn't only a description of the lifeways of young Samoans. Rather, she used her research to define the nascent field of anthropology as enabling us to understand that "aspects of behavior which we had been accustomed to consider invariable elements of our humanity . . . [are] merely a result of civilization, present in the inhabitants of one country, absent in another country."[6] Similarly, Crate isn't in Kiribati to study young girls, but this brief moment and the ceremonial scene that follows paint a fuller picture of the I-Kiribati. They become more than one-dimensional people struggling with the dread of losing their entire island to climate change, as they appear to be in *Before the Flood*.

This kind of curiosity about cultures being studied is brought out more directly in a later scene in Peru, when Crate visits her colleague, medical anthropologist Patricia Hammer. Together they explore how the melting glaciers are affecting agriculture in that area. During a conversation with a local farmer, they ask about native plants that are used "to provoke an abortion," "for vaginal discharge," and for help with "postpartum depression." This moment ties climate change directly to women's health: if these medicinal plants stop growing due to rising temperatures, it would be a disaster for women's healthcare in the region. *The Anthropologist* has not been focused on women's health in particular. But these details allow the film to widen the scope of the climate catastrophe, which isn't only about rising sea levels and melting glaciers. Ordinary observers, the scene suggests, might not have asked questions about plants that induce abortions or help with postpartum depression because they may treat climate change and women's health as distinct issues. But a participant observer can "watch her own actions, the behavior of others, and everything she could see in this social situation."[7] In other words, Crate uses what James P. Spradley has called "a wide-angle lens, taking in a much broader spectrum of information."[8] By observing these smaller and more personal details that may not seem significant, she reflects on the bigger picture.

Intriguingly, *The Anthropologist* ties this type of anthropological observation to maternal observation. Mead and Crate are both introduced as mothers. Bateson sets up a projector in the opening scene, and we see images from home movies—of Mead nursing, playing with, and giving swimming lessons to a young Mary Catherine. Visually, Mead is first shown as a mother while her daughter's disembodied voice reminds us that for about thirty years she was the most influential anthropologist in the world. This is true of Crate as well; she walks into the next shot with her daughter Katie, whose voice-over tells us, "My mom is a cultural anthropologist." They are in Siberia, learning about the effects of the melting permafrost. We see Crate as a participant observer, asking questions about and photographing local artisans. In the opening credits that follow, she turns her camera on Katie, who also becomes a subject being observed.

The parallels between Crate's work as an anthropologist and as a mother are established early. Right after Bateson explains how anthropologists understand human subjects by studying their "learned behavior," the film cuts to the Crate home, where Katie reads "How I Am Different," a poem she wrote in second grade that is still on their refrigerator, while her mother goes through old photographs and newspaper clippings in albums spread out all around her on the floor. At first, there is nothing striking about this shot of a mother introducing us to her family through photographic memories. But this documentary is keenly invested in how photography is used to record a way of life. The camera, for anthropologists, is a crucial apparatus for seeing others in their own worlds and trying to understand those worlds through the images they take. Eric Gable explains the ties between anthropology and photography:

> The camera is an extension of the eye. The camera takes visual notes. Anthropologists use these visual notes later to illustrate a lecture, to illuminate the words on the page of a book or journal article; we use these images to prove a point or as an aid to memory—we look at them to conjure up the place again, to recall it. Because the camera takes visual notes for us, and because these notes are a sort of document, we can justify the time we take snapping shots. But we also take pictures or make sketches for the sheer pleasure of the activity.[9]

Throughout *The Anthropologist* we see Crate with camera in hand. Photography becomes a way of documenting her fieldwork as well as of reflecting on what we have already lost to climate change and what we must strive to preserve. As she says on her trip to the Sakha Republic in Siberia, there have been "lots of studies, charting, modeling, trying to understand climate change. The missing part is the human face." Photographs provide that human face, and Crate later uses them to offer a fuller picture of how this geopolitical crisis affects people locally when she attends a town-hall style meeting in Siberia and when she gives a lecture at George Mason University.

In light of these moments, the scene in Crate's home takes on an autoethnographic tenor. The family pictures do not merely record or document Katie's youth; they also show how mothers keep and tell stories of their children. As her daughter's friend Carly listens curiously, Crate explains that she embodies the concept of "going native"—she met and married Katie's dad while doing research in Siberia, and Katie was born there while her mother was still doing fieldwork. There are pictures of Katie being bottle-fed by her dad, of Katie with other Sakha women, presumably her aunts, and so on. Among these images is a local newspaper article in Sakha, whose headline Crate translates as "Our American Bride Had a Baby Girl." There are two pictures accompanying that story: of Katie lying in Crate's lap and of Katie being held. These pictures with their smiling subjects are similar to the other images of their little family in the album. They are visual notes, as Gable calls them, helpful for remembering and marking an entire childhood and young adulthood. But they are more than that. Family photography is often considered trivial, regarded suspiciously as illustrating a fake image of happiness, or dismissed for promoting nostalgia. But taking photographs and making albums, a task primarily undertaken by mothers, is hardly just about keeping a sentimental record of one's family. Like scrapbooking, it is a form of reflection through storytelling. Danille Elise Christensen has argued that scrapbooking ought to be seen as "the autoethnographic shaping of lives as performances," for "scrapbooking—like ethnography—is also in itself a reflexive, metacultural activity."[10] Crate's picture albums function that way too. Collectively they illustrate, as her daughter's poem had done, how Katie Yegorov-Crate is different and how she might find her place in different worlds.

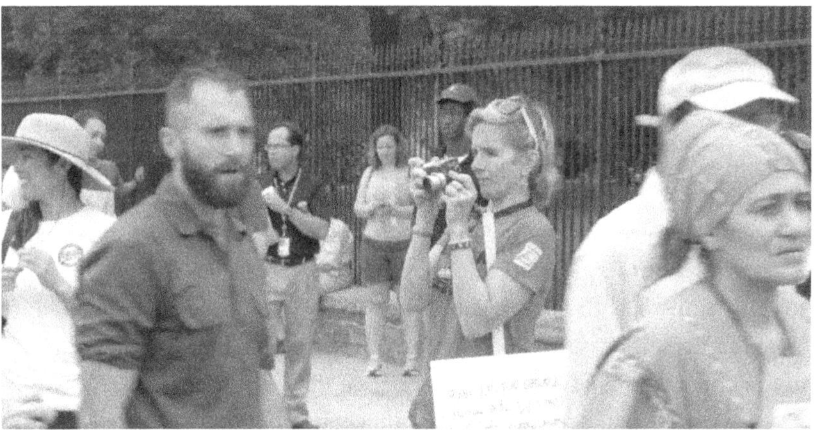

Crate photographing as a cultural anthropologist and a mother, *The Anthropologist* (Seth Kramer, Daniel A. Miller, and Jeremy Newberger, 2015).

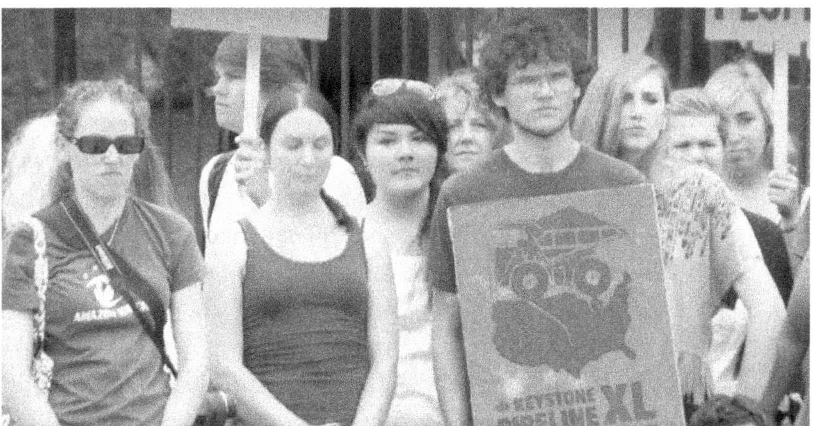

Katie being photographed as a subject and a daughter, *The Anthropologist* (Seth Kramer, Daniel A. Miller, and Jeremy Newberger, 2015).

Just as her anthropological photography is intertwined with mothering, Crate's fieldwork is also connected to her work as a mother. When they head to the White House to protest the Dakota Access Pipeline, Katie stands with a group of protesters after the rally while Crate photographs the scene. Is this Crate-as-cultural-anthropologist or Crate-as-mother photographing Katie in this moment? She is, of course, both—or rather, there is no clear distinction between her role as a mother and as an anthropologist. The resulting reverse shot shows Katie among the protesters; Crate is focusing on her daughter, but the shot also becomes a way of reflecting on the demonstration, a visual response to a speaker's emotional question from moments earlier: "Look at your little girls: what will you tell them about this day in history?" This is exactly the kind of dynamic Spradley describes in relation to the participant observer, who may become more of a participant on one occasion and more of an observer on another. "Doing ethnographic fieldwork," he suggests, "involves alternating between the insider and outsider experience, and having both simultaneously."[11] Crate similarly oscillates between trying to gain intimacy with the subjects of her observation and maintain distance from them: looking outward and inward, documenting and reflecting, aware of the intersection between the personal and the cultural.

Even the final scene, where Crate sends Katie off to college, works this way. As Katie packs her bag, we see glimpses of her young life, especially through photographs that Crate has taken over the years. While these shots zoom in on her growth, her mother reflects on change more broadly. As Katie gets in her packed car and pulls out of their driveway, Crate goes over all the things one expects a mother to say: how she loves her with all her heart, how Katie should drive safely and text when she gets there, and so on. As the shutter of her camera keeps clicking, we hear her saying in voice-over, "We're headed for some pretty big change"—a sentiment that connects Katie's story to the global story. She is off to college to study (what else?) anthropology, but the changes she will experience are much larger than that transition. While marking Katie's transition to adulthood, Crate contemplates how it is her daughter's generation that will have to deal with and hopefully find a solution to climate change.

Though Crate is professionally a cultural anthropologist, she is hardly the first mother to document and reflect on her child from an autoethnographic perspective. In order to theorize the relationship between maternal observation and autoethnography further, I want to move through three reflections on maternal perspective. Writing about the birth of her granddaughter Sevanne Margaret at the very end of her autobiography, Mead argues that becoming a mother gives women "a special and perhaps transient sensitivity."[12] When her daughter Mary Catherine was born, Mead notes, she worried that she had become a biased observer of children, as she "saw each of them as older or younger, bigger or smaller, more or less graceful, intelligent, or skilled than my own child."[13] But what initially felt like a loss of objectivity was actually an ability to "visualize . . . with new comprehension."[14] Seeing and knowing her own child, Mead suggests, leads a mother to become acutely sensitive to other children's behaviors or characteristics, to "grasp the meaning of puckered eyebrows, a tensed hand, or a light flick of the tongue."[15] It is through understanding and loving a particular child, she concludes, that one becomes capable of considering sensitively other children—and thereby of thinking and writing about the work of childbearing and mothering.

Sara Ruddick similarly theorizes that mothering leads to distinctive maternal modes of perceiving the world. In particular, she writes about mothers who connect with other mothers to discuss their everyday experiences; what may appear to be mundane conversations about their children's daily lives lead to deeper cultural observations. Ruddick argues that mothers often "practic[e] together attentive noticing and disciplined reflectiveness about what they notice"; they "share and elaborate their observations, making a coherent, often amusing, dramatic, or poignant story of their children's particularities"; and they "establish continuities in their nurturing activities."[16] Maternal observation here involves moving from the particularities of one's own children to reflecting overtly or implicitly on the cultural practice of motherhood.

Patty Sotirin emphasizes precisely this double move while focusing on the momoir—popular memoirs written by moms—which are typically marketed to a mainstream audience and are seen as more entertaining than serious autoethnographic studies. Sotirin's careful analysis shows that, beyond superficial differences, momoirs exhibit the key features of autoethnography: "introspective inquiry into the emotional depths of personal experience, resonances of significance moving from personal to cultural relations and back again."[17] In order to make this move, they foreground a kind of Deleuzian "radical specificity of living a life, not in the sense that we all live our own lives but in the sense that life is lived in the flows, multiplicities, and provisionality of each moment, event, emotion. Such radical specificity is difficult to communicate without reframing it as something shared and understandable."[18] This ostensible paradox, of communicating something completely individual that must be analyzed in relation to the general, resonates in momoirs because the ongoing exceptional experience of individual mothers makes sense only in relation to the shared understanding of motherhood. In the analysis that follows, I use these insights to analyze the work of maternal observers in digital media. Like Crate's thought-provoking reflections, these observations are extremely individual, and yet they reflect on how the work of mothering is grounded in and resistant to cultural expectations.

Maternal observations found on social networks tend to be brief and ephemeral. In the popular media, mothers who engage in posting online are often chided for being banal or exploitative in oversharing their children's lives. But as Lorin Basden Arnold and Bettyann Martin argue, mothers use social media in order to create a sense of community. Instead of being self-indulgent, mothers use Facebook, Instagram, Twitter, blogs, and public or private online forums for "informational and emotional support."[19] Beyond offering support, some digital spaces facilitate a resistance to traditional expectations of motherhood. That is why many online participants have declared their work as radical, even feminist. More recently, scholars have begun analyzing the digital work of mothers more seriously. May Friedman argues that "mommyblogs borrow from and extend the tradition of *écriture féminine* by allowing for the formation of the self under observation from both within and beyond the individual doing the writing."[20] Drawing on Hélène Cixous's *écriture féminine*, which sees writing about the self as performative, Friedman makes the case for seeing mothering blogs as simultaneously observing and reflecting through the process of writing. I would suggest that all forms of maternal writing perform this work of observing and reflecting. As Meika Loe, Tess Cumpstone, and Susan B. Miller argue, mothers who post on online forums about their experiences do so as "informal participant observers in the world of childrearing."[21] Their frank, not always polished, and often ambivalent postings about their lived experiences reveal how maternal observers wrestle with the institution of motherhood and try to create spaces that might contribute to a cultural rethinking of maternal practice. And that is what makes their work autoethnographic.

Consider this Instagram post by Alice Bradley, who writes online about motherhood and creative practice as Finslippy. Upon taking down her Christmas tree in January 2018, she shared two pictures of ornaments made by her son Henry. They carried this caption: "It is a truth universally acknowledged that it is impossible to toss out any Christmas ornaments that were made by your child, no matter how half-assed they were, or how much the cat gnawed on them."[22] The first image is of a round ornament, with Henry's picture in the middle and some glitter around; the second image is of a snowman, with teeth marks showing where the cat must have nibbled on it. Bradley's post is ostensibly about her son's childish crafts and his mother's sentimental attachment to them. It undercuts its sentimentalism, however, by expressing a frustration with her desire to hold on. But her post isn't aligned with the popular Twitter hashtag #BadMom or #BadMommy, where moms happily post about their own screwups. Here is an example: "2nd kid starts preschool . . . and I forgot to take pictures :). #badmommy."[23] As Lorin Basden Arnold puts it, these posts are not in any way remorseful, as the smiley face at the end indicates. They underscore "violations of the intensive mothering expectation of always prioritizing the child's needs and desires," but with gleeful satisfaction.[24] This is certainly not Bradley's sentiment.

Having said that, her ironic sentimentalism is also in contrast to Anna Quindlen's, who likewise writes about the challenge of giving up a child's things. In "Tag Sale," Quindlen compares parting with "the box of crib sheets, yellow with milk stains, yellowing just a bit with age" to "giving away a part of my life that I am not ready yet to relinquish."[25] This is clearly not the way Bradley's attachment to her son's old ornaments functions. So, what is the "truth universally acknowledged" in her post? I would say that it is one that is not actually acknowledged. In the photographs, her partially visible hand is holding the "half-assed" ornaments. It looks outsized, especially next to a young Henry, who must've been three or four when these crafts were made. He is fifteen at the time of the post, which becomes also about a mother's tough task of holding on and letting go—not only of things but also of the people to whom those things once belonged. Bradley seems aware that the larger conversation about motherhood tends to be either intensely romantic or provocatively cynical. Her brief post emphasizes that her maternal experience lies somewhere in between those polar extremes. In fact, it underscores the ambivalence she feels about mothering, and her vacillation allows us to see that the tug of mothering can be a contradictory experience.

Blogs offer a similar space for reflecting on the intense, exhilarating, and always inimitable experiences of mothering. In one way or another, all introspective mothering blogs wrestle with the ideal of motherhood. These contemporary moms may not feel as restricted by what Adrienne Rich identified as the patriarchal construction of motherhood, which "demands of women maternal 'instinct' rather than intelligence, selflessness rather than self-realization, relation to others rather than the creation of self."[26] But the shadow of what Susan J. Douglas and Meredith W. Michaels have called "the new momism" haunts their work. Though at first it seems liberatory, new momism implies that the only true choice for a woman is to become a mother and, more than that, to become a perfect mother, "to bring to child rearing a combination of selflessness and professionalism that would involve a cross cloning of Mother Teresa and Donna Shalala."[27]

Mother-bloggers overtly take issue with this model of motherhood, which appears suffocating and unreal. Ilana Wiles, who blogs as *MommyShorts*, reminds new moms not to believe the glossy images of "perfectly clean houses with their beautifully dressed babies" or "the pictures of Kate [Middleton] emerging from the hospital, a day after she had each baby, looking perfectly put together and like she had somehow lost every ounce of baby weight overnight." In "How to Survive Your First Year of Parenting," she argues that these images are deliberately choreographed and cannot possibly be replicated in real life.[28] Marsha Takeda-Morrison's *Sweatpantsmom* also critiques fantastical representations of motherhood. Her nom de plume itself connotes this opposition, as a sweatpants-wearing mom is one who isn't invested in keeping up appearances; she is casual and laid-back and clearly imperfect. In "Regrets: Teaching Them How to Read Nutritional Labels," Takeda-Morrison notes that "when I am too lazy to make the girls lunch," she pretends that cafeteria food is good for them. Here's how she makes corn dogs sound suitable: "Look—they're having corn dogs!! Corn. Dog. That's a vegetable and a protein."[29] Of course, her girls do not fall for this trick. This short post at first appears confessional, but the tongue-in-cheek title suggests otherwise. *Sweatpantsmom* is implicitly critiquing the school lunch program, which can leave busy moms with having to choose convenience over nutrition for their children. However, she is not insisting that the right response would be to pack a healthy lunch from home. The internet is filled with advice columns, blogs, and websites on how to pack healthy school lunches, the vast majority of them directed toward mothers.

Because her specific anecdotal experience leads her to implicitly comment on public policy, Takeda-Morrison's resistance pushes further than Bradley's or Wiles's.

This kind of resistance is inherent to online forums or communities that are organized thematically, many of which are set up as explicitly feminist interrogations of normative representations of mothering. Take, for instance, *Hip Mama*, a space for thinking about mothering as practice and as activism. In "Mermaid," Meg Weber writes on that forum about trying to raise her nine-year-old daughter to love her body by a mother who was taught "that my body was too big, not feminine enough, unacceptable, and undesirable." She observes her daughter swimming as she "speeds through the water, fearless."[30] But when she steps out, "Kai uses one arm to cover her belly and my heart tumbles." How to teach her daughter to embrace her body when she herself struggles with acceptance? That question is at the heart of this piece, which isn't a self-help column about losing weight or making peace with one's body. Weber describes how she feels in her body and then turns to how she sees others seeing her and her daughter. At a party, her sister's friend, who has just returned from Hawaii, suggests insouciantly that "[fat] women should not wear that little clothing in public." After a family vacation on the Pacific coast, her sister-in-law sends her photographs of them on the beach. The post critiques fat shaming and an insistence on a perfect slender body for women, a treacherous norm that led to her sister's suicide. But Weber also turns the critical gaze on herself, realizing that, though her "own mother taught me fear, self-hatred, and 'thin at any cost,'" she needs to learn to encourage her daughter's "sense of waterborne freedom and grace." The post concludes open-endedly, with her putting Kai to bed and heading off to write a story, presumably another piece about her lived experience as a white lesbian divorced mother raising an adopted daughter with "long limbs" and "light brown skin" who loves to swim. By ending on that note, Weber subverts normative descriptions of motherhood and any expectations of a decisive resolution. Indeed, this post demonstrates exactly how the autoethnographic process functions in the work of maternal observers. Weber details her specific experience; this is not a broader essay on body shaming or adoptive mothering or racial difference. Rather, to use Sotirin's terms, its "radical specificity opens unfamiliar connections and relations that move both beyond and against the familiar storylines."[31] Unlike the generalities and prescriptions that fill parenting websites, mothering here becomes an ongoing act with multiple, sometimes contradictory, iterations.

Of course, the radical specificity of autoethnographic maternal writing is not limited to realistic anecdotes or sketches. Kelly O'Brien uses an impressionistic approach for rendering her maternal observations. Her *How Does Life Live?* (2017) is a contemplative op-doc that gives voice to her children's questions about life, death, poop, butterflies, and whatever else their young minds drift to. While her daughters Emma and Willow play near a gravel site, they ask questions in voice-over. These questions don't exactly match the visuals, and there is no overarching argument. O'Brien shot the film on an old 16 mm Bolex camera, and it feels more like a home movie than a short documentary. Still, given the sparseness of the landscape and Emma's and Willow's repeated questions about the environment, the film does more than document O'Brien's children. At one point, during a series of questions about the natural world, young Willow asks: "Why is the world so messy?" Then, right as her older sister reaches the very top of the pit, she wonders: "What does extinct mean?" These moments reflect on how (O'Brien's) children see the world, but they also implicitly ask us to consider what kind of world they will inherit. Like any participant observer, O'Brien looks both inward and outward. What we see is her critical observation of the way her daughters observe the world around them. Like other maternal observers, she begins with her children and then moves centrifugally toward the world. In speaking about her practice, O'Brien confirms this move, noting that she tries "to make work that captures the poetry of the everyday and finds universal themes through my family's experiences."[32]

But "universal" here does not imply the loss of essential difference. Susan Schalge has argued that "earlier anthropologists assumed that motherhood was biologically determined." Because "the act of mothering was considered instinctual . . . it was also assumed to be universal."[33] Autoethnographic work by maternal observers counters this enduring propensity for universalizing motherhood. Autoethnographies, as we have seen, are rooted in incredibly specific and therefore specifically non-normative versions of mothering. Instead of a singular version, they offer multiple lenses for thinking about the work of mothering. They raise pragmatic questions about what mothers do and ontological questions about who mothers are. If their reflections on mothering connect with other mothers and establish new communities, it is because of their "ability to make observations without prescriptively writing mothering for the audience."[34] Thus, maternal observers write and rewrite tales about mothering, undermining the larger cultural narrative about motherhood. By focusing intensely on their own lives, they move beyond the self and visualize alternative maternal possibilities with new comprehension. More than anything, they demonstrate what the work of participant observers looks like for individual mothers. As Christie Tate puts it, using her teenage daughter's stories on her blog is part of her "creative labor."[35] That is to say, documenting and reflecting on their lives as mothers is a fundamental part of maternal work.

Notes

1 Anna Prushinskaya, *A Woman Is a Woman until She Is a Mother: Essays* (Des Plaines, IL: MG, 2017), 71.
2 Matthew Engelke, *How to Think Like an Anthropologist* (Princeton, NJ: Princeton University Press, 2018), 3.
3 Engelke, *How to Think*, 3.
4 Deborah E. Reed-Danahay, introduction to *Auto/Ethnography: Rewriting the Self and the Social*, ed. Deborah E. Reed-Danahay (Oxford: Berg, 1997), 2.
5 Carolyn Ellis, *The Ethnographic I: A Methodological Novel about Autoethnography* (Walnut Creek, CA: AltaMira, 2004), 37.
6 Margaret Mead, *Coming of Age in Samoa: A Psychological Study of Primitive Youth for Western Civilization* (New York: Perennial, 2001), 5.
7 James P. Spradley, *Participant Observation* (Long Grove, IL: Waveland, 2016), 54.
8 Spradley, *Participant Observation*, 56.
9 Eric Gable, *Anthropology and Egalitarianism: Ethnographic Encounters from Monticello to Guinea-Bissau* (Bloomington: Indiana University Press, 2011), 97.
10 Danille Elise Christensen, "'Look at Us Now!' Scrapbooking, Regimes of Value, and the Risks of (Auto)Ethnography," *Journal of American Folklore* 124, no. 493 (2011): 179, 180.
11 Spradley, *Participant Observation*, 57.
12 Margaret Mead, *Blackberry Winter: My Earlier Years* (New York: Kodansha Globe, 1995), 282.
13 Mead, *Blackberry Winter*, 281.

14 Mead, *Blackberry Winter*, 282.

15 Mead, *Blackberry Winter*, 282.

16 Sara Ruddick, *Maternal Thinking: Toward a Politics of Peace* (Boston: Beacon, 1989), 98.

17 Patty Sotirin, "Autoethnographic Mother-Writing: Advocating Radical Specificity," *Journal of Research Practice* 6, no.1 (2010), jrp.icaap.org/index.php/jrp/article/view/220/189.

18 Sotirin, "Autoethnographic Mother-Writing."

19 Lorin Basden Arnold and Bettyann Martin, "Mothering and Social Media: Understanding, Support and Resistance," in *Taking the Village Online: Mothers, Motherhood, and Social Media*, ed. Lorin Basden Arnold and BettyAnn Martin (Bradford, ON: Demeter, 2016), 6.

20 May Friedman, *Mommyblogs and the Changing Face of Motherhood* (Toronto: University of Toronto Press, 2013), 23.

21 Meika Loe, Tess Cumpstone, and Susan B. Miller, "Feminist Parenting Online: Community, Contestation, and Change," in Arnold and Martin, *Taking the Village Online*, 180.

22 Alice Bradley, "Photos of Handmade Ornaments," *Instagram*, January 7, 2018, www.instagram.com/p/BdqQZOnFWQYi0M7gTKpOhfgdo rAsVZIAiBAtj00/.

23 Quoted in Lorin Basden Arnold, "Confession in 140 Characters: Intensive Mothering and the #BadMom Twitter," in Arnold and Martin, *Taking the Village Online*, 50.

24 Arnold, "Confession in 140 Characters," 49.

25 Anna Quindlen, *Living out Loud* (New York: Ballantine, 1988), 98, 96.

26 Adrienne Rich, *Of Woman Born: Motherhood as Experience and Institution* (New York: Norton, 1976), 42.

27 Susan J. Douglas and Meredith W. Michaels, *The Mommy Myth: The Idealization of Motherhood and How It Has Undermined Women* (New York: Free Press, 2004), 5.

28 Ilana Wiles, "How to Survive Your First Year of Parenting," *MommyShorts* (blog), May 15, 2018, www.mommyshorts.com/2018/05/survive-first-year-parenting.html.

29 Marsha Takeda-Morrison, "Regrets: Teaching Them How to Read Nutrition Labels," *Sweatpantsmom* (blog), September 21, 2006, sweatpantsmom.blogspot.com/2006/09/regrets-teaching-them-how-to-read.html.

30 Meg Weber, "Mermaid," *Hip Mama*, January 10, 2018, hipmamazine.com/meg-weber-mermaid/.

31 Sotirin, "Autoethnographic Mother-Writing."

32 Kelly O'Brien, "How Does Life Live?" *New York Times* March 21, 2017, www.nytimes.com/2017/03/21/opinion/how-does-life-live.html.

33 Susan Schalge, "Maternal Practice: Mothering and Cultural Variation in Anthropology," in *Maternal Thinking: Philosophy, Politics, Practice*, ed. Andrea O'Reilly (Toronto: Demeter, 2009), 244–45.

34 Lisa Hammond, "'Mommyblogging *Is* a Radical Act': Weblog Communities and the Construction of Maternal Identities," in *Mothers Who Deliver: Feminist Interventions in Public and Interpersonal Discourse*, ed. Jocelyn Fenton Stitt and Pegeen Reichert Powell (Albany: State University of New York Press, 2010), 80.

35 Christie Tate, "My Daughter Asked Me to Stop Writing about Motherhood. Here's Why I Can't Do That," *Washington Post*, January 3, 2019, www.washingtonpost.com/lifestyle/2019/01/03/my-daughter-asked-me-stop-writing-about-motherhood-heres-why-i-cant-do-that/.

6

"You Have Absolutely No Control over Your Mind and Body Anymore"

Pregnancy, Autonomy, and Prepartum Anxiety in Alice Lowe's Prevenge

Alice Haylett Bryan

The 2016 horror comedy *Prevenge* was born out of actor Alice Lowe's need to keep working during her pregnancy. Faced with a long period of unemployment due to the imminent changes to her body, Lowe decided to take matters into her own hands and write a screenplay for a film she could star in while pregnant. *Prevenge* is the story of Ruth, a pregnant woman suffering from prepartum psychosis after the death of her partner. Her baby is talking to her, instructing her to kill all those implicated in the death of its father. Lowe made her directorial debut with the feature, leading to a film that is fully embedded, both in narrative and production, in the mind of a pregnant woman. But whereas Ruth is experiencing the extremes of prepartum psychosis, I propose that the film can also be read as a text of prepartum anxiety: the anxiety of Ruth, the anxiety of Lowe, and my own pre- and postpartum anxiety watching it for the first time just months after giving birth.

I didn't enjoy pregnancy. I suffered from severe morning sickness for the first twenty weeks, and then, as my son grew bigger, his movements became more and more uncomfortable, at times even painful. Once he was born, I found mothering a baby monotonous and frustrating. I didn't love him like I thought I should, like a mother should. I felt broken and selfish. Overwhelmed by responsibility, yet with little to do. And bored—so, so bored. If I admitted this boredom to friends or colleagues, I would be told, "You are loving it, though, aren't you?" as if I were not even allowed to voice my own discontent. When I replied that I loved my son but that I did not love motherhood, people did not know what to say. But even this was partly a lie as I didn't love him then, yet to acknowledge that would mark me as a monster. How can a mother not love her baby? How can a mother be bored? Mothers are expected to rejoice in mothering, to fall instantly in love with their child moments after giving birth. Mothers should want to devote everything to their child, to willingly say good-bye to their previous lives as an act of their unconditional love.

Di Winstanley argues that the cultural "myth" of motherhood renders such thoughts of discontent unspeakable.[1] When women are surrounded with images of happy mothers gazing lovingly at their children, they feel as though any thoughts counter to total love and contentment must be kept secret. Winstanley suggests that this mothering myth is ultimately one of social coercion whereby patriarchal society actively promotes the happy mother as a model of successful womanhood. "If the image can become powerful enough, it could condition and socialise women into striving to fulfill their ordained roles in society. To fall from grace, to deny this model, is to be an outsider, un-natural and despised. So strong is this image, that the template can be internalised into the psyche of women, to be passed from generation to generation."[2] This myth, which seeks to perpetuate the figure of the perfect mother, also feeds prepartum and postpartum anxiety and depression. Parents, especially mothers, must hide feelings of discontent for fear of being labeled abnormal, even monstrous. If they felt more able to talk about such thoughts, to realize that they are not alone in their sense of loss and anxiety, maybe they would not suffer so keenly.

The personal experiences of three mothers guide this chapter: Lowe, the French psychoanalyst Julia Kristeva, and my own. In her book *Of Woman Born* Adrienne Rich argues that it is impossible for a mother to write a book on motherhood without it being autobiographical.[3] The same must be true for a pregnant woman making a film about pregnancy and a psychoanalytic theorist writing about motherhood after having given birth to her own child. But this self-reflexivity in work on motherhood by mothers should not be seen as a descent into subjective indulgence. Instead, as Rich suggests, the embracing of such personal narratives is the only way women can shed the myth of motherhood and "create a collective description of a world which will truly be ours."[4] Rich calls *Of Woman Born* a "vulnerable" text due to its movement across disciplines, selecting what is of use without specializing in any one subject. The book crosses back and forth between historical research and personal reflection, always asking what motherhood is like for living women. But the book also feels vulnerable because Rich reveals her own personal story of motherhood, a story of suffering, joy, anger, love, and fear.

I watched *Prevenge* for the first time with a young baby. My pregnancy and time spent raising a newborn undoubtedly shaped the way that I read the film. But instead of running away from this subjective response back to the warm welcoming arms of objective critical theory, I am going to embrace my own personal experience. I watched *Prevenge* as a mother who was not enjoying motherhood. I watched *Prevenge* as a person whose life and freedom had been swept away in the service of another. This is my vulnerable text.

"Nature's a Bit of a Cunt"

Lowe came up with the concept for *Prevenge* when she found herself jobless and pregnant for the first time, with little hope of employment due to her changing body. She had wanted to develop her own feature for a number of years, but once pregnant she believed that she might never have the chance to direct: "I knew plenty of male directors with young babies, but no female directors. It's notorious how under-represented female directors are in the industry. Making your first feature is a labor of love, and I was resigned to the idea that two labors—filmmaking and babymaking—were incompatible. Something had to give."[5] However, when director Jamie Adams (whose film *Black Mountain Poets* [2015] Lowe had previously starred in) told her that a production company was looking for a low-budget, short-shoot picture, Lowe started to think about the roles she could play as a pregnant woman. She went on to submit a one-page pitch to Western Edge Pictures and was surprised when they took on the project. She quickly finished the whole script, and then shot the film a month later with a schedule of just eleven days to maintain continuity with the size of her bump. Lowe had originally intended Adams to direct, but he decided that the film was "her story to tell," and suggested that she take the helm for her directorial debut.[6]

Lowe wanted to move away from the typecasting that she believes women are increasingly pushed into (the dowdy mother, the emotional partner, the meek caregiver); *Prevenge* is a story about an outcast: a pregnant Travis Bickle seeking revenge on a world that just does not care enough anymore, or rather does not care about the right things. Lowe's refusal to typecast women is dramatically symbolized in the film's opening scenes. After the introductory credit sequence that suggests Ruth's recent bereavement, she is shown entering a reptile and insect store. Ruth is dressed in a manner that suggests the typical "mumsy" mum so common in television and films, wearing a floral dress, baggy cardigan, and oversized scarf. In contrast to the shop owner's repugnantly suggestive comments—he (Dan Renton Skinner) tells her about a pair of lizards who "come together" and asks her if she wants to touch his "big fat snake"—Ruth is overly squeamish about the creatures she sees. Speaking in a gentle, almost childlike manner to the overbearing man, she informs him that she is nervous and doing "it" for her child—the "it" obviously being the brutal act she is about to carry out, not the purchasing of a spider. When they enter the shop's back room, Ruth grabs a knife and swiftly cuts the man's throat. She watches as the blood drains from his body, kisses him on the forehead, and leaves.

In the next scene Ruth burns the clothes she wore when killing the shop owner. For Lowe, this destruction of clothing symbolizes much more than getting rid of evidence. She wanted the audience to burn their preconceptions about Ruth, to throw away any belief that Ruth is another stereotypical representation of a two-dimensional "mumsy" mum. In Lowe's own words, "She doesn't have to be constrained by [the audience's] ideas of what she is."[7]

As the film continues, Ruth kills four other people who were involved in her partner's death (and one innocent bystander). It is revealed that her partner died in a climbing incident—the other members of the group cut his rope, killing him to save themselves. Under her baby's instruction, Ruth seeks to rid the world of these selfish people. The fetus talks to her, encouraging her to reject the world around her as corrupt and depraved. In the film's final stages, as Ruth starts to go into labor, she confronts the climbing instructor who led the group. It is revealed to the audience that her husband was going to leave her before his death; instead of killing her final victim, Ruth breaks down and the instructor comforts her. Once the baby is born, her psychosis lifts. Or does it? The film's ending is ambiguous, leaving the extent of Ruth's illness and/or monstrosity up to the audience.

One of the strengths of *Prevenge* is that Ruth is an incredibly likeable character, aided by Lowe's usual funny, deadpan performance. Even though Ruth is linked to monstrosity via her on-screen viewing of the film *Crime without Passion* (Ben Hecht and Charles MacArthur, 1934) and her re-creation of the facial expressions of its furies (the three goddesses of vengeance and retribution), she actually works her way through her kill list in a very normal and unmonstrous fashion. It is almost as though she is ticking items off a to-do list or scrapbooking. Although on the surface Ruth is the castrating and avenging monstrous feminine (she does actually castrate one of her victims), this monstrosity is countered and even overpowered, first though the humor in the script and performance, and second through the confirmation that she is indeed suffering from a mental illness and not under the sway of any demonic force. Ruth's psychosis may be the root of her monstrosity, but it also negates it.

For Lowe, "film is poetry"; its imagery should have layers, however obvious: "A lot of filmmakers don't use symbolism anymore, they see it as really gauche and film school, but I was like, why not?"[8] She did not want to make a schlocky horror film with images of an evil baby but a psychological thriller that penetrated the subjectivity of a pregnant woman. Although a very superficial reading of *Prevenge* may take it as an example of the monstrous feminine *à la* Barbara Creed, this combination of Lowe's lived experience with a narrative of psychosis allows for a multifaceted interrogation of not only pregnancy but also society's view of pregnant women and mothers.[9] Film critic Simon Abrams rejected the film for forcing the audience to enter Ruth's subjective reality, but as Lowe herself states, is this not the point of cinema?[10] Or is it the case that the viewing public is so used to the white heterosexual male subjectivity that anything else is too much to bear? Lowe explains that she wanted to carry the audience along with Ruth on her mission: "You're not pregnant? You're not a woman? Doesn't matter—you are going to come on this journey."[11] This is pregnancy-centered horror *à la* Pier Paolo Pasolini's cinema of poetry.[12]

Because, let's face it, pregnancy is not normal, even for women. Even those with the largest of families spend only a small proportion of their lives actually pregnant, and for many it is a process that is experienced only briefly. Pregnancy does things to your body; it can make you sick, incontinent, tired, emotional, turned on. It changes your posture, your joints stretch, and your hips and feet change shape. You lose weight, put weight on, retain water, sweat. You can get hemorrhoids, thrush, anemia, urinary tract infections, gestational diabetes, hypertension, preeclampsia. For the first few months all you want to do is sleep, and then in the final few months, almost like a cruel joke from Mother Nature, sleep becomes impossible. You are told not to sleep on your back, not to eat unpasteurized cheese, not to drink, smoke, get stressed. (And yes, some women do have lovely pregnancies but even for them, pregnancy is not a normal state.) All this comes with the knowledge that you are about to go through one of the most intense experiences of your life—childbirth—and afterward your life will never be the same again. As Ruth puts it to her midwife, when it comes to pregnancy, "nature's a bit of a cunt." Pregnancy may be a natural process, but this does not mean that it feels "normal" for women.

Maternal Mental Health

However, it *is* normal to feel anxious during pregnancy. Statistics show that the vast majority of women will experience some form of anxiety, depression, or stress during pregnancy. Up to 80 percent of pregnant women report what are classed as negative mood symptoms during pregnancy, with up to 17 percent meeting the diagnostic criteria for depression.[13] In his review of the prevalence of mental disorders in pregnant women, Uriel Halbreich suggests that rates in pregnant women are comparable with the rates of non-childbearing women of the same age.[14] But, as Anita Riecher-Rössler and Anke Rohde note, depression during pregnancy can have more severe short-term and long-term consequences on both mother and child, and it is difficult to treat with medication.[15] The correlation between prepartum depression and depression in the wider female public is also countered by the work of Bennett et al.[16] In their overview of existing case studies on the topic they report that 7 percent to 9 percent of the surveyed general female public suffer from depression, but among pregnant women depression rates rise from 7.4 percent in the first trimester to 12.8 percent in the second and then drop back to 12 percent in the third.[17] They also report on studies showing that between 8 percent and 51 percent of pregnant women present depressive symptoms (the difference between depression and depressive symptoms coming partly from the method of data collection used: interview in the former, questionnaire in the latter). Therefore, even if we take into account that a woman is likely to suffer depression during pregnancy if she has a previous history of it, there is still a large number of women for whom depression is a direct consequence of pregnancy, be that due to hormonal changes, stress and anxiety caused by the pregnancy, or a combination of the two. Further, there are even more women (in many studies a majority) who suffer depressive symptoms or anxiety during pregnancy. It is surprising, then, that in comparison with postnatal depression there is very little awareness of prepartum anxiety and depression. Ruth's prepartum psychosis is an incredibly rare condition, but many women will be able to identify with the anxieties and loss that fuel it.

Although thankfully only a few women will suffer such a severe mental mental illness as Ruth does during pregnancy, the loss of control over her body and life that feeds her psychosis is one felt consciously or unconsciously by nearly all expectant mothers. As a counter to the bloody violence of each death, the film intersperses mundane scenes of Ruth's visits to her midwife. Here Ruth's psychosis most clearly merges with the more common anxieties of pregnancy.

During her first visit her midwife (Jo Hartley) informs her: "You have absolutely no control over your mind and body anymore; this one does," pointing to her bump. On one level the midwife is unknowingly suggesting the control that the unborn child has over its mother through her psychosis, but her words mirror phrases that are familiar to all mothers-to-be from baby

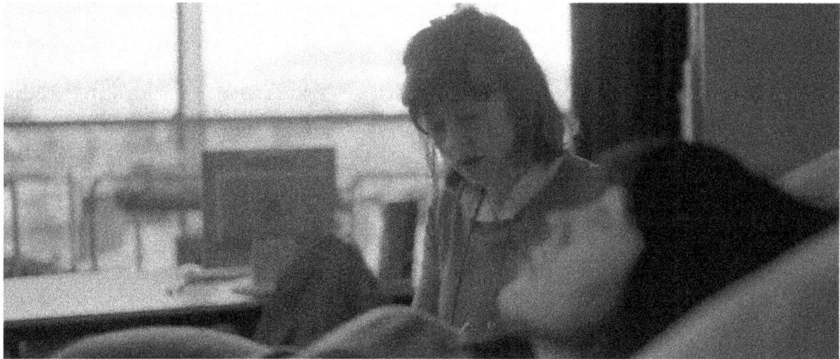

Ruth visiting her midwife in *Prevenge* (Alice Lowe, 2016). (© Alice Lowe / Western Edge Pictures.)

books, websites, and their own midwives. Pregnant women are constantly told that their body will know what to do, that it can grow and deliver the baby almost as though it is a machine or organism removed from the mother's control. But a dialectic is created. At the same time that Ruth (indeed, like pregnant women in general) is told that the baby is in control, that it knows what to do, the midwife also tells her that she must be "[R]uthless" in her attempts to keep her unborn baby safe and well. She needs to selflessly put another life before hers, even though that other life can cause sickness, pain, and permanent changes to her body and lifestyle. A pregnant woman's body is no longer her own. She is both self and the site of another; an *other* that she is at once completely responsible for yet has little control over. It is no wonder that Kristeva called pregnancy an institutionalized psychosis.

Kristeva, Pregnancy, and the *Other*

Kristeva describes pregnancy as a form of "alterity within." In her famous essay "Women's Time," Kristeva writes, "Pregnancy is a dramatic ordeal: a splitting of the body, the division and coexistence of self and other, of nature and awareness, of physiology and speech. This fundamental challenge to identity is accompanied by a fantasy of wholeness, of narcissistic self-containment. Pregnancy is a sort of institutionalized, socialized, and natural psychosis."[18] Pregnancy, for Kristeva, is a state that is both abject in its processes and akin to abjection through its theoretical parameters. Like abjection, pregnancy is a borderline phenomenon. Pregnancy is abject in nature due to the common physical side effects and symptoms that are experienced, many of which involve expulsions from the body such as morning sickness, spontaneous nosebleeds, hemorrhoids, and incontinence. Pregnancy is also abject because the baby actually crosses the border of the body as it is born, with the mother undergoing an experience of pain, blood, and hormonal chaos. For some women, the experience of childbirth is "magical," but for many more it is a drawn-out and difficult act. That the mind clouds over parts of the experience in the months after birth suggests that such a cognitive activity needs to operate to cover over the nasty bits of childbirth or else we would die out as a species. But even more importantly, pregnancy can be seen as an abject state because the baby is an *other* that resides within the borders of the female form. It is, as Kristeva notes, the blurring of identities, both self and other, known and unknown. Is it me, or am I it? It is this inability to separate self and other that, in Kristeva's view, marks pregnancy as a form of psychosis.

Kristeva writes that during pregnancy this experience of alterity within is bound up with the mother's sense of the loss of autonomy. Pregnancy is something that happens *to* women, occurring at the level of the organism rather than engaging with the mother's agency or identity: "Cells fuse, split, and proliferate; volumes grow, tissues stretch, and body fluids change rhythm, speeding up or slowing down. Within the body, growing as a graft, indomitable, there is an other. And no one is present, within that simultaneously dual and alien space, to signify what is going on. 'It happens, but I am not there.' 'I cannot realize it, but it goes on.'"[19] Therefore conception and gestation, like the abject, are processes of splitting, merging, fusing, and fragmenting that are beyond the control of the mother herself. Women may be active in trying to conceive, but they still actually have no control over whether they get pregnant, or whether the fetus will develop properly. Pregnant women have no control over what grows inside of them, yet at the same time they are completely responsible for it.

This relates to how Kristeva regards the ability to give birth as positioning women on the pivot of sociality. Pregnancy is abject, it is everything that patriarchy wishes to label as monstrous because it is unknown, uncontrollable, purely within the realm of woman in a biological sense, yet simultaneously it is the only means by which society can survive and perpetuate itself. As Elizabeth Grosz writes in her work on Kristevan theory:

> The woman-mother finds that it is not her identity or value as a woman which maternity affirms, but her position as natural or as a hinge between nature and culture. Pregnancy betrays any tenuous identity she may achieve as a subject and a woman. In pregnancy, she is positioned as space, receptacle, matter; in lactation and nurturing functions, she takes on the position of part-object, complement, and anaclitic prop. In a sense, "she" is a screen onto which the child's demands are projected and from which images are introjected. "She" does not exist as such.[20]

For Kristeva this necessitates a split in the patriarchal conception of the mother. If she is only abject—a bleeding, lactating, monstrous split-self—then that would entail that patriarchy is abject too, for it is born of woman.

Kristeva argues that in order to negate this, patriarchal society simultaneously mythologizes the mother, making her virginal, clean, and good. Yet this mythical mother figure has no real power, as her position is only granted through her total self-sacrifice to her child.

It is this abject nature of pregnancy, of not only having an *other* within, but also the loss of subjecthood in the need to totally give oneself over to that *other*, that can be read into *Prevenge* as a text of general prepartum anxiety. Common feelings of a lack of control or power in pregnancy are amplified in a narrative where a woman's unborn child is ordering her what to do. The manner in which pregnancy is spoken about during the film compounds this loss of control, of an inhabitation within one's body of an *other*, and of the tightrope women are forced to walk between responsibility and powerlessness. Ruth calls her pregnancy a "hostile takeover," likening herself to an old car that the baby is driving. Pregnancy is also referred to as a state where the mother must hand herself over like a human sacrifice to the will of the baby. The midwife constantly tells Ruth that the baby is in control, that the baby will decide when it wants to come, but ultimately, as with Ruth's belief that the baby is speaking to her, this is a fallacy. The baby has no real will; it is just a fetus. Such declarations increase this sense of responsibility and powerlessness, as they encourage a conception of the unborn child as a developed psyche rather than a life-in-process that is still, biologically speaking, an extension of the mother's body.

Lowe herself admits that she suffered from moments of depression during pregnancy, and her anxiety can be read into the narrative. During her first trimester she would lie in bed and worry about the state of the world, the election of Donald Trump, the reelection of the Conservative Party in the United Kingdom, and the European referendum. At the same time, she was researching the work of Thomas Hobbes and his assertion that human nature is naturally selfish, destructive, and violent, and that people should not be allowed to govern themselves. Lowe channeled these ideas into Ruth's psychosis. Ruth is not just seeking revenge on those who were responsible for her partner's death; she has loftier notions. Lowe thought it would be too easy to have an avenging mother-figure, so instead she presented a character who was more of a disciplinarian. For Ruth, those she kills represent the worst of society, people who selfishly put their own needs and lives first. Lowe explains that Ruth kisses each of her victims because she

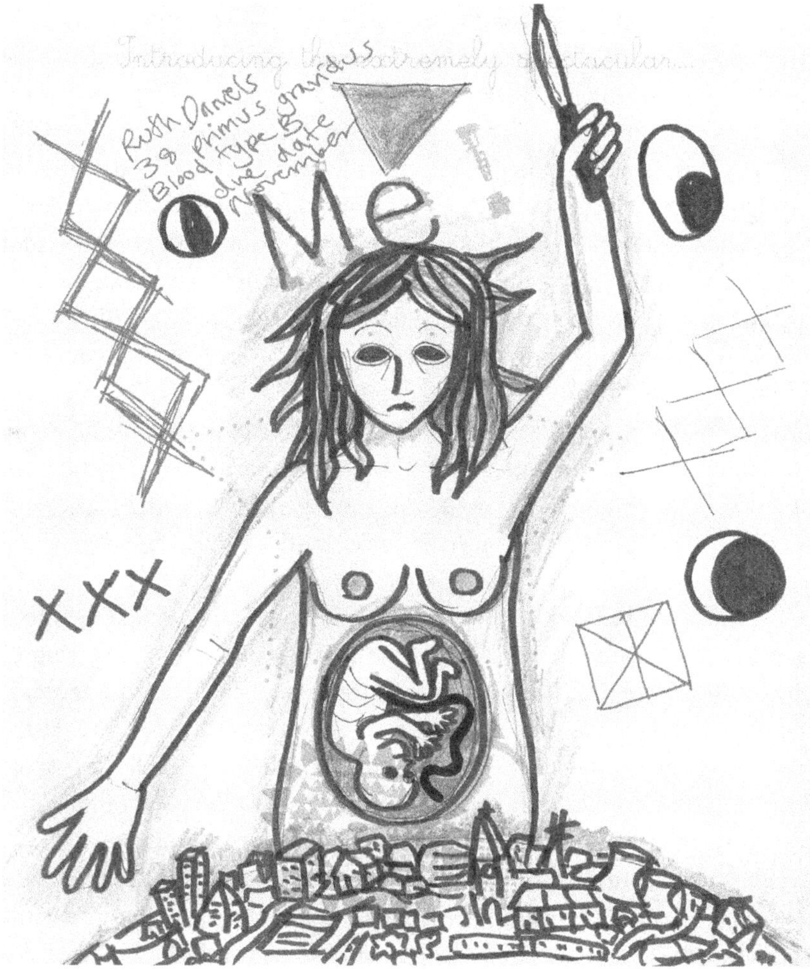

Ruth's scrapbook self-portrait, a re-creation of the frontispiece from Thomas Hobbes's *Leviathan* (1651). (© Alice Lowe.)

has some regret over what she is doing, but her actions are meant to serve a higher purpose. Ruth believes that the world will be a better place without them. She is not evil; she has a job to do—to improve society. Lowe wanted to move away from the petty concerns of the "mumsy" mum stereotype and instead present a woman with lofty personal ideas. The baby is Ruth's philosophical alter ego, a projection of her desire to clean up society and set it on a straight and true path.

So again, Ruth's psychosis is an inflation of the common anxieties of pregnancy. The familiar parental worry about the state of the world that the child is going to be born into is amplified in Ruth, a figure who takes matters into her own hands and kills those whom she deems society could do without. This flux between anxiety and psychosis, monstrosity and maternity, can be seen in Ruth's killing of DJ Dan (Tom Davis). The offensive and misogynistic Dan invites Ruth back to his flat for sex, only for it to be revealed that he actually lives with his mother (Leila Hoffman). In this instance we have another mother experiencing a psychological disorder, as the elderly woman is obviously suffering from dementia. There is a reversal of care, with Dan "mothering" in the loosest sense of the term his own mother, who herself has returned to a childlike state. He speaks of his mother as nothing more than a hindrance, claiming that he is waiting for her to die so that he can receive his inheritance. In contrast, his mother continually tries to do his washing, demonstrating her need to "mother" her child even after having reverted to semi-infancy.

After Ruth has castrated and killed Dan, the mother enters the room and informs her that she will "need a bit of bleach on that," referring to the blood-soaked rug. This matter-of-fact statement could be read as representing not only the breakdown of the mother-child relationship but also a similar blurring of the line between reality and mental instability, as we see in Ruth. Dan's mother does not react at all to the bloody body of her son on the floor, and at first it seems almost as though this is attributable to a sense of relief at his death because of his confinement and mistreatment of her. But of course, this failure to react could also be due to her dementia, mirroring Ruth's flux between reality and psychological dysfunction. At this point we actually see Ruth's ability to mother. She reassures the old woman, tucking her into bed with her teddy and kissing her goodnight. Ruth even puts a load of washing on for her, despite the fact that Dan obviously no longer has a need for the "knickers" his mother was trying to wash. Here Ruth exhibits a caring touch that is detached from the horrific act she has just carried out, encouraging the audience to feel sympathetic toward her. Ruth is not devoid of the potential to love and care—to mother—and indeed it is not motherhood itself that is represented as monstrous, as is often the case in horror cinema, but rather a lack of empathy between people, or the refusal of ethical responsibility toward the *other*. In this light, Ruth's partner's death becomes symbolic of the ethical weight of pregnancy as a whole. Those involved in cutting the rope put their own lives first, denying their responsibility toward the *other*.[21]

Conclusion

As part of her research for *Prevenge* Lowe did not look into prepartum psychosis, but instead explored work on women who had lost their partners during pregnancy. She found that they often spoke of being unable to grieve, as other people expected them to find solace in, and be happy about, the pregnancy. This experience of grief and mourning can be seen to spread out from the terrible example of those losing partners to a more general feeling of loss during pregnancy and after birth. Paula Nicholson focuses on this sense of loss in her research on postnatal depression. She argues that the condition is a healthy response to the losses felt when motherhood is entered into: "Daily life can be devastating. It might feel to the mother that she has lost everything she once had and expected for the future. But there is no going back. You cannot return the baby. Motherhood, with its dilemmas and stresses, is not any indication of feeling for the baby. It is common to love the baby, but hate the things you have to do for it and the domestic 'captivity' that motherhood frequently imposes."[22] This feeling of loss is supported by the work of Stefanie Zaers. In her research she records a significant decline in the subjective quality of life for women during pregnancy and post-birth.[23] Her data reveals that women feel as though they have experienced a decline in their quality of life across a range of areas, including energy, physical and mental capabilities, profession, leisure time, and sexuality. Rather depressingly, she states that after childbirth, women may never return to the same subjective quality of life that they had pre-pregnancy.

However, as noted at the start of this chapter, women are encouraged not to talk about such feelings. So oppressive is the myth of motherhood that mothers do not realize that we share such feelings of discontent and loss, of self-hatred and guilt. Instead we post another picture on Facebook or Instagram of a smiling happy family, telling the world how contented we are. So oppressive is the myth that mothers perpetuate it for fear that we will be revealed as monstrous, as backward, as a bad parent. But if we shared such stories more frequently, if we refused to keep on telling everyone that it is all fine, that we are happy, that we love our babies so much, then maybe we could realize that we are, or can be, good parents too. A word of hope for new mothers: you do get there eventually, just give yourself time. And fuck the myth! It is okay not to love motherhood and your baby all the time, or even half the time. But hopefully sometime, some of the time, you will. As Kristeva writes, we should not think of motherhood as an experience of instant and overwhelming love, but instead as a "slow, difficult, and delightful apprenticeship in attentiveness and gentleness, in forgetting oneself."[24]

This essay has been composed of the self-reflexive words of mothers: Lowe's, Kristeva's, my own. As with any major life event, pregnancy and childbirth leave a lasting imprint on the psyche. Once experienced, it is difficult to discuss them objectively. Just as Lowe's own prepartum anxieties morphed into Ruth's psychosis, my experience of a loss of control in pregnancy, of being occupied by a thing that kicked me all day and night, that made me sick and necessitated the loss of my independence, inflected my reading of *Prevenge*. But these are *shared* experiences. Patriarchal society may wish for women to suppress negative feelings about motherhood and to aspire to be the perfect mother—and indeed women are often unconsciously complicit in this process—but the pregnant subjectivity found in *Prevenge* allows for a counter to this. Mothers may not identify with Ruth's psychosis, but they will identify with the anxieties that drive it. *Prevenge* offers a space for mothers to shed the weight of the myth of motherhood. Maybe it is time that we, like Ruth, burn our clothes and start again.

Notes

1 Di Winstanley, "Existential Stories on the Myth and Reality of Motherhood" (paper read at the Critical Management Studies Conference, Manchester, July 11–13, 2001), citeseerx.ist.psu.edu/viewdoc/download?doi=10.1.1.523.8414&rep=rep1&type=pdf.

2 Winstanley, "Existential Stories."

3 Adrienne Rich, *Of Woman Born: Motherhood as Experience and Institution* (London: Norton, 1986). As a mother I found *Of Woman Born* a liberating text; as a feminist who believes that trans women are women, I find her links to transmisogyny deeply troubling. Discussions of motherhood and pregnancy can lend themselves to biologism (as well as assumptions that women all want to have children), and this should be questioned at every point when writing on the subject. As Jos Truitt

writes: "Being able to make a baby and being a woman are not the same thing," in "The Ways of Talking about the 'War on Women' That Leave People Out," *Feministing*, March 19, 2012, feministing.com/2012/03/19/the-ways-of-talking-about-the-war-on-women-that-leave-people-out/.

4 Rich, *Of Woman Born*, 16.

5 Alice Lowe, "Delivering Results: How Alice Lowe Wrote *Prevenge* in a Week and Shot It in 11 Days . . . while Pregnant," *Moviemaker*, March 24, 2017, www.moviemaker.com/archives/moviemaking/alice-lowe-pregnant-prevenge/.

6 Lowe, "Delivering Results."

7 Alice Lowe, telephone conversation with the author, May 7, 2017. I would like to thank Alice Lowe for taking the time to speak to me extensively about *Prevenge*.

8 Lowe, conversation with the author.

9 Barbara Creed, *The Monstrous-Feminine: Film, Feminism, Psychoanalysis* (London: Routledge, 1993).

10 Simon Abrams, "*Prevenge*," RogerEbert.com, March 24, 2017, www.rogerebert.com/reviews/prevenge-2017; Lowe, conversation with author.

11 Lowe, conversation with author.

12 Pier Paolo Pasolini, "The Cinema of Poetry," in *Heretical Empiricism*, trans. Ben Lawton and Louise Barnett (Bloomington: Indiana University Press, 1988), 167–86.

13 Sami Shawer, "Mental Disorders in Pregnancy," *SlideShare*, July 17, 2013, www.slideshare.net/samishawer/mental-health-disorders-in-pregnancy-24348303; Hanna-Leena Melender, "Experiences of Fears Associated with Pregnancy and Childbirth: A Study of 329 Pregnant Women," *Birth* 29, no. 2 (2002): 101–11.

14 Uriel Halbreich, "Prevalence of Mood Symptoms and Depression in Pregnancy: Implications of Clinical Practice and Research," *CNS Spectrums* 9, no. 3 (2004): 177–84.

15 Anita Riecher-Rössler and Anke Rohde, "Diagnostic Classification of Perinatal Mood Disorders," in *Perinatal Stress, Mood and Anxiety Disorders: From Bench to Bedside*, ed. Anita Riecher-Rössler and Meir Steiner (Basel: Karger, 2005), 6–23.

16 Heather A. Bennett et al., "Prevalence of Depression during Pregnancy: Systematic Review," *Obstetrics and Gynecology* 104, no. 4 (2004): 698–709.

17 These are average figures, with their research showing that in some surveys up to 17 percent of women suffer from prepartum depression.

18 Julia Kristeva, *New Maladies of the Soul*, trans. Ross Guberman (New York: Columbia University Press, 1995), 219.

19 Julia Kristeva, "Motherhood according to Giovanni Bellini," trans. Thomas Gora, Alice Jardine, and Leon Roudiez, in *The Portable Kristeva*, ed. Kelly Oliver (New York: Columbia University Press, 2002), 303.

20 Elizabeth Grosz, "The Body of Signification," in *Abjection, Melancholia and Love: The Work of Julia Kristeva*, ed. John Fletcher and Andrew Benjamin (London: Routledge, 1990), 96.

21 I would like to stress at this point that this discussion of pregnancy as an ethical responsibility to the other is in no way challenging the right of a woman to choose whether she terminates a pregnancy. If anything, the opposite is true, as an ethical discussion of pregnancy should arguably consider the mother's wishes first and foremost, as she is a life that is living rather than a life that is not yet formed. As this piece is about women who chose to continue their pregnancies, the fetus has been referred to as a "baby" occasionally when discussing the earlier stages of pregnancy, but this suggests not any pro-life subtext but instead the subjective nature of pregnancy for a woman who decides to continue her pregnancy. If a pregnancy is planned, wanted, or even just accepted, a fetus may become a "baby" in the woman's mind at any point during the process: when it is just a few cells, when she hears the heartbeat, or when she first feels a kick. For some women the fetus may not feel like her baby until it is born, or even weeks or months after the birth.

22 Paula Nicholson, *Postnatal Depression: Facing the Paradox of Loss, Happiness and Motherhood* (Chichester: John Wiley & Sons, 2001), 7.

23 Stefanie Zaers, *Psychosocial Adaptation to Pregnancy and Delivery: Course, Predictors and Outcomes* (Göttingen: Cuviller Verlag, 2007).

24 Kristeva, *New Maladies of the Soul*, 219.

7

Pregnant Situations in Agnès Varda's and Anne Claire Poirier's Film Creations

Tessa Ashlin Nunn

With their representation of two creative processes, works on the subject of pregnancy link an individual woman's life to the universal fact of human life born of mothers by shining light on the links between acts of social reproduction and artistic production.[1] As Adrienne Rich began her 1976 feminist exploration of motherhood, *Of Woman Born: Motherhood as Experience and Institution*, the common experience of having developed inside a woman's body unifies all men and women because "all human life on the planet is born of woman."[2] Cinematographic representations of maternity risk essentializing women as mothers, yet films presenting pregnancy as a complex creative process, similar to conceiving and creating an artistic work, recognize pregnancy as a phenomenological experience that, like most human experiences, is simultaneously generalizable and specific to an individual. Drawing from theories of feminist phenomenology, the present essay analyzes representations of pregnant experiences in films directed by Agnès Varda and Anne Claire Poirier: *L'Opéra-Mouffe* (Varda, 1958), *Réponse de femmes* (Varda, 1975), and *De mère en fille* (Poirier, 1968). These three films, each portraying an aspect of the director's embodied existence as a pregnant or formerly pregnant woman, present possible experiences of pregnancy and childbirth. In this essay, I examine how Varda and Poirier, as mothers and film directors, create objects over which they cannot claim complete control while also existing in and through the process.

Current scholarship on pregnancy in cinema tends to focus predominantly on commercial films whose pregnancy narratives often neglect the corporeal experience of pregnancy and reduce it to a series of events leading up to childbirth.[3] Turning to auteur cinema, we see an attempt to go against the grain and break with normalized notions of pregnancy. Varda's and Poirier's films zoom in on the bodily experience of pregnancy, giving little attention to the dramatization of a linear pregnancy narrative and thereby allowing the films' pregnant women to project themselves and to be projected in different temporalities. These three experimental films, combining elements of documentary and narrative cinema, explore the filmmakers' multiple creative processes incorporating the natural and cultural world. In the same way, pregnant women creatively readjust their biological and cultural body's phenomenological presence in the world.[4]

The directors' embodied involvement in these films, as creators, images of bodies, and voices of experience, reminds us that the time-based art of filmmaking, much like pregnancy, is a creative activity originating in the body. For this reason, I draw from feminist phenomenology, specifically the work of Simone de Beauvoir, Iris Marion Young, and Vivian Sobchack, to examine how these films represent the situated body's lived experience of being pregnant. Phenomenology allows me to consider how pregnancy changes a woman's experience of time, space, and movement as she grapples with being her body and creating another body within her body. Moreover, I consider how the more generalizable experience of living in a female body in patriarchal Western societies persists during pregnancy. A phenomenological approach also opens up the possibility of a cinematic aesthesis soliciting the creator's and spectator's corporeal and affective experience of the world. The films studied in this essay demonstrate the directors' questioning of what it means to be seen in film and in everyday life as an image of a woman, and as an image of a pregnant woman, in contrast to the phenomenological experience of living as a subjective individual who is pregnant.

At a time when few female directors received recognition for their films, Poirier and Varda were two of the first Francophone filmmakers, after Alice Guy-Blaché, to create cinematic representations of pregnant experiences.[5] The short film *L'Opéra-Mouffe*, composed of ten vignettes, begins with images of Varda, visibly pregnant, sitting on a bench nude before showing various images of elderly people in the street and a young couple indoors. Contrasting unborn life and the approach of death, the film acts as "a fecund surrogate" for a pregnant woman's "anxieties about the ultimate destiny of the life she carries within her."[6] At the dawn of second-wave feminism, Varda's short essay film *Réponse de femmes* explicitly addresses the problematic homogenization of women's bodies as bodies for reproduction. Across the Atlantic, Poirier fueled the nascent Quebecois feminist movement with her first feature-length film, *De mère en fille*, which documents the bodily transformation of Liette Desjardins during and after her real pregnancy. Without showing her body, Poirier incorporated her own pregnancy into the film. As we view Liette's lived experience of pregnancy, we hear Poirier reading a revised version of her diary entries written while she was pregnant with her first child. These three films prioritize women's subjectivity by addressing the phenomenon of human reproduction from the perspectives of individual women. I study how the films represent pregnant bodies in relation to pregnant women's subjective relation to movement and space in addition to the factors that transform pregnancy into an alienating experience. In the conclusion, I examine the spectator's embodied experience watching pregnant women in what I qualify as a haptic cinema. By exploring experiences of pregnancy, these films present pregnancy as a project that, like the production of a film, involves giving one's body to another or others in a unique but also generalizable experience.

Pregnant Women as Mobile Subjects

Varda's and Poirier's films deal with pregnant and nonpregnant women's freedom to move in public spaces and in filmed spaces. I turn to Iris Marion Young's 1980 essay on female bodily motility, "Throwing Like a Girl," to consider how these films complicate and confirm North American and European anxieties surrounding women's bodily movements during the second half of the twentieth century. Women, Young claims, are subjects free to participate in transcendence but are often in situations denying their subjectivity. Consequently, their modalities of corporeal comportment exhibit a tension between acting as a subject and being an object. Treating her body like a thing, a woman inhibits her movement's intentionality and disconnects it from her surroundings. According to Young, who draws on the work of Simone de Beauvoir and Maurice Merleau-Ponty, a woman often experiences her body as a "fragile encumbrance" rather than a medium through which she can realize existential projects.[7] Instead of directing her attention to how she will use her body to accomplish her aims, a woman frequently feels impelled to focus on her body to ensure that it/she does what it/she is supposed to do and avoids injury. She experiences her body first as a representation—the object of other people's imagined or real gaze—and then as intentional movement split between achieving her aim and matching an image. As long as women are married to beliefs about how their bodies should be, seen as objects and not as capable instruments for accomplishing tasks, they cannot fully embody a transcendental state of moving toward their goals.

This inhibition in a woman's motility informs her relation to space as it encloses her instead of proposing distant horizons. During pregnancy, a woman can inhabit an inner space while also creating an inner space within herself. Like all bodies, she is an expanse of corporeal surface within a space. According to Young in a later essay, "Pregnant Embodiment: Subjectivity and Alienation," pregnancy creates a split subjectivity in which a pregnant woman is aware of herself as an objective body and a subject pursuing projects, as a source and a creator.[8] She is her body, and she makes her body. The vignette of *L'Opéra-Mouffe* entitled "De la grossesse" (On Pregnancy) proposes shots from different angles of a dove captured in a fishbowl. Then, in opposition to this image of entrapment, a young woman in a deserted garden runs toward the camera. This juxtaposition of confinement and freedom closely aligns with Young's concept of a pregnant experience split between passively entrapping something else and actively moving toward something. Similarly, a film cradles the director's concept and offers it to the audience.

In patriarchal Western societies, many women, like the dove, experience others' gazes as a form of enclosure. Young posits in "Throwing Like a Girl" that instead of existing in space or inhabiting space, a woman experiences her body as positioned in a bounded, inner space, as if she were only an object to be looked at. Situated in space, a pregnant woman becomes the space in which she creates, places, and moves a nascent life; at the same time, she takes up space as an object to be examined. Like a filmed woman, she appears limited to a certain frame, yet she experiences this space as her site of action.

Drawing attention to her body as a vessel, the visible signs of pregnancy lead observers to forget a pregnant woman's invisible creative effort.

A woman's to-be-looked-at-ness intensifies as the visual gains a more prominent rank among our sensory modes of experiencing the world. Film theorist Laura Mulvey made the term *to-be-looked-at-ness* synonymous with the erotic objects of the male gaze.[9] Avoiding an argument about scopophilia, I use this term to highlight the tendency to value visual observations of individuals, particularly in film, over other forms of perception. The cultural dominance of vision over other senses transforms the body into an image instead of an embodied, sensate situation. For film theorist Vivian Sobchack, "increasing valorization of the visible" in Western culture has reduced "the sensual thickness of lived experience" to a single "soulless dimension."[10] A woman's attention to her body in relation to culturally constructed images of how women should be seen can prevent her from existing as a free subject in the world. These images, what Simone de Beauvoir calls *myths*, can prod a woman into inhabiting an image of what dominant culture defines as female being. As a result, she is her body, "but her body is something other than she is."[11] Pregnancy further complicates this situation as a pregnant person shares her body with another *other* and attempts to imitate a new image—the image of a pregnant woman, a woman who is no longer a woman alone. As Beauvoir wrote in *The Second Sex*, "Tenanted by another, who battens upon her substance throughout the period of pregnancy, the female is at once herself and other than herself."[12]

Poirier's and Varda's films present possible experiences of pregnant women's increased bodily inhibition and heightened bodily self-consciousness. Borrowing from Maurice Merleau-Ponty's location of intentionality in motility as a bodily "I can," Young contends that a woman often fails to access bodily possibilities due to "an *inhibited intentionality*, which simultaneously reaches toward a projected end with an 'I can' and withholds its full bodily commitment to that end in a self-imposed 'I cannot.'"[13] On the one hand, the social norm of treating pregnancy as if it were a disorder can intensify a pregnant woman's attention to her body as an object and, consequently, further inhibit her movements' intentionality. On the other hand, a pregnant woman's elevated awareness of her body and its creative capacities can draw her focus away from socially constructed images of female bodies to her personal bodily situation.

In *De mère en fille*, Liette reflects on her situation as subject and object for others and for herself. While dancing at a nightclub with her husband and friends, she suddenly pauses on the dance floor. The voice-over accuses other people of reminding her that she is different through their excessive attentiveness to her bodily situation. Liette experiences her body as capable of dancing, but when she sees other people perceiving her as a body that *should not* dance, she retreats from the dance floor. Responding to a "You should," she replaces her "I can" with an "I cannot." The voice-over compares the pregnant body's effort to the nonpregnant dancing body's effort: the pregnant body, through its invisible work, dispenses significantly more energy moving and creating than the nonpregnant visibly active bodies. We see an inhibition of Liette's motility but hear a recognition of a pregnant woman's unseen creative movements. Later, Poirier's voice-over, in which she speaks as if she were Liette, articulates a concern about her pregnancy being neglected. Admitting the inanity of this concern, Poirier says, "It's absurd. I indeed know that no one can give birth for me" ("C'est absurde. Je sais bien que personne ne peut accoucher à ma place"). She is the only person capable of creating her child, but others' increased attention to her body makes her question the *correctness* of her creative body.

The pregnant woman is the performer of her child's creation and birth; however, social norms and medical institutions remove any sense of intentionality in her bodily experience by convincing her that she is fragile, ill, or disabled.[14] Furthermore, through the prominent concerns with the visual effects of pregnancy on a woman's body, consumerist culture influences a woman's attitude toward pregnancy as a problem to be solved.[15] Although *De mère en fille* demonstrates how a pregnant woman conforms to normalized images of pregnancy, it also portrays a desire to break free from these images and exist as a mobile, intentional body in space.

Throughout the film, Liette has a series of dreams in which she grapples with the relationship between space, her body, and the freedom to move. In the first dream scene, Liette finds herself on a beach where a group of women, who do not seem to be pregnant, appear frozen in different poses as children run around and a man adjusts some of the women's outfits. A large sculpture consisting of numerous twisting rods stands in the middle of this scene. Separated from the women behind a fence, Liette stands motionless; however, the camera's gaze races throughout the tableau from one woman to another. Traveling shots through the convoluted sculpture repeatedly interrupt a quick series of close-ups and zoom-outs of the women's frozen bodies as well as a store mannequin placed among them. The camera's fast movements create a sense of violence, as if its gaze forced the women to

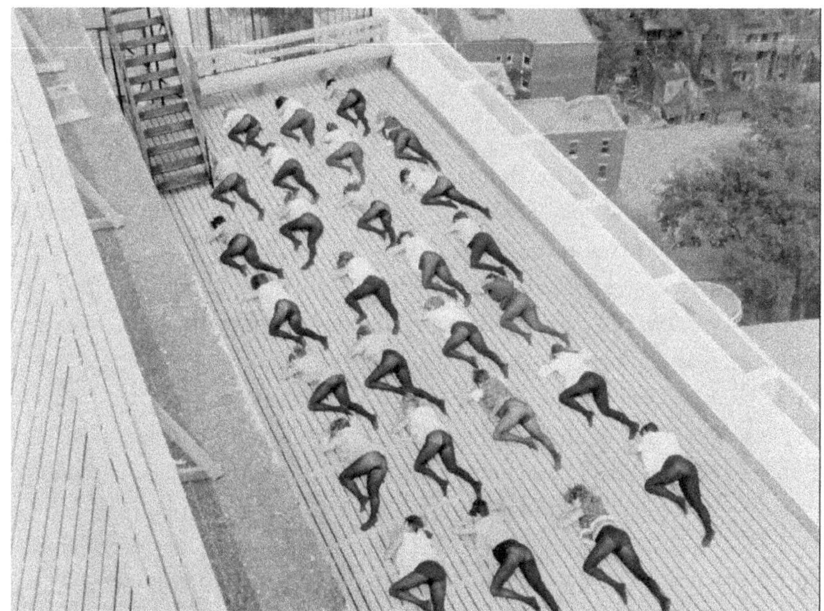

Women on the rooftop in *De mère en fille* (Anne Claire Poirier, 1968).

transform into mannequins. Bordering on a nightmare, the dream reveals a fear of immanence, of losing one's humanness to become a static creation. In the ensuing dream sequence, Liette and several other women lie motionless on their stomachs during an exercise class on a skyscraper's rooftop. An extradiegetic voice guides the women through breathing exercises as they gradually begin to move and create audible breath. As the class continues, their movements become larger and faster. Moving through space, the women project themselves toward a distance. The contrast between the frozen glamorous women on the beach and the moving women in the class transforms the rooftop into a utopic space above the city where the women are liberated from immobilizing forces.

Split Subjectivity

In many ways, pregnancy forces women to be more attentive to their experiences as bodies. According to Young's essay on pregnant embodiment, pregnant women become increasingly aware of their bodies as the mobile force carrying another body and as an immanent object to be moved. Augmenting a woman's perception of her rootedness to the earth, pregnancy heightens her consciousness of her body's physicality as she moves her corporeal material weight. To recognize our physical weight and power, we compare the work of our body against its potential to move objects through space.[16] A pregnant woman's body contains both the power to carry the fetus through space and the fetus itself, making her body the mover and the moved object as well as the creator and the created object. Young writes, "The pregnant woman experiences herself as a source and participant in a creative process. Though she does not plan and direct it, neither does it merely wash over her; rather, she *is* this process, this change."[17] In the same way, Liette performs in a film about pregnancy and experiences pregnancy in the film. Similarly, the concepts for *L'Opéra-Mouffe* and *De mère en fille* originate in Varda's and Poirier's experiences of pregnancy, which they incorporate into the films. The directors are both sources and participants in the filmmaking.

Recounting Poirier's lived experience, the voice-over constructs "female subjectivity as film discourse" in *De mère en fille*.[18] In the opening shot, Liette swims and plays with her three-year-old daughter. Her pregnancy is not evident until she climbs out of the pool and reclines on a lounge chair with her hands cupping her round belly. We see her as a physical body moving through space before seeing her as a pregnant body. As soon as she leaves the pool, extradiegetic music begins to play, and we no longer hear Liette's voice. In fact, from this point forward, we rarely hear Liette speak in the diegesis, with the exception of a few brief conversations she has with her daughter and husband. Once her pregnancy is visible, its presence precedes her as her body's materiality obfuscates her voice's subjectivity within the visual field. Yet, Liette's character is pure transcendence in the immaterial space of the voice-over, the space exceeding the visible that the spectator can imagine but cannot access.[19] Poirier's narration in the voice-over escapes the constraints of the visual while also connecting her lived experience to that of Liette.

Further creating a mistrust of the visual, the camera angles disfigure Liette's pregnant body as a split being, a self and other joined in a material mass. In the second scene of the film, Liette rubs her naked self with a washing mitten in front of a mirror. An oblique low-angle shot emphasizes her relation to a body that is at once her own and other to her as her chest and face appear in the mirror while an extreme close-up of her pregnant belly dominates the foreground. In a medium-long shot, Liette, contemplating and rubbing her body, is visible from behind. Since the camera captures this shot at an angle from behind the bathroom door, her body is not visible in the mirror as a pregnant body. A full-profile shot cuts to a series of extreme close-ups of her caressing her face and her torso. Occasionally, distorted images of both her belly and chest appear in the mirror. The break between the foreground and her reflection not only presents the shape of her body as ambiguous but also creates a disconnection between her subjective gaze and her object-like belly.

Throughout this scene, the voice-over describes a feeling of alienation as well as amazement at the capacity to create human life through the body. Acknowledging that Liette is probably no longer attractive in the eyes of others, Poirier's narration describes her body as simultaneously beautiful and frightening ("d'une beauté effrayante"). This sequence encourages haptic viewing as alternating shots of Liette's eyes and hands investigate the sensations of her body. The intensity of her hand motions, the distortion of the images, and the ambiguous direction of her gaze create a split between her subjective body and her creative body generating, housing, and nourishing an-other life. She perceives, enacts, and communicates her existence and consciousness of being-in-the-world as both an individual body and

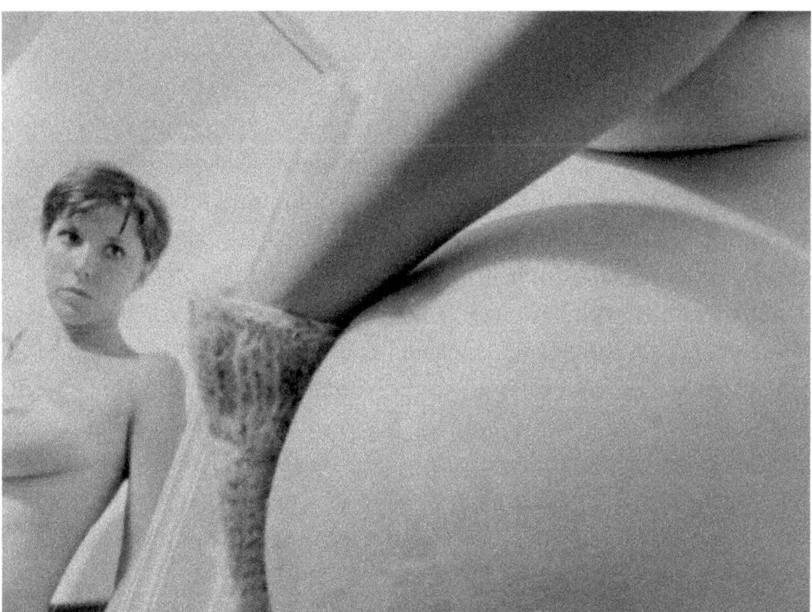

Liette in front of the mirror in *De mère en fille* (Anne Claire Poirier, 1968).

a pregnant body. As a result of the visual distortion and emphasis on the tactile in this scene, the film's viewers are nudged into a haptic form of looking, in which we are "more inclined to graze than to gaze."[20] This sequence gives valence to the lived experience, in particular the feeling of being split between transcendence and immanence, represented by the cinematography rather than the actual images of a body.

The dissonance between the sound of Liette's rarely heard on-screen speaking voice and Poirier's voice-over, which masquerades as Liette's inner dialogue, compounds Liette's split subjectivity as a woman and a woman carrying an-other. In line with Young's generalizations, Liette compares her body to the images of what a woman's body is supposed to be. However, this comparison manifests itself through a voice that is not her own—the voice of the film's creator—and a gaze that is not her own: the camera's gaze. These substitutions for Liette's personal evaluation of her body highlight her unique but also generalizable bodily situation of being a pregnant woman, as well as the broader existential dilemma of being the subject of one's body that becomes the object of other people's gazes and speech acts.

The film's movements between the universality of pregnancy and the uniqueness of an individual pregnant woman's experience contrast with popular tendencies to prioritize the creation of human life over the individual's gestation. In a rare moment of speaking in the film's diegesis, Liette attempts to discuss the process of pregnancy with her young daughter by focusing on the fetus's development rather than the pregnant woman. They look through an issue of *Life* magazine displaying various sonogram images. Liette explains to her daughter Josie how sonograms depict the development and growth of the fetal body. The magazine includes only sonograms, no images of a pregnant or birthing woman. Consequently, Josie struggles to understand how the fetus receives nourishment from the mother and how these images illustrate what is inside living women. The rising interest in sonogram images, according to Young, devalues pregnant women's bodily experiences: "Sonogram technology has revolutionized the experience of pregnancy and expectant parenting by putting a visual representation of the fetus at the center, in the context of a modern epistemological system that has always given priority to the visual over the tactile or even the oral."[21] For Sobchack, imaging technologies reveal the "unforthcoming mystery" of human bodies instead of information about bodily situations.[22] The film, however, acts in opposition to the sonogram image. As spectators, our only knowledge of the fetus comes from our perception of Liette as she experiences her bodily interactions with it. The film spotlights the pregnant body's experience without showing the mysterious image of the fetus, thereby prioritizing the process of creating life over the life created.

Creative Women

Just as Poirier's voice and writing about her own pregnancy infiltrate her film, Varda represents herself in *L'Opéra-Mouffe* and *Réponse de femmes* as a creative woman—a creator of films and a creator of children. She utilizes her own bodily situation to question its uniqueness and its commonalities with other women's bodies. *Réponse de femmes* opens with a shot of Varda carrying a transparent sign on her shoulder identifying her as the creator of the *ciné-tract*.[23] She appears as both a body-object of the film and the body-agent of the film's creation. In another shot, a group of women hold a translucent sign asking, "Qu'est-ce qu'être femme?" (What is it to be a woman?). Up to this point, the soundtrack of a woman singing a wordless melody saturates the film's aural sphere. While a nude baby lies on her back with her genitals exposed to the camera, a female voice-over defines a woman as a human born with female genitals. The definition of being woman, *être femme*, then expands from *having* female genitals to *living* in a woman's body as a nude woman standing in an empty white space announces this second definition.

Shining light on the inextricable entanglement of culturally and physiologically situated ways of existing, this montage differentiates the situated body, the biological body, and the subjective body. First, the fully clothed silent women question their social label; then the visible nude baby rocks as we hear the female voice-over; finally, the nude woman speaks as a subjective biological body. This last woman defines her whole body, not just her breasts and genitals, as a woman's body. As she speaks, a man holds a clapper board on which Varda's name is written next to extreme close-ups of the woman's breasts and pubic region. These shots point to the director's role in transforming women's bodies into filmed parts. As the director, Varda transforms women into images, but in the first shot she also presents herself as an image of a woman. Standing behind the transparent sign, she draws our attention to the multiple mediators—the screen, the camera, and the eye of the viewer—implicated in transforming her lived body into a visible image.

The women in *Réponse de femmes* contest the relationships between existing in a woman's body, a pregnant woman's body, and a woman's body defined by the capacity to reproduce. Two clothed women hold a transparent sign that asks if all women wish to be mothers. One woman answers *yes*; the other says *no*. The following long shot shows a nude pregnant woman laughing and caressing her body as we hear a nondiegetic sound of young children and the singing voice from earlier. In a scene similar to the mirror scene in *De mère en fille*, the pregnant woman's exploration of her body through touch accentuates the invisible, sensuous experience of pregnancy. Her apparent joy derived from her bodily experience reminds us that, as viewers and listeners, we can perceive only limited knowledge of her body as a lived and inhabited situation. We gaze upon her as a body or a rounded shape, whereas she experiences her body as a site of movement and creative activity.

Varda presents and explores the contours of her own pregnant body in the first images of *L'Opéra-Mouffe* as the film's credits appear over an image of her sitting on a bench with her back facing the camera. As in the opening credits of *Réponse de femmes*, her name announced as the filmmaker is superimposed on her body. A profile shot of her pregnant body follows. The movement of her breath resonating through her round torso brings our attention to her body's fullness of life and its active movement fixed in space. Rather than moving through space, she moves through her creative and creating body. Discussing her choice to appear pregnant in this film, Varda explains in an interview, "I had a very happy pregnancy, I translated what could be the pregnancy of a woman from la Mouffe. It tends toward not what one feels, but what one can feel."[24] Indeed, it is a film about the possibilities of pregnant existence as well as those of mortal human life. Throughout her long career, Varda has taken provocative approaches to filming motherhood, pregnancy, and the experience of living creatively in a woman's body.

As the first sequences of *L'Opéra-Mouffe* progress, a shot of a large squash, resembling the shape of Varda's pregnant belly, replaces a close-up of her reclined torso rising and falling. A man slices the squash in half and pulls out its seeds and placenta (the fibrous material inside such a squash is indeed called the placenta in both French and English). The music, composed by Georges Delerue, becomes more urgent, increasing in tempo during a montage of close-ups of the emptied squash, the pile of seeds and placenta, and finally slices of squash on display at the market. The transitions between these shots likewise follow a faster tempo than the series of shots showing Varda's breathing belly, creating a contrast between the calmness of nascent life and the anxiety of a looming death. While more urgency surrounds the images of the vegetable, the pregnant belly evinces a movement toward development in contrast to the destruction and distribution of the squash. In addition to their similar form as rounded, hard materials housing a softer material, both the squash and the pregnant woman provide human nourishment. As Hélène Rouch suggests in a conversation with Luce Irigaray, pregnant women "offer their body as food" to another.[25] The emphasis on vegetality throughout the film coincides with its focus on cycles of approaching birth, represented by the two pregnant women in the film, and approaching death, silently looming in the shots of elderly people. Feminist film scholar Sandy Flitterman-Lewis interprets the glorification and idealization of the pregnant woman's body as supporting an essentialist ideology despite the fact that the "film offers a powerful contrast to traditionally codified images of maternity."[26] This different perspective investigating the anxieties and complicated emotions surrounding a woman's pregnancy as a phenomenological experience, I argue, acknowledges the possibilities of pregnancy as a lived experience. Instead of hiding the pregnant body and extolling the fact of reproduction, *L'Opéra-Mouffe* accentuates the body's situated, subjective, creative presence in gestation.

The Spectator and the Pregnant Body as Flesh

In this final section, I will shift the focus from the screen to the spectators and consider the bodily experiences of watching pregnancy and childbirth in film. Sobchack compares film to Merleau-Ponty's definition of philosophy as "an expression of experience by experience," meaning a film is an act of seeing, hearing, and reflecting that makes itself seen, heard, and reflexively understood.[27] Poirier's and Varda's films provide viewers the opportunity to experience pregnancy through perception. As explored in depth by Sobchack and Laura Marks, we should not limit perception of films to the visual. As Liette rubs her body, as a woman screams while delivering her baby, as the pregnant woman eats a rose to satisfy her cravings at the end of *L'Opéra-Mouffe*, we perceive possible tactile, aural, kinetic, and gustatory sensations that a pregnant woman can feel. Viewing the films through our bodies, we do not possess the films in thought or project an idea on them. We abandon ourselves to the sensations created by the films and allow them to think themselves within us.

The address of our vision responds to the cinematic expression of an experience that becomes our bodily sensation as we grasp "the perceptual expression, the seeing, the direct experience of that anonymously present, sensing and sentient 'other.' Thus, the film experience is a system of communication based on bodily perception as a vehicle of conscious expression."[28] Our bodies respond to Varda's and Poirier's expressions of how they perceive their bodily experiences and other women's bodily experiences of pregnancy. If, as Merleau-Ponty explains in *Phenomenology of Perception*, we can understand the function of the living body only by enacting it ourselves, can we understand pregnant or birthing bodies without having experienced pregnancy and childbirth?[29] Perhaps not. The bodily experiences of spectators inhabiting bodies that have been pregnant, bodies that can become pregnant, and bodies that can never become pregnant inevitably differ. Yet all human spectators can experience the bodily situation of having been born. In response to Jean-Luc Nancy's claim that the ontology of the body is ontology itself, I disagree with his assertion that nothing precedes or underlies the phenomenon of being.[30] For being begins with becoming, with being birthed into the world.

In her essay "Creating Life, Giving Birth, and Learning to Die," Brooke Schueneman posits that almost all humans have potential access to discussions of motherhood from a variety of perspectives. In contrast, those who have never given birth or can never give birth struggle to think about "the lived experience of creating life."[31] As the films' pregnant women caress their stomachs, spectators who have never been pregnant bodies cannot easily imagine what those women feel growing and moving inside of them or the sensation of carrying an-other body inside their own. Watching the extreme close-ups of the vaginal delivery and the Cesarean section in *De mère en fille*, these spectators may feel a bodily sensation of discomfort but most likely struggle to fathom the physical pain or numbness of such experiences in the same ways as spectators who have lived through similar situations. Nevertheless, all spectators can watch these films "as a *visible performance* distinguishable from, yet included in" their own experiences as bodies in the world.[32] As bodies "engaged in intentional acts of perception in an intended world," all spectators "have a *place* of viewing, a *situation*."[33] The differences in their bodily knowledge of pregnant existence, as well as their bodies' biological capacity to become pregnant, alter their situations and the places from which they view the experience of pregnancy in the films. As Sobchack explains, these differences allow for distinct perceptional experiences that permit us to "speak back to the cinematic experience" from our bodily situation: "Both the problem and the pleasure of embodiment is that embodiment marks our differences as well as our similarities, that is—as we watch a film and its signifying and significant movement—we are suddenly, yet frequently, conscious of an implicit incarnation, an 'other's' consciousness embodied both *like* and *unlike* our own, as a Here situated There upon the screen."[34] Spectators who have never been a pregnant body can see a pregnant body on the screen as different from their body but also similar, as a human body, a breathing body, a self-conscious body, a frightened body, a laughing body.

Perceiving pregnant women in films as bodies in the world, as bodies born into the world, and finally as bodies birthing bodies into the world, a spectator who has never given birth can find phenomenological unity-in-difference. Spectators can experience what Merleau-Ponty calls *intercorporeity*, meaning a sensibility shared among distinctly different bodies of flesh.[35] For him, *flesh* is a *general thing*—not matter, mind, or substance—but an element "midway between the spatio-temporal individual and the idea, a sort of incarnate principle that brings a style of being wherever there is a fragment of being. The flesh is in this sense an 'element' of Being. Not a fact or a sum of facts, and yet adherent to *location* and to the *now*."[36] This turn to the *element of Being* in a discussion on pregnancy could be misconstrued as essentialist. It is not my intention to reduce pregnant women to merely the creators of the organic material constituting humans. Rather, I argue that by viewing our bodies as flesh, born into the world, with similar and different experiences of space, time, and sensations, we can see our bodily existence as connected to all human bodily existences that at one time emerged into being.

Recognizing and valuing this intercorporeity as we watch pregnant women in film, we can revalue the place of childbirth in our own lived experiences. Philosophers frequently fail to address the ontological significance of the obvious fact that all human beings are born.[37] As Rich argues, patriarchal institutions have subjugated the concept of "maternal power" to make reproduction the source of women's powerlessness.[38] These three films, however, divorce pregnancy from institutions and present it as a creative process. The experience of perceiving pregnant bodies in films can remind us of our constant bodily connections to the fact that sensate pregnant bodies created and delivered our sensate bodies into the world. Therefore, these films are not films about pregnant bodies. They are films about all created and creating human bodies thrown into existence.

Notes

1 Throughout this essay, I use the terms *woman* to designate both individuals who identify as such and individuals who identify differently but have also experienced pregnancy.

2 Adrienne Rich, *Of Woman Born: Motherhood as Experience and Institution* (New York: Norton, 1976), 11.

3 Kelly Oliver, *Knock Me Up, Knock Me Down: Images of Pregnancy in Hollywood Films* (New York: Columbia University Press, 2012).

4 On the phenomenological existence of pregnant women interacting with the natural and cultural world, see Carol Bigwood's "Renaturalizing the Body (with the Help of Merleau-Ponty)," *Hypatia* 6, no. 3, "Feminism and the Body" (Autumn 1991): 54–73.

5 Although women's issues are certainly not the only subjects tackled in Varda's and Poirier's often highly political films, the lived experiences of women are at the forefront of their respective canons. When Varda first began making films, Jacqueline Audry was the only other active female filmmaker in France. Regarding Poirier, some scholars credit *De mère en fille* as having incited the feminist movement in Canada, where Poirier was one of the few Quebecois women film directors in the early 1960s.

6 Kierran Argent Horner, "Intersubjectivity in the Pregnant Self: Maternity from Simone de Beauvoir's *The Second Sex*, through Agnès Varda's *L'Opéra Mouffe* to Contemporary Feminist Thought," *Studies in European Cinema* 18, no. 1 (2021): 4.

7 Iris Marion Young, *On Female Body Experience: "Throwing like a Girl" and Other Essays* (New York: Oxford University Press, 2005), 32–35.

8 Iris Marion Young, "Pregnant Embodiment: Subjectivity and Alienation," *Journal of Medicine and Philosophy: A Forum for Bioethics and Philosophy of Medicine* 9, no. 1 (1984): 45–62.

9 Laura Mulvey, "Visual Pleasure and Narrative Cinema," *Screen* 3 (1975): 6–18.

10 Vivian Sobchack, "'Is Any Body Home?' Embodied Imagination and Visible Evictions," in *Home, Exile, Homeland: Film, Media, and the Politics of Place*, ed. Hamid Naficy (New York: Routledge, 1999), 48.
11 Beauvoir, *The Second Sex*, trans. H. M. Parshley (Harmondsworth, UK: Penguin, 1972), 61.
12 Beauvoir, *The Second Sex*, 22.
13 Young, *On Female Body Experience*, 36; Maurice Merleau-Ponty, *Phenomenology of Perception*, trans. Colin Smith (London: Routledge & K. Paul, 1962), 137.
14 See Kerreen Reiger and Rhea Dempsey, "Performing Birth in a Culture of Fear: An Embodied Crisis of Late Modernity," *Healthy Sociology Review* 14 (2006): 364–73; Katherine Beckett, "Choosing Cesarean Feminism and the Politics of Childbirth in the United States," *Feminist Theory* 6, no. 3 (2005): 251–57.
15 Reiger and Dempsey, "Performing Birth in a Culture of Fear," 366.
16 Merleau-Ponty, *Phenomenology of Perception*, 314–15.
17 Young, *On Female Body Experience*, 54.
18 Joan Nicks, "Anne Claire Poirier's Cinema," in *Gendering the Nation: Canadian Women's Cinema*, ed. Kay Armatage, Kass Banning, and Brenda Longfellow (Toronto: University of Toronto Press, 1999), 227.
19 See Michel Chion's *The Voice in Cinema* (1982), trans. Claudia Gorbman (New York: Columbia University Press, 1999); and Mary Anne Doane's "The Voice in the Cinema: The Articulation of Body and Space," *Yale French Studies* 60 (1980): 33–50.
20 Laura Marks, *The Skin of the Film: Intercultural Cinema, Embodiment, and the Senses* (Durham, NC: Duke University Press, 2000), 162.
21 Young, *On Female Body Experience*, 61.
22 Sobchack, "Is Any Body Home?" 49.
23 The short film genre of *ciné-tracts* developed during and after the events of May 1968.
24 "J'ai eu moi une grossesse très heureuse, j'ai traduit ce qui pourrait être celle d'une femme de la Mouffe. La sensibilité n'est pas ce qu'on éprouve, mais ce qu'on peut éprouver." Agnès Varda, quoted in Alison Smith, *Agnès Varda* (Manchester: Manchester University Press, 1998), 94.
25 Luce Irigaray, "On the Maternal Order," in *Sexes and Genealogies*, trans. Gillian C. Gill (New York: Columbia University Press, 1993), 43.

26 Sandy Flitterman-Lewis, *To Desire Differently: Feminism and the French Cinema* (Urbana: University of Illinois Press, 1990), 217.
27 Vivian Sobchack, *The Address of the Eye: A Phenomenology of Film Experience* (Princeton, NJ: Princeton University Press, 1992), 3.
28 Sobchack, *The Address of the Eye*, 9.
29 Merleau-Ponty, *Phenomenology of Perception*, 75.
30 Jean-Luc Nancy, *Corpus* (1992), trans. Richard. A. Rand (New York: Fordham University Press, 2008).
31 Brooke Schueneman, "Creating Life, Giving Birth, and Learning to Die," in *Philosophical Inquiries into Pregnancy, Childbirth, and Mothering: Maternal Subjects*, ed. Sheila Lintott and Maureen Sander-Staudt (New York: Routledge, 2012), 167.
32 Sobchack, *The Address of the Eye*, 11.
33 Sobchack, *The Address of the Eye*, 179.
34 Sobchack, *The Address of the Eye*, 287–88.
35 Maurice Merleau-Ponty, *The Visible and the Invisible: Followed by Working Notes*, trans. Alphonso Lingis and Claude Lefort (Evanston, IL: Northwestern University Press, 1968), 141.
36 Merleau-Ponty, *The Visible and the Invisible*, 139–40.
37 Christine Battersby, *The Phenomenal Woman: Feminist Metaphysics and the Patterns of Identity* (New York: Routledge, 1998), 3.
38 Rich, *Of Woman Born*, 68.

8

Fetal Imagery and Alternative Maternities in Jane Campion's *Top of the Lake*

Missy Molloy

A striking sequence in the television program *Top of the Lake: China Girl* occurs early in its second episode, when Robin (Elisabeth Moss), prowling the upscale Sydney neighborhood where the daughter she placed for adoption seventeen years earlier now lives, catches sight of Mary (Alice Englert, Jane Campion's daughter) for the first time since her birth. Slowing the car to a crawl, Robin stares at her daughter through the open window, mesmerized. Attention to the intensities and dysfunctions of mother-daughter bonds unifies *Top of the Lake*'s two seasons, the first released in 2013 and the second, subtitled *China Girl*, in 2017. In the first, Robin's return home to New Zealand's South Island is motivated by her mother Jude's (Robyn Nevin) fight against cancer; however, Robin becomes so engrossed in investigating the pregnancy of a twelve-year-old girl, Tui (Jacqueline Joe), that she neglects her mother. Pursuing Tui, who has disappeared into the wilderness surrounding Robin's hometown, Robin is not present for Jude's death, experiencing her mother's good-bye secondhand over voicemail: "I'm imagining your face," Jude says softly, "I'm looking at you, kid . . . Good-bye, my little girl."

In *China Girl*, Robin's passionate gaze at Mary, her long-absent daughter, recalls the emotion audibly expressed in Jude's voicemail message, thereby linking *Top of the Lake*'s two seasons via the painful intensity of a mother's feelings for her daughter, which are depicted as excessive and lacking any other outlet. In both scenes, the camerawork centralizes the suffering apparent in Robin's face: as a daughter ravaged by loss and as a mother overwhelmed by desire. In the latter scene, the cinematography and editing illustrate conventions typically reserved for romance; a close-up of Robin's intent gaze precedes a slow-motion, medium-long shot of Mary from Robin's perspective, followed by a cut to capture Robin's fervent look in medium close-up as Mary disappears down the block. The editing stresses Robin's rapt attention, which viewers are invited to share. Like Jude's, Robin's desire for her daughter will far exceed what her daughter returns, and Robin's efforts to protect Mary will only partly succeed. This chapter reads *China Girl* as the culmination of Jane Campion's career-long attention to the convolutions of the mother-daughter bond, and *Top of the Lake* as a whole as confirmation of Campion's status as the contemporary screen author most committed to the peculiar complexities of motherhood, which *Top of the Lake* closely scrutinizes through portraits of alternative maternities, including early teen pregnancy, adoption, and surrogacy.

Scholarship on Jane Campion's work more or less demonstrates consensus regarding what unifies her oeuvre, in particular its sustained attention to the subjectivities of women in violent, patriarchal societies.[1] The writer/director's move to emphasize reproduction more explicitly lines up with her twenty-first-century adoption of the crime genre to explore unconventional maternities that straddle legal boundaries, which complements her early-career focus on women fighting for autonomy and creative opportunities in hostile worlds (for example, in the Cannes- and Oscar-winning feature film, *The Piano* [1993], which she wrote and directed, and in her cinematic portrait of New Zealand writer Janet Frame, *An Angel at My Table* [1990]). Scholars have additionally noted masochistic and destructive tendencies in Campion women. Kathleen McHugh's synopsis of Campion's authorship up to *In the Cut* (the 2003 feature marking Campion's first effort in crime drama) outlines the definitive features of Campion's authorship:

> Controversial and edgy themes . . . have dominated her work from her first student films up to the present: how power and violence permeate familial and sexual relationships, confound self-expression, and reify and distort gender roles. . . . Her oeuvre explore[s] characters' agency,

> sexual desire, and drive for self-expression—forces that set them at odds with each other, with the environment, and also, particularly in the case of female characters, with themselves.[2]

In *Top of the Lake, China Girl* in particular, maternal drives take priority over Campion's earlier fixation on struggles for "self-expression"; moreover, this unprecedented focus on maternity enhances the masochism evident in many Campion protagonists. In addition, *Top of the Lake*'s spotlight on maternity produces a startlingly original aesthetic of maternal devotion bordering on obsession, one that situates Campion's characteristic "foreground [of] female interiority" in the context of women longing for children, real and imaginary, in scenes that "suspend clear distinctions between objective and subjective viewpoints."[3] In other words, the characteristics that McHugh identifies in Campion's films feature differently, and distinctly, in Campion's work in crime drama, specifically in *Top of the Lake*, wherein the genre enables the screen author to figure transgressive dimensions of maternity from a variety of provocative angles. In the series, the aesthetics of maternal subjectivity underscore the ambivalence women experience in the desire for children and toward the children they reproduce and/or parent. Maternity in *Top of the Lake* appears exceptionally attractive and risky, and I argue that it provides the masochistic outlet offered by illicit romance and the drive for self-actualization in earlier Campion productions.

Patriarchal Abuse, Masochistic Desire, and Crime

In a review of *China Girl*'s first episode, Laura Hudson writes, "Sexism, rape culture, and exploitation aren't new themes for *Top of the Lake*, but this season seems primed to explore the dark side of another facet of womanhood: the relationship between mothers and daughters, and what it means to give birth to or raise a girl in a world that is primed to eat her alive."[4] The distinction Hudson makes between the two seasons isn't entirely apt, as Robin's struggles in the first season are also rooted in maternity—in being a daughter and mother, and in supporting other mothers: Simone (Mirrah Foulkes), for one, who loses her only child, Jamie (Luke Buchanan), in the search for Tui, and Tui herself, whose traumas revive Robin's history as a teenager made pregnant by rape. Furthermore, Hudson identifies "the dark side" of motherhood as *China Girl*'s focus, no doubt in consequence of the season's consistent reiteration of maternal desire as dangerously intense to the extent that mothers are singularly vulnerable to suffering and even psychosis. Yet visually, the series casts maternity in an eerie, extraordinary light. For instance, Robin's psychological and emotional struggles manifest in maternal hallucinations that end in her outrage at their disappearance; in one such episode, the spectral figure of a young woman caring for a toddler lounges alongside Robin, who cuddles an infant-shaped outline in a ghostly blue. The image depicts maternity as surreal; Robin is compelled to experience imaginary encounters with her lost child at different stages of development, and these encounters inspire intense pleasure and pain.

If the first season is, as many have suggested, a complex treatment of the crime of rape that stresses its deep cultural roots and social connotations, then *China Girl* handles motherhood's implication in various crimes: initially in the black market surrogacy service that replaces the first season's rape ring as central to the crime plot, but additionally in the extreme behaviors of mothers that consistently illustrate maternity as a threat.[5] These include Robin suffering nightly from the loss of her child; Julia (Nicole Kidman), Mary's adopted mother, constantly professing devotion to the daughter who, Julia alleges, now "hates" her; Miranda (Gwendoline Christie), Robin's new partner on the police force, who is eventually exposed as a client

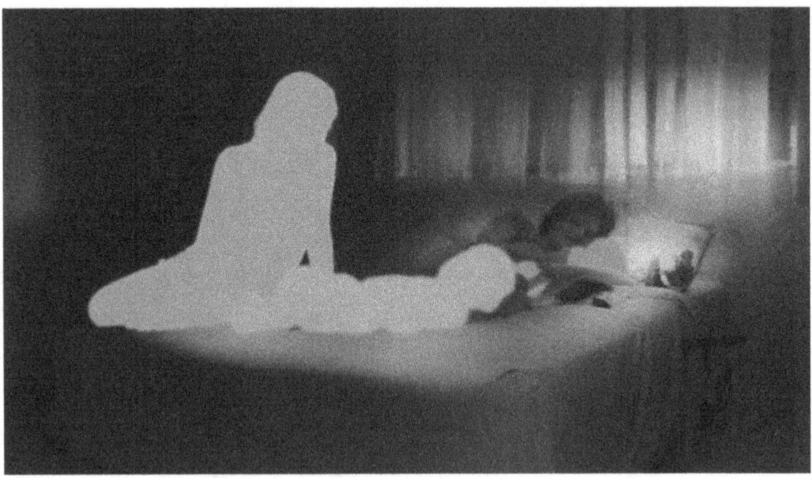

Robin hallucinates maternal scenarios that end with her screaming in outrage in "The Loved One," episode 2 of *Top of the Lake: China Girl* (created by Jane Campion, 2017).

of the illegal surrogacy scheme; and Felicity (Helen Thomson), a mother related to the main case, who is picked up by police in the throes of a psychotic episode, overcome by an experience of love and anxiety depicted by *China Girl* as borderline criminal. Escaped from a psych ward, Felicity desperately shouts, "My baby's missing . . . hasn't been fed in two days, I'm very worried," to the first officer on the scene. "You can't be here," he replies, his words and actions conveying a contradictory urge both to protect her and to protect others *from* her. Does Felicity's desperate desire for her imaginary child make her dangerous? When the investigation leads Robin to an IVF clinic, a doctor she interviews cynically observes, "The drive to reproduce is manic; it can become a vortex."[6] While both seasons of *Top of the Lake* foreground pregnancy and maternity, the second season interrogates from manifold perspectives the various costs—emotional, psychological, financial—of motherhood.

In an interview published in the *Guardian*, Campion stressed the impact of losing a newborn baby, Jasper, in 1993, on her personal life and career: "I am incredibly grateful for having that whole experience of that baby that did not live, because it put me in touch with that kind of suffering. It just changed my perspective forever."[7] Her interview with Kate Muir implies that *Top of the Lake*, and *China Girl* in particular, represents Campion's most direct expression of the "change of perspective" inspired by Jasper's loss: "The experience resonates in [Campion's] more recent work in *Top of the Lake*, in which Robin reveals that in the past she was raped and gave the baby away for adoption. She searches for her lost child, and other stories feature surrogacy, miscarriages and loss. 'This whole area of female experience is so unknown, but it's like the equivalent of going to war, except no one makes movies about it,' says Campion."

Campion's "going to war" analogy resonates most explicitly in *China Girl*'s main criminal case, in which a young woman nicknamed "China Girl" by a forensic pathologist is murdered, the fetus she had been carrying dying with her.[8] The idea that the physical and psychological tolls of maternity are akin to war also resonates in the harsh criticism and emotional abuse motherhood exposes women to in *China Girl*; for example, in the episode titled "Surrogate," Mary tells Julia, who adopted Mary after not being able to carry a fetus to term, to "shove it [Julia's opinion of Mary's boyfriend] up [your] cunt where everything dies and nothing lives," and in the following scene, Julia says of Robin, "She's a wasteland; you'll get nothing from her."

These vicious remarks underscore the special cruelty of insults that explicitly target maternal failures. Moreover, Campion's likening maternity to war is supported by *Top of the Lake*'s illustration of motherhood as devastating at every point in its long arc: from failed efforts to get pregnant to the many challenges of gestation and labor, and far into the experience of parenting, with Robin's neglect of Jude marking death as the end point of that mother's suffering.

A recurring feature of Campion's work is its focus on sex, power, and violence, and how they are perceived by and affect women. While these issues were often taken up in an art cinema context early in her career, in 2003 she turned her attention to genre cinema with the crime drama *In the Cut*, which gave her the opportunity to pay particular attention to women's experience and desires, especially their traumatic and masochistic dimensions. *In the Cut* underscores the destructive capacities of romantic ideologies that target women, the plot's criminal case centered on a serial killer who places engagement rings on his victims' fingers before dismembering them. The film's protagonist, Franny (Meg Ryan), becomes involved in the investigation on multiple levels, including through her witness of a victim fellating the killer and later her affair with a detective on the case, Giovanni Malloy (Mark Ruffalo). In my view, the serial killer investigation is subordinate to the film's interest in Franny's passions for poetry, sex, and risk, and in the aggression and sadism of the men she encounters. *In the Cut* depicts the sexism and misogyny Franny routinely faces as widespread and banal, the serial killer's actions only exaggerations of cultural norms. In this sense, Campion's experiments with crime drama in *In the Cut* and later in *Top of the Lake* develop organically from her previous work, allowing for an intensification of her decades-long investigation into "female interiority" in a genre that complements her fixation on introspective women confronting hostile, male-dominated environments.

McHugh connects the "ongoing motif of bad choices" in Campion's treatment of "women's desire" to a mother's influence on her daughter: "In all of Campion's films, but particularly from *The Piano* onward, mothers determine the erotic character of their daughter's relationships. In this film and her most recent, *In the Cut*, that character is profoundly masochistic, and associated with a lost or absent mother whose heartbreak and traumas are relived, repeated in their protagonist daughters' lives."[9] *Top of the Lake* adds to the thread McHugh traces from *The Piano* to *In the*

Cut, the two seasons encompassing a full cycle of maternal desire—fueled by obsessive love, suffering, and masochism—via Robin's character arc, as she struggles with the traumas of a rape-induced pregnancy and of giving birth to a child she immediately places for adoption; the guilt and regret of failing to reach closure with Jude before her mother's death; and the emotional rollercoaster of testing out the maternal role for the first time with a nearly grown daughter. Building on this interpretation, Robin's hallucinatory episodes in *China Girl* function as imaginative efforts to reconcile what was lost, fantasies at various stages of Mary's development substituting for missed mother-daughter encounters. Notably, *China Girl* depicts both Robin and Julia, the birth and adopted mothers, as "driven mad" by love for Mary, which suggests that motherhood is psychologically devastating in fact and fantasy, the season blurring distinctions between the two to underline maternity's comprehensive psychological upheaval. Every mother is also a daughter: Robin's two-season arc represents maternal masochistic desires as cyclical and reproductive, their high-frequency circulation abetted by women's subordinate status in patriarchal societies.

In *In the Cut*, the risky behaviors of Franny and her half sister, Pauline (Jennifer Jason Leigh), stem from their mothers' traumas, the film indicting conventional romance for its harmful effects. At a key moment in the film, Pauline gives Franny a charm bracelet of a baby carriage that pops open to reveal a little infant, which she calls a "courtship fantasy." Pauline's gift prompts Franny to recount her mother's version of her engagement to their father, concluding with her belief that the story reflects her mother's romantic fantasy rather than fact: the memory "killed her [because she] just couldn't believe it when [their father] left." *In the Cut* firmly attributes the half sisters' masochistic behaviors to their mothers' romantic fantasies, and indeed, both Pauline's reckless pursuit of romance and Franny's attraction to risk put them in the serial killer's path. Through Robin's development over *Top of the Lake*'s two seasons, Campion crafts a character who embodies a broader spectrum of maternal drama—trauma, disillusionment, loss, and desire—a product and producer of maternal ambivalence who keeps the wheel turning.

Campion's overall stance on maternity is explicitly and consistently ambivalent, her proclivity for shaping women's subjectivities through trauma animating her representations of mothers and daughters on-screen.

Top of the Lake, which takes significant advantage of crime drama's focus on darker dimensions of human behavior, frames sexuality as traumatic—as in, for instance, Tui and Robin carrying pregnancies caused by rape to term. The second season, set five years after Tui gives birth, contributes additional maternal traumas to the series' repertoire by simultaneously focusing on Robin's fledgling relationship with Mary and her investigation of an illegal surrogacy scheme. This brief sketch demonstrates that Campion's turn to crime drama is affinitive in that it allows her fixation on the traumas that influence women's behaviors to thrive, particularly in *China Girl*'s depiction of maternal desire as uniquely corrupt. The second season additionally portrays Robin's emotions toward Mary as devotional and erotic, their intensity augmented by startling images of fetuses and infants that appear in loose coordination with a sprawling plot unified by unconventional, and often dysfunctional, maternity. Thus, in crime drama Campion's unique perspective on women's subjectivities flourishes in a genre where it is narratively and stylistically at home. Furthermore, *China Girl*'s casting of maternity in a criminal light aligns with Campion's view of women's experiences—as mothers, lovers, and daughters—as dangerously intense and spectacularly transgressive.

An "Ovarian" Series

Paratextual accounts of Campion's inclusive direction highlight that it nurtures long-term, supportive, and familial bonds, which markedly contrast her screen fixation on dysfunction. In fact, Campion has a history of working with family; she collaborated on multiple productions with her sister, Anna Campion, who directed Jane in the 1989 short, *The Audition*, and co-wrote the 1999 feature *Holy Smoke!* with Jane, who also directed the film. Additionally, Campion has a history of developing long-term creative partnerships that she and others characterize as familial.[10] Making *Top of the Lake*, Campion reunited with multiple actors instrumental to her career, including the star of *The Piano*, Holly Hunter, and the star of *Sweetie* (1989), Genevieve Lemon, in the first season, and Nicole Kidman, star of *The Portrait of a Lady* (1996), in the second. In interviews, Hunter likens working with Campion to "falling in love," while Kidman, who nearly starred in one of Campion's student films three decades ago, asked to be cast in the second season of her close friend's television production.[11]

Both women, along with Elisabeth Moss, characterize Campion's direction as supportive, even if the material she writes propels the actors into traumatic scenarios. Moss attributes her decision to take on the difficult role of Robin a second time to her "love for Jane" and "passion" for the series, as well as her trust in Campion's "in-tune way of guiding me through a scene," concluding that the "deep" and "intense relationship" they share is fundamental to their successful collaboration. After shooting the first season in New Zealand, Moss described the process of preparing for and performing Robin's traumatic experiences: "I remember calling my mom and saying, 'I don't know if I can do this.' . . . And Jane just held my hand and Garth [Davis, co-director of the first season] held the other one and we learned how to do it."[12] Moss's description makes it clear not only that *Top of the Lake* foregrounds maternity, but that the production process operated with maternity as a model.

In addition, Campion's move into television production aligns with an unmistakably maternal shift in her creative attention. With *China Girl* (which Campion refers to as an "ovarian" series), Campion took the propensity to approach creative collaboration as familial a step further when she wrote the role of Robin's daughter, Mary, with her own daughter, Alice Englert, in mind to perform it.[13] Publicly she describes this decision as "brave," while adding that she found the process of directing her daughter challenging, so much so that she asked second-season co-director Ariel Kleiman to direct the scenes featuring Mary that she found too "distressing."[14] In fact, in honing in on diverse experiences of maternity via *China Girl*, Campion appears remarkably clear-sighted about the personal risks she and her collaborators exposed themselves to, commenting, for instance, on Kidman's bravery in "taking on the material" given the actor's experiences as a mother, which include adoption and surrogacy.[15] Campion, it seems, shares the risks of delving into maternity with her co-workers, especially the other mothers. Johanna Gondouin, Suruchi Thapar-Björkert, and Ingrid Ryberg's statement on *China Girl* supports this conclusion: "The focus on motherhood is bolstered by both the biographical background and public and fictional personae of Campion and the female leads in the series."[16]

In describing maternal loss, Campion segues with ease from addressing motherhood as experienced by other women to her own experiences and finally to maternity's broader connotations: "But it's not just the children you bear; you have miscarriages that are so disturbing you can't even talk about them—I personally had three miscarriages and a baby who died—and all of that really isn't in our cultural discussion because most of that discussion is run by guys. So it was great to tell a story that has maternity at the centre of it."[17] Campion obviously regards the profound treatment of maternal experiences on-screen as culturally valuable and personally risky, and views emotional vulnerability as essential to the process of making *China Girl* for her and the series' creative team. In her words, "That's the challenge of filmmaking, you're so often on that precipice, just risking your life to get to that top rock."[18] As supportive as Campion's directing style is purported to be, she is obviously comfortable leading her collaborators into difficult and challenging terrain, her work consistently demonstrating a compulsion to mine personal traumas for creative rewards and to gently—with affection and humor—persuade others to do the same.

A Sharper Focus on Maternity as Criminal

Top of the Lake's long-form narrative allows for great variety in its dissection of mothers, daughters, and dysfunction—and the communities that breed them. In the first season, Robin's fractured relationship with Jude epitomizes the bleakness of a paranoid and divided community. For example, the scene of Robin listening, too late, to her mother's good-bye cuts to the season's main antagonist, Tui's father, Matt (Peter Mullan), at his mother's grave, where he honors her memory by whipping himself with the belt she had used to discipline him. Robin's eventual discovery that Matt is her biological father completes a bizarre family tree. In this model of family, Robin and Tui represent a variant of Franny and Pauline; as in *In the Cut*, the half sisters have different mothers and share a father, the older sister filling a maternal role for the younger, and the younger sister's traumas reviving the elder's. Also in the case of each pair, the narrative implies that their mothers' experiences, actual and imaginary, compel their daughters' actions. Conversely, *China Girl* demonstrates its emphasis on mothers over daughters by focusing on two mothers, Robin and Julia, both fixated on Mary as the primary target of their frustrated desires. Unfortunately, and surprisingly, the titular pregnant woman who opens the series—nicknamed "China Girl" by the police and later referred to by her brothel nickname, "Cinnamon" (Thien Huong Thi Nguyen)—is not a significant subject of *China Girl*'s attention; this despite the fact that her pregnancy's function in the seasonal arc resembles Tui's, and her status as a gestational carrier is essential to the season's framing of maternal desires as borderline criminal. This oversight is difficult to reconcile with the depth of attention *China Girl* pays to other, non-Asian mothers.

Top of the Lake's distinct title sequences indicate overlaps between the two seasons, yet *China Girl*'s highlights that season's more pronounced focus on maternity and reproduction. In the title sequence of *Top of the Lake*'s first season, a lake is suddenly breached, its water pouring down in a stream animated by a series of sketches: most notably of a buck head (resembling many mounted on walls in the first season), which cedes to a curled fetus that develops into an infant before it disappears, a photograph of Tui replacing it as the water empties, ending the sequence. The uterine connotations of the title sequence, which the fetus literalizes, gradually become apparent in the parallels drawn between Tui and Robin, both pregnant as a result of rape at perilously young ages. Thus McHugh's analysis of the title sequence concludes as follows: "It is that relation between Robin Griffin and Tui Mitchum [*sic*], albeit enigmatically expressed, that will be the central subject matter of the investigation pursued in *Top of the Lake*."[19]

The title sequence also "enigmatically" expresses the centrality of pregnancy and maternity to the series, which the second season's focus on illegal surrogacy reinforces. Thus the pronounced emphasis on fetal imagery in the second season's title sequence suggests pregnancy and its aftermath—including varied forms of maternity—as *Top of the Lake*'s overarching concern. Moreover, the different aesthetic of *China Girl*'s title sequence previews the season's visual approach to maternal desires as startling and uncannily bright, in contrast to the darkness of the first season's lake and barely sketched fetus. As stated above, the fetus's origin in rape is the central crime the first season investigates, whereas the fetus in *China Girl* originates in maternal desires desperate to a criminal extent; therefore, it is significant that the liquid, uterine environment of the second season's title sequence is oceanic (in contrast to the first season's titular lake). Alongside the shift from lake to ocean, the revised color palette of *China Girl*'s fetal and infantile imagery conveys the second season's distinct take on maternity, while corroborating the series' overall fascination with maternal ambivalence.

Multiple reviews of *Top of the Lake*'s second season suggest that the series' shift from the rural grandeur of New Zealand's South Island to Sydney,

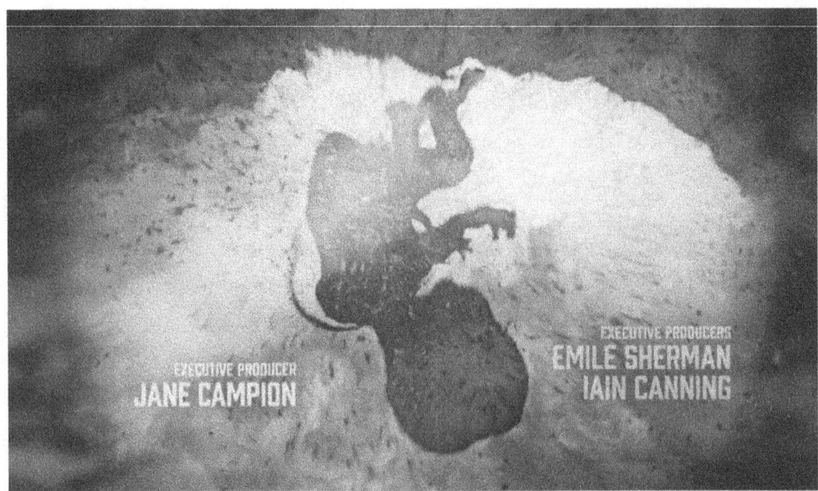

The fetus in *Top of the Lake: China Girl*'s title sequence is more prominent than, but reminiscent of, the brief sketch of a fetus that drains along with the lake's water in the celebrated title sequence of the first season, *Top of the Lake* (created by Jane Campion, 2013).

Australia, blunted its impact. Without a doubt, *China Girl's* transportation of Robin from vast, "otherworldly" landscapes to a dense urban environment dramatically revised the series' iconography. Sophie Gilbert's review in the *Atlantic* exemplifies the tendency to account for *China Girl*'s weaknesses by citing the location change: "Set around Sydney's Bondi Beach, the six-hour drama feels unmoored by its new location. The characteristic obsessions are all there—motherhood, misogyny, self-actualization—but removing them from the context of South Island's dramatic scenery has somehow neutered their narrative potential."[20] Gilbert concludes that the series' critique of misogyny becomes "comical" in the large-city setting, although she accurately notes that the second season concerns itself less with misogyny than motherhood: "what it means, what it costs, and the lengths women will go to when they're denied it."[21]

In a *New York Times* interview, Campion articulates her perspective on the second season's setting: "It was always in my mind that the ocean is the major uterus of the whole thing. It's a feminine space."[22] Meanwhile Moss, in a "behind the scenes" video, "*Top of the Lake*: Shooting Sydney," stresses *China Girl*'s "temperamental" and constantly changing ocean in comparison to the stillness of the first season's lake.[23] "To me the ocean is the other character," Moss concludes, while Kleiman offers several provocative and vague claims: "Jane and I talked about [the ocean] being the womb of the series. It's full of pureness; it's full of freedom. . . . In a way it is this season's wilderness."[24] These statements convey the significance the creative team placed on *Top of the Lake*'s bodies of water; however, Kleiman's characterization of the ocean as "full of pureness . . . [and] freedom" is strikingly at odds with *China Girl*'s ocean, in particular the season's inciting incident, which is the depositing of China Girl/Cinnamon's body (crammed inside a blue suitcase) in the ocean—a scenario that implies precisely the opposite of purity and freedom.[25]

Despite the criticism the new setting inspired, Sydney is well suited to *China Girl*'s canvas of the reproductive black market and the gender, racial, and class dynamics that fuel it. The visual approach to Sydney recalls Campion's portrait of New York City in *In the Cut*, which Sue Thornham interprets as defined by the "tangib[le] presen[ce]" of "sadistic masculinity": "In this city, the visual symbols of male power are crude, even parodic, but what they display is a socially sanctioned dominance with powerful material effects."[26] Like *In the Cut*'s New York, *China Girl*'s Sydney is distinguished by "excessive" performance(s) of "masculinity," which women are forced to navigate along with the urban geography. The main settings include the brothel Cinnamon worked in, where men habitually capitalize on the services of mainly housebound Asian girls (who appear to perennially lounge, scantily clad); the various institutions of Sydney's police force, in which the overrepresentation of men inspires harassment of women at every level of the organization; an internet café where a group of socially awkward, porn- and prostitute-obsessed young men meet to trade gossip about sex workers; and the domestic spaces of Robin's apartment and Mary's childhood home. The different socioeconomic classes the season depicts are framed as parasitic, the lifestyles of the affluent creating the market for sex and surrogacy that employs the Asian women. Relevant statistical research on the Australian sex industry indicates a sharp increase in Asian migrant sex workers since the early 1990s, perhaps attributable to "a decrease in Australian-born sex workers."[27] Apparently responding to that increase, *China Girl* draws attention to various aspects of Asian sex workers' social roles and political precarity without delving deeply enough into the brothel workers' characters to present a clear position on the issues that their presence and occupation in Australia raise.

China Girl's opening scenes involve Cinnamon's transport from brothel to sea in a battered suitcase, which a man and woman (later revealed as managers of the brothel where the surrogacy scheme is based) nudge into the sea from atop a dramatic cliff top, the man's repeated failure to tip the suitcase over the edge played for dark humor. In subsequent murky images of the suitcase settling to the ocean floor, long, straight black hair escapes from a gaping hole, thus garishly anthropomorphizing the suitcase. In a sense, then, *China Girl*, like *Top of the Lake*'s first season, uses the dangerous submergence of a pregnant girl to initiate its drama, yet it adapts the formula to a dead girl (thus closing the narrative in one direction) in an ocean (a space figurally much vaster than the first season's lake). However, like the first season, *China Girl* exploits the aesthetic appeals of liquid imagery and the vulnerability of a young, pregnant woman to generate suspense.

Maureen Ryan, writing for *Variety*, describes *China Girl* as about "what it is to be a parent or to want a child—and how wrenching it is to crave a connection with a child who has turned away (or has been given away) . . . [and] what it feels like for a woman to be viewed through the lens of her sexual availability, her looks and her ability or desire to become pregnant." Her review concludes, "Once again, *Top of the Lake* is unusual in that it gives unquestioned primacy to thorny, ambiguous questions that surface constantly in almost every woman's life."[28] Incidentally, the sense that China Girl/Cinnamon's experiences might be perceived as foreign to the series' target audience might have contributed to her (and her brothel companions') narrative marginalization in favor of the white women (Robin, Julia, Miranda, Felicity) who suffer as a result of maternal desires. Therefore, to Ryan's conclusions, I would add that *China Girl* emphasizes the economically and politically privileged end of the reproductive black market to the detriment of the comparatively slight Asian characterizations occupying the other end. Gondouin, Thapar-Björkert, and Ryberg's analysis of *China Girl* arrives at a similar conclusion: "An intense emotional drama about white women's experiences of sexual violence, reproduction, and motherhood[,] the affective economy of the series . . . attaches great value to white femininity as precious, emotionally fragile, and at risk of abuse—against the flat backdrop of passive and emotionally indifferent Asian sex workers."[29]

In contrast, the fetal images in *China Girl*'s psychotic maternal sequences are depicted with sensitivity and depth, shedding welcome light on the masochism at the heart of Campion's portraits of maternal subjectivity. For instance, in the grip of psychosis, Felicity holds a gaunt, horrifying infant whose disappearance motivates the desperate pursuit through heavy traffic that results in her arrest. Comparing this to Robin's dream infant exposes a world of difference, yet the infants—compelling, repulsive, otherworldly—emphatically express the ambivalence many mothers experience: their children's dependence is dreadful and delightful, and often a precursor to their own mixed feelings of dependence.

Conclusion

I sympathize with reviews that fault *China Girl* for the incredibility of its main case, the plotting of which often makes or breaks crime drama.[30] Moreover, Cinnamon's shockingly thin characterization undermines the promise many read in *Top of the Lake*'s Tui, perhaps the most developed woman of color Campion has characterized to date. However, reflecting on the series as a whole, Campion's crime dramas, and her history as revelator of women's experiences from surprising angles reveals *China Girl*'s significance to the ever-evolving portrait of Campion's authorship, in particular its unique vision of maternity.

One way of interpreting *China Girl*'s desperate mothers is that they are all victims of excessive, intense desires for children, and engage in careless, destructive behaviors in consequence. *China Girl* undeniably presents maternal desires as singularly vulnerable to corruption; it also frames mothers as obsessive to a masochistic extent, and is thereby consonant with Campion's stance on women's desires. In Campion's work, awareness of and empathy with the psychotic potentials of maternity energize social potentials that oppose what So Mayer refers to as "heteropatriarchal colonialist capitalism" in their reading of *Top of the Lake*'s first season.[31] In that season, an alternative community took literal shape in Paradise, a newly established wilderness settlement of traumatized, rebellious women. In its finale, Tui and her newborn emerge to join a society significantly altered by events that her criminal pregnancy set in motion. Paradise, by undermining the patriarchal control exercised by Laketop's police and criminals, had apparently opened space for matriarchal and anarchic social practices—for instance, Jamie's memorial at Paradise in episode 5, which resembles both a millennial activist gathering (Jamie's young friends' memorializing his tragic death by writing "NO" on their foreheads) and a neo-pagan rite (mourners swimming out in the dark lake among burning pyres).

In comparison, *China Girl* lacks an alternative community akin to Laketop's Paradise; instead, it presents mothers desperate for babies who require other women's bodies to carry and deliver them, the dynamic in this association of women based on steep economic and political disparities. Also, in lieu of magnificent scenery, *China Girl* offers the Pacific—and fetuses and infants lit on the bright end of an oceanic palette—to signify the unbounded provocations of maternity. It is the latter that recommend *Top of the Lake*'s second season, namely, their uncanny expression of maternal ambivalence without glimpses of utopia to soften its painful manifestations.

Notes

1 For example, see Dana B. Polan, *Jane Campion* (London: British Film Institute, 2001); Hilary Radner, Alistair Fox, and Irène Bessière, eds., *Jane Campion: Cinema, Nation, Identity* (Detroit: Wayne State University Press, 2009); and Alistair Fox, *Jane Campion: Authorship and Personal Cinema* (Bloomington: Indiana University Press, 2011).

2 Kathleen McHugh, *Jane Campion* (Champaign: University of Illinois Press, 2007), 1–2.

3 McHugh, *Jane Campion*, 127; 50.

4 Laura Hudson, "*Top of the Lake: China Girl* Recap: The Destiny of Man," *Vulture.com*, September 10, 2017, www.vulture.com/2017/09/top-of-the-lake-china-girl-recap-episode-1.html.

5 See Emily Bullock, "Interrogating Gender in Crime TV: *Top of the Lake*," *Screen Education* 77 (2015): 116–23; and Natalie Wilson, "*Top of the Lake*: A Non-Watered-Down Depiction of Rape Culture," *Ms.*, April 18, 2013, msmagazine.com/2013/04/18/top-of-the-lake-a-non-watered-down-depiction-of-rape-culture/.

6 *China Girl* episode 3, "Surrogate."

7 Kate Muir, "Jane Campion: 'Capitalism Is Such a Macho Force. I Felt Run Over,'" *Guardian*, May 20, 2018, www.theguardian.com/film/2018/may/20/jane-campion-unconventional-film-maker-macho-force.

8 We later discover she was a paid surrogate.

9 McHugh, *Jane Campion*, 107.

10 Writing *Top of the Lake* also revived Campion's collaboration with Gerard Lee, who co-wrote both seasons as well as early Campion short *Passionless Moments* (1983) and feature *Sweetie* (1989).

11 Diane Haithman, "Holly Hunter on Working with Jane Campion Again—'You Can't Say No,'" *Deadline*, January 5, 2013, deadline.com/2013/01/holly-hunter-jane-campion-top-of-the-lake-tca-397447/.

12 Laura Prudom, "*Top of the Lake*: Elisabeth Moss on Working with Jane Campion and Holly Hunter," *HuffPost: TV & Film*, March 18, 2013, www.huffpost.com/entry/top-of-the-lake-elisabeth-moss_n_2899064.

13 For Campion's use of "ovarian," see Jennifer Vineyard, "*Top of the Lake: China Girl*: Jane Campion on Her 'Ovarian' Series," *New York Times*, September 12, 2017, www.nytimes.com/2017/09/12/arts/television/top-of-the-lake-china-girl-jane-campion.html.

14 Kate Whiting, "*Top of The Lake* Director Campion 'Wanted to Go in a Darker Direction,'" *Belfast Telegraph*, July 22, 2017, www.belfasttelegraph.co.uk/entertainment/news/top-of-the-lake-director-campion-wanted-to-go-in-a-darker-direction-35948465.html.

15 Meredith Blake, "Jane Campion Explores the 'Secret World of Motherhood' in *Top of the Lake: China Girl*," *Los Angeles Times*, September 8, 2017, www.latimes.com/entertainment/tv/la-et-st-jane-campion-top-of-the-lake-20170909-story.html.

16 Johanna Gondouin, Suruchi Thapar-Björkert, and Ingrid Ryberg, "White Vulnerability and the Politics of Reproduction in *Top of the Lake: China Girl*," in *The Power of Vulnerability: Mobilising Affect in Feminist, Queer and Anti-racist Media Cultures*, ed. Anu Koivunen, Katariina Kyrölä, and Ingrid Ryberg (Manchester: Manchester University Press, 2018), 117.

17 "*Top of the Lake*'s Elisabeth Moss and Jane Campion on the Gender War That Brought Them Together," *Radio Times*, July 27, 2017, www.radiotimes.com/news/2017-07-27/top-of-the-lakes-elisabeth-moss-and-jane-campion-on-the-gender-war-that-brought-them-together/.

18 Blake, "Jane Campion Explores."

19 Kathleen McHugh, "Giving Credit to Paratexts and Parafeminism in *Top of the Lake* and *Orange Is the New Black*," *Film Quarterly* 68, no. 3 (2015): 19.

20 Sophie Gilbert, "The Strange Confusion of *Top of the Lake: China Girl*," *Atlantic*, September 12, 2017, www.theatlantic.com/entertainment/archive/2017/09/top-of-the-lake-china-girl-review/539367/.

21 Gilbert, "The Strange Confusion."

22 Vineyard, "'*Top of the Lake: China Girl*.'"

23 The video is available through Hulu, one of the series' main distributors ("*Top of the Lake*: Shooting Sydney," See-Saw Films, Sundance TV, Hulu and BBC Worldwide, 2017). Robin's characterization of the lake does not align with the Māori narrative of Lake Wakatipu's origin, which is referenced in the first season and stresses its tidal nature. So Mayer, "Paradise, Built in Hell: Decolonising Feminist Utopias in *Top of the Lake* (2013)," *Feminist Review* 116, no. 1 (2017: 102–17) interprets the first season with an emphasis on the lake's connotations.

24 "*Top of the Lake*: Shooting Sydney."

25 China Girl's birth name, Pathma, is offhandedly revealed in the penultimate episode, "Who's Your Daddy?"

26 Sue Thornham, "Starting to Feel Like a Chick: Re-visioning Romance in *In the Cut*," *Feminist Media Studies* 7, no. 1 (2007): 37.

27 B. Donovan et al., *The Sex Industry in New South Wales: A Report to the NSW Ministry of Health* (Sydney: Kirby Institute, University of New South Wales, 2012); "The Australian Sex Industry," *Australian Institute of Criminology*, November 3, 2017.

28 Maureen Ryan, "*Top of the Lake: China Girl*," *Variety*, September 5, 2017, 88.

29 Gondouin, Thapar-Björkert, and Ryberg, "White Vulnerability," 128.

30 See James Donaghy, "*Top of the Lake: China Girl*: Is This Mess of a Series beyond Repair?" *Guardian*, August 11, 2017, www.theguardian.com/tv-and-radio/2017/aug/11/top-of-the-lake-china-girl-is-this-mess-of-series-beyond-repair; Brian Lowry, "*Top of the Lake* Adds to Peak for Women's TV Roles," *CNN*, September 8, 2017, edition.cnn.com/2017/09/08/entertainment/top-of-the-lake-womens-roles/index.html.

31 Mayer, "Paradise, Built in Hell," 115.

III

Forms of Collectivity

9

Crow, Child, Stranger

Radical Mothering in Bashu

Sara Saljoughi

Rising from a verdant field in northern Iran, N'ai (Susan Taslimi), the mother in Bahram Beyzai's *Bashu, Gharibe Kuchak / Bashu, the Little Stranger* (1986), gazes directly at the camera with piercing eyes. She is framed to appear as if from nowhere, the close-up our first glimpse of her. Framed by her white *hejab* in mid-wrap, N'ai has risen in response to her children's call. She is a singular character, and her direct look is a historical anomaly of form. Through an encounter with the racial and linguistic difference of a young orphaned boy—the titular Bashu (Adnan Afravian)—N'ai undergoes a dynamic process that reveals mothering as not only an act of care for an *other* but also a recuperative psychological, social, and political process that extends beyond the mother-child relationship with the potential to forge new collectivities. This essay analyzes how *Bashu*, one of the most important contemporary Iranian films, explores the intersubjective possibilities of mothering.

Mothers at War

Bashu was both a critical and popular success. While in some ways the film is exemplary of the well-known tropes of post-revolutionary Iranian cinema (child protagonist, rural setting, use of nonactors, Iran-Iraq War), closer examination suggests it departs from convention in significant ways. The film's critical stance on the rhetoric of war and martyrdom and its depiction of a fractured society separate it from its contemporaries. Like the acclaimed 2016 war horror film *Zeer-e sāye / Under the Shadow* (Babak Anvari), *Bashu* links the war with maternal trauma, unease, and familial loss.

The narrative of *Bashu* offers a traumatic representation of the Iran-Iraq War that displaces the centrality of martyrdom. Production on the film was stalled several times due to the state censors requesting changes, which Beyzai refused to make.[1] The film's unapologetic stance on the trauma of war put it at odds with the ideology of the state. Kamran Rastegar has discussed the Iranian state's repression and censorship of films that present the war with ambivalence.[2] The official state-sanctioned version of war representation was the new genre of Sacred Defense cinema. This genre was positioned to create ideological support for the war by unifying the nation and uplifting martyrdom. Sacred Defense cinema represented the war primarily in terms of religious ideology that provided a justification for the war and allowed Iranians to unite around the notion of protecting the homeland (*vatan*).[3] Although many readings of *Bashu* consider it a war film, it is marginal to the codes of Sacred Defense because, as Rastegar notes, it "produces a counternarrative to the state's project of war memory."[4] This is vividly demonstrated by the ways in which the memory of Bashu's mother, killed in a missile attack, haunts and devastates the young orphan. The image of his mother, clad in a chador, abruptly enters the frame, visualizing how the trauma flashes into Bashu's mind. Her appearance disrupts any progress Bashu makes in his new environment and his developing relationship with N'ai. When he sees his dead mother, he is overcome with emotion: cringing and covering his eyes, wailing, and running away. Bashu's dead mother as a displaced sign of the war is a contrast to the heroic memorialization of war suggested by murals and statues of martyrs. The damage caused to subjects left in the wake of war, the film suggests, cannot be healed through the empty rhetoric of martyrdom.

Bashu makes this intervention primarily by focusing on the underrepresented experiences of women during the war. Women's participation in the war has been mired in the politics of visibility. In her discussion of motherhood and the Iran-Iraq War, Roxanne Varzi discusses how Iranian mothers took disproportionate responsibility for the care of families and households, making significant sacrifices that were not always visible or appreciated in the shadow of the war. Only the act of women's mourning was registered in the state's representation of war.[5] Rastegar also notes how "the sacred defense field valorizes the transcendent sacrifices [of martyrs] . . . while giving less priority to those of the home front, which are the memories of the war that most Iranian women have."[6] Against the public commemoration of military service, the work of Iranian mothers during the Iran-Iraq War is, according to Varzi, a "living martyrdom [that] is uncounted and uncommemorated."[7] In *Bashu*, the domestic setting of N'ai's home brings women into the frame of war; they are far from the terrain of the war yet deeply affected by its events. N'ai's experience of the war is dramatized through the absence of her husband (Parviz Poorhosseini), her witnessing of Bashu's trauma, and the expansion of her worldview. But N'ai is not the typical mourning mother of Iranian war cinema; she is resourceful and matter-of-fact about her husband's absence. "Maybe *he* can be my family, since I don't have one," she says of the stranger Bashu.

Departing further from the conventions of contemporary Iranian cinema, *Bashu* utilizes linguistic difference as a launching point to depict a fractured society. The decisions to set the film in Gilan and to have the dialogue be primarily in Gilaki—a Caspian language that would not be understood by the millions of Iranians who live outside Gilan—challenge the state's vision of a unified, homogeneous Iran. Nasrin Rahimieh has discussed the ways in which the Gilaki language acts as an agent of displacement in the film.[8] Bashu is alienated by the language spoken all around him—he asks, "Is this Iran?" when he arrives in Gilan—and he speaks an equally unfamiliar Khuzestani Arabic dialect. Both languages are minor; neither evokes the nation or nation-state.[9] By largely eschewing the Persian language, the film challenges ideals of national unity through aural articulations of difference.

The disorienting use of Gilaki works dialectically with the film's setting in Gilan. The province's lush, vibrantly green landscape holds a privileged place in the Iranian national imaginary. Gilan is associated primarily with the Caspian Sea, which is the source of many elements of Iranian national culture and a popular holiday destination. Several of Beyzai's most acclaimed films are set in Gilan: *Gharibe va Meh / Stranger and the Fog* (1974) and *Tcherike-ye Tara / The Ballad of Tara* (1979); they also feature mothers as their protagonists.[10] In *Bashu*, however, the primary use of the Gilaki language defamiliarizes this setting for viewers. It also allows the war to hover just outside the frame: it is visible only in Bashu's hallucinations and flashbacks. In Iranian cinema, this region has ordinarily been cast as a safe refuge during the time of war.[11] Pointing to Rakshan Bani-Etemad's *Gilaneh* (2005) as well as films such as *Bashu*, Varzi describes the Caspian as a "feminized space of escape from the male nation at war." She goes on to describe the Caspian Sea in terms of a mother's womb that functions as both "a space of return" and "a space of rehabilitation from the horrors of war."[12]

Bashu's displacement to the northern village is a narrative device that allows the film to operate outside the rhetoric of societal unification during wartime. The village is isolated, exclusionary, and racist. Bashu is harassed by children and adults alike for the color of his skin and his "strange" language. The villagers seek to control, if not eliminate, Bashu's presence in their community. Acting as surrogates for her absent husband, the villagers also try to control N'ai's relationship to Bashu. In their failure to imagine an Iran beyond what they already know, the villagers can be read as a microcosm of the nation. Their various acts of racism in the film are all the more disturbing because they target a child.

The figure of the child has a central place in post-revolutionary Iranian cinema. Scholars have read this emphasis on child protagonists as a way for filmmakers to circumvent the limitations posed by state censorship.[13] Understood in this manner, the child leads of celebrated films such as *Khane-ye doust kodjast? / Where Is the Friend's Home?* (Abbas Kiarostami, 1987) and *Badkonake sefid / The White Balloon* (Jafar Panahi, 1995) can be read as possessing the universal, nonpoliticized subjectivity that is often conferred upon the figure of the child. *Bashu* has been described as focusing on "the traumatic effect of war on civilian children" and "driven by the narrative of an orphaned child," but in fact the film foregrounds the mother to whom Bashu is the little stranger.[14] Whereas the child is a depoliticized figure with claims to universality, the mother is the furthest from the child in terms of her politicization. As the figure of the mother has long been cast as allegory of the nation, what happens to the mother is at the core of national politics.[15] The focus of Beyzai's film, I argue, is *not* Bashu, the titular child, but rather N'ai, the mother.

The emphasis placed on the mother figure in *Bashu* significantly shifts the discourse of motherhood in Iranian cinema. In what follows, I examine how *Bashu*'s depiction of mothering differs from the treatment of mothers in Iranian cinema in general and in Iran-Iraq War films in particular. Finally, I demonstrate the specificity of N'ai's radical mothering as it constitutes her worldview and marks her difference within her community. The trajectory of her radical mothering provides in the film a potential for newly formed collectivities.

Bashu's Mother

Mothers in Iranian cinema have often been assigned minor roles lacking complexity or nuance. Many scholars have discussed the ways in which the figure of the mother has come to stand in for the homeland (*vatan*) across the landscape of Iranian cultural production, including in cinema.[16] This allegorical representation can be summarized, according to Hamid Reza Sadr, as "iconic."[17] Yet the iconography of the mother/homeland on whose behalf male characters act is always "loyal, obedient, and self-sacrificing."[18]

In *film farsi*, the popular cinema active prior to the 1979 Iranian Revolution, mothers were portrayed as the "axis of morality in a family, neighbourhood, or society."[19] Their lack of complexity, which served the ideological function of cinema, was lulled by the notion that they were primarily "patient," "nourishing," and able to "endure hardship to safeguard their family."[20] This so-called positive representation obscured the ways in which maternal characters were written without desire or agency. Visually, the notion of mothers as submissive was emphasized through the depiction of "hopeless women in weeping and pleading scenes."[21] While maternal characters in *film farsi* fall within some of the patterns of representation accorded to women characters, the importance of the mother for maintaining tradition and morality gave those characters a specific function within the films.

In the Iranian New Wave, the oppositional film movement contemporaneous with *film farsi*, the absence of mothers as a structuring presence in cinematic inquiries of sex and the family is striking. In Ebrahim Golestan's *Khesht va Ayneh / Brick and Mirror* (1965), for example, the runaway mother who abandons her baby is unseen and yet pivotal to the film, for it is her abandoned baby who drives the rest of the story. Fereydoun Rahnema's *Pesar-e Iran az Madarash Bikhabar Ast / The Son of Iran Has No News from His Mother* (1976) takes the occurrence of "Iran" as a feminine first name in the Persian language to allegorize mother as nation.

Beyzai's pre-revolutionary films *Stranger and the Fog* and *The Ballad of Tara* enter this landscape with a dramatically different representation of mothers. Khatereh Sheibani cites Beyzai's works as ushering in a new discourse of motherhood in Iranian cinema.[22] Describing Rana, the maternal protagonist of *Stranger and the Fog*, as a "character that stands alone" among representations of women, Eldad J. Pardo suggests the film puts forth women's desire, agency, and leadership in realist terms that counteract dominant societal ideas.[23] *Bashu* brings Beyzai's tradition of strong female characters into the early period of post-revolutionary Iranian cinema. The women of Beyzai's films, notes Hamid Dabashi, "hold a place of dignity through their work."[24] Beyzai's turn to the subject of war allowed him to directly tackle the question of the invisibility of women, mothers, and their work.

In the context of Iranian war cinema, the lack of nuance ascribed to maternal characters has furthered what many scholars describe as a pattern of writing simplistic female characters. The dominant cinema presented as ideal models only mourning mothers who could be ideologically folded into the state's regime of control over representations of the war. When depicted at all, women were often shown as "bound to the cemetery, alone, with very well-scripted and acceptable lines of lament," portrayed as the "spectral, invisible good mother, sister, or wife."[25] Women are largely absent in Iranian war cinema because many scenes take place at the front lines, designating any nondirect experience of war as minor. But these absences pointedly ask us to question the aesthetics and politics of invisibility. Hamid Naficy describes the mid-1980s as a period in which women were represented in Iranian cinema as "ghostly presences in the background or as domestic and domesticated subjects in homes (often as housekeepers, daughters, and mothers)."[26] Putting aside this seeming equation of the domestic and the ghostly, which recuperates for the dominant ideology the notion that the domestic is always already ghostly, we will turn to how *Bashu* confronts this politics of invisibility.

In *Displaced Allegories: Post-revolutionary Iranian Cinema*, Negar Mottahedeh also conjures the "ghostly" by way of her analysis of the destruction of veiled female bodies (including Bashu's biological mother) in *Bashu*'s opening scenes of missile attacks on southern Iran. Mottahedeh argues the film "draws on both the shocks of warfare and the presence, movement, and ultimately annihilation of veiled female bodies to produce its own narrative building block."[27] The argument is deployed here in support of Mottahedeh's broader claims about the ways in which film technology produces a "woman's cinema" in the Islamic context. Annihilation is an extreme form of rendering invisible that mobilizes the logic of Mottahedeh's argument in support of our investigation of the maternal. In other words, Mottahedeh says the destruction of the veiled female bodies annihilates them, but the key is that it does so *visibly*. The very annihilation draws our attention to those bodies. In the same way, showing this violence against women's bodies in the context of war cinema intervenes by making women visible. Although they appear and are killed within the same shot, the act of showing the effects of war on women, *and especially* a mother, is singular in the Iranian cinematic context.

Two Mothers

By showing us the scene at the home front, *Bashu* invites us not only to think about women's experiences of war but also, quite simply, to look at women. The film's visual politics augment the singularity of N'ai's character. As Mottahedeh has discussed, our first illicit view of N'ai subverts the codes of modesty enacted by the newly established Islamic Republic of Iran.[28] In the film's infamous opening, N'ai looks directly at the camera, thereby breaking the fourth wall and challenging the Islamic visual grammar by appearing in medium close-up. She appears to be caught in the action of folding her *hejab* around her face, and the film teases the limits of censorship by positioning her *hejab* as a frame. In other words, the film conforms to the censorship guidelines while also suggesting to us that it is pushing against them by letting us know she isn't fully covered.

The film thus begins by showing us the death of Bashu's biological mother and the (literal) emergence of N'ai, a figure who challenges the norms of looking. The film's politics of visuality vis-à-vis the maternal are highlighted through this contrast between N'ai and Bashu's biological mother, for even as it celebrates one and annihilates another, the film forces us to associate war with these mothers' experiences. In the first half of the film, Bashu continually sees his biological mother, but it is unclear whether she is a ghost or he is hallucinating. Her body remains present in the text through his visions of her. Clad in her black chador, the traditional Islamic dress for women in Iran, Bashu's biological mother haunts the frame, passing behind and through scenes where he attempts to connect with N'ai. The dead mother's chador has a striking visual presence while also eliciting a pious look-that-does-not-look. Its appearance in the background of key scenes set in Gilan is paradoxical: she is absent from Bashu's life but present in his memory. N'ai's immense formal presence in every scene in which she appears (afforded by mise-en-scène, especially acting) is augmented by the persistent presence of this "other" mother who skirts the periphery of the frame. The biological mother appears in the frame when Bashu is resisting N'ai's motherly advances. Her appearance reminds Bashu of what he has lost, serving as a foil for establishing N'ai's eventual warm and enthusiastic embrace of Bashu. Through her inclusion in the composition of the image, Bashu's biological mother continues her work of mothering by relaying it to N'ai. The two mothers' appearance in the same frame allows Bashu the continuity of being with his biological mother even as he is held by N'ai, a new mother.

Represented visually alongside N'ai, the insertion of the dead mother in the frame thus forms a collective of mothers who are positioned outside the state's discourses. Though visually distinct, they are depicted together, pointing to their collaborative work. The film challenges what Joan Raphael-Leff describes as the "dread of the archaic mother on the one hand, and of

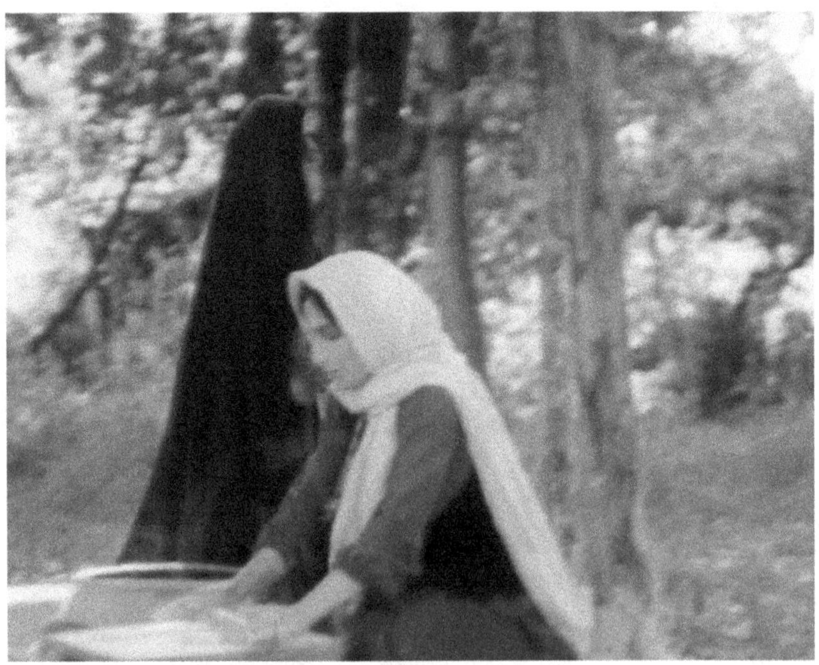

N'ai and Bashu's mother in *Bashu Gharibe Kuchak / Bashu, the Little Stranger* (Bahram Beyzai, 1986).

the dependent baby on the other, are fueled both by Western valorisation of autonomy, and by the intensely dyadic relationship generated within nuclear families."[29]

If, as Mottahedeh suggests, the annihilation of Bashu's biological mother is a narrative building block, then this analysis makes it possible to consider the mother as mourned object. As I've elaborated above, women, and especially mothers, were often absent from Iranian war films because these films largely took place on the front lines of war. *Bashu* is thus singular in bringing together the signs of mother, woman, and war removed from the discourse of mourning. Not only does the stereotype of the mourning mother who celebrates an absent son's martyrdom disappear, but the mother herself is the object of the son's mourning. It is precisely because we have been able to witness her death and remember her through Bashu's hallucinations that we can see an *other* space for mothers in the visual regime of the Iran-Iraq War. Departing from dominant Iranian war cinema, *Bashu* imagines an experience of war that complicates existing narratives of suffering, mourning, and responsibility. The influence of *Bashu*'s maternal war narrative is evident in recent Iran-Iraq War films such as *Under the Shadow*, in which the absence of the protagonist's mother, signified through numerous visual objects, looms over her own actions as a mother and weighs heavily on the horrific events that take place in her apartment.

N'ai and Bashu

In *Bashu*, N'ai's subjectivity is presented as singular and peculiar. She is unique, different from the other mothers in the village: autonomous, independent, and rather weird. She communicates with animals. Part of this autonomy is structural, due to the absence of her husband. With her husband away at war, N'ai manages life on her farm in isolation, doing domestic work and work outside the home, selling her garlic, eggs, and rice at market. N'ai's situation signals the ways in which women in Gilan have historically been indispensable to the region's agriculture. Shahla Lahiji describes the rice paddies of northern Iran as "the undisputed domain of female power" and "the place where in the absence of women, there is no agriculture, no food, no home and no happiness."[30] The absence of the husband, in other words, is only partly responsible for N'ai's autonomy, which also stems from her important societal role.

N'ai's unique qualities are joined by her troubling acquiescence to the village's xenophobia. She participates in the racist worldview of her fellow villagers. When N'ai first sees Bashu, she throws rocks at him. Her fear of this outsider is affirmed by the way she can't stop turning back to look at him as she walks away. We are horrified to hear her ask him, "What did you do to become so black and so dirty?" Yet these unfortunate interactions and her seeming distrust of Bashu are from the beginning countered by her acts of motherly care. Shortly after this first confrontation, N'ai leaves him bread from her family dinner. Continuing in this vein, over the next days she leaves him a bowl of rice, water, and clean clothes.

The sequence "crow, child, stranger" invokes the shift and expansion of N'ai's mothering. The range of her maternal devotion is dramatized by a scene that features N'ai speaking to the crows. She is by the riverside with the children when her words are interrupted by the cawing of a crow. Stopping what she is doing, her thought and speech are displaced as she caws back, head lifted to the sky. The call of the crow is clear enough to her that she must respond. The film gestures here to N'ai's ability to shift from the unknown (Bashu) to the familiar (the crow), suggesting that the unknown is not as threatening to her as it is to her fellow villagers. To someone else, the crow would be another unknown, but N'ai's ability to hear and understand the crow foreshadows her willingness to understand Bashu. In the next sequence of the film, Bashu attempts to explain to N'ai what happened to his parents. She doesn't understand his dialect, but through attentive listening to Bashu's emotional testimony, N'ai recognizes the depth of what he is trying to communicate. She is framed in medium close-up, staring intensely at Bashu while she listens, as the camera zooms in to give us a better sense of her affective experience. It is after Bashu narrates his story that N'ai begins to defend him to the village shopkeeper, calling him her guest. Her ability to communicate in modes that exceed her linguistic ability (with both the crows and Bashu) suggests she is finely attuned to life around her and mutable in accordance with the situation at hand. The dyad of her relation to her biological children is exceeded by the crows and other animal life, which is subsequently exceeded by her relation to Bashu.

Cawing to the crows reflects the importance of play to N'ai's worldview. Playfulness emerges in her domestic work, her relation to animals, and her particular form of mothering. Her willingness and desire to play are what help her overcome the Gilaki-Khuzestani language barrier she experiences with Bashu. In an early scene in the film, N'ai sets out to understand who Bashu is by creating a simple game involving everyday household objects. She holds the item up, names it in Gilaki, and asks Bashu what he calls it in his language. Each time Bashu responds, N'ai attempts to repeat the unfamiliar word. She mimics his words as though sounding them out with her own voice will help her to understand him. But in fact, this game does not do much to bring the two closer to understanding each other. It allows them to be themselves in proximity to each other, but because they cannot understand each other's language, their speaking is a form of parallel play. The game brings into the aural track of the film a welcome laughter from both N'ai and Bashu as they hear the other call familiar objects by names they do not recognize or understand. Simply put, they are so strange to one another at this point that even to know that the other has a name for this thing is to inch closer to some form of recognition; the other's possession of language makes them recognizable, if not understood. In the Winnicottian view of things, play is how we access our creative, "authentic" selves—that is, our less defended selves. This dynamic is clearly at work insofar as neither subject is defensive of their name for the object, nor of their inability to understand the other's language. Both actors employ a relaxed body language, which is mirrored by the film's more conventional use of shot-reverse-shot framing to include both characters in each shot. Contrasted with the techniques of distanciation used in much of the rest of the film's framing (for example, the constant presence of a direct gaze at the camera), the strategy used in this scene formally supports the idea that it is in the presence of the other that each (and most importantly Bashu) is able to feel supported and relaxed enough to laugh and play. Correspondingly, the inability to understand the other's language becomes less alienating, even something to delight in.

The film positions racial difference as the means by which N'ai sees the community around her differently. Playing a game with Bashu, who is trying to resist N'ai's attempts to bathe him, N'ai enacts a hide-and-seek scenario. She pretends she has gone but in reality she has hidden behind a haystack, from which she emerges to drag Bashu to the river. There she aggressively lathers his hair and body with soap, holding him underwater for an unsettling length of time. When he emerges still black, N'ai is shocked, for she has never met a black person. Embodying a trait of maternal care, she catches herself and scales back her emotional reaction. She is aware of Bashu and her biological children watching her. Despite her initial participation in racist behaviors, N'ai's encounter with Bashu transforms her through the process of expanding her circle of maternal care. The trajectory of N'ai's encounter with racial difference reasserts the possibility posed by the maternal relation: that lived experiences of care and living in common together can allow for the emergence of new affiliations. N'ai's process of overcoming her own limitations coincides with her "attempt to break through the limitations the linguistic and social order impose on her subjectivity."[31] N'ai's openness to Bashu is pre-indicated by her relation to the world. While we can't forgive her for her racist behavior toward Bashu, we can consider the transformative potential of maternal care. Through the act of providing maternal care, she is able to see how troubling her limitations were.

In N'ai's case, the encounter with Bashu works to upend her sense of the world around her. She becomes autonomous in a way she was not before, taking her power in the nuclear family and the larger community. She is asked to confront linguistic and racial difference and surprises herself by overcoming her limitations. N'ai rises to the occasion to meet Bashu, setting aside her own reticence so that her "good enough" mothering eventually circles back to allow her to sit with the discomforts of the encounter. Jacqueline Rose writes that motherhood gives one the experience of feeling "turned inside out" and that it is precisely this property of maternal joy "which shatters the carapace of selfhood."[32] If the maternal can splinter notions of the self, the ethics of maternal care are poised to potentially alter the consequences of this dynamic far beyond mother and baby. In a scene where N'ai tries to learn Bashu's name, she describes her children as "this one" and "that one," a gesture that implies a circle of intimacy (only those in proximity to and in relation to her could be called this way) but also implies a capaciousness to her maternal care. At the level of language, the use of "this" one or "that" one suggests her maternal subjectivity extends beyond the dyadic relation she has with each of her children and with the two of them as a unit.

N'ai plods through what Rahimieh calls her trouble "communicating Bashu's humanity to the other villagers."[33] Instead of bending to the will of her neighbors by pushing Bashu out, N'ai rushes the crowd out of her house when she can no longer abide their judgment. Rahimieh argues that together, N'ai and Bashu pose an ethical challenge to a symbolic system intolerant of difference.[34] They eventually arrive at a place of being singular alongside each other. Their resistance, which becomes their insistence to go on being (in the Winnicottian sense), models for the village and (through the spectator-screen relation) the nation a potentially new way of living in common.

Yet the most significant element of N'ai's radical mothering is not *who* falls under the umbrella of her maternal care but how *far* her care resonates and reproduces itself. Although the film establishes N'ai as an eccentric character to whom people are sympathetic but not necessarily loyal, her example coaxes people to emulate her ethics of care. This happens at the first level with Bashu. In his vulnerable, recently orphaned state, Bashu is wary and reticent with N'ai. She speaks a language foreign to him, behaves in unusual ways, and rejects him. He moves cautiously around her, often backing away slowly. His need for a maternal figure does not immediately produce in him a willing acceptance of her. It is through the repeated, everyday acts of care such as providing food and shelter that he begins to trust N'ai. This trust is taken to its pinnacle when he understands how tenderly she has cared for him during his illness. Their lack of a shared language doesn't allow N'ai, or us, the opportunity to hear Bashu express his gratitude. Instead, he shows his gratitude by emulating her ethics of care when N'ai falls ill. Bashu, stricken

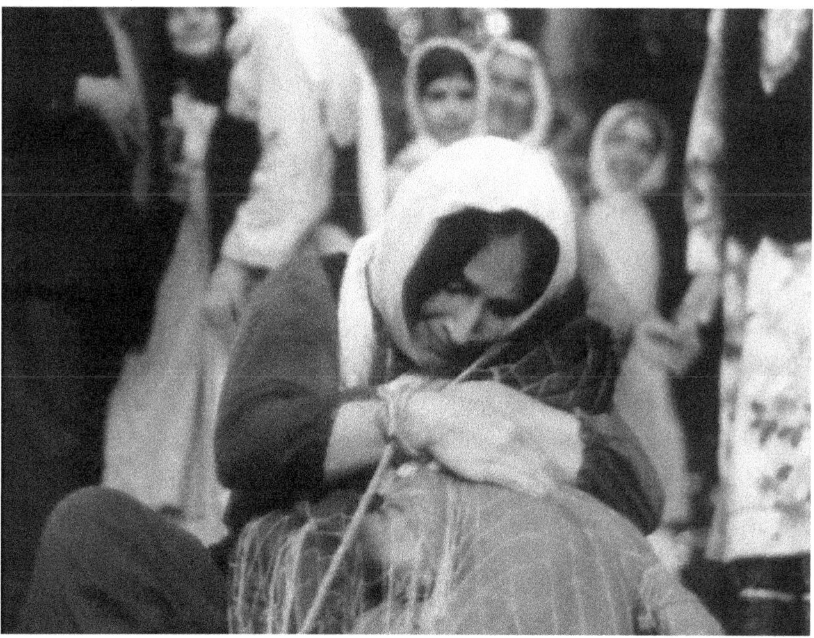

N'ai and Bashu embrace in *Gharibe Kuchak / Bashu, the Little Stranger* (Bahram Beyzai, 1986).

with worry, runs through the village calling for the doctor. No one opens their door to him. In a moving montage, we see Bashu perform the physical rituals and ceremonies of his biological mother and his maternal homeland (region) in order to bring N'ai back to health. We see how the work she has done is reproduced and returned to her.

What N'ai brings forth in the context of her encounter with Bashu initiates a chain of affiliations. As Rahimieh points out, N'ai's subversion is subordinated to questions of survival because she is not free to extend her acts of subversion to all realms of village existence. But she does make the villagers question their xenophobia and ethnocentrism.[35] Notably, it is the village children who reject their parents' xenophobia and befriend Bashu. They provide a counterpoint when their parents try to complain about Bashu: the camera turns and shows us Bashu and the village children playing cooperatively and laughing together. The camera's neutral point of view on the situation counters the parents' insistence that Bashu is a problem. Given the ways in which children typically represent futurity, the village children's acceptance of Bashu indicates how radical care can create collectivities even in the midst of extreme hostility and racism. The children, after all, are not their parents, and in making this distinction, the film points to their potentiality.

Radical Mothering

The work of mothering as presented in *Bashu* is thus a precursor to the possibilities of new collective relations. It suggests that mothers are more than figures of mourning and sacrifice and that they are transformed beyond their relation to their babies. Lisa Baraitser argues that the word *motherhood* "seems to offer a form of living in the elongated suspended time of staying alongside another's erratic, unprincipled and unpredictable growth and change whilst managing one's own experiences of love and hate as they veer in and out of relation to one another."[36] This conception of motherhood pivots it away from uncritical representations of the mother as a uniformly devoted figure, for Baraitser is especially concerned with thinking of "the maternal as a principle or model in social and psychic life that speaks to this impossibility of love without hate, an impossibility that has the potential to mobilise guilt, gratitude, and reparative wishes."[37] Radical mothering, therefore, is not simply about the ability of a mother (or mother figure) to provide care, but also about moving toward a more intersubjective model of relations.

The possibility of maternal subjectivity changing, expanding, and having broader social effects is integral to how the film understands relations between maternal and child figures. N'ai's unsettling behavior is especially difficult because the process of its unfolding and change occurs during her care for Bashu. N'ai's process of maternal becoming entails specific acts of mothering that extend maternal ethics into a recuperative social process beyond the dyadic relation of mother and child.[38] N'ai's mothering work commences a process that deepens their relation through the way care reverberates back to her from Bashu. The recuperative element of this process is part of disentangling the work of care from gendered notions of femininity. Baraitser writes, "Maternal encounters (encounters between those who identify as 'mothers,' and those whom we come to name and claim as our 'children') could hold open the potential for a radical form of ethics running counter to capitalist modes of productivity, temporality, and exchange, without this form of ethics necessarily re-suturing femininity to an ethics of care."[39] In *Bashu*, the context of the maternal encounter is the condition of possibility for this ethics as a recognition of the other. Wendy Hollway reads this possibility as one that is born from the mother's experience. She asks, "In what ways, if at all, does maternal subjectivity permeate a mother's (and other's) subjectivity more generally and extend beyond the relations of mothers and their children?"[40] N'ai's experience as mother is born from the work of mothering, which begins with her biological children and expands to include animals and a stranger. But the consequences of her mothering point to an ethical model of care that is expansive and infectious. The film does not fully realize this possibility, but it points to the potential of its becoming.

In the film's moving final scene, N'ai's husband has returned home from the war and the couple are fighting about Bashu continuing to stay with them. When Bashu joins the scene, he approaches the husband cautiously, brandishing a large stick, and asks, "Who is this man?" When the husband responds, "Father," Bashu asks, "Where have you been?" To everyone's surprise, the father responds, "Looking for you." Bashu sees that the father has lost one of his arms and he weeps while embracing the older man. The formation of the new family is underway. Suddenly, N'ai begins to sniff the air with exaggeration. As she gets up from her seat on the porch, her body stiffens to attention and she begins to bark loudly. She has smelled a wild boar. One by one her family joins her and we see everyone barking, yelling, and waving as they run into the fields to chase the boar away. N'ai leads the way for the collectivity in formation. The final frame of the film contains each family member, making different sounds, gesturing in different directions, performing the work that brings them together.

Notes

1 Hamid Naficy, *A Social History of Iranian Cinema*, vol. 4: *The Globalizing Era, 1984–2010* (Durham, NC: Duke University Press, 2012), 37.

2 Kamran Rastegar, "Treacherous Memory: *Bashu the Little Stranger* and the Sacred Defense," in *Moments of Silence: Authenticity in the Cultural Expressions of the Iran-Iraq War, 1980–1988*, ed. Arta Khakpour, Mohammad Mehdi Khorrami, and Shouleh Vatanabadi (New York: New York University Press, 2016), 61–87.

3 Michelle Langford, "Tending the Wounds of the Nation: Gender in Contemporary Iranian War Cinema," *Screening the Past* 35 (2012), www.screeningthepast.com/2012/12/tending-the-wounds-of-the-nation-gender-in-contemporary-iranian-war-cinema/.

4 Kamran Rastegar, *Surviving Images: Cinema, War, and Cultural Memory in the Middle East* (New York: Oxford University Press, 2015), 144. Elsewhere Rastegar notes it is important to distinguish the ideological differences between "war cinema" and "Sacred Defense cinema." See "Treacherous Memory," 63–65.

5 Roxanne Varzi, "Iran's Pieta: Motherhood, Sacrifice and Film in the Aftermath of the Iran-Iraq War," *Feminist Review* 88 (2008): 89.

6 Rastegar, *Surviving Images*, 137.

7 Varzi, "Iran's Pieta," 96.

8 Nasrin Rahimieh, "Marking Gender and Difference in the Myth of the Nation: *Bashu*, a Post-revolutionary Iranian Film," *Thamyris: Mythmaking from Past to Present* 3, no. 2 (1996): 264.

9 In her reading of the linguistic politics of the film, Rahimieh discusses how the establishment of Persian as the official national language correlated with a rise in nationalism. "Marking Gender and Difference," 262.

10 *The Ballad of Tara* also stars Susan Taslimi, who plays N'ai in *Bashu*.

11 *Under the Shadow* repeats the trope of escaping to the Caspian region, away from the attacks on Tehran.
12 Varzi, "Iran's Pieta," 91.
13 Hamid Reza Sadr, "Children in Contemporary Iranian Cinema: When We Were Children," in *The New Iranian Cinema: Politics, Representation and Identity*, ed. Richard Tapper (London: I. B. Tauris, 2002), 227–37.
14 Philippa Lovatt, "Breathing Bodies: Sounding Subjectivities in the War Film," *Music, Sound and the Moving Image* 10, no. 2 (2016): 173; Rastegar, *Surviving Images*, 146.
15 Mohammad Tavakoli-Targhi, *Refashioning Iran: Orientalism, Occidentalism, and Historiography* (London: Palgrave Macmillan, 2001); Firoozeh Kashani-Sabet, *Conceiving Citizens: Women and the Politics of Motherhood in Iran* (Oxford: Oxford University Press, 2011).
16 See Afsaneh Najmabadi, "The Erotic *Vatan* [Homeland] as Beloved and Mother: To Love, to Possess, and to Protect," *Comparative Studies in Society and History* 39, no. 3 (1997): 442–67; Eldad J. Pardo, "Iranian Cinema, 1968–1978: Female Characters and Social Dilemmas on the Eve of the Revolution," *Middle Eastern Studies* 40, no. 3 (2004): 29–54; Tavakoli-Targhi, *Refashioning Iran.*
17 Hamid Reza Sadr, *Against the Wind: Politics of Iranian Cinema* (Tehran: Zarrin, 2002).
18 Minoo Derayeh, "Depiction of Women in Iranian Cinema, 1970s to Present," *Women's Studies International Forum* 33, no. 3 (2010): 152.
19 Khatereh Sheibani, "The Aesthetics of (Dis)Empowered Motherhood in Iranian Cinema (1965–1978)," in *Screening Motherhood in Contemporary World Cinema*, ed. Asma Sayed (Bradford, ON: Demeter, 2016), 391.
20 Sheibani, "The Aesthetics of (Dis)Empowered Motherhood," 391.
21 Sheibani, "The Aesthetics of (Dis)Empowered Motherhood," 378.
22 Sheibani, "The Aesthetics of (Dis)Empowered Motherhood," 412.
23 Pardo, "Iranian Cinema, 1968–1978," 42.
24 Hamid Dabashi, *Close-up, Iranian Cinema: Past, Present and Future* (New York: Verso, 2001), 96.
25 Varzi, "Iran's Pieta," 94; Homa Tavassuli, quoted in Derayeh, "Depiction of Women in Iranian Cinema," 155.
26 Naficy, *A Social History*, 114–15.
27 Negar Mottahedeh, *Displaced Allegories: Post-revolutionary Iranian Cinema* (Durham, NC: Duke University Press, 2008), 23.

28 Mottahedeh, *Displaced Allegories*, 21–22.

29 Joan Raphael-Leff, "Maternal Subjectivity," *Studies in the Maternal* 1, no. 1 (2009): 3.

30 Shahla Lahiji, quoted in Sheibani, "The Aesthetics of (Dis)Empowered Motherhood," 410.

31 Rahimieh, "Marking Gender and Difference," 268.

32 Jacqueline Rose, *Mothers: An Essay on Love and Cruelty* (New York: Farrar, Straus & Giroux, 2018), 200.

33 Rahimieh, "Marking Gender and Difference," 264.

34 Rahimieh, "Marking Gender and Difference," 264.

35 Rahimieh, "Marking Gender and Difference," 275.

36 Lisa Baraitser, "Postmaternal, Postwork, and the Maternal Death Drive," *Australian Feminist Studies* 31, no. 90 (2016): 398.

37 Baraitser, "Postmaternal," 395.

38 My reference to "maternal becoming" is inspired by Margrit Schildrick's notion of becoming-maternal. In "Becoming-Maternal: Things to Do with Deleuze," *Studies in the Maternal* 2, no. 1 (2010), Schildrick asks, "If we accept the inter- and indeed intra-dependency of the maternal dyad, then can we not extend that further to take on the model of connectivity that intrigues Deleuze when he writes of desiring machines and assemblages?" (3).

39 Baraitser, "Postmaternal," 394.

40 Wendy Hollway, "From Motherhood to Maternal Subjectivity," *International Journal of Critical Psychology* 2 (2001): 9 (in PDF).

10

Confessions of an Aca-Fan-Mom

Jane the Virgin, Motherhood, and Community

Corinn Columpar

Writing about motherhood and media as both a mom and a film and media scholar is challenging. Much like an ardent devotee trying to engage critically with a favorite text, a fraught balancing act both evoked and elided by the identity of "aca-fan," used to denote a hybrid of academic and fan, I find myself unable to negotiate a proper distance from my object of study. No experience in my life has been as consuming and disorienting—emotionally, physically, and intellectually—as motherhood, and writing about its mediation only redoubles that effect. Indeed, I sometimes feel like my students when first confronted with Vivian Sobchack's "What My Fingers Knew: The Cinesthetic Subject, or Vision in the Flesh."[1] In that situation, they ask how something as specific and potentially idiosyncratic as their affective engagement with a film can serve as grounds for a broader claim. In this context, I ask something similar: if my experience of conception, pregnancy, birth, and parenting has been so particular (and it has), and that experience conditions the way that I engage with media (and it does), how can I help but be trapped in a hall of mirrors as I tackle the topic of motherhood and media?

Yet rather than attempt, in vain, to overcome my admittedly particular vantage, I am doubling down on it, writing from a position that is not just *like* that of a fan, but *is* that of a fan—as well as a mom. Specifically, I am writing about a media text that has given me hours of desperately needed pleasure, clarity, comfort, insight and, most crucially of all, community ever since having a child: the (melo)dramedy *Jane the Virgin*, which premiered in 2014 on the CW network and ended in 2019 at the conclusion of its fifth season. As a media text that is structured by the logic of motherhood and that enfolds it characters and viewers alike in a group hug, all to feminist ends, *Jane the Virgin* provides ample opportunity not only to have a resonant viewing experience, but also to assume the doubly hybridized identity of "aca-fan-mom." In the essay that follows I reflect on this identity as well as certain terms of critical analysis that it, like *Jane the Virgin* itself, raises. Indeed, if aca-fan already "acknowledges and interweaves both intellectual and emotional cultural engagements," adding mom to the mix acknowledges and interweaves other terms as well, including distance and absorption, particularity and universality, individuality and collectivity.[2]

Telenovelas and the Politics of Taste

In 2011 Henry Jenkins, the scholar most readily associated with aca-fandom, posted to his blog, *Confessions of an Aca-Fan*, multiple installments of a roundtable discussion wherein invited scholars weigh in on the topic of "Aca-fandom and Beyond." While multiple contributors express a degree of discomfort with aca-fandom for various reasons, Alisa Perren voices concern instead over that which it includes and excludes: "To what extent has aca-fandom legitimated the study of certain tastes over others?" Noting that select texts, such as the television shows *Buffy the Vampire Slayer* (1997–2003), *Battlestar Galactica* (2004–9), and *Lost* (2004–10), are privileged points of reference, she continues her line of questioning by asking pointedly, "What does it mean that these particular media products are the objects of so much discussion, while shows like *Law & Order* [1990–2010] and *The Good Wife* [2009–16] (two personal favorites of mine) are far less likely to be examined at panels devoted to aca-fandom? Does 'aca-fandom' have a responsibility to expand its scope beyond the genre or 'quality' texts that it has tended to radiate toward?"[3] These queries have particular salience in a discussion of *Jane the Virgin*, which journalist Kathryn VanArendonk calls "anti-prestige in every way." Between its candy-colored production design, unique combination of silliness and sincerity, virtuous titular protagonist and, in the words of VanArendonk, "radical premise that good people can also be interesting," *Jane the Virgin* is out of step with a contemporary mediascape wherein "quality" television is dominated by anti-heroes navigating a neo-noir world.[4] Further adding to its anti-prestige status is its source material: *Jane the Virgin* is an adaptation of the Venezuelan telenovela *Juana la virgen* (2002) and, as such, shares the relatively low cultural status of other media forms associated with women, including chick flicks and romance novels. As much as these forms constitute genre fare, they have not typically elicited the aca-fan treatment, which tends to be reserved for less feminized genres.

In light of this tendency, it is noteworthy that one person Jenkins distinguishes himself from when articulating the scholarly project of the aca-fan is Janice Radway. In his groundbreaking book *Textual Poachers: Television Fans and Participatory Culture*, he acknowledges Radway's *Reading the Romance: Women, Patriarchy, and Popular Literature* as a foundational influence on his own work and "otherwise exemplary," but takes issue with the "academic distance" she maintains from the fan community she studies, arguing that it enables her "either to judge or to instruct but not to converse with" that community.[5] In contradistinction, Jenkins employs an approach that "requires greater proximity and the surrender of certain intellectual pretensions and institutional privileges."[6] Yet it is not just his approach that differs throughout *Textual Poachers*; it is also his object of study. Rather than revisit Radway's readers of romance, he tends to foreground texts and consumers associated with science fiction and fantasy when modeling his position of greater proximity. While this shift can be chalked up to Jenkins's individual taste, which dictates the objects of his fandom, the fact that so many scholars have followed in his footsteps, thereby creating and entrenching the canon Perren references, suggests that the issue at hand has a systemic dimension as well. Indeed, it suggests that there may be significantly more risk, both intellectually and interpersonally, in declaring one's fan relationship to certain genres and texts than to others, especially in academic discourse.

Scholars of media associated with women, including melodramatic serials, are well aware of those risks, just as they are aware of the exceptionally low regard in which their objects of study are often held. Diana I. Rios and Mari Castañeda, for example, begin their edited collection *Soap Operas and Telenovelas in the Digital Age: Global Industries and New Audiences* by noting the reaction with which their work is regularly met:

wonderment and even laughter. In response, they ask, "Why does the study of this televisual genre incite such reactions that other media topics would not?"[7] If simply assuming soap operas and telenovelas worthy of study is widely considered to be bewildering, even in 2011, when Rios and Castañeda's volume was published, it is not difficult to imagine the line of questioning that an aca-fan framing of that study might elicit: what self-respecting scholar, particularly feminist scholar, could ever find sincere pleasure in such texts?! Yet, unlike Radway, multiple scholars of soap operas and telenovelas do, in fact, use a personal connection to their object of study as a jumping-off point for their work, and interestingly, that personal connection is predicated not only on an appreciation of the texts at hand but also on the feminine, familial, and intergenerational bonds they foster. To wit, when justifying their field of inquiry in the face of the wonderment mentioned above, Rios and Castañeda identify soap operas and telenovelas as the "television programs that we, the editors, have utilized as ways for spending time with our *abuelitas* (grandmothers)."[8] Likewise, in the very first line of *Women and Soap Opera: A Cultural Feminist Perspective*, Dannielle Blumenthal uses the first person to invoke a tight-knit group of viewers of which she is an integral part: "Soap operas . . . a connection with other women, beloved to me: my mother, grandmother, aunt, sister . . . a steady stream of modern folktales that symbolically link us together."[9] Later in her study, after providing ethnographic evidence that her experience of soap operas is not unique, she extrapolates, "Watching the soaps with one's mother sets the stage for thinking of soap operas as having an innately social quality," and then identifies that social quality as part of the form's empowering effect.[10]

Working in the same spirit as these scholars, *Jane the Virgin* performs its investment in telenovelas while also commenting on them; for this reason critic Emily Nussbaum identifies it as "the latest in a tradition of ambitious shows that both emulate and deconstruct established TV genres."[11] Yet while an aca-fan's ability to engage simultaneously in both of these operations—investment and commentary—stems from the dual position they occupy, the series' ability to do so is largely due to its status as, in the words of Courtney Brannon Donoghue, a "multi-layered transnational media product."[12] Donoghue uses this description in reference to *Ugly Betty*, which aired on ABC from 2006 through 2010, but it applies equally to *Jane the Virgin*, which is strikingly similar to its predecessor as both an industrial product and a textual object. First, both are based on

Latin American telenovelas that have been adapted in several countries and thus are part of global franchises that serve as significant counterexamples in narratives of U.S. media imperialism.[13] Second, rather than being "literal telenovela translation[s]," both are "hybrid" texts that strategically retain certain aspects of the telenovela—its dramatic tropes and modes of address, for example—while changing others to suit the cultural context and media traditions of the United States.[14] In particular, they not only displace their action from Latin America to the United States, they also supplant certain defining attributes of the telenovela structure, such as daily installments and delimited stories, with conventions derived from U.S. prime-time television: the use of weekly episodes and multiple seasons to narrate relatively open-ended narratives. Fittingly, in the case of *Ugly Betty* this process of hybridization was the result of a cross-cultural collaboration: the series had two showrunners, one Cuban American (Silvio Horta) and one Anglo American (Marco Pennette). In comparison, *Jane the Virgin* has a single Anglo showrunner, Jennie Snyder Urman, but she has consistently ensured that a significant portion of her writing staff—four out of thirteen in 2019—are Latinx; of that group, one (Carolina Rivera) has significant experience working on Spanish-language telenovelas.[15]

Rooted in a particular cultural tradition while also moving beyond that tradition demographically and formally, *Jane the Virgin* addresses a wide and varied audience. As a result, the series, especially through its most metatextual moments, serves as both a self-conscious celebration of the telenovela for the genre's knowing fans and a tutor text for those who are new to it. For example, at least once per episode, the narrator (Anthony Mendez) draws the viewer's attention to genre conventions by asking some variation of "Straight out of a telenovela, right?" Sometimes the event prompting this question is related to Jane's father, Rogelio (Jaime Camil), a telenovela star whose story lines often revolve around his career and who brings a melodramatic flair to every action he performs. Most of the time, however, it is an occurrence involving other characters. The most outlandish and prominent is the mix-up that sets the series in motion, an accidental artificial insemination that results in Jane (Gina Rodriguez) becoming a pregnant virgin, but there are numerous other plot twists befitting a telenovela as well, including a love triangle whose resolution is always only provisional, identical twins scheming to displace each other, and a crime lord who masquerades as other people in order to evade capture. In addition to acknowledging the process of producing telenovelas and featuring tropes typical of the genre, *Jane the Virgin* also contains self-reflexive moments that foreground telenovela spectatorship, especially its communal nature. For example, in a resonant echo of the scholarship cited above, the series presents a tableau within the first ten minutes of the pilot ("Chapter One") that recurs with regularity throughout its five seasons: a shot of Jane, her mother, Xiomara (Andrea Navedo), and her grandmother, Alba (Ivonne Coll), seated on a couch in the home they share watching a telenovela love scene with rapt attention. While this scene captures the experience of more seasoned fans of *Jane the Virgin*, a second scene involving iconic actress River Fields (Brooke Shields) is offered up as a potential mirror image for the uninitiated: originally disdainful of telenovelas, even after being cast in an American adaptation of one, River watches them in Xiomara's company for one day and then declares, "I love telenovelas so much. . . . They're everything. They surprise you and move you and make you feel alive" ("Chapter Eighty").

With this scene *Jane the Virgin* lays bare the proposition that it consistently advances: that telenovelas deserve respect, not only because they are popular and profitable the world over, but also because they have a unique ability to affect viewers profoundly. For Nussbaum, the implications of this proposition are far-reaching, involving the redemption of women's media. In making her case, she places *Jane the Virgin* at the center of a network

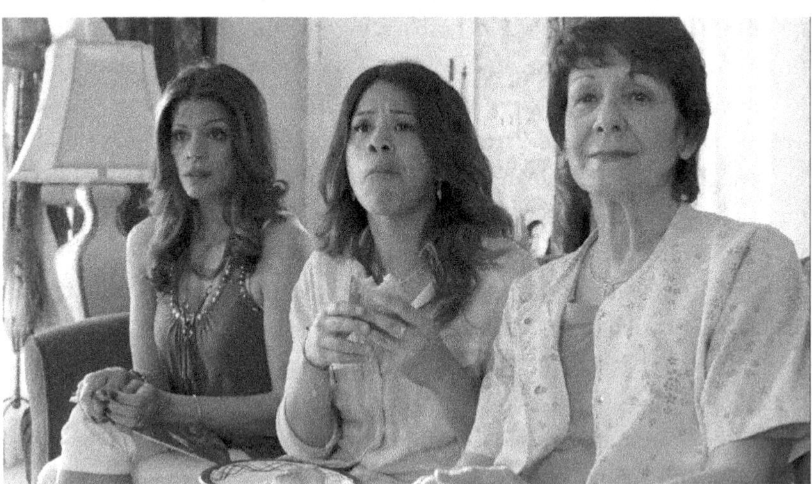

Xiomara, Jane, and Alba watching a telenovela together in "Chapter One," the first episode of *Jane the Virgin* (created by Jennie Snyder Urman, 2014–19).

of genres, including not only telenovelas but also "the soap, the rom-com, the romance novel, and, more recently, reality television," all of which "get dismissed as fluff, which is how our culture regards art that makes women's lives look like fun." In response to charges that such genres qualify as "guilty pleasures," Nussbaum identifies *Jane the Virgin* "as a joyful manifesto against that very putdown, a bright-pink filibuster exposing the layers in what the world regards as shallow."[16] To be sure, many of the layers exposed by *Jane the Virgin* relate to romance, which figures centrally in the worldview, if not the very name, of the genres Nussbaum identifies. Accordingly, when Jane first meets Michael (Brett Dier), her fiancé at the series' start, she explains her love of telenovelas in terms of their ability to create scenarios that are the "epitome of romance" ("Chapter Six"). Yet one of the most interesting ways that *Jane the Virgin*, in its hybridity, transforms the telenovela is by making motherhood, even more than romance, its single most important structural element. As a result, in the recurring tableau mentioned above, it is the three generations of women on the couch rather than the love story they are watching that take center stage.

The Logic of Motherhood in *Jane the Virgin*

In an episode from the fourth season ("Chapter Seventy-Seven"), *Jane the Virgin* makes explicit the logic that has been animating it all along. At the start of the series Jane is an aspiring author; by the fourth season she has published a romance novel based on her relationship with Michael, who has since died (or so she thinks), and is facing writer's block as she contemplates her next project. In response to this situation she joins a writers' group and throws herself into its first exercise: to tell a story from her life from the perspective of a side character. Jane decides to narrate the originating event of the series, her accidental artificial insemination, from the vantage of Luisa (Yara Martinez), the doctor who was responsible for the mix-up and who also happens to be the sister of Rafael (Justin Baldoni), the resulting baby's father and Jane's current boyfriend. As she does so, the episode itself follows suit, using Jane's discovery of a deposition Luisa gave in the immediate aftermath of her malpractice as a way of reviewing the events originally presented in the pilot through a different lens. At the conclusion of the episode, which serves as a savvy and self-reflexive primer on narratology, Jane has a breakthrough: she explains to her writing group, "I want to write about my mom, our relationship." When a fellow writer responds with surprise, "So no more romance?" Jane identifies that relationship as "a romance *of sorts*." While Jane's progress on this project is piecemeal throughout the rest of the series, the fragments of it that are presented are reenactments of events seen in earlier seasons, suggesting that the work Jane is creating is a narrative strand of the very series the audience has been watching. Yet while Jane's work may be, as she says, "about my mom, our relationship," the story of Xiomara and Jane is just one particular variation on a resonant theme when it is embedded in the sprawling and multifaceted world of *Jane the Virgin*.

In understanding the role that motherhood plays in *Jane the Virgin*, the language Teresa de Lauretis employs when describing Chantal Akerman's *Jeanne Dielman, 23, quai du Commerce, 1080 Bruxelles* (1975) in her canonical essay "Rethinking Women's Cinema: Aesthetics and Feminist Theory" seems uniquely apt: this film, she argues, "defines all points of identification (character, image, camera) as female, feminine, or feminist."[17] Similarly, *Jane the Virgin* defines all its points of identification as maternal, matriarchal, or motherly. First, the series presents myriad maternal figures with its wide array of biological, adoptive, and stepmothers, all of whom have highly cathected relationships with their children and exercise considerable influence over them, even in absentia. Of those figures, four—Jane, Xiomara, Petra (Yael Grobglas), and Darci (Justine Machada)—have pregnancies, one of which is terminated and three of which are carried to term, and the series details those pregnancies across several episodes. In addition to foregrounding so many maternal figures, the series also represents the texture of their experience, especially during pregnancy and a child's early years, with a candor and consistency that is unprecedented on television. For example, along with certain incredible events that suit a telenovela, such as an accidental insemination or the kidnapping of a newborn, the pregnant women and mothers on the series deal with a whole host of mundane issues related to maternity as well, including amniocentesis, stalled labor, postpartum depression, a plugged milk duct and mastitis, cluster feeding, nipple confusion, plagiocephaly, and an ADHD diagnosis. Therefore it is fitting that when Jane finally goes into labor in the finale of season 1, the series refuses the cliché of having her water break, opting for a less dramatic, but more commonplace and thus relatable, series of contractions.

Second, as already suggested by the tableau discussed above, at the center of *Jane the Virgin* is a matriarchy comprised of Alba, Xiomara, and Jane, all of whom start the series as unmarried women living together on terms that they establish collectively, without the input of any male figures. Crystallizing this is a scene in "Chapter Two" wherein Jane welcomes Michael to his first family meeting. When Michael ceremoniously notes that he is "proud to be representing the male point of view," Jane replies, "Oh, see, I wouldn't lead with that because that's not going to do well in our meetings." In response, Michael resigns himself to "mostly" observing. Over time his role in the family, and his say in family matters, grows considerably, as is the case for Rafael, Rogelio, and Jorge (Alfonso DiLuca) too, but it never eclipses that of the women, around whom the family (and the series) is organized. Moreover, as significant as the Villanueva family is, it is not the only matriarchy that *Jane the Virgin* features. Even the crime network that provides the series with its more action-oriented elements is conceived of as such: at its head is a woman known as Mutter (German for "mother") and among its many members is Rose (Bridget Regan), also known as Sin Rostro, who is Mutter's stepdaughter and the series' recurring villain.

Third, turning patriarchal values on their head, the series normalizes those attributes associated with motherliness, even in the case of characters who might seem far removed from this quality. One example is Rose. In addition to being a sociopathic criminal, she is also embroiled in a complicated personal relationship with Luisa: she is both Luisa's stepmother and her lover, and in this dual capacity she takes care of Luisa, albeit in ways that are also, at times, self-interested. While the series lays much greater emphasis on the sexual side of Rose's devotion, the motherly side is significant as well, as is made clear when Luisa is at her most vulnerable. In "Chapter Seventy-Seven," the episode mentioned above wherein Luisa's deposition helps lay bare the series' maternal logic, Luisa explains how a perfectly timed phone call from Rose once prevented her from committing suicide; as she narrates it, "I realized I still had someone who cared about me. Not my mom, my stepmom." Even more significant than Rose, however, are the various male characters in *Jane the Virgin*, who are also largely defined in terms of their motherly qualities. Indeed, it is their capacity as caregivers more than anything else that determines their romantic appeal and, by extension, their narrative value; this goes for the male characters with a leading role—Rafael, Michael, and Rogelio—as well as those who are less prominent, from Esteban (Keller Wortham), Rogelio's acting rival cum doting co-parent, to Adam (Tyler Posey), Jane's boyfriend until he expresses ambivalence about children. On this count, the endpoints of Rogelio's and Rafael's developmental arcs are telling: each concludes the series with a declaration regarding a change in priorities. After realizing that parenting is more satisfying than fame, Rogelio announces his contentment with being "the spice, not the dish"—that is, a supporting character in his new television series, not its star—"so I can enjoy other parts of my life" ("Chapter Ninety Six"), while Rafael, two episodes later, explains his decision to pass on a demanding and high-status job by noting, "My dream has changed. I want time with my family" ("Chapter Ninety Eight").

When de Lauretis describes *Jeanne Dielman* in "Rethinking Women's Cinema," she does so in order to illustrate "an aesthetic of reception" and to propose an understanding of women's cinema as "a cinema for, not only by, women."[18] In other words, she is interested in certain textual qualities related to both the profilmic drama and its cinematic rendering, but only to the extent that they add up to a film that assumes and constructs a particular spectator—more specifically, to a film that "addresses its spectator as a woman."[19] In order to expand on the nature of that spectator, she appeals to another feminist film, Lizzie Borden's *Born in Flames* (1983), "whose images and discourses project back to the viewer a space of heterogeneity, differences and fragmented coherences that just do not add up to one individual viewer or one spectator subject, bourgeois or otherwise."[20] Just as de Lauretis's language when describing *Jeanne Dielman*—"points of identification"—is uniquely suited to capturing a defining attribute of *Jane the Virgin*, her larger argument is resonant as well. By defining all points of identification as maternal, matriarchal, or motherly, *Jane the Virgin* addresses its spectator as a mother; when doing so, however, its conception of that identity is capacious, encompassing a diverse array of parenting possibilities. In sharp contradistinction to the mother that ironically haunts the series, the Virgin Mary, the mothers who figure explicitly in *Jane the Virgin* do not conform to any ideal; rather, they are individuated, complex, and widely varying in their identities, experiences, behavior, values, and life choices. As a result, the series, much like *Born in Flames*, allows for a broad range of spectating mothers to be "addressed intermittently," all of whom become part of an audience defined by its points of both difference and commonality.[21]

Creating Community, Socializing Happiness

In recent years there has been a rash of media texts that, like *Jane the Virgin*, feature the experience of motherhood in a manner that is both comedic and dramatic and that foreground its embodied and social dimensions. Moreover, many of these texts are also concerned with community, both its representation and, by extension, its creation in the form of a mass audience that can relate to the parents on-screen. While the most prominent of such texts may be American films like *Bad Moms* (Jon Lucas and Scott Moore, 2016), *A Bad Moms Christmas* (Lucas and Moore, 2017), and *Fun Mom Dinner* (Alethea Jones, 2017), the most interesting, I would argue, are two television series that have been airing since 2017: the Canadian production *Workin' Moms*, which Catherine Reitman produces, writes, and stars in, and the Australian production *The Letdown*, which Alison Bell and Sarah Scheller created and write together and which features Bell as its lead. At the center of both series is a protagonist, Kate (Reitman) in *Workin' Moms* and Audrey (Bell) in *The Letdown*, who starts attending a moms' group while adjusting to life with their first child. Not only does that moms' group provide her with a number of things she desperately needs, including advice, friendship, empathy, and adult conversation, it also becomes the cornerstone of her social life. As a result, it figures prominently in each series, serving as a recurring structural element: it is introduced within the first five minutes of the pilot; subsequent narrative action is organized around its regular meetings; and the supporting characters are drawn from its membership.

These two series are engaged in significant ideological work insofar as they frankly represent the challenges, compromises, and vulnerabilities associated with motherhood from a female perspective. Yet the limits of that work are thrown into fresh relief when *Workin' Moms* and *The Letdown* are read against *Jane the Virgin*; of particular note are the communities each series represents and, in turn, addresses, which differ dramatically on multiple counts. One difference relates to the range of subject positions and experiences those communities accommodate. In contrast to the highly unusual Jane, who, throughout season 2, for example, is a single Latina mother who has never had sex and works multiple jobs to make ends meet, Kate and Audrey are white, economically secure, professionally established, and part of a nuclear family wherein parenting responsibilities are shared with their child's father. Moreover, the diversity of the communities surrounding these relatively conventional protagonists pales in comparison to that created by *Jane the Virgin*, with its sprawling network of maternal, matriarchal, and motherly figures: in each moms' group featured at least one other mother differs from the norm embodied by Kate and Audrey on some key count, but the specificity of that identity is rarely explored in a sustained manner. As a result the decentered plurality that de Lauretis associates with *Born in Flames*—and that I associate with *Jane the Virgin*—is not a defining component of these other texts, which, on the contrary, devote the majority of their attention to, and in the process shore up, a subject position that is familiar in Anglophone mainstream media.

A second, and related, difference between the communities at issue in *Jane the Virgin* and in *Workin' Moms* and *The Letdown* is the functions they serve. Indeed, the moms' groups in the latter are strikingly similar to the communities that Julie A. Wilson and Emily Chivers Yochim discuss in *Mothering through Precarity: Women's Work and Digital Media*. They draw on ethnographic research involving an array of mothers living in Pennsylvania and various associations to which they belong, including a local chapter of Mothers of Preschoolers (MOPS) and the online initiative Momastery, in order to understand the role that community plays in the lives of contemporary mothers. They conclude that as much as the various moms' groups studied, and the communities they engender, may "appear countercultural, they are in no way about disrupting the grammars and scripts of family autonomy."[22] For Wilson and Yochim, the implications of this conclusion are far-reaching since those grammars and scripts work against the best interests of mothers by abetting two phenomena associated with neoliberalism: the privatization of happiness, wherein the burden of cultivating happiness is placed on the individual family unit rather than society as a whole; and the experience of economic and social precarity, which is the norm when social safety nets unravel. Similar to the communities that Wilson and Yochim study, those in *Workin' Moms* and *The Letdown* also serve to preserve family autonomy. Both series take shape around the protagonist's movement between her community of mothers on the one hand and her nuclear family on the other. Yet despite this movement—or, as Wilson and Yochin suggest, because of it—the line between the two realms remains intact. In other words, as much as Kate and Audrey may gain from the group in which they find camaraderie and as much as they may modify their behavior under its influence, their mothering activity continues to occur within the context of, and in service of, a family unit that is narrowly conceived. Consequently, that unit remains the locus of emotional and economic life, thereby perpetuating the conditions of family life under neoliberalism.

To be sure, an argument could be made that *Workin' Moms* and *The Letdown*, by virtue of their focus on moms' groups, serve to lay bare, rather than actively participate in, the ideological work just described; in other words, they could be read as texts that reveal a great deal about the burdens of mothering under neoliberalism, burdens that can be temporarily alleviated, but not systematically eliminated, with the support of certain kinds of community. Yet as Wilson and Yochim write, "Moving beyond family autonomy ultimately requires more than critiquing," never mind laying bare, "dominant ideologies. . . . It requires new sensibilities of what might make a livable life and new configurations of care and collectivity."[23] New sensibilities and configurations are precisely what *Jane the Virgin* offers. To continue adapting the language of Wilson and Yochim, the series creates family collectives rather than family units, and it socializes happiness rather than privatizing it; in so doing it provides a compelling blueprint for a kind of community with the power to put into place "new sensibilities of belonging, new affective infrastructures" and thus to transform motherhood—indeed, parenting more broadly—as both an institution and an experience.[24]

As already mentioned, Jane is, at various points throughout *Jane the Virgin*, a single mother; yet she also actively co-parents with a wide array of other people: Rafael, Xiomara, Alba, Rogelio, and sometimes Michael. Moreover, as much as her family is understood to include all of these people, it also extends far beyond them, encompassing their many relatives by blood, marriage, or some other kind of commitment, and some of those relatives also assume occasional caregiving duties involving Jane's son, Mateo (Elias Janssen). A particularly significant case in point is Petra. At the start of the series, Petra is married to Rafael, but they split up and get back together multiple times after Jane becomes pregnant with Rafael's baby and starts her own on-again, off-again relationship with him. This dynamic, in conjunction with Petra's capacity to be unapologetically conniving, positions her as Jane's rival, and the tension between the two women only escalates when, in season 2, Petra uses Rafael's sperm sample to become pregnant and then gives birth to twin daughters, Anna and Elsa (Mia and Ella Allen).[25] When she learns of the pregnancy, Jane realizes that any baby Petra gives birth to will be Mateo's half sibling and thus she begrudgingly but definitively reframes her relationship to Petra (and eventually Anna and Elsa) as familial. As early as "Chapter Twenty-Eight" Jane invites a pregnant Petra to the quintessential family dinner, Thanksgiving, and from that point on their family bond grows steadily, such that by season 5 the intimacy they share, as both friends and "aunties" to the other's offspring, is one of the series' most significant themes.

In addition to those who are closest to Jane, including Petra, there are at least a dozen other characters who are a part of Jane's extended family, as is captured succinctly in the photos taken after Jane and Rafael's wedding in the series' finale ("Chapter One Hundred"). The result is an expansive web of relations that, as already discussed, is distinguished by its diversity. Yet as individual as each member of that web may be, especially in terms of the way they occupy the role of mother, they nonetheless tend to cultivate actively a sense of familial community and, in the process, contribute to an affective infrastructure that is anything but insular. Consequently, *Jane the Virgin* manages to create a community that is both expansive and tight-knit and to which many people can rightfully belong. Crystallizing this dual impulse is a formal strategy that is a hallmark of every episode: the repeated use of some element—for example, a word, a situation, or a gesture—to bridge any edit that conjoins two different lines of narrative action; sometimes that element stands on its own while other times the narrator draws attention to it, usually by announcing, "Speaking of . . ." In keeping with Nussbaum's understanding of *Jane the Virgin* as a whole, these playful and clever transitions may seem facile but in fact serve profound ends: they acknowledge the co-presence of commonality and difference, thereby fortifying the connections, be they causal, affective, or thematic, between various characters and events but never at the expense of the plurality on display. As a result they are integral to the horizon of possibility that *Jane the Virgin*, through myriad formal means, manages to represent, one organized around a family collective with the capacity to socialize happiness, one that serves to "project back to the viewer a space of heterogeneity, differences and fragmented coherences" while simultaneously making that space the site of community.[26]

When occupying that space, I find myself not only thinking in new ways about caregiving, to both personal and professional ends, but also feeling cared for, as *Jane the Virgin* enfolds me in its spirit of generous, and moreover radical, inclusivity. The series addresses me as a mother, however I may inhabit that role, and creates the conditions needed for a conjunction

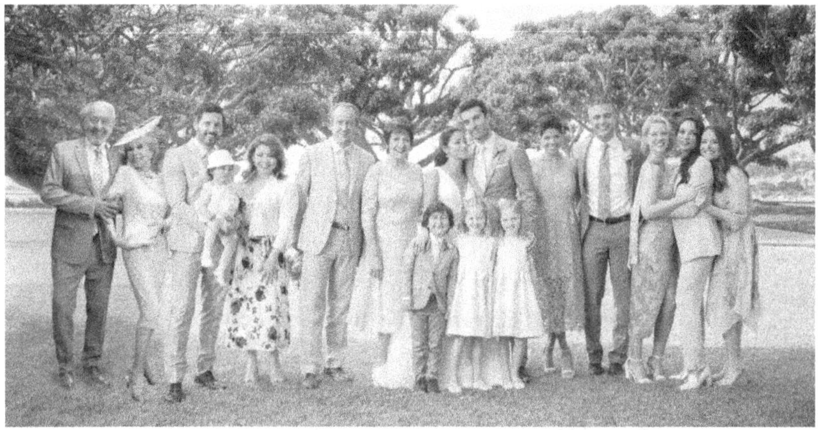

Jane surrounded by her expansive and tight-knit community in "Chapter One Hundred," the final episode of *Jane the Virgin* (created by Jennie Snyder Urman, 2014–19).

between the identities of aca-fan and mom. I may not have, in my daily life, a community as expansive as that in which Jane is enmeshed, but as an aca-fan-mom I can experience its affective potential and begin to imagine the shifts, both intellectual and material, both personal and systemic, that building such a community in the future would entail. Moreover, in the meantime, I can, like *Jane the Virgin* itself, invest myself in a collective practice of both meaning making and world building wherein the labors of caregiving and critique are not only acknowledged and interwoven but also mutually sustaining.

Notes

1 Vivian Sobchack, "What My Fingers Knew: The Cinesthetic Subject, or Vision in the Flesh," in *Carnal Thoughts: Embodiment and Moving Image Culture* (Berkeley: University of California Press, 2004).

2 Jason Mittell, "On Disliking *Mad Men*," *Just TV* (blog), July 29, 2010, justtv.wordpress.com/2010/07/29/on-disliking-mad-men/.

3 Alisa Perren, "Aca-Fandom and Beyond: Jonathan Gray, Matt Hills, and Alisa Perren (Part One)," *Confessions of an Aca-Fan* (blog), August 29, 2011, henryjenkins.org/blog/2011/08/aca-fandom_and_beyond_jonathan.html.

4 Kathryn VanArendonk, "The Anti-prestige Showrunner," *New York*, March 27, 2019, www.vulture.com/2018/09/jane-the-virgin-jennie-snyder-urman-profile.html.

5 Janice Radway, *Reading the Romance: Women, Patriarchy, and Popular Literature* (Chapel Hill: University of North Carolina Press, 1984); Henry Jenkins, *Textual Poachers: Television Fans and Participatory Culture* (New York: Routledge, 1992), 6.

6 Jenkins, *Textual Poachers*, 6.

7 Diana I. Rios and Mari Castañeda, *Soap Operas and Telenovelas in the Digital Age: Global Industries and New Audiences* (New York: Peter Lang, 2011), ix.

8 Rios and Castañeda, *Soap Operas and Telenovelas*, ix.

9 Dannielle Blumenthal, *Women and Soap Opera: A Cultural Feminist Perspective* (Westport, CT: Praeger, 1997), 3.

10 Blumenthal, *Women and Soap Opera*, 106.

11 Emily Nussbaum, "*Jane the Virgin* Is Not a Guilty Pleasure," *New Yorker*, March 5, 2018, www.newyorker.com/magazine/2018/03/12/jane-the-virgin-is-not-a-guilty-pleasure.

12 Courtney Brannon Donoghue, "Importing and Translating *Betty*: Contemporary Telenovela Format Flow within the United States Television Industry," in Rios and Mari Castañeda, *Soap Operas and Telenovelas in the Digital Age*, 271.

13 Exactly how significant is a matter of debate, as discussed by Daniël Biltereyst and Philippe Meers in "The International Telenovela Debate and the Contra-Flow Argument: A Reappraisal." Therein they write, "On the one extreme of the debate some scholars claimed a revision of the cultural imperialism and dependency thesis, even going so far as launching idea[s] about a 'reverse cultural imperialism.' For other, especially critical scholars, such a revisionist framework tended to overestimate the range of the changes in global production and contra-flow." In *Telenovelas*, ed. Ilan Stavans (Denver, CO: Greenwood, 2010), 34.

14 Donoghue, "Importing and Translating *Betty*," 264.

15 VanArendonk, "The Anti-prestige Showrunner."

16 Nussbaum, "Not a Guilty Pleasure."

17 Teresa de Lauretis, "Rethinking Women's Cinema: Aesthetics and Feminist Theory," in *Technologies of Gender* (Bloomington: Indiana University Press, 1987), 133.

18 de Lauretis, "Rethinking Women's Cinema," 141, 135.
19 de Lauretis, "Rethinking Women's Cinema," 133.
20 de Lauretis, "Rethinking Women's Cinema," 143.
21 de Lauretis, "Rethinking Women's Cinema," 143.
22 Julie A. Wilson and Emily Chivers Yochim, *Mothering through Precarity: Women's Work and Digital Media* (Durham, NC: Duke University Press, 2017), 144.
23 Wilson and Yochim, *Mothering through Precarity*, 178–79.
24 Wilson and Yochim, *Mothering through Precarity*, 180.
25 While Petra and Rafael give their daughters the names of the sisters in *Frozen* (Chris Buck and Jennifer Lee, 2013) without realizing it, *Jane the Virgin* knows exactly what it is doing. In light of this intertextual reference, Disney princess films should be added to the list of genres that Nussbaum associates with *Jane the Virgin*.
26 de Lauretis, "Rethinking Women's Cinema," 143.

11

Obstetric Violence and the Creative Exploration of Alternatives in Guadalupe Sánchez Sosa's *La primera sonrisa*

Elissa Rashkin

For centuries, midwives and natural healers in Mexico have used a wide range of therapeutic techniques to assist pregnant women in the birth process: massages, plant-based tonics, steam baths, and many other practices form part of a repertoire associated with this area of feminine medicine. Traditional healers also possessed and utilized knowledge of herbal birth control and abortion methods long before the introduction of the pill, condoms, and other contraceptive technologies, and in quiet defiance of the abortion prohibition that persists in every state of the country except the district of Mexico City. At the same time, contemporary Mexican women are subjected to one of the world's highest rates of cesarean sections and, in hospitals and clinics, have little control over childbirth.

This situation is symptomatic of a context in which women's bodies are objects of violence, both physical (rape, murder, and torture as facts of everyday life in social conditions dominated by organized crime and judicial indifference and/or complicity) and symbolic. Reproduction, as the production of offspring for the satisfaction of paternal and patriarchal desire, takes place within a status quo in which women are exalted as caregivers but denied agency, subject to overlapping regimes of ideological control via church, state, family relations, and an authoritarian medical system that denies women's knowledge and participation in the elemental process of giving birth.

In this context, Guadalupe Sánchez Sosa's documentary *La primera sonrisa / The First Smile* (2014) denounces obstetric violence in Mexico while focusing on the heritage of midwifery and the contemporary possibilities of natural delivery, exemplified in the work of Veracruz midwife Naolí Vinaver. Vinaver has delivered numerous babies in loving collaboration with mothers and sometimes their partners, and has also become a visible advocate for natural childbirth and for restoring women's control over their own sexuality and reproduction. The documentary traces Vinaver's work with various mothers and families as well as her leadership in workshops in Mexico and Brazil. Verbal and visual testimony are key to the film's construction, but beyond the individual subjects portrayed, *La primera sonrisa* makes a forceful argument against the violent imposition of obstetric intervention, an argument that the director has since aired in numerous public forums.

My analysis of *La primera sonrisa* addresses the film's documentary strategies, also focusing on the role of the filmmaker herself as midwife and mother of a unique creative process. Sánchez Sosa, a former member of the pioneer feminist film collective Cine-Mujer, has a long history as an art director and animator. In *La primera sonrisa*, her luminous animated drawings add an intimate dimension to the film, weaving multidimensional, metaphorical ties between corporeal and artistic creativity.

Guadalupe Sánchez Sosa and Feminist Documentary in Mexico

As Siboney Obscura Gutiérrez indicates in her article "El documental mexicano dirigido por mujeres," documentary making by women formed part of their early, if sporadic, participation in filmmaking as a whole: the sisters Dolores and Adriana Ehlers, for example, worked under contract during the early 1920s to produce documentaries on the oil industry, Mexico City's water system, the Teotihuacan pyramids, and other subjects; later, the multifaceted Elena Sánchez Valenzuela, hired by then president Lázaro Cárdenas, directed *Michoacán* in 1936.[1] However, feminist documentary as such arose with the women's movement of the mid-1970s as well as the introduction of cinema studies at the university level, an environment that allowed women to bypass the obstacles that excluded them from the male-dominated commercial film industry.

Specifically, the Colectivo Cine-Mujer was born in 1975 as an interdisciplinary project linking film students and women in fields such as sociology and anthropology. Its perspective was both Marxist and feminist; its films reflected gender and class consciousness and were intended to generate reflection and debate.[2] The collective continued its activities until the mid-1980s; upon its dispersion, many of its members continued to work in film, including the group's sole animator, Sánchez Sosa, who directed the animated shorts *Mentirosa / Liar* (1976) and *Y si eres mujer . . . / And if You Are a Woman . . .* (1977) and collaborated on films with other members of the collective.[3] Isabel Jiménez Camacho describes *Y si eres mujer . . .* as "a short film that, using frame-by-frame animation and collage, describes, criticizes, and analyzes the ways in which gender roles are assigned to women from birth to adulthood, in the home and the mass media."[4] Interestingly, ideas expressed in this early work recur decades later in *La primera sonrisa*, particularly in its animated sequences.

In 1988, Sánchez Sosa starred in Marisa Sistach's *Los pasos de Ana / The Footsteps of Ana*, one of the first feature films made by an emerging cohort of women directors utilizing noncommercial, cooperative, university- and/or state-supported production strategies. Sánchez Sosa went on to work primarily in art direction, in films directed by women (Sistach's *El cometa / The Comet* [1999] and *Perfume de violetas / Violet Perfume: No One Is Listening* [2001], Maricarmen de Lara's *El país de no pasa nada / In the Country Nothing Happens* [2000]) and others by Arturo Ripstein, Paul Leduc, and Felipe Cazals, highly regarded male figures of the New Mexican Cinema of the 1970s onward. Costume design, makeup, special effects, and still photography are other areas that appear on her diverse résumé. As a creator of animation, she directed two shorts in 2005 for the Consejo Nacional para Prevenir la Discriminación, and capsules for Disney Channel in 2001. In order to promote this largely marginalized area of filmmaking, she published *Guía para los animados: Animación tradicional con ayuda de herramientas digitales* (2011), a guide to film animation using traditional and contemporary digital methods. Like other members of Cine-Mujer, her early work with the collective laid the groundwork for a solid trajectory within and on the margins of the Mexican film industry.

Neglected for several decades, Cine-Mujer has begun to resurface in screenings, press, and scholarship, as documentary making by women flourishes—supported by festivals such as Ambulante and the Muestra Internacional de Cine con Perspectiva de Género, or MIC-Género—and as students as well as filmmakers rediscover feminist history.[5] It is significant, in this regard, that one of the collective's first productions, *Cosas de mujeres / Women's Issues* (1978), directed by Rosa Marta Fernández, focused on the issue of abortion: then, as now, an illegal yet widely practiced procedure in Mexico. Other Cine-Mujer films addressed prostitution, sexual violence, domestic labor, and women's organizing, all of which, like abortion, remain unresolved subjects of struggle. *La primera sonrisa*, Sánchez Sosa's first documentary, thus emerges not only at a time of effervescence in the documentary field but also at a time of feminist renewal in Mexico. Current feminist activism has focused on combating sexual violence (from street harassment to femicide), patriarchal control of women's bodies, and denial of reproductive rights, including state-level abortion bans and widespread obstetric violence.

Obstetric Violence

Although obstetric violence is not the direct subject of *La primera sonrisa*, Sánchez Sosa's decision to focus on positive models of sexuality, childbirth, and midwifery was motivated by a negative context in which feminist practices function necessarily within the realm of the "alternative." In an interview published in Mayka Martín's blog *Crianza con apego natural*, the director comments, "One thing that I encountered making the film was obstetric violence, this disconnect with our nature, not only on the part of the healthcare system or the doctor involved, but also the fear the women have of giving birth." She adds, "In Brazil I saw a package that offered cesarean section, liposuction, and breast surgery."[6] The medicalization of pregnancy and childbirth, and the concomitant devaluation of traditional knowledge and practices as well as women's control over what happens to their bodies in the process, is exacerbated by consumer capitalism's ever-expanding paradigm of the impossible. In this case, the physiological changes accompanying birth, and indeed birth itself, are framed as aesthetic disturbances to be "corrected" as soon as possible, rather than normal aspects of a life event that other cultures have assumed to be natural.[7]

It is important, however, to note that the discussion of medicalized versus traditional childbirth in Mexico has taken place in a complicated context in which the tendency toward medicalization has clashed with the absence of an efficient healthcare system in many regions, especially in rural and/or Indigenous zones. As Hilda Argüello-Avendaño and Ana Mateo-González show in their study of the framing of the argument by international healthcare organizations over two decades, 1970s tendencies favoring the incorporation of midwifery as part of institutionalized healthcare were reversed when the same organizations found that maternal mortality had not decreased, and determined that such a decrease could best be achieved through an increase in medical intervention, especially delivery via cesarean section.[8]

The lack of access to formal medical services has meant, in practice, that rural women continue to depend on traditional birth assistants. Indeed, the federal health department sponsors a certification program for traditional midwives whose guidelines begin with a highly positive description of traditional Indigenous medicine as a "complete healthcare system" based on the relation between humans and nature.[9] The requirements for certification, however, are restrictive in that the midwife must be able to read and write, provide numerous documents, undergo training, recertify every two years, inform the agency of changes of residence, and deliver regular reports.[10] The ensuing clash of cultural systems is predictable; as Argüello-Avendaño and Mateo-González show, depending on the outcome being measured, the definition of "qualified personnel" may or may not include traditional birth attendants, whether or not these have undergone officially recognized training.[11]

Overall, policy vis-à-vis traditional healthcare practices reflects a long-standing ambivalence toward Indigenous cultures on the part of national institutions: at times intercultural, multicultural, and pluralist rhetoric favors programs that enlist midwives and other traditional practitioners as welcome allies of an underfunded healthcare system that is viewed with little confidence by potential patients, yet at other times that same cultural knowledge is deemed backward and counterproductive to efficient policy development. In this scenario, rural and Indigenous women may utilize traditional healthcare due to preference, custom, and/or necessity, with or without the blessing of the state; on the other hand, they may be channeled into a hospital or clinic that may subject them to obstetric violence in the form of unnecessary medical intervention, sterilization without informed consent, disregard for their wishes, verbal denigration, separation of the newborn from the mother, and other forms of physical and psychological abuse, all of which constitute gender discrimination as well as flagrant violation of the patients' rights.[12]

Discussions regarding the acceptability or not of traditional midwifery have mostly occurred in the context of rural and Indigenous populations; in urban areas, medicalized hospital births are the norm. Yet, as is the case with rural clinics and hospitals, urban public health services are also chronically underfunded, understaffed, and overcrowded. Roberto Castro and Joaquina Erveti, reviewing twenty-five years of research on obstetric violence in Mexico, posit not only the systematic violation of what they call women's "reproductive citizenship" but also the failure to recognize cultural norms or habitus within the healthcare sector, in which gender discrimination and power disparities are normalized.[13]

Castro and Erveti argue that the "sensitivity" or "awareness" training that medical personnel receive in order to improve "quality of care" has little impact in that it fails to address the disciplinary structures that shape everyday practice within the institution, normally in the name of "efficiency."[14] Similarly, María Teresa Silvia Tinoco Zamudio argues that the primary problem is the "omnipotence of the doctor as representative of hegemonic patriarchal power," said power wielded in a socioeconomic context in which "health becomes a commodity, principally in private services, while in public services we find dehumanization of medicine, situations that favor the presence of institutional violence in obstetric care in spite of global policies regarding human rights and discrimination against women."[15]

This panorama of violence and violation of women's human rights and "reproductive citizenship" is the background against which the alternative midwifery and women's health movement documented in *La primera sonrisa* has gained momentum. It is important to bear this in mind, given that the film's portrayals of women's gatherings featuring massage and belly painting, beachside consciousness-raising, dream work, water births, and the like sometimes seem both idyllic and exclusive. Yet its overall message, a message that has resonated with a variety of publics, is one of love toward the female body, personal and collective reconnection with traditional and corporeal wisdom, and valorization of the birth process in resistance to social structures that treat pregnancy, childbirth, and the very fact of being female as pathological.

Birthing Documentary Processes

La primera sonrisa centers on the activities of midwife Naolí Vinaver during workshops in Mexico and Brazil, along with conversations with mothers and birth activists, including midwives, doulas, and medical personnel. It culminates in two home births recorded, as we shall see, with great sensitivity by Sánchez Sosa's camera. Traditional wisdom, women's feelings about their bodies and sexuality, fear and repression, and the birth experience itself are some of the themes addressed—via interviews, voice-over, and on-screen discussions, but also through the evocative use of music and, especially, sensuous visual language.[16] Close-ups of hands, feet, bellies, faces; bodies interrelating and flowing into one another in guided exercises, dance, birth preparation, and the birth process itself; the group in the individual, the individual in collectivity. These images, moreover, interact with a series of landscapes that work not only to link sequences and provide attractive backdrops but also to impart a primordial, almost paradisiacal sense of spiritual connection between women and the Earth.

After the animated, musicalized sequence that introduces the film's title, the first live images show, in turn, a pregnant woman's belly painted with a design echoing the animation; a low-angle shot of treetops in a round spiral pattern, mirroring the roundness of the belly; and a woman's feet submerged in flowing water, followed by other images of the bathing suit-clad woman in attitudes of sensuous relaxation in the river. This subject turns out to be Vinaver, who narrates in voice-over her introduction to midwifery through dreams: three months of dreams of different kinds of births, each presenting a specific problem; taken together, she interpreted them as indicating her calling. This initial imagery of the midwife (and other women) in water introduces an idea that will recur in different ways before being explicitly articulated, again in the voice of Vinaver, toward the end of the film: the idea that in the birth process, the woman herself is reborn. Moreover, the reclaiming of midwifery traditions, as a challenge to patriarchal values and practices that deform women's experiences of sexuality and motherhood, is also a rebirth, in this case of women's self-knowledge and autonomy.

The two workshops documented in the film illustrate this holistic feminist philosophy. The first, in Rancho Viejo, Mexico, takes place in and around a simple wooden kitchen, in which Vinaver and other *parteras* show a selection of plants and explain their uses: calendula, arnica, plantain peel, espinosilla, rosemary. A tincture is displayed, and an herb-infused chocolate is prepared as it would be for a woman in labor. The camera examines the plants, hovers over the pot of chocolate, and follows the women's activities, dwelling on their hands in close-up, involved but unobtrusive. Throughout the film, the camera assumes the role of participant observer, focusing on details and gestures while listening to the diversity of voices represented in the workshops and gatherings. Occasionally, the filmmaker's eye strays from the women's activity to gaze at the remarkable and notably nonurban surroundings: in Rancho Viejo, the lush vegetation characteristic of the state of Veracruz; in Florianopolis, Brazil, the paradisiacal beach that serves as backdrop for the second workshop.

At this second gathering, Sánchez Sosa deploys the same complicit camerawork as in the previous workshop, keeping her documentary eye and ear close to the level of the participants. Here at the beach, freed temporarily from the productive processes of everyday life, the utopian possibilities of women's community seem even greater: an ideal setting for the discussion of sexuality that opens the sequence. The valorization of women's intimate experiences (masturbation, orgasm, late-life sexual awakening) implicitly counteracts a common institutional scenario in which women who express discomfort during the birth process suffer verbal abuse under the premise that, since pregnancy is the result of a sexual act, pain is a just

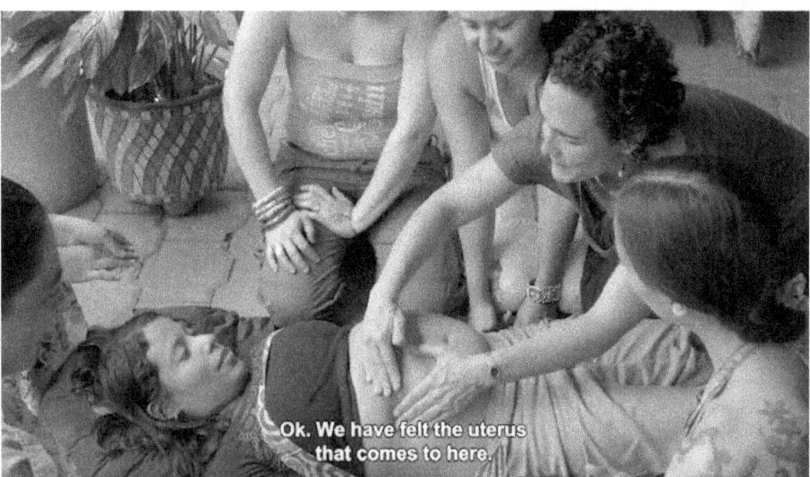

Naolí Vinaver leads a midwifery workshop in Rancho Viejo, Veracruz, Mexico, in *La primera sonrisa* (Guadalupe Sánchez Sosa, 2014).

punishment.[17] While certainly not all health workers moralize or are hostile to their patients, obstetric violence research indicates that pregnant women, not unlike rape victims, are often intimidated and subjected to humiliation. The sharing of sexual knowledge at the midwives' workshop is thus a feminist act that reframes and reclaims the place of sexuality, along with (though not forcibly attached to) pregnancy, birth, and motherhood, in the histories of women as speaking subjects.

In the segments that follow, activities from the workshop are intercut with testimonies in which women tell their birth stories, joined in some cases by their male partners, who in one scene read aloud their letters of gratitude to Vinaver. A relatively long sequence depicts a woman sitting on the mosaic floor of an unfurnished room, narrating her experience of pregnancy and giving birth. The story takes place in Berlin, but rather than intercutting contextual imagery, Sánchez Sosa uses the enclosed space as an opportunity to illustrate the narration with drawings. The back wall becomes a screen-within-a-screen onto which drawings are projected; when the speaker relates her dream of a saber-toothed tiger announcing her pregnancy, an animated drawing of a tiger appears next to her, laughing, as in the dream. The connection between pregnancy/birth and creativity is emphasized in this sequence, as is the importance of dreams as an alternative form of knowledge.

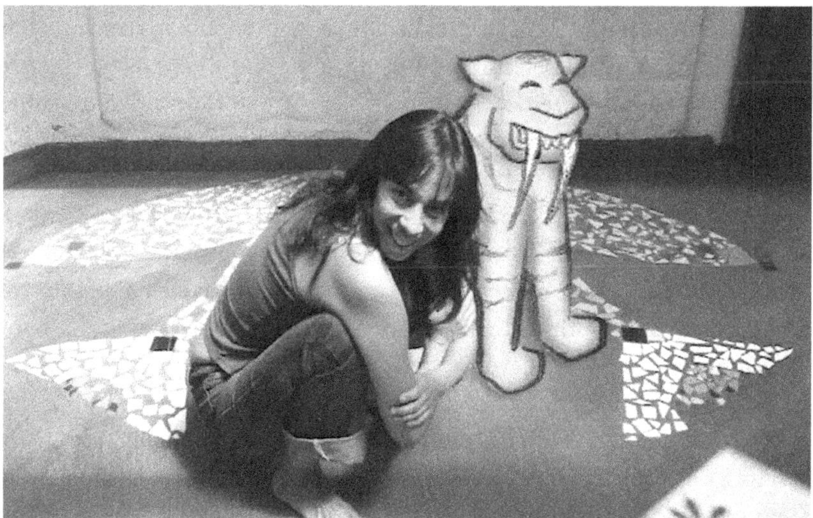

"And I woke up and I said to myself: I am pregnant": animated drawings accompany women's stories in *La primera sonrisa* (Guadalupe Sánchez Sosa, 2014).

Along with these imaginative and intimate sequences, *La primera sonrisa* includes interviews with midwife and ob-gyn nurse Guadalupe Laderreche, doula and perinatal educator Glenda Furszyfer, and midwife Eva Valero, all of whom critique the mentality in which giving birth is seen as a dangerous event that needs to be controlled. This way of thinking leads to the medicalization of birth within a hierarchical institutional structure that Valero likens to the feudal estate, and thus to various forms of violence. Furszyfer points out, for instance, that episiotomy is performed in virtually all hospital births in Mexico, even though current research shows that this procedure is rarely necessary. Vinaver, in a workshop scene inserted into the discussion, suggests that specialized jargon naturalizes practices that would otherwise be clearly perceived by the patient as violent: "cutting your vagina with a knife" or, in Furszyfer's term, genital mutilation.

At this point, the filmmaker intervenes with an animated sequence depicting episiotomy as a vertical red gash, bleeding and being stitched; as Laderreche explains that the procedure is unnecessary in part because the baby's head helps to stretch the vaginal canal as it moves down, the wound becomes a black circle, the head crowning. This image gives way to a new circle, the world, upon whose surface appear two buildings, a hospital and a house, as Laderreche argues for collaboration between medical personnel and midwives in the event that complications make it unsafe for a woman to give birth at home. Sánchez Sosa's simple animation complements the more traditional "expert testimony," using color and geometry to suggest a transition from the vertical and the violent to the rounded and gentle, representing the horizontal practices advocated by the film's protagonists.

Finally, this section of the film shows two male doctors taking part in the beach workshop in Florianopolis; later, gynecologist Gilberto Ramírez shares an interview with Laderreche, both commenting on the high number of cesareans performed in Mexico: 85 percent of hospital births, among the highest rates in the world. This number implies that many medical school students graduate having never witnessed a natural birth; moreover, according to Furszyfer, the practice of scheduling surgery without regard for the baby's readiness to be born has produced an "epidemic" of premature births resulting, in turn, in babies who require special care as well as separation from their mothers in the first moments of life. The routine abuse of the cesarean section, as opposed to its use as an emergency measure, points to an ideological rationalization in which the inherent liminal nature of the birth process (in between life and death, or life and not-yet-life) is recast as dangerous and needing to be controlled by means of preprogrammed surgical intervention. The woman as subject is absent; her objectified body becomes the terrain on which patriarchy, via the male-dominated medical establishment, asserts its power over life itself.

Having established through the voices of these varied witnesses the grim scenario that constitutes conventional birthing practices in Mexico and other parts of the world, the film moves on to explore the complicated relationships between women and their histories, particularly family histories shadowed by generations of "baggage." The segment is introduced by a close-up of turtles stacked one on top of the other, a voice-over explaining that when a woman is pregnant, she bears the weight of her family heritage, much of which must be released in order to free her to give birth. She must pass through a dark tunnel in order to reach the light. This idea is expressed first in a fluid animated sequence and then in a ritual from the Florianopolis workshop in which participants pass under and between the legs of their companions in emulation of the birth process. In being pregnant and giving birth, the sequence suggests, one is necessarily reborn; moreover, this rebirth, assumed as a conscious experience, implies transgenerational healing.

The final section of this segment gives way to the film's "big moment," in which Sánchez Sosa's camera accompanies two couples and their midwife (Vinaver) during birth. Here, the challenge for the filmmaker and her crew is to document an extremely intimate process without replicating the violation of intimacy that commonly takes place in the operating theater. The film approaches the event gradually: a red screen with a pattern of white lights, a dark room lit with red, the darkness and quiet music honoring the privacy of the mother-to-be undergoing contractions, her partner supporting her as she takes steps to walk through the pangs. Transition to the second couple, the woman also moaning from contractions, her male partner also playing a supporting role. The film will move between these two scenarios; throughout, the handheld camera is positioned at a respectful distance, creating anticipation and empathy with the early stages of the process.

The film then transitions away from this focus, as if creating space and, in the meantime, allowing women to tell their birth stories. What is interesting here is how the women speak about themselves, their feelings of strength and purpose: one describes herself as "a bear," while another remembers yelling with all her might in the taxi on her way to the hospital, scaring the driver. This scene is animated on the wall behind her until, with her arrival at the hospital, the animation stops as she tells of the birth itself. These stories illustrate what Vinaver describes in the previous sequence as "taking off the mask," a crucial moment of self-knowing and realization.

They are also important given that in the scenes that follow, the women do little talking. In the case of Yahil and Sael, both *son jarocho* musicians, it is clear that the inclusion of music at the birth was a decision made by the couple ahead of time; initially they sing together in traditional call-and-response style, but as Yahil's contractions grow stronger, Sael's singing and playing seem to compete with her for center stage. His improvised strumming on the jarana continues as we watch the baby's head crowning in a stunning shot indicative of the level of trust existing between filmmaker and subjects by this point in the documentary. When the baby, assisted by Vinaver, emerges from Yahil's body and gives its first cry, Sael stops playing and cries as well. The father too, it would seem, has been reborn.

The other couple, whose water delivery sans music is filmed with equal tact and visual surety, is less verbally expressive, yet here too the male partner plays a prominent role. These scenes, though powerful, cannot help but feel somewhat alienating to spectators (for example, myself) with little confidence in the male as collaborator in a society in which literal or figurative paternal abandonment is arguably more the norm than the exception. One is left to assume on faith that the alternative championed by Vinaver and her circle also includes single women, lesbian couples, and/or the participation of other women, not necessarily parental, in the birth process. At the same time, it is understandable that Sánchez Sosa would wish to highlight the active role of the fathers, given that in hospital births in Mexico, men are generally excluded from the delivery room, their role culturally limited to celebrating, among their friends or relatives, the arrival of their preferably male offspring. Care of both the new baby and its mother, the latter presumably recovering in many cases from a cesarean section, is left in the hands of other women. The notion of men as attuned to women's feelings during pregnancy, knowledgeable about contractions and breathing, or visibly moved to tears by the appearance of the newborn is, in this context, a radical one.

Animation

As the descriptions above have already indicated, Sánchez Sosa's talent as an artist and animator is brilliantly deployed throughout the film in the form of a complementary visual discourse that reinforces and/or elaborates on selected aspects of the documentary material. This artisanal intervention, a significant mark of authorship, connects *La primera sonrisa* to its immediate antecedent in the director's oeuvre, the 2008 short film *Niño de mis ojos / The Apple of My Eyes*, a frank and humorous reflection on female sexuality and intimacy.

In *Niño de mis ojos*, the protagonist lives with a miniature companion, a literal "boy toy" who accompanies her in the shower, at the table among fruits and chocolates, and in bed, pleasuring her under the sheets. When a man moves in upstairs and invites her to a party, however, she begins an affair, commenting to her miniature lover, "I love you, but I don't know where to put you." The displaced "niño" is jealous until he discovers that the rival comes complete with a "niña" his own size. The regrouping of the couples seemingly imposes conventional order, but the protagonist's Giaconda smile at the end suggests that the possibility of new sexual combinations is not foreclosed. The film is not carried so much by the plot line as by the fluid lines and colors of Sánchez Sosa's animated drawings and by the fragments of son jarocho performed by Luis Felipe Luna of the group Sonex. The traditional song lyrics generate a changing emotional landscape that largely replaces dialogue. The world thus created is familiar—filled with everyday objects and activities such as eating and bathing—and unique, a visual and aural creation that privileges sensuality on multiple levels.

The same elements appear in *La primera sonrisa*: music, color, sensuality, fluidity of design and experience. Not only do animated sequences serve as transitions or title material, they are, in fact, key to the film. In the opening sequence, for instance, translucent red ink or paint, blood-like, swirls abstractly before forming a flower, dissolves once again into liquid, bubbles, filling the screen, displaying different grades of density and translucence. Rosa Zaragoza's "Carta a las estrellas" is heard; the Catalan singer's lullaby, from her album *Nacer renacer* (2005), intensifies the sense of drama as the primordial visual abstraction becomes a multicolored drawing of a fetus in the womb, growing, moving—an image of transformation and multiplicity.

Not all the artwork in *La primera sonrisa*, however, is feminine mysticism. About twenty minutes into the film, another sequence illustrates gender construction as a lifelong process of discrimination suffered by girls and women: a cartoon bow, dress, and shoes become the garments of an adult, followed by an iron, washing machine, clothesline, and other domestic implements in rapid succession, suggesting the overwhelming burden placed on women; the kitchen becomes the house, the house becomes smaller, further and further away until it is a tiny structure on a round planet, while on the soundtrack Vinaver explains how from birth on, women are devalued until, "day by day, gesture by gesture," we lose the capacity to recognize our right to self-discovery and self-determination. The sequence highlights the ways in which the construction of the feminine in relation to domesticity is naturalized to the point of invisibility, even as it contributes to the heavy baggage that women bring to the birth process and their subsequent roles as mothers.

Finally, the blue designs at the end of the film and during its final credit sequence echo the red ink of the beginning and also the beach landscape of Florianopolis, the last photographic image before the return to animation. The clear blue, now forming water, now flowers, now adding new colors, connotes serenity, even transcendence. The song "Pra Nené Nanar," performed by MU with Rosa Zaragoza, similarly contrasts with the earlier "Carta a las estrellas": the baby has been born, the soft bossa nova-style melody describes the father lulling her to sleep, reinforcing the film's message in support of paternal involvement. The ending is thus not only hopeful but utopic: a peaceable kingdom of liquid light, a projected reinvention of maternity and community.

Midwifery and/as Creativity

The narrative detailed above is held together not only by the continuity of place—the Florianopolis and Veracruz landscapes in particular—and the subjects who appear and reappear to tell their stories or provide contextual information, but also by the consistent multifaceted emphasis on creativity. Pregnancy, birth, and midwifery are seen as dynamic processes in which women invent and reinvent themselves in communion with family, supportive community, nature, and dreams. Music and dancing, along with painting, are prominent: workshop participants sing and dance, and at one point a son jarocho group plays while women dance on the wooden platform, or *tarima*. Conversely, a moving close-up in the Florianopolis workshop frames an older woman singing in Portuguese, sharing intergenerational knowledge and memory through song.

All of this music, color, light, scenery, and effervescence is compelling, especially given the implicit contrast with the typical environment in which most mothers give birth: the sterile setting of the hospital, mentioned but not portrayed in *La primera sonrisa*. The possibly exclusionary implications of this utopic audiovisual discourse are not entirely ignored by the film; indeed, when midwife Eva Valero comments that for the movement to be successful it can't be limited to "four hippies giving birth at home," she points to a contradiction that the film does not attempt to resolve. Very different, for example, is another documentary from the same year, Alessandra Zeka and Holen Sabrina Kahn's *Una inquisición silenciosa / A Quiet Inquisition*, set in a hospital in Nicaragua in which ob-gyn doctor Carla Cerrato deals on a daily basis with the violent effects of the country's absolutist abortion ban: pregnant women, many of them adolescents, suffer complications that put their own lives in danger, yet medical personnel are prohibited from taking action as long as the possibility of fetal viability exists, regardless of the consequences for the mother.

Although the issue in Zeka and Kahn's film is not obstetric violence per se but rather the drastic suppression of women's rights to life and health under the administration of President Daniel Ortega, Dr. Cerrato's fight against a policy that leaves her staff paralyzed—legally obstructed from carrying out the basic lifesaving mandate of the medical profession—exposes the patriarchal context of medicine in contemporary Nicaragua as well as the conditions of sexual abuse and subjection in which pregnancy often occurs in the first place. In contrast, *La primera sonrisa* opts for a positive depiction of alternatives.[18] If the latter at times seems confined to the "four hippies" invoked by Valero, the hope voiced by the film's subjects is that the recuperation of traditional feminine wisdom and creativity, and the rejection of medicalized and depersonalized obstetric intervention, will become a broad social demand, a women-led movement and, eventually, a reality.

Feminist Documentary in the Public Sphere

After its release, the activist message of *La primera sonrisa* was picked up in the press, with nearly every article mentioning the 85 percent cesarean statistic among other data foregrounded in the film. This led to circulation not only in university and art house cinemas like the Cineteca Nacional and festivals such as Ambulante, but also in contexts such as a screening in the Senate in May 2016, followed by a discussion with Sánchez Sosa, Asociación Mexicana de Partería president Cristina Alonso, and three women senators, and another at the National School of Nursing and Obstetrics at the National Autonomous University of Mexico (UNAM) in October 2017. In November, the film was featured in the Primer Festival por la Salud de la Mujer y la Tierra (First Festival for the Health of Women and the Earth) in Mexico City. It has shown in numerous cities outside of the capital, and screenings have often included discussions with health professionals and/or midwifery advocates.[19] In the spirit of the feminist cinema pioneered by the Colectivo Cine-Mujer in the 1970s and '80s, *La primera sonrisa* has been taken up as a consciousness-raising tool with the potential—in conjunction with other voices and actions—to influence public policy and question the habitus in the medical establishment that, as Castro and Erveti argue, tend toward the perpetuation of forms of obstetric violence and patient dehumanization.[20]

As I have sought to demonstrate in this essay, the film's creative depiction of women's self-knowledge and community surrounding the birth process, guided by midwives like Vinaver, represents a positive, even utopic moment in a much less idyllic overall scenario; yet this moment, multiplied by *La primera sonrisa* in each projection and by the many other actions taken by women and men in Mexico and elsewhere working to transform the conditions in which children are born and mothers give birth, may well help to define a future in which women, whatever their socioeconomic circumstances, are assured the right to well-being and self-determination.

Notes

1 Siboney Obscura Gutiérrez, "El documental mexicano dirigido por mujeres," *Ciencia*, April–June 2014, 47–48, www.revistaciencia.amc.edu.mx/images/revista/65_2/PDF/DocumentalMexicano.pdf. On the Ehlers, see also Patricia Martínez de Velasco Vélez, *Directoras de cine. Proyección de un mundo obscuro* (Mexico City: Instituto Mexicano de Cinematografía and CONEICC, 1991), 31–37; and Elissa Rashkin, *Women Filmmakers in Mexico* (Austin: University of Texas Press, 2001), 34–40. Patricia Torres San Martín's *Elena Sánchez Valenzuela* (Mexico City:

Universidad de Guadalajara, Cineteca Nacional, Universidad Nacional Autónoma de México, 2018) is a superb study of this feminist pioneer.

2 Rashkin, *Women Filmmakers*, 68–74.

3 "Guadalupe Sánchez Sosa," Perfiles, *CorreCamara.com.mx*, accessed August 6, 2020, www.correcamara.com.mx/inicio/int.php?mod=perfiles_detalle&id_perfil=438. Dates for these films vary among the sources consulted.

4 Isabel Jiménez Camacho, "De cines y feminismos en América Latina: El Colectivo Cine Mujer en México (1975–1986)" (BA thesis, Universidad Nacional Autónoma de México, 2018), 136. Translations are mine unless otherwise noted.

5 Ambulante, an annual traveling documentary festival, exhibited *La primera sonrisa* in 2016 in a section on motherhood that also included Juliet Jordan's *Miriam: Home Delivery* (2014) and Irene Lusztig's *The Motherhood Archives* (2013). For feminist history, see, for instance, Jiménez Camacho's 2018 thesis, "De cines y feminismos," a study of the Cine-Mujer collective. See Obscura Gutiérrez, "El documental mexicano," 51–52, on the twenty-first-century wave of documentary production by women.

6 Mayka Martín, "*La primera sonrisa*, documental sobre sexualidad femenina, partería tradicional y violencia obstétrica," *Crianza con apego natural*, May 3, 2016, https://crianzaconapegonatural.wordpress.com/2016/05/03/la-primera-sonrisa-documental-sobre-sexualidad-femenina-parteria-tradicional-y-violencia-obstetrica/.

7 I use the word "*natural*" guardedly, recognizing that the cultural constraints on women's "choices" are not to be taken lightly. The criminalization of abortion is a case in point. In Mexico, abortion became legal in the national capital in 2007; in response, many states have strengthened laws penalizing women who abort and medical personnel who perform abortions. Mortality from clandestine abortions remains high, while women have been jailed for aborting and even for spontaneous miscarriages; notorious cases have involved Indigenous women with little command of Spanish, due to the shortage of interpreters in the judicial system. An article in the Mexican edition of *El país* reviewed abortion policy in the thirty-one states that penalize it, finding that in six of these, penalties are determined by moral judgments regarding the woman's behavior and "reputation." In some cases, women may shorten

or avoid jail time by submitting to therapy designed to reinforce their appreciation of maternity and family values (Zorayda Gallegos, "Seis estados mexicanos reducen las penas por abortar 'si la mujer no tiene mala fama,'" *El país*, May 11, 2017, elpais.com/internacional/2017/05/06/mexico/1494025710_367931.html). Although the Mexican government recognizes separation of church and state, it tends to allow the Catholic Church and the religious right, rather than public health experts or women's organizations, to define discussion of the matter.

8 Hilda E. Argüello-Avendaño and Ana Mateo-González, "Parteras tradicionales y parto medicalizado. ¿Un conflicto del pasado? Evolución del discurso de los organismos internacionales en los últimos veinte años," *Revista liminaR. estudios sociales y humanísticos* 12, no. 2 (2014): 13–29.

9 Secretaría de Salud, *Guía para la autorización de las parteras tradicionales como personal de salud no profesional*, December 11, 2017, 2, www.gob.mx/cms/uploads/attachment/file/103624/GuiaAutorizacionParterasTradicionales2016.pdf.

10 Reglamento de la Ley General de Salud en Materia de Prestación de Servicios de Atención Médica, artículos 102–14, cited in Secretaría de Salud, *Guía*, 5–7.

11 Argüello-Avendaño and Mateo-González, "Parteras tradicionales," 19–20.

12 Laura F. Belli, "La violencia obstétrica: Otra forma de violación a los derechos humanos," *Revista redbioética* (UNESCO) 1, no. 7 (2013): 30–32, ri.conicet.gov.ar/bitstream/handle/11336/12868/Art2-BelliR7.pdf?sequence=2&isAllowed=y.

13 Roberto Castro and Joaquina Erveti, "25 años de investigación sobre violencia obstétrica en México," *Revista CONAMED* 19, no. 1 (2014): 39–40, https://dialnet.unirioja.es/descarga/articulo/4730781.pdf.

14 Castro and Erveti, "25 años," 40.

15 María Teresa Silvia Tinoco Zamudio, "Propuesta para la prevención y atención de violencia institucional en la atención obstétrica en México," *Revista CONAMED* 21, supplement 1 (2016): 52, https://www.medigraphic.com/pdfs/conamed/con-2016/cons161f.pdf.

16 On the DVD, *La primera sonrisa* is divided into chapters, titled as follows: Looking for Help; Traditions and Sexuality; Woman, Emotions, and Sensations; Teachings of Colors; Midwifery United with Medicine; Connections; The Big Moment. The titles do not appear in the film itself,

yet they provide a guide to its representational strategies, even as the themes mentioned overlap and intertwine.

17 Belli, "La violencia obstétrica," 32; Tinoco Zamudio, "Propuesta," 49.

18 Again, it is worth emphasizing that abortion is illegal in most parts of Mexico. State laws are not as extreme as those in Nicaragua and generally allow for therapeutic abortion in order to save the mother's life; nevertheless, as long as interruption of pregnancy is not a legal option, giving birth, whether by cesarean or natural delivery, cannot be considered a choice.

19 A "second round" of screenings in various locations in 2019, again with discussions and the presence of midwives and advocates, points to *La primera sonrisa*'s impact both as a film and as a teaching tool.

20 Castro and Erveti, "25 años," 39–40.

12

"We Insist on This Project of Life"

A Conversation with Loira Limbal

Maria Cabrera

Loira Limbal is an Afro-Dominican filmmaker, DJ, and the senior vice president of programs at Firelight Media, a nonprofit documentary production company that supports the making of films by and about communities of color. *Through the Night* (2020), her latest feature documentary, is an intimate look at the running of a twenty-four-hour daycare in New Rochelle, New York. Working from their home, Deloris and Patrick Hogan, known by the children as Nunu and Pop Pop, have run Dee's Tots Daycare for twenty years while raising their own family. Welcoming children to their warm and joyfully decorated home at all hours, the two work tirelessly, providing a safe haven for children of different ages and their parents. While depicting the thoughtful embrace Nunu and her partner provide for those that walk through their door, the documentary also illuminates the load carried by caregivers, particularly those who are Black and/or Latin American, as parents work longer hours to provide for their families and, notably, to afford childcare. The stories of two single mothers and their children are also included, revealing the difficult realities they face balancing multiple jobs and minimal healthcare, emphasizing the tremendous support Nunu's daycare gives them.

I feel grateful for the opportunity to have had a virtual conversation with Loira about her film, which I watched during quarantine on my small computer screen. The film touched me deeply, revealing and reflecting back to me a lot of questions and answers I had as I went through doula training and started to look back at my family and the essential role my aunties, cousins, and neighbors played in shaping who I am. Talking to Loira was equally clarifying. Here she generously discusses the making of the film, the role of caregiving, and what we can learn about mothering in its many forms, as well as how caregiving can gift us with valuable strategies and perspectives that can significantly shift our lives and creative work.

MC: I saw that you have another event today as well this interview. So it's a full day.

LL: It is. These days have all been pretty full. And I have my kids here too: my seven-year-old and nine-year-old in virtual school right now.

MC: Thank you so much for taking time to do this interview. I saw your film at Blackstar [Film Festival, at 2020's virtual edition] and just absolutely loved it. I stayed up till 1 a.m. to watch it because of the time difference [between the United States and the United Kingdom].

LL: Oh my goodness!

MC: I was so glad that I saw it because I currently work in film education, and I'm training to be a doula, so it was something that's of massive interest to me; and I'm Latin American as well. It showed a lot of things that I haven't really seen represented. To start: I read that you heard about Deloris through a mothers' group.

LL: I'm part of an online group, and someone posted an article in the group about their daycare. So that's how I came to know about them. At the time my own children were in daycare—although my children were going to a daycare with standard hours, 8 a.m. to 6 p.m. I work a full-time job, but it's office hours, so I work 9 to 5. But when I read the article it did make me think about my childhood because my mother was a home health aide and worked the night shift while we were growing up, and so a lot of the stories in the article made me think of my mother and our childhood.

MC: Was the article specifically about how long the hours were, or was it general coverage of the daycare?

LL: The article called it the rise of extreme childcare or the rise of extreme daycare. It was looking at precisely the fact that people in the U.S. now have to work multiple jobs to make ends meet, or they have to work on nonstandard hours. In light of that, it was posing a question of who takes care after people's children, looking at labor and the economy from that lens.

MC: What I found most interesting was how you managed to depict Deloris doing so much labor, emotional and physical, but at the same time you weren't positioning her as a victim—neither her nor her partner. Sometimes you grow up with these kinds of caregivers, and you don't see them that way. It's just, this is what they do—which is also slightly problematic. But I was wondering how you achieved that?

LL: I am completely obsessed by what I regard as a really kind of stubborn and subversive and radical commitment to life by Black and brown women, particularly working-class women. . . . There's this ethos that we have adopted in our society that literally works us to the bone and disrespects us and disregards us and dismisses us and invisibilizes us, and yet still: we insist on this project of life, and nurturing and caregiving. So that for me is something that I'm really enthralled with and by, and something I want to explore.

That's how I see us, so I think the film is very much just a reflection of that gaze, which is my gaze, because I'm looking at Deloris, Shanona, Marisol in the film, but I'm looking at my mother, I'm looking at my neighbor, I'm looking at my co-madre, I'm looking at my sister, who is also the childcare provider for my kids, who is also the woman who works at the supermarket, who is also the nurse that I come to at 2 a.m. when my child has a 104-degree fever. These are the women that keep our communities alive in the face of societies that try to do the opposite with us. I see this work as work that's been invisibilized by society, but it's a shortcoming of society. It's a flaw in society that people are not able to read—see, perceive, behold—this ingenuity.

And for me that definitely means not reducing anyone to either a victim or a martyr. I think both ends of that spectrum are super problematic and reduce people's lives to two-dimensional flattened pictures or portrayals, and I do think I'm very aware that, particularly within nonfiction, most of the films about our lives are about a social issue. And there's the common phrase of putting a human face on a social problem, and so you tell a character-driven story to illuminate some sort of social issue. I understand the practice and I understand the concept, but I am troubled by the fact that when you look cumulatively at the body of work that exists about us, it really does limit us to the things that ail and kill us.

So then our bodies become synonymous with that problem that needs to be fixed in society, as opposed to portrayals of our lives that also just include our humanity: our everyday sorrows

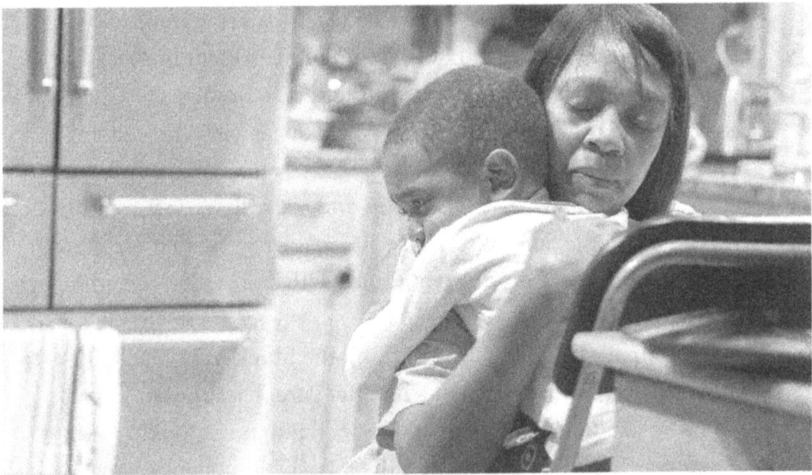

Nunu holding a child in *Through the Night* (Loira Limbal, 2020).

and our joys, our triumphs, our victories, our failures, our shortcomings, the things that we're unsure about, are insecure about. Just the complexity of what it is to be human. We don't have the benefit of many films that do that. And so I went into it thinking about all of those things. I know for a fact, because these are my people, that no one there is just the victim or just the hero or just a martyr; they're all of those things, and so, so much more.

MC: The film took a long time to make, right? It was four years of filming. How did you feel filming in the daycare because, for me, I think it would have been very emotional and also stressful seeing someone extending themselves in such a way. How did you feel as a filmmaker in that space?

LL: It was actually really emotional at times because we developed relationships, and I deeply care about Nunu, Patrick, their family, the children, the daycare, the mothers who I spent time with. We got to know each other. Obviously they shared the things that you see on the camera, but they also shared a lot more that I chose not to include in the film—and I shared a lot of myself with them. The experience of making this film has been an experience of creating this two-way mirror, where everyone that's been involved is able to reflect on their own lives through seeing or witnessing the lives of others that are part of this collaboration.

That was the case for me, watching Shanona and her exhaustion and the dilemma of having a good career. She's a pediatric ER nurse; that's a good, honorable, important career. It's one that she chose, it's one that she likes, and it's still very hard to parent as a single mother. You're exhausted and at times you feel guilty, and you are very unsure if you're doing things right or if you're giving your children enough. The weight of that as a mother is huge because I think there's perhaps nothing more harmful or insulting that you can say to a woman who is a mother than to call her a bad mother. So you're walking around physically exhausted and depleted and drained, because our economy requires that kind of labor under those conditions, but emotionally as well, because on top of the physical, we have the nerve to then judge women, to question them and critique them at every turn. That's something I constantly experience myself. So there were ways in which I was trying to make sense of my own experience through bearing witness to their experience.

I think that's something that has happened for everyone that was involved. The crew was an all-women of color team that worked on the film, and many people had stories of feeling reflected because their mothers worked really hard and struggled with childcare. One of our camerapeople, her mother used to run a daycare out of their house, and she worked as her mother's right hand when she came home from school. Everybody had this very intimate, personal connection to the story: just being able to reflect on their relationship with their mother, or look at their mother's motherhood differently because of being part

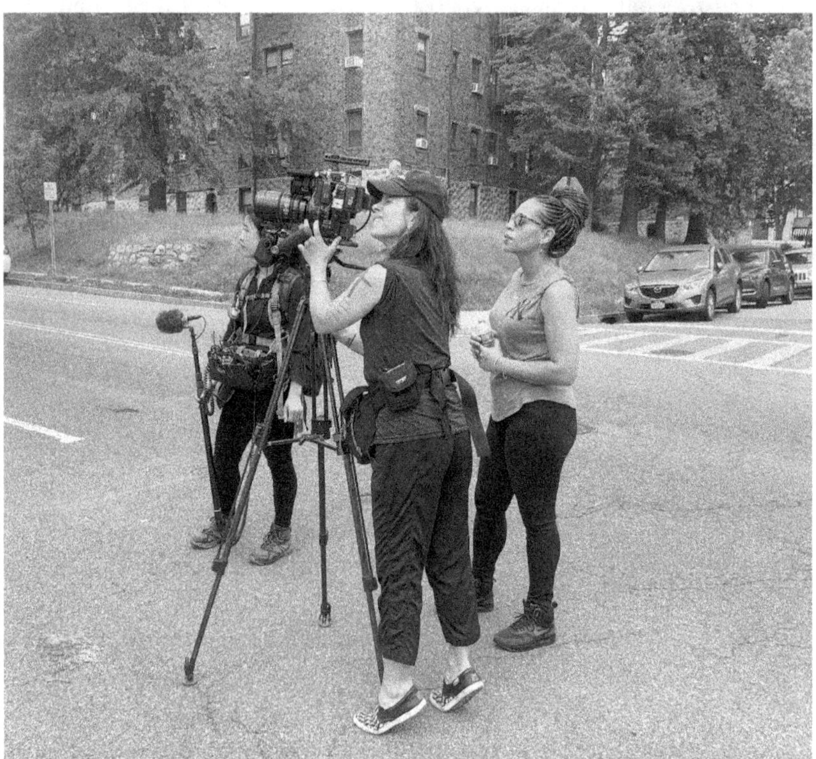

Loira Limbal and her crew at work in New Rochelle, New York.

of this experience. That, of course, is vulnerable and emotional and very raw, so that's sort of what it felt like a lot of the time that we were there.

At the same time, it was everyone's happy place because the love and warmth that comes across on the screen—that was not constructed by us. That is truly what it feels like at their daycare. And it feels like that for children and adults alike, and it felt like that for us as a film crew. It is very much like this sanctuary and safety for everyone that steps in there.

MC: It feels so special. Some of the bits that really stood out for me were really small moments, like when Marisol would come in the evening to pick up her children and Deloris would pat her on the back, as if saying, "You know, it's okay." There's this mothering of mothers and this continued support; I recognize that within my own family and the support the women have given each other. Also Marisol's daughter: I loved watching her. I felt like you could just see what it meant to have this place, and how it also made her appreciate her mother as well.

LL: Hearing you talk about the support within your family, there's this way that motherhood, mothering is such a huge part of the human experience, whether you're a biological parent or not. This work of mothering is such a critical part of the human experience. Because it's work that is gendered and associated with the feminine, it gets treated in the same way that everything that is associated with the feminine does. On the one hand we have these symbolic gestures of it mattering, like Mother's Day, all this symbolism that is completely devoid of any kind of structural support that people actually need in order to live with dignity and health and safety, and to be able to fulfill their full potential. We do the opposite: we penalize women and we make it nearly impossible to live a life of dignity, particularly if you are navigating the experience of mothering as a woman of color, as a poor woman, as a working-class woman.

The only people that take care of us are other people like us. It's this work that happens and it's completely left to the individual, and society and the government takes no responsibility for providing anything that mothers need. At least in the U.S. context; I won't assume that it's the same everywhere, but that's pretty much what it feels like here. It's like, "Yeah, you do this work, it's the most important work in the world, but we're gonna make it hard as hell and make it impossible for you to actually do the things that we want to celebrate you for, but we want to kill you in the process." It's such a huge contradiction. In a moment like this, with COVID-19, you're seeing, one, that caregiving is the work that makes all the work possible. And two, that the work that keeps the society functioning is, in the U.S., by and large performed by low-wage workers who are women of color. And three, that there's predictions now in the U.S. that an entire generation of women are going to fall out of the workplace. Because of the demands of caring for children and schooling in a pandemic, women are leaving the workforce left and right.

It's completely unsustainable. It was unsustainable before. The brunt of that burden is shouldered by our communities, but it is a problem for everyone. It doesn't work for anyone. I think there's no recovery without taking these issues into account. There's no way forward post-pandemic if we don't deal with these issues.

MC: What has it been like to bring the film to audiences during this moment?

LL: The premiere was set to be at Tribeca Film Festival this year [2020] in April. That was the first big festival scheduled to happen post-quarantine, and it got postponed. So we've done everything virtually, which is not at all the vision or the hope. This is definitely a film that I was really looking forward to sharing in community with folks. It's been interesting. I think the film, for the people that do see it, resonates; the response has been really positive.

Part of me was initially very panicked about: What now? I spent four years working on this and now the world has been turned upside down. But I've settled into having a sense of surrender and having faith that the film will do what it needs to do in the world. Ultimately, I hope that it can serve as a balm, as a bit of medicine and a love offering, a love letter to the women that it is about, and to the women that I made it thinking about. I also hope that it can be used by movements that are working to improve the material lives of these communities. I think that those things hopefully can still happen, it just has to look very different than we were accustomed to. But now I'm in a place of surrender: having faith and surrendering, and believing that we will form a community and create connection and meaning in whatever ways we can.

MC: With a lot of my friends, Black and/or Latin American, we've been talking a lot about how there was this initial panic when the pandemic started, but for us, this is the work of community we do all the time, looking after each other. We don't even think about it.

LL: Mutual aid, right? Well, that's how we've survived, because there has been an ongoing apocalypse for our communities. This is not the first time we're here. I think a lot about that too with regards to New York City. I was raised in New York and my family came here when I was three. People are like, "Oh, this is the end of New York City. New York is not going to be able to recover." I grew up in Harlem and the Bronx during the height of the crack epidemic in New York City, which was a time of extreme devastation, and the people who couldn't leave or who wouldn't leave took that devastation and we created hip-hop. And we made New York City the place that everybody wants a part of. The city might be dead to those who were never really essential to the city to begin with, to the soul of the city, but for those of us that make the place what it is, we've been through devastation before. The optimist part of me is like, we'll create something amazing out of this.

But I'm scared. I battle the optimism and the pessimism, because things are very, very bleak right now on multiple fronts and levels. We've lost so many people already, and a lot of our folks are not going to make it, and we're going to lose more people. It's hard trying to hold to both those things at the same time. I go between taking a little bit of comfort, and wanting to just be like, "Look, we've been telling y'all. I told you so. You kept thinking that because Obama was president, something had fundamentally changed." Meanwhile we know that the day-to-day life and lived reality of our communities is really harsh, but y'all were not listening to us when we were saying it. And now you're like, "Oh, we weren't listening, now we get it." The petty part of me wants to get on a soapbox and say, "I told you so, I told you so, I told you so."

But the mother in me, the pragmatist and the advocate and activist in me, is like, "No, this is an opportunity." This is a moment when people are forming analysis. It's an opportunity to help shape that analysis, and bring to light the things that have been ignored to date, and hopefully use this moment to shift consciousness and to move the needle on some of these structures and systems that wreak havoc in our lives.

MC: I saw on the website for the film that you have a campaign and an ongoing commitment to uplifting organizations and movements and groups that are uplifting all types of caregivers.[1] You said it is the work that will shape our futures. I want to discuss a bit more about you as an artist who is prioritizing mothering in your work and in your whole life—because obviously being an artist is part of your life. What have you learned about yourself through the process of making the film? And is there's anything you've reevaluated about your practice?

LL: I learned a lot about myself in the process of making the film. I think the first thing that comes to mind is just how symbiotic my experience of mothering has been to my experience of creating. I would have all these stretches of time when I would get into a good groove on the home front: things are going well with the kids and they're growing and maturing, or demonstrating things that, for me, signal that they're healthy, they're doing well. So that would be happening on the home front, and that would always mirror or parallel something similar happening with the film. Then similarly, when things got really hard with the film, oftentimes things would be rocky on the home front.

Sometimes I got advice from my kids about the film that was really critical. And sometimes I got advice from Nunu or Marisol that was really critical for the home front. So I feel like there is, for me, a real parallel between the way that both creative work and mothering require you to show up fully, warts and all. There's nowhere to hide. When it comes to your kids, it's not social media, it's not your day job, it's not someone you're dating; there's no way to hide any parts of yourself in motherhood. The exercise of mothering requires that you confront some of your shadows, or confront the skeletons in your closet, or confront the things that you're really struggling with or trying to work on. Mothering does that constantly: it forces you to face yourself in a way that very few other relationships in life, at least in my life, have required me to. I think the same is true about filmmaking. There is that James Baldwin quote that says—I'm paraphrasing, but it's something along the lines of—all good art is a form of confession.[2]

Good art, or art that is resonant and moving and compelling, is that, is if you are vulnerable and if you are willing to confront not just others in the world but yourself, your biggest flaws, your biggest fears, and your biggest doubts. You have to do that in motherhood. I felt like whenever I was doing that on the home front, it was like an exercise to gain muscles. I moved up from a three-pound weight to a five-pound weight. And that five-pound weight that I gained at home, I can use in this situation, in navigating this relationship or in quieting the demons in my own head to figure out a way forward when my fear was threatening to paralyze me.

That was a revelation for me, because I had only thought about motherhood and filmmaking up until I worked on this film as things that were not compatible, as things that were in competition with each other. It's harsh, but I think in my head, some part of me had bought into the idea that being a mother is a liability to being an artist. In this process, I have found that the opposite is actually true. I think that what is a liability to being an artist in the body that I reside in in this world is being Black, is being from the community I'm from, is being a woman. Those are the liabilities; it's not anything inherent to motherhood. And those very same things are a liability to being a mother. That's probably my biggest epiphany.

Then there were a couple of other things that are quieter, but were equally earth-shattering for me. Along the way, I landed on the idea of tenderness as an aesthetic, wanting to create visual language that captures and depicts what tenderness looks and feels like, wanting to show that and convey that. So I was consumed and having conversations with my DP and my editor about how to do that, trying this and trying that, then just being really fierce, saying I just want some kind of tenderness and some ease and some rest for Nunu and Shanona and Marisol because they're working so hard. Probably towards the end of the process, something clicked for me in realizing that if I believe that they are all worthy of tenderness and ease, then I'm no different, and I'm also worthy of those things, which I don't necessarily— That was a big shift for me. I'm worthy of that too, but why did that never occur to me before? That continues to have some ripple effects in how I'm living my life.

When we finished the score of the film, it's delicate and very airy and very tender. Sometimes it has ranges and you feel fear, doubt, trepidation, remorse, or joy, but overall it stays in a tender space. When we finished it, I was like, "Oh my god, I am capable of this kind of tenderness," which I had also not seen in myself in that way. I think in an interesting way it is all related to having grown up in the Bronx, poor, as the oldest child of a working single mother, where I, in many ways, was my mother's right hand and my mother's caregiver and definitely my siblings' caregiver. Things were rocky and so my role became to be a rock, to be of service to my mother. That's where I derived my self-esteem from, and my worthiness was from being able to be depended upon and helping my mother and protecting my mother. But that didn't leave a whole lot of space for some of my own needs, or for me to understand that I had needs as a child, or to articulate them. Not because my mother was saying, "No," but because there wasn't space. So these things around being worthy of tenderness and being capable of tenderness are real shifts in how I've gotten used to seeing myself, and that all came from this process of working on this film.

MC: This brings it back to the idea of the film as a mirror: for me, when watching the film, because I have the experience of seeing so many women in my family becoming ill or stressed and eventually burning out, it wasn't a surprise to see it happening. You would have had to recognize that in yourself in some way.

LL: In this whole process, one of the things that happened was my mother apologized to me. She said, looking back, "I can't believe I put you in that position," and she said, "I can't believe I did that to you and I'm sorry." Until she said it, I didn't even recognize it as something that was wrong or a kind of violence that happened in my childhood. I tried to deflect, to tell her, "No, Ma, I don't need you to apologize to me, you did the best that you could with what you had." My mother was and is an amazing mother, and we have a great relationship. And she insisted, and then I realized, "Okay, I have to let her apologize because this is something that *she* needs to do." But even as she first apologized, I was not in a place where I could accept it, because again I held on so strongly to this narrative of being my mother's protector, my mother's keeper and helper.

Then she did it, and then that also unleashed an opportunity for me to look back on the ways in which I was harmed as a child. Not because I'm seeking to blame her, but to acknowledge that in these conditions that we force women into they have to make impossible decisions. There has to be space for that: for her, for her to grieve that and to feel that. But there also needs to be space for the child in it; there has to be space for all of us, [to realize] that ultimately none of this stuff is our fault. It's not due to any individual shortcomings or flaws that we have as mothers or as families. It's structural and it happens. This is by design.

MC: I feel that deeply because I'm going through a similar process with my parents. You can acknowledge that it's no one's fault, but there's still the power of having your experience seen and recognized: that did happen; this wasn't imaginary. Did the apology come from her after watching the film, or was it in the process of making it?

LL: She watched some clips and then we started talking. I was telling her what prompted me, but I was saying it as a laundry list of things. Up until that point, if you had asked me, all of my childhood trauma was related to the fact that my father abandoned us. There was no childhood trauma related to anything to do with my mother; my mother was perfect—a saint, even. Even in all her flaws, she did the best she could, so she was beyond reproach in my mind. Then watching some of the footage, and us talking, and me being like, "When I heard about this, it made me remember when I was nine . . ." She sat down and took it in, and then two days later sent me two audio messages on WhatsApp, and I called her right away, like, "What are you talking about? No!" Then it unleashed this whole process: like you're saying, you have to be able to acknowledge that this did happen. Not to seek who to blame but to be able to heal, because you can't heal that which you cannot face. It's what I hope happens for everybody. It's happened for me. I know that it has happened in multiple ways for Nunu and Marisol.

After she first watched it, Marisol's first comment was, "Wow, I really didn't know my value. But now I do." She was talking about the job interview scene, that was the first thing that she thought about. And then Nunu recently said, "Thank you for letting me see myself." I hope that happens for other people that watch the film as well.

MC: That's beautiful, and I'm really glad that all these things were able to happen, because sometimes everyone is so busy that you end up not having these conversations at all, but they're so transformative. And going back to what you said about your mom, that you were like, "No, it wasn't traumatic!" It's testament to your mother, and to maybe other caregivers, that you had that. It makes me think about how maybe Marisol's children, because they also had Nunu, were cared for and that's why mothering is so important—because it literally saves people.

I just really love this idea of tenderness, and it's so exactly what I think aesthetically about the film. Do you have anything that you're working on now or researching that you want to use to explore tenderness?

LL: I am working: I have two short film ideas and a feature idea. They're all really in early development. One of them is connected to *Through the Night*, and it's about the cycle of sacrificial care in the lives of women of color, and wanting to do more of an essay kind of film that is able to connect some historical dots to the present day. I think a lot about how today in the U.S.'s brand of capitalism, we demand that some people work so much that they're not able to even sleep. I draw a direct line between that and slavery, and the idea of slavery as stolen labor where rest was denied to people. There's this continuum that goes back to the very founding of the nation. And so I want to do an essay, a slightly more experimental film that connects those dots, from the nursemaid to the essential worker, if you will.

Then I have another, very different kind of film, also a short film, also more experimental, that I'm thinking about which is about looking at the traditional African spiritual practices in Cuba, Dominican Republic, and Puerto Rico as a point of connection between these three islands, and as this retention that, despite so much persecution, is still very alive and very dynamic and vibrant—then using that as a framework to feature the words, the ideas of some key Afro-Latinx leaders throughout time. I often think about the conversation about Blackness within Latinx spaces, and I think sometimes the conversation remains at a very 101 level: are Latinos Black, and can Black people be Latino? We kind of stay there, and there's all this other stuff that we need. I feel like part of the work of an artist is to create culture that helps shift imagination. I think in terms of cinema we have a real dearth of Afro-Latinx stories and we need a multiplicity of them, and so there are ideas in that space that I want to work on.

And then the feature is a feature documentary, which is also really early in development, about two mothers, one from the Dominican Republic, one from Jamaica. One of them works as a restaurant worker, and the other one as a hotel housekeeper in a resort town here in New York—in Montauk, New York. They basically split their year between home—their islands—and the "season," the vacation season here. That's a look at mothering across waters. It's also about labor again, but also immigration and how do you parent across borders, literally.

Notes

1 See the #CareForCaregivers campaign, *Through the Night*, accessed November 6, 2020, www.throughthenightfilm.com.

2 The original quotation is "All art is a kind of confession, more or less oblique. All artists, if they are to survive, are forced, at last, to tell the whole story; to vomit the anguish up." In Studs Terkel, "James Baldwin Discusses His Book, *Nobody Knows My Name: More Notes of a Native Son*," WFMT, broadcast July 15, 1963, studsterkel.wfmt.com/programs/james-baldwin-discusses-his-book-nobody-knows-my-name-more-notes-native-son, 00:47:39.

IV

Alternate Genealogies

13

From (An)other Mother

Maternal Genealogies and Experimental Film History

Elinor Cleghorn

If we are not to be accomplices in the murder of the mother we also need to assert that there is a genealogy of women.

—Luce Irigaray, *Body against Body: In Relation to the Mother*, 1980

In 1979, a group of British filmmakers, curators, and researchers, including Lis Rhodes, Annabel Nicolson, and Felicity Sparrow, co-authored a statement titled "Women and the Formal Film" for the exhibition catalogue of *Film as Film: Formal Experiment in Film, 1910–1975*, a major Arts Council-supported survey presented at London's Hayward Gallery. Rhodes, and later Nicolson, were the only women officially involved in the organizing committee. They wanted to create a collective space within the exhibition itself where women could come together to present their work, share personal histories, and discuss future projects. Rhodes and Nicolson invited Sparrow, their friend and collaborator, to participate with research that would form the basis of a feminist genealogy foregrounding the subjective experiences of women filmmakers from past to present. This project was a communal endeavor. Rhodes, Nicolson, and Sparrow also engaged their network of friends and colleagues, along with researchers working in the United States and Europe, to build a collection of original and translated archival statements by women who had been misrepresented, overlooked, and ignored in dominant scholarly and curatorial assessments of film history. But before the exhibition opened, the women decided to withhold their research and leave their gallery space empty. As they explain in "Women and the Formal Film," the exhibition committee continually disregarded their requests for more women to be involved and represented, stifled their ambitions for their gallery space, and undermined their organizational skills and intellectual rigor. "We made the decision not to carry on, not to continue working in a situation that was hostile and ultimately fruitless for the individual women involved," they write. "It is better that the historical research be published elsewhere and the work of contemporary women film-makers, artists and critics be presented in a context where they are valued."[1]

Throughout the 1970s, Rhodes and Nicolson were active filmmakers and important contributors to British independent film and video culture through their work with the London Filmmakers' Co-op. Film, for both women, was a resistant art form, a set of material, technological, perceptual, and intellectual possibilities for political intervention. They came to the organization of *Film as Film* as part of a wider community of artists, scholars, researchers, and curators emerging from the galvanic social energies of the women's movement who had been resituating film and video as a feminist technology since the early 1970s. The question of women artists' representation in institutional and pedagogical canons was crucially important to the formation of film feminism, both in Europe and the United States. *Film as Film* purported to be a cohesive assessment of "artisanal" modes of film production since 1910, yet it acknowledged the work of just eight women, some of whom were mentioned only in passing in the catalogue essays. Nicolson was invited to join only after Rhodes requested that more women be involved. By extending the authorship of their statement of withdrawal to the circle of women who had contributed with them behind the scenes, Rhodes and Nicolson asserted their objection to the exhibition's curatorial tokenism, while at the same time exemplifying that the broader project of film feminism was a social movement, forged through mutual participation, communal support and, crucially, multiple voices.

In her essay "Whose History?," included after "Women and the Formal Film" in the catalogue, Rhodes reflects on the version of history presented in the *Film as Film* exhibition. This version, underpinned by the broader "hierarchy of film history," is merely a "reconstruction of events," a pattern manipulated according to overarching critical and theoretical assumptions.[2]

And this history, which claims the contributions of only eight women and thus perpetuates the myth of scarcity, a history that positions women outside of its jurisdiction, in obscurity, in the margins, is not *her* history. The women film artists whose work was included in *Film as Film* were consigned to what Rhodes terms the "historicised past," their work enfolded into a system of definitions that, as she states, only serves to "testify" to their "exclusion" from the present.[3] In addition to Rhodes's essay and their joint statement of withdrawal, Rhodes, Nicolson, Sparrow, and their peers presented original writing by Alice Guy-Blaché, Germaine Dulac, and Maya Deren, three pioneering "historical" filmmakers whom they had intended to "re-present" in their gallery space. Dulac and Deren were featured elsewhere in the exhibition, but Guy-Blaché appeared only in a scant filmography in the catalogue. By offering these writings in the stead of direct participation, the women opened up a "different presentation of history" within the reductive constraints of *Film as Film*, "a history made by women about women."[4] In this history, *her* history, Guy-Blaché, Dulac, and Deren appear on their own terms, in their own words, as foremothers in a matrilineal genealogy where their art and influence is not buried in the past but renewed and validated in the present. As Rhodes writes, "History is not an isolated academic concern but the determining factor in making 'sense'—'nonsense'—of now."[5]

In 1978, the feminist film theorist Laura Mulvey gave a lecture titled "Film, Feminism and the Avant-Garde" as part of the series "Women in Literature" organized by the Oxford Women's Studies Committee, in which she reflected on the growing importance of film as a medium around which the creative and social consciousness of feminism was being questioned and explored. The women's movement provided the impetus, as Mulvey writes, for women involved in the making and exhibition of experimental films to examine the impact of oppressive cultural ideologies on their "past culture." Like Rhodes and Nicolson, Mulvey was speaking as both a filmmaker and a theorist, advocating for the construction of histories of women in film through the lens of feminism's urgent evaluation of the present and its hopes for the future. As Mulvey remarks with reference to her film *Riddles of the Sphinx*, made in 1977, the concerns of feminist filmmaking since the early years of the decade were predicated upon "a constant return to women, not indeed as a visual image, but as a subject of inquiry."[6] A growing counterculture within the "experimental sphere" of films made by women, for women provided, for the first time, a context in which women filmmakers of the past could be meaningfully recovered from historical obscurity. Filmmakers such as Deren and Dulac were of important interest to the project of film feminism because of their acknowledged association with the so-called avant-garde, the intense period of nonindustrial film experimentation that began in Europe in the 1920s and migrated to the United States in the 1940s. These artists were part of the "tradition" with which Mulvey, Rhodes, and Nicolson aligned their own work; yet under the eyes of "male chroniclers" of the avant-garde, the extent of their contributions was diminished, and the resonance of their films was ignored by the limited scope of patriarchal analysis. As Rhodes writes, this "is the history that defines the present, the pattern that confirms and restricts our position and activities."[7] Re-presented as formative enunciations of a feminist "interior consciousness," as Mulvey puts it, filmmakers like Deren and Dulac were recovered in histories created by women, for women, about women: histories that enmeshed the past with the present and thus prioritized, above all else, the political and subjective experiences of existing in the world as a woman.[8]

In the late 1980s, queer and feminist theorist of film and media Teresa de Lauretis introduced the term "symbolic mother" to describe "a guiding concept of feminist practice [that] . . . permits the exchange between women across generations and the sharing of knowledge and desire across differences."[9] For de Lauretis, feminist history making necessitates the creation of genealogies of women untethered to patriarchal structures of lineage and descent. This intentional statement on how to *do* feminist history guided my ambitions in 2008, while I was in the early stages of formulating my PhD project. I was focusing on three female filmmakers, working experimentally across the first fifty years of cinema, who were interested in dance, movement, and choreography: Deren, Lotte Reiniger, and Loie Fuller. I didn't have a background in film studies, but I had learned from my undergraduate and master's degrees in art history to be innately suspicious of the terms of women artists' inclusion in extant theoretical histories. I wanted to present a robust argument for bringing these artists together as examples of the significance of women's technical and aesthetic innovations in experimental film to the history of cinema. Each of these women appear to a greater or lesser extent in accounts of key movements in the history of experimental film: Fuller in proto-cinema and the cinema of attractions in Paris in the late nineteenth century; Reiniger in Weimar animation in 1920s Berlin; and Deren in the New York avant-garde of the 1940s and 1950s. So, I combed the indices of the canon, trying in vain to meaningfully accommodate Fuller's pre-cinematic dance spectacles, Reiniger's flat fantasies of shadow and silhouette, and Deren's choreographic exploration of ritual and dream within what Rhodes calls the "acceptable facts" of history.

My PhD supervisor, who had been taught by Rhodes at the Slade School of Art in the early 2000s, suggested that I look into her research into women's film history, principally because she had engaged with Deren's films and writings. In Rhodes's and her peers' statements I found, for the first time in my academic life, an articulation of women's filmmaking that resonated beyond my scholarly interests and spoke to my experience as a woman. They gave me permission to question the "relevance and authority" of the terms imposed by male critics and historians and affirmed my intuitive sense that what was important about Fuller, Reiniger, and Deren was being hidden from me. They valorized my need to collapse the impersonal stance and critical distance deemed necessary for "proper" academic work and get as close to my subjects as possible. They taught me that I could foreground my own subjectivity in my research and write about how the work of these artists made me *feel*. And, most crucially, they showed me that *doing* film history from a feminist perspective meant addressing not only everything that male-authored history disavowed, but also all that it simply couldn't contain. In "Women and the Formal Film," the authors explain that they included writings by Dulac and Deren in order to "relocate their work within the context of their own concerns, giving it a complexity and fullness that the 'Film as Film' exhibition denied by excluding."[10] This sentence was a complete revelation to me. History-with-a-capital-H gave me nothing to connect Fuller, Reiniger, and Deren other than a generational chronology and the "fact" that they were all women. But these artists were intimately, subjectively *concerned* with dance and choreography. By bringing them together in a matrilineal genealogy of dance/filmmaking, I could create a history that prioritized the context in which each woman made her work, but that also situated those artists in what de Lauretis termed a "symbolic community."[11]

Rhodes et al. re-presented Deren, Dulac, and Guy-Blaché in *Film and Film* as part of their "symbolic community." As de Lauretis explains, genealogies of women are "generated, and indeed en-gendered" through "feminist practices of reference and address."[12] The women's choice of texts enabled Deren, Dulac, and Guy-Blaché to be represented in the exhibition in the context of their own concerns. Their writings were made available because of the research labors of women working elsewhere, in Europe and the United States, who were also "conserving their own histories, creating their own sources of information."[13] The extract from Deren's notebook of 1947, an account of her experience of possession in Haiti, and her "statement of principles" from 1946 were provided by Catrina Neiman, Francine Bailey Price, Millicent Hodson, and VèVè Clark, a collective of women working across different disciplines at the University of California, Berkeley. Since 1973, they had been working toward *The Legend of Maya Deren*, a documentary biography drawn from the collection of Deren's personal materials donated by her mother to an archive of "notable figures" housed at Boston University's Mugar Memorial Library. *The Legend* began with the intense work of cataloguing a vast "confusion of boxes and papers," a labor that ensured Deren's life and work were archivally available for generations of scholars.[14]

A translation by Sparrow and Claudine Nicolson of Dulac's essay "Du sentiment à la ligne," her articulation of cinematic form, rhythm, and movement first published in the journal *Schemas* in 1927, was accompanied by an unpublished article titled "Germaine Who?" by Ester Carla de Miro, an Italian professor of cinema who had been researching Dulac for several years. De Miro explores how Dulac's feminism, activated through her participation as a journalist in the early 1900s at *La française*, one of the first feminist magazines, was expressed through her formal and aesthetic experiments with film as the "ideal vehicle for the full realisation of the female spirit" in all its complexity: sensitive, poetic, active, and self-affirming.[15] Guy-Blaché's article "Women's Place in Photoplay Production," originally published in *Moving Picture World* in 1914, attends to the suitability of women working in film direction and production, and addresses the societal and misogynistic obstacles encountered by women trying to enter such a male-dominated industry. Sparrow found Guy-Blaché's article during her research, when she also translated a report from Guy-Blaché's biography that was originally written for a publication proposed by Leon Gaumont, head of the Gaumont film company, detailing the technical innovations she made while working as the company's head of production between 1896 and 1906.

As Rhodes writes, dominant ideology "predetermines information and its availability." Historical theses such as those enforced by *Film as Film* largely privilege a system of values codified by male promulgators of film culture and criticism, through whose theoretical "terms" certain filmmakers and works have accrued pedagogical and institutional legitimacy over time.

The women's decision to withhold their labors from the exhibition but to assert them in the catalogue was a gesture of insistence upon the enduring visibility and availability of information about women's filmmaking, writing, and research. Film, materially speaking, is a precious medium, and the economies of film conservation, distribution, and exhibition can be restrictive. Writings, on the other hand, can circulate democratically. The feminist genealogy presented by Rhodes et al. exemplified the importance of not only stating the existence of women filmmakers from the past but of positioning them within de Lauretis's "symbolic community," a community that emerges through the citational acknowledgment of multiple genealogies of feminist research labor. As de Lauretis writes, the "feminist practices" underpinning the methodologies of genealogies of women depend upon "the reading or re-reading of women's writing, taking other women's words, thoughts, knowledges, and insights as a frame of reference for one's analyses, understanding, and self-definition; and trusting them to provide a symbolic mediation between oneself and others, one's subjectivity and the world."[16]

I interpreted "Whose History?" as a call to arms and a generous invitation. I came to film feminism forty years later, one of the symbolic daughters Rhodes hoped would go on to "discuss and describe our histories, in our own ways, on our own terms."[17] *Her* history needed me, not to reiterate her ambitions but to attest to their continued relevance in the present, my present. I decided to structure the methodology of my thesis according to the context of Rhodes's concerns. I made the decision to cite only female-identifying scholars, researchers, and artists and to prioritize the writings of Fuller, Reiniger, and Deren in my interpretations and analyses. I learned quickly that film feminism is, in itself, an act of mothering. Resituating the neglected women of film's history as "symbolic mothers" in genealogies of women entails *work*.

In 2004, in a special issue of the cultural journal *Signs* dedicated to recent approaches in film feminism, feminist film historian Patrice Petro addressed the trend among scholars of my generation to turn toward early histories of women in film and cinema. Referencing the introduction by fellow film historian Jennifer M. Bean to *A Feminist Reader in Early Cinema*, a volume she co-edited in 2002, Petro writes that feminist "work on early cinema is an act of historical retrieval and recovery."[18] My own motivations, like Bean's, arose from what Mulvey described as "a fascination with the unspoken history of women."[19] But I would argue, forty years later, that feminist scholars also seek to situate themselves in a community with our "symbolic mothers" by continuing and expanding their efforts to insist upon, and fight for, the enduring relevance of our histories, the significance of our thoughts, and the validity of our existence as speaking subjects, as speaking women. Film feminism, for me, is a means of activating and exploring the genealogy of our contemporary feminism, of honoring the maternal legacy undergirding our capacity to intervene, and expressing our freedom to determine who we are and how we think.

It's no coincidence that my academic feminist consciousness was raised when I became a mother for the first time. My eldest son was born at the end of my first year of PhD study. I always planned to be an academic, but I didn't plan to be a mother. My own mother, a socialist second-waver, made the decision to raise me alone, and for the first six years of my life it was just us. There's a space in my mind where the memories of my earliest years of life are protected. I can recall with perfect clarity the feeling of sharing a Victorian wrought-iron bed with my mother, of her reading to me every night and stroking my arm until I fell asleep. I often wake up with a start from a recurring dream where I'm plonked into the steel and leather seat perched on the back of her antique Pashley bicycle. My mother didn't make films or write about them, but she was empowered to parent me on her own, the way she wished to as a woman, by the collective conversations of the women's movement. De Lauretis remarks that feminism's basic assumption is that it is "historically constituted in the present."[20] Rhodes, Mulvey, and other leading figures in film feminism are of my mother's generation; becoming part of their "symbolic community" was as important to my determination of my identity as a mother as it was to my academic ambitions.

My son was born with two parents, into a vision of socially appropriate heteronormativity that had been alien to me as a child. My husband is, and always has been, a genuine ally, a feminist in deed, not merely word, who shared the labors of raising our first and second sons equally, with pride and love and not a shade of resentment. I am exceptionally lucky. But the notion that mothering—parenting—belonged to the intimate, desiring, queer space between mother and daughter was part of my identity, inscribed in me from birth when my own mother gathered all the strength she had left and pushed me into life. Reading, rereading, and writing from the enunciations of film feminism made in the late 1970s enabled me to inhabit a kernel of my selfhood that resisted the constraints and polite presentation of the "nuclear" family. My symbolic mothers had constructed feminist genealogies that aligned with the *version* of motherhood that shaped who I am, that pulse through my blood and cells. Motherhood, to me, isn't a state-determined role decided by a biological imperative and defined by its relation to men. If I was to be a mother, I had to be free to determine my identity through *production*, not *reproduction*. In my research and writing I could "discover and construct" the symbolic mother-daughter relationship that de Lauretis identifies as integral to genealogies of women, relationships that "extend beyond the natural and domestic to enable an alliance, a social contract."[21]

In an interview with feminist art historian Griselda Pollock in 2010 about the "role of the feminine in maternal subjectivity and the role of the mother in culture," Mulvey explains how important the question of motherhood was to the women's movement in preempting "the more abstract questions and principles of feminism."[22]

> Motherhood was central to this debate first of all as specific to the female body and female experience—parenting was almost exclusively divided by gender in those days. But there was also a "topography" of motherhood: it occupied a space, the domestic, enclosed, interior space of the home that existed in binary opposition to the public space of social and political discourse as well as male work across all classes. Metonymically, this interior, the isolation of women's work within the restricted and defined space of the home, led to the interiority of the maternal "mentality" associated with sentiment and suffering, that feminine feeling that existed, once again, in binary opposition to masculine rationality. From a practical point of view, one of the first questions that emerged was how to challenge the isolation of domestic space and the isolation of domestic labour? How political organisation should and could involve collectivity and women working together?[23]

Writing my PhD was made possible not in spite of but because of my becoming a mother. And it had nothing to do with the old adage *If you want something done, ask a mother*. I wasn't able to write like I used to, through the night in a semi-delirious fugue. I couldn't participate in the social scene of talks and events and screenings. My swift grasp of concepts softened with my ligaments, my deft ideas loosened with my limbs. But my body was no longer separated from my mind. I did much of my early thesis writing with one hand, the other clasped around my baby's tiny tree frog body. I went for walks along the seafront with him strapped to my chest in a sling, and the weight of him expanded my thoughts. I read books and essays and watched films as he suckled at my breasts, oxytocin swelling as Deren plunged into the sea, Reiniger articulated the uncanny tenderness she felt for the silhouette figures she made, Fuller described the sensation of extending the energy of her muscles into her immense projections-screen costumes. I was interested in how each of these artists exemplified dance as a particular "tendency" among women filmmakers, as Mulvey identified in 1978.[24]

But through my mothering body I was beginning to understand that dance, for these women, wasn't merely an aesthetic or formal conceit, or an articulation of some essentially "feminine" sensibility. Dance, as feminist film historian Antonia Lant writes in her edited volume *Red Velvet Seat: Women's Writing from the First Fifty Years of Cinema*, "was a form of expression residing in the body."[25] I started to think about dance and choreography as symbolic of the embodied labor of filmmaking, where films came into being through the specificities of individual female bodily experience, not as some affective transcendent ideal but as exhaustion and pain, close-looking and desiring, trembling and trying and yearning toward the creation of something *else*. As Luce Irigaray wrote in 1980 in a discussion of the necessity of genealogies of women, "It is crucial that we keep our bodies even as we bring them out of silence and servitude. . . . Let us try to situate ourselves within that female genealogy so that we can win and hold on to our identity. Let us not forget, moreover, that we already have a history, that certain women, despite all cultural obstacles, have made their mark upon history and all too often have been forgotten by us."[26]

Throughout the history of women's experimental filmmaking, economic necessity and social duty have inevitably tied women artists to their domestic spaces. As a site of production, the home has constituted the locus of feminine and feminist invention and innovation since the earliest decades of cinema. Fuller's garden studio and laboratory rivaled that of Edison. Reiniger created an entire genre of film animation at her home studio *tricktisch* ("trick-table"), a glass table lit from underneath from which she shot the frame-by-frame movements of her flat figures made of cardboard or soft lead. From her tricktisch, Reinger extended the traditionally feminine craft of *scherenschnitte* ("scissor cutting") from the privacy of the parlor to the public space of projection. Deren's apartment, on Morton Street in Manhattan's West Village, served as her editing studio, exhibition venue, and shooting location throughout the late 1940s and 1950s. When experimental and independent cinema became consolidated in the 1950s, many female artists retreated into domestic space as both a resource for filmmaking and a mode of subjective enquiry. In *Points of Resistance: Women, Power & Politics in the New York Avant-garde Cinema, 1943–71*, feminist film historian Lauren Rabinowitz situates the home as a sort of symbol of the familial relations structuring emergent experimental film culture in New York. As Rabinowitz puts it, the female members of the avant-garde film community "outwardly opposed the dominant ideology of the 1950s" in their artistic and activist practices, yet their social positions within that community were nonetheless constrained by "social subordination."[27] For women hindered by the lack of access and recognition afforded to their male peers, the home was essential not only to the practical *making* of film, but to the investigation, through film, of what it meant to inhabit the world as a woman.

From the home, women artists revolutionized the postwar filmic landscape. Yet the relegation of women's work to the homespun sphere of inherently "feminine" crafts and tasks has historically trivialized its value and significance. The women's movement "reoriented," as Mulvey puts it, the isolated, invisible labors of maternal servitude into the social, political, and public discourse of art and film. The nurturing responsibilities associated with making homes and sustaining lives were being conceived of as the locus of interior and collective consciousness-raising, as having a value and significance entirely separate from that enclosed by the patriarchy. From the mid-1960s, artists including the American filmmaker and painter Marie Menken and the Canadian filmmaker and multimedia artist Joyce Wieland drew upon the social and spatial constraints of women's domestic roles in their radical expressions of female labor, subjective perception, and embodied experience. Wieland, who came to filmmaking after years of making art that utilized and enlarged "women's" domestic craft skills, could not afford to have her own studio when she married the painter and later structural filmmaker Michael Snow in 1956. She made her film *Water Sark* in 1965 at her kitchen table. Filming through glasses of water and magnifying lenses to create a choreographic vision of feminized domestic space as a "site of feminine self-discovery," Wieland performed, as she put it, "the high art of the housewife."[28] For the American filmmaker and activist Marjorie Keller in the 1970s and the Swedish filmmaker Gunvor Nelson, who began making films in 1965, the transformative temporal and motile capabilities of film enabled powerful meditations on the social and psychical implications of motherhood and the work of mothering.

In 1977, Mulvey's *Riddles of the Sphinx*, an experimental feature directed with her husband, theorist and filmmaker Peter Wollen, eschewed narrative conventions to depict the specifically feminist psychical negotiations with domesticity and motherhood. Discussing *Riddles* with Pollock, Mulvey reflects on the way that the aesthetic and temporal languages made possible in film enabled explorations of the "riddle" of motherhood as the "absolute centre of social and individual experience but somehow undervalued and relegated to the cultural margins." Experimental film practice, as she explains, questioned "how motherhood could be articulated within a culture that defined itself by excluding the maternal. . . . Intuitively, at the time, it felt as though this might begin to be possible through a gradual evolution of elusive images, almost lost memories, half articulated words and phrases and so on. Something like that."[29]

For Rhodes, like Mulvey, feminist filmmaking and research interrogated the predominant ideology that annexed feminine and maternal labors to a separate sphere of cultural production. The role allocated to her as the only woman originally included on the organizing committee of *Film as Film* was to "take care" of the overtly masculine bias both on the committee and in the exhibition. But as curators and researchers Lina Džuverović and Irene Revell write in their essay on feminist curation and its histories, "We Falter with Feminist Conviction," Rhodes "diffracted" the maternal role assigned to her and multiplied "the question of representation at the very first turn."[30] By refuting tokenistic participation and sharing the productive labor of curation and research among her friends and peers, Rhodes retransmitted the caring role assigned to her *as* a woman, transferring her energies from solo servitude within an overtly masculine representational structure to the collective coalition of her real and symbolic communities. Rhodes initiated a matrilineal genealogy as an activist intervention within *Film as Film*. But through her insistence upon making visible the *work* that it takes to present a different version of history, and the collective graft of "retrieval and recovery" necessary to reinstate women filmmakers from historical margins, she instigated a genealogy of women's filmic labor from the early twentieth century to the present. Guy-Blaché, Dulac, and Deren all helped formulate complex questions of what it meant not only to make films as women but to live *as* women in the face of social, political, and cultural opposition. They made films that can be viewed and read as articulations of female embodiment and lived experience, sure, but they also *labored* to create conditions in which women could become producers of films and subjects of discourse in their own right, on their own terms.

The *Film as Film* collective transmitted the impulse of their research into Circles, a distribution organization dedicated to promoting and supporting women's filmmaking. Circles ran from 1979 as the only feminist distributor of experimental films in the United Kingdom. In 1992, when its funding from the British Film Institute (BFI) was cut, the organization merged with Cinema of Women, a distribution network focused on the intersection of filmmaking and the activist concerns of the women's movement, to form Cinenova. Over the last twenty-five years, Cinenova has developed into a volunteer-run charity that continues to preserve and distribute contemporary and archival feminist film and video work as well as stage exhibitions and events that bring the conditions of feminist distribution practices into public discussion. This genealogy of feminist film distribution in the United Kingdom was initiated by the recognition that women's work requires a separate approach: not only to methods of production and modes of exhibition but to the presentation of its history. Reflecting on the formation of Circles, Rhodes writes, "Circles was based on consensus and a mutual support network of discussion and practical help which redressed the hierarchies which had marginalised many women filmmakers in other film production and distribution models."[31] By presenting films by historically obscured artists such as Deren in the context of contemporary feminist concerns, Rhodes et al. initiated the "rehabilitation" of women's filmmaking from the margins of a History that threatened its obfuscation.

The queer feminist film scholar B. Ruby Rich, in her 1998 book *Chick Flicks: Theories and Memories of the Feminist Film Movement*, describes the way that women artists have been manipulated into and out of the canon of film history as "Derenesque bury-the-mother-maneuvers."[32] Deren is indeed the paradigmatic buried mother. Her status as "The Mother of the Avant-Garde," assigned to her by male peers (maybe Hollis Frampton, maybe Stan Brakhage, probably the poet James Broughton) after she died in 1961, has been deemed by feminist scholars a dubious honorific. As Rich observes, the theoretical definitions and historiographic assessments of New York-based avant-garde film practice of the 1940s and 1950s that appeared in the early 1970s by critics and journalists, including P. Adams Sitney and Parker Tyler, were predicated upon a scramble to "masculinize" the tradition of New American Cinema that followed in the 1960s. In a memorial issue of the Cinema 16 journal *Filmwise*, edited by Sitney and published in 1962, Deren is raised into mythological motherhood by a chorus of male voices, including her peers Tyler, Brakhage, Rudolph Arnheim, and Willard Maas. The tributes and eulogies to "My Maya" and "Our Girl" diminish the value not only of her films but of her exhaustive efforts to structure and consolidate the conditions through which film art became a viable art form. When she died, Deren was running the Creative Film Foundation, an organization she founded, single-handedly from her apartment in 1956, to provide advocacy and generate funding for independent film artists. Since the early '50s, she had been working to unify the milieu of film-art makers, first with a film group predicated upon "mutual action and protection" by and between its members. Between 1953 and 1955, under Deren's guidance and leadership, the group evolved into the Film Artists' Society and then the Independent Film Makers Association. As Rabinowitz has shown, Deren not only provided a communal space for "hitherto isolated film artists" to come together; she developed and defined a "support structure for artistic practice" that foregrounded "production, distribution, and promotion."[33]

Deren's apartment was the nerve center of these organizations; she turned her own home over to her community as meeting place, office, screening room, and archive. Most of the *Filmwise* contributors either participated in or benefited from Deren's creative vision and administrative labors. But the emphasis in *Filmwise* is not on what Deren did but on what she *represented* to "us," those men who orbited around her. Her achievements are eclipsed by the authors' intimate familiarity with her, which they attempt to authenticate through anecdotes embellishing the more dramatic aspects of her persona. In doing so, they perform subtle and not so subtle vitiations of Deren's agency by amplifying her femininity to mythological proportions. She is memorialized variously as beloved goddess, vengeful harpy, gentle confidante, siren of artistic energies, mystic priestess and, of course, "The Mother of Us All."

In 2011, the year of the fiftieth anniversary of Deren's death, I found myself sitting on the couch in her old apartment, talking to the couple who lives there now. Somehow, I had managed to talk my way in. I had nearly finished writing my thesis. I'd spent days in Deren's archive at Boston University, combing through papers and journals and drafts and notebooks painstakingly catalogued by the women of *The Legend of Maya Deren*. I'd listened to tapes of Deren's interviews, lectures, music, and strange sounds transferred by Rich from delicate wire recordings in 1973. I was in the midst of organizing a season of educational and screening events to commemorate Deren's anniversary at the BFI, for which I'd invited women scholars, artists, researchers, and filmmakers to reflect on the impact her films, writings, and activism had on their own practice. I had curated a special program of films made by women associated with Circles and the London Film-maker's Co-op in the mid-1970s to examine how Deren was a symbolic mother: both a mentor in filmmaking and film-cultural activism, and a powerful formative interlocutor of the capacities of experimental film to enunciate feminist subjectivity. This was all made possible for me through feminist genealogical thinking, by the film feminists who, since before I was born, had labored to intervene within and disrupt the reductive constraints of patriarchal Histories.

Barbara Hammer, the pioneer of lesbian cinema who identified Deren as "mother," expressed in an interview in 1991 that her practice of watching and rewatching Deren's films and reading and rereading works by de Lauretis and Irigaray "sustains and propels me into a community of discourse." For Hammer, symbolic maternal identification with women who have been her "mother[s], mentor[s], progenitor[s]" through decades of filmmaking, research, reading, writing, and speaking creates "a genealogy of *survival*."[34]

By the time I submitted my thesis in autumn 2012, I had two children, sons, then aged three and five. When I tried to trace the genealogy of my own thinking over those five years, it formed into this tentacular map of names of filmmakers and researchers and scholars and activists but also of conversations, snatches of gossip, arguments, frustrations, sensations, laughter, and hot tears. All of this was folded into the blue hardbound book, trembling beneath the sentences and paragraphs I'd spent years drafting and polishing, fueled by my blood and milk and refusal to limit who I was, or how I thought. The examiners told me it was too much of a love letter. They told me I wasn't critically distanced enough, that my prose was prolix, my engagements with the films overly indulgent. But after two agonizing hours, the examiners returned their verdict. I passed the PhD. Though they "doubted the quality of the thesis," they had never experienced such an impassioned defense. For a while I was heartbroken, not because I had confronted criticism but because the labor I had invested in that work, the extent to which my sense of self had been determined and shaped by it, had been undermined by the same marginalizing ideologies I was striving to overcome. The thesis has remained at the back of the wardrobe ever since, but it also exists in the world, on a library shelf, as part of a "genealogy of *survival*." I've continued the conversations, the thoughts, the energies that my thesis engendered in the years since. Doing feminist histories through the creation and acknowledgment of maternal genealogies has become my vocation. I owe so much to my symbolic mothers. I hope I become one someday.

Notes

1 Lis Rhodes et al., "Women and the Formal Film," in *Film as Film: Formal Experiment in Film, 1910–1975*, exhibition catalogue (London: Hayward Gallery, 1979), 118.

2 Lis Rhodes, "Whose History?" in *Film as Film*, 119.

3 Rhodes, "Whose History?" 119.

4 Rhodes, "Whose History?" 119.

5 Rhodes, "Whose History?" 119.

6 Laura Mulvey, "Film, Feminism and the Avant-Garde" (1978), in *Visual and Other Pleasures*, 2nd ed. (London: Palgrave, 2009), 130.

7 Rhodes, "Whose History?" 119.

8 Mulvey, "Film, Feminism and the Avant-Garde," 118.

9 Teresa de Lauretis, "The Practice of Sexual Difference and Feminist Thought in Italy," in *Sexual Difference: A Theory of Socio-Symbolic Practice*, Milan Women's Bookstore Collective (Bloomington: Indiana University Press, 1990), 11.

10 Rhodes et al., "Women and the Formal Film," 118.

11 de Lauretis, "The Practice of Sexual Difference," 2.

12 de Lauretis, "The Practice of Sexual Difference," 2.

13 Rhodes, "Whose History?" 120.

14 VèVè Clark, Millicent Hodson, Catrina Neiman, and Francine Bailey Price, *The Legend of Maya Deren*, vol. 1, part 1: *Signatures (1917–42)* Anthology Film Archives/Film Culture (New York: Anthology Film Archives, 1984), xiv.

15 Ester Carla de Miro, "Germaine Who?" in *Film as Film*, 127.
16 de Lauretis, "The Practice of Sexual Difference," 2.
17 Rhodes, "Whose History?" 120.
18 Patrice Petro, "Reflections on Feminist Film Studies, Early and Late," *Signs* 30, no. 1 (2004): 1273. See Jennifer M. Bean and Diane Negra, eds., *A Feminist Reader in Early Cinema* (Durham, NC: Duke University Press, 2002).
19 Mulvey, "Film, Feminism and the Avant-Garde," 116.
20 de Lauretis, "The Practice of Sexual Difference," 19.
21 de Lauretis, "The Practice of Sexual Difference," 11.
22 Griselda Pollock and Laura Mulvey, "Laura Mulvey in Conversation with Griselda Pollock," *Studies in the Maternal* 2, no. 1 (2010): 1 (in PDF), www.mamsie.bbk.ac.uk/articles/abstract/10.16995/sim.101/.
23 Pollock and Mulvey, "Laura Mulvey in Conversation," 2 in PDF.
24 Mulvey, "Film, Feminism and the Avant-Garde," 117.
25 Antonia Lant, "Part Two: Introduction," in *Red Velvet Seat: Women's Writing from the First Fifty Years of Cinema*, ed. Antonia Lant with Ingrid Perez (London: Verso, 2006), 145.
26 Luce Irigaray, "Body against Body: In Relation to the Mother" (1980), in *Sexes and Genealogies*, trans. Gillian C. Gill (New York: Columbia University Press, 1993), 19.
27 Lauren Rabinowitz, *Points of Resistance: Women, Power & Politics in the New York Avant-garde Cinema, 1943–71* (Urbana: University of Illinois Press, 1991), 3.
28 Rabinowitz, *Points of Resistance*, 159.
29 Pollock and Mulvey, "Laura Mulvey in Conversation," 13.
30 Lina Džuverović and Irene Revell, "We Falter with Feminist Conviction," *On Curating* 29 (May 2016), www.on-curating.org/issue-29-reader/we-falter-with-feminist-conviction.html#.W87u49uZPow.
31 Lis Rhodes, statement on the history of Circles, LUX Online, accessed August 6, 2020, www.luxonline.org.uk/histories/1970-1979/circles.html.
32 B. Ruby Rich, *Chick Flicks: Theories and Memories of the Feminist Film Movement* (Durham, NC: Duke University Press, 1998), 282.
33 Rabinowitz, *Points of Resistance*, 80.
34 Barbara Hammer, "Interview: Barbara Hammer," *Art Papers*, September–October 1991, 3, https://barbarahammer.com//wp-content/uploads/2019/11/Interview-Julia-Hodges-1991.pdf.

14

Mother-Storyteller

Jules Arita Koostachin

I acknowledge that *we*, those who identify as Indigenous documentarians,* express ourselves from our *Ancestral* connection, homeland, social location, and also from a cultural position—we are claimed. Furthermore, I recognize that *we* define ourselves from an *ourstory*;† one that is weaved within a collective memory, a memory that links the past to the present, and the present to the future. What we speak to is in context, and for the most part positioned. As a cis Cree woman I speak from a distinct social location in regards to Indigenous *documemory*.‡ A few years ago I was in conversation with the late James Luna where I was reminded that stories also act as a memorial, a remembrance of our lives prior and perhaps even our pre-settler (for lack of a better word) ways of being. Throughout this chapter I will alternate between *documemory* and documentary; *documemory* captures the birth

* I respectfully acknowledge the work of Indigenous documentary storytellers and the impact of their work.

† Defining our stories as *ourstory* or as *theirstory* includes all members of community.

‡ In 2018, I met with the late artist James Luna, a Payómkawichum, Ipi, and Mexican American performance artist, photographer, and multimedia installation artist whose work is best known for challenging the ways in which conventional museum exhibitions depict Native Americans. We spoke about documentary, asking each other how to say the word in our Indigenous languages. We then discussed how documentary and memory were interconnected; we both realized that documentary is a means to capture our memories. In using the term *documemory*, I am honoring James. The teachings in our exchange will always be with me.

of memories—or memories yet to be. We as Indigenous documentarians carry an important role in community, and I would even go far as to argue that we, those who identify as IsKweWak documentarians, carry an inherent right to carry stories for the generations to come. We challenge the very core of colonialism just by telling our stories, strategically dismantling the colonial influence not only on our daily lives, but also on our families; we use story to remember who we are and to honor where we come from.* Even though colonial dams have diverted our streams of stories, our stories continue to carry agency and sustain our communal ideals, principles, and our well-being.

My position is one of an InNiNew IsKwew† mid-career filmmaker whose practice embodies my cultural teachings and lived experience. I also carry a herstory‡ of working within the arts sector, as well as in the field of social services where I worked closely with marginalized communities, and in some cases, specifically with Indigenous women and children fleeing from violence. My knowledge as a documentarian has also been informed by my InNiNeWak§ relations, who include my mother, a residential school warrior, and my Nanan (grandmother), whom I often refer to as my *medicine bundle*; both relationships have shaped my arts practice and the person I am today. I write this chapter against the backdrop of a life of working in the arts as a documentarian, and as the mother of four sons, and the bundle of narratives I share is deeply rooted within an intricately woven InNiNeWak belief system. My teachings advise me not to speak for others, but only to offer further insight into the significance of story, which I recognize as an act of *MooNaHaTihKaaSiWew*,¶ reclamation, resilience, and, of course, resurgence. Articulating Indigenous knowledge and ways of being from within the limitations of the English language is often a challenge—therefore, I carefully chose to use the word *unearth*.** In addition, I have chosen to use

* We are using the camera to remember for the next generations.

† IsKwew translates to MoshKeKo AsKi Cree woman.

‡ I identify as a cis woman; therefore I will use *herstory* to share my story.

§ InNiNeWak translates to people from the Ancestral lands of MoshKeKoWo AsKi.

¶ *MooNaHaTihKaaSiWew* translates to *Unearthing Spirit*—My PhD research focus.

** I am not a fluent InNiNiMoWin (Cree) speaker, so my mother gifts me with Cree words bundled with teachings.

spirit throughout this chapter, in hopes of honoring the essence and agency of our Indigenous stories. When referencing Indigenous story and identity, the word *unearth* symbolizes an action, and speaks to the belief that our stories are alive and with us; they are protected within our *Ancestral* lands known to many Indigenous people as Turtle Island, renamed by settlers (without our consent) the Americas.

Furthermore, I recognize that the English words *reclamation* and *resurgence* may potentially be read as though our *cultural ways of knowing* were conquered, but I have been taught otherwise: I have learned that the embers of our *Ancestral* stories have been reignited. Our cultural ways of knowing were and continue to be cared for and protected—we have always been active in our responsibility to story. We have always strategized, resisted, and most significantly, we have stayed connected. Regardless of the constructs of time, we connect through our ceremonies, relations, and our relationship to our stories. Over the years, I have come to embrace that our *truth* lives in *spirit*, and therefore, our *spirit* lives in our connections to each other, and to our ancient stories—also referred to as our *orality* in all its forms. My path as a documentarian has led me to a world of creating content, where I focus solely on stories that matter to me as an InNiNew IsKwew, and this journey has also led me to academia where, interestingly enough, I often struggle to find my voice. I am faced with many questions, and without getting into the complexities of identity politics, I am often left wondering about our positionality as it relates to the stories we share. Hence, my PhD dissertation "MooNaHaTihKaSiWew: Unearthing Spirit" explores the importance of following protocol, and declaring our relationships to the stories we tell as Indigenous documentarians.

As a *documemory* filmmaker, I understand documentary as a storytelling platform to be quite similar to the protocols in relation to orality. Also, *documemory* can be used as a tool, one that provides opportunity to intervene by piercing our own stories through the veil of colonial narratives. Once we collectively confront and dismantle misrepresentations, we have set things right. As a documentarian, I am intrigued by this notion of *documemory* because it allows me the opportunity to share stories that are important to my community and to me, not only as an IsKwew but also as a caretaker—I want my children to remember who they are, always. As a mother-storyteller, utilizing documentary as a storytelling platform has proven to be manageable and accessible—I can have my children with me as I work. It is a creative avenue that ensures that I am true to my family, my community, and myself. My family have always been a part of my documentary practice; they are, for the most part, with me on set helping me tell the story. I have had my children support me in several capacities: operating the camera, assisting production, and even supporting me with administrative tasks. I was raised by my grandparents, who sustained themselves by living off the land. We as a family supported each other, and we, my siblings and I, learned of their skills by observing them while they worked, and so—*Why would it be any different for me as a mother-storyteller, and for my children?* I am sharing the skills I have acquired with my own children, and they, in turn, are learning the importance of Indigenous documentary protocols, practices, and approaches.

Again, it is also important to stress that when referencing protocol I am also speaking to our positionality, as our relationship to story is an integral part of Indigenous storytelling. My position as a mother-storyteller most definitely guides how I would like my children to become part of my practice.* My work teaches them about the significance of incorporating Indigenous methodology into their own artistic expression, whatever that may be; it also informs them about respect, accountability, and responsibility to our stories. Being a *documemory* storyteller with family responsibilities has been more than challenging, and it has even forced me to be more innovative in my approach to documentary. All through my career, I have dealt with financial challenges, time constraints, and, as other women have experienced, even discrimination. I have been overlooked because of my family responsibilities. Being made to feel invisible as an InNiNew IsKwew with children comes with the territory; unfortunately, we as caregivers must often sacrifice time with our families to work in the industry. We have become experts at strategizing.† If we are still creating content despite all the barriers, I argue, we have found creative ways to make it work for us. If there are more of us in key creative roles, the industry will be forced to change and become more inclusive for people with families—we make the rules as the key creatives

* My arts practice is a huge part of who I am as a person. The stories I share are important to me, and so I want my children to be part of that experience and to understand the importance of following protocol.

† There are times when artists without children have questioned why I chose to have a family and work in this field; this is awkward because I am uncertain how to respond. My children inspire my work, and I create for them.

on projects. Take, for example, my narrative short *OChiSkwaCho* (2018): although it was a small production, I ensured that there was money allotted in the budget for childcare—for myself and other caregivers working on my film. I understand the barriers, and I know very well what needs to occur for me to be able to work comfortably; we have a long way to go for meaningful change to transpire, but there is hope. I have owned my own production company since 2010, VisJuelles Productions, Inc. Although it is just me for now—as producer, writer, and director, I hold all the key creative roles, which is significant—it means that I create opportunity and support for others. We all need to start somewhere, and sometimes we need to do it ourselves. We are the experts in our own lives, so we are well aware of the disparity that exists in our fields, and what needs to change.

I recognize that there are talented trailblazers across Turtle Island, other IsKweWak filmmakers who are capable of changing perspectives and, in some cases, legislation. There is one individual whom I feel it is important to acknowledge; customary practice suggests that I pay tribute and my respects to her role as an Indigenous documentarian. Through my academic research, I have learned of an Inuk woman named Nancy Columbia, one whose very existence challenges the *his-story* of documentary practice. Sadly, the stories of her are few and far between; there are few accolades surrounding her contribution to the documentary movement. Based on my own research, it seems that Columbia surpassed the legendary Robert Flaherty, otherwise known as the architect of documentary. Flaherty was documented as the very first documentary filmmaker with *Nanook of the North* in 1922; remarkably, Columbia's work predated his by eleven years. Columbia wrote the treatment and starred in, perhaps, the very first documentary: *The Way of the Eskimo* in 1911. Both Columbia and her mother participated in a well-established troupe of Labradorean Inuit performers.[1] Historians assert that Columbia stared into the camera lens right from childhood; she was born into the human exhibit, and astonishingly, she never diverted her eyes from the colonial gaze. According to Kenn Harper, *The Way of the Eskimo* "was the first Inuit-written and Inuit-cast film ever made, ninety years before . . . *Atanarjuat*, the previous claimant to this honor. Eleven years before Robert Flaherty's ground breaking work in *Nanook of the North* brought Inuit to mainstream audiences, Nancy Columbia appeared on screen in a film that she had written."[2]

Although the film is unavailable, I was able to locate a brief synopsis, which describes an unsettling *romantic* affair between a white settler and an

Inuk woman. Based on the synopsis, I imagine that Columbia operated from a set of cultural ideas, artistic values, and conceptions of what she considered to be relevant at the time. Columbia's understanding of Inuit life may be understood as complicated due to the fact that she spent her young life in a human exhibit under the scrutiny of whiteness. Conceivably, being so far from her *Ancestral* lands, she weaved together narratives of her own understandings of Inuit identity, rooted in the gathered knowledge shared with her by her colleagues. Columbia, an arts practitioner herself, acquired her language, narratives, and survival skills; seemingly, her affiliates contributed to her understanding of Inuit life rooted in their own experiences, supporting her understandings of Inuit identity. Though that identity can be seen as possibly skewed by performativity, I would argue that it was informed by her homelands through memory and orality (regardless of place), that she did indeed derive her culture from her *Ancestral* lands. Through these reenactments of cultural practices in front of a white audience, she was at the very least exposed to memories of home—through the collective memory of her stage family. Columbia embodies an Inuit narrative: her very *being* carried the knowledge of her people, and in essence she was a collector of story through the art of performance. Regrettably, her life was severely impacted by and subject to the colonial gaze. Nonetheless, not unlike Flaherty, she set the parameters of her story line; the difference between the two is that Columbia was an Inuk woman in the position of authority, the documentarian. She was in a position of *power*, actively negotiating with settler paradigms and their notions of her *truth*. Undeniably, she had a comprehensive understanding of the entertainment industry; she might have foreseen the benefits of her filmic intervention, employing a tool that she perhaps recognized as a method to better inform on Inuit life.

Long after the last human exhibit, documentary continued to be relevant for Indigenous peoples; communities with similar experiences shared a collective interest. Documentary as a tool conjures a response, doing away with biased Western beliefs, particularly as it pertains to the telling of Indigenous story. Scholar Mary Norris reminds us that IsKweWak hold the role of *knowledge* keepers, and they also play a key role in the revitalization of culture: "Women have generally been viewed as the traditional keepers of their languages and cultures, customs, and Indigenous knowledge."[3] Indeed, IsKweWak have taken to producing sociopolitically charged works, documentaries that work to sustain cultural knowledge systems. All the while, their stories continue to replace Western constructs with an alter*native* account of what it is to be Indigenous.

Our practice is rooted in *ourstories*, the bloodline of story flows through the words and visions of IsKweWak. In 2012, I wrote and directed *PLACEnta*, a short documentary regarding birthing ceremonies; the film was a personal story about my experience of being severed from my rights as an InNiNew mother. I filmed my journey attempting to locate an appropriate place to conduct an InNiNeWak placenta ceremony. *PLACEnta* captured the interruption of culture, knowledge transmission, and family. Since its release, the film has been traveling, crossing international borders, sparking necessary dialogue in regard to the importance of restoring and sustaining our birthing ceremonies.

Documentary by IsKweWak is recognized as a mode of transmitting knowledge, one that is in constant motion, mobilizing community into action. *PLACEnta* has created a pathway for caregivers like myself, both Indigenous and non-Indigenous to speak out. We as IsKweWak documentarians have adopted a digital approach for its capacity to travel through time and space—reaching far beyond the present with the hopes of connecting with our descendants—our children's children.* In a way, through *PLACEnta* I am hoping to connect with the next generations of mothers through my personal story of reclamation. Documentaries like *PLACEnta* strategically communicate the complexity and resiliency that exist to this day, as is the case with several of my other films, which discuss an array of issues, from language revitalization to land-based learning, family, wellness, and ceremony. Indeed, colonialism has disrupted our documentary practices, yet IsKweWak,† such as Alanis Obomsawin, Tasha Hubbard, Loretta Todd, and several others, have respectfully embraced their role as documentarians in community—and all have established a space to share, examine, and honor the diverse lived experiences of Indigenous people.

In terms of creating content that relates to Indigenous lived experience, my documentary practice has fueled my drive to produce work that reflects my own reality. I have found ways to include my children, and in doing so have guaranteed the completion of my productions because they

* All children of our communities.

† IsKweWak translates to Cree women, but for me, it refers to those who identify as Indigenous women.

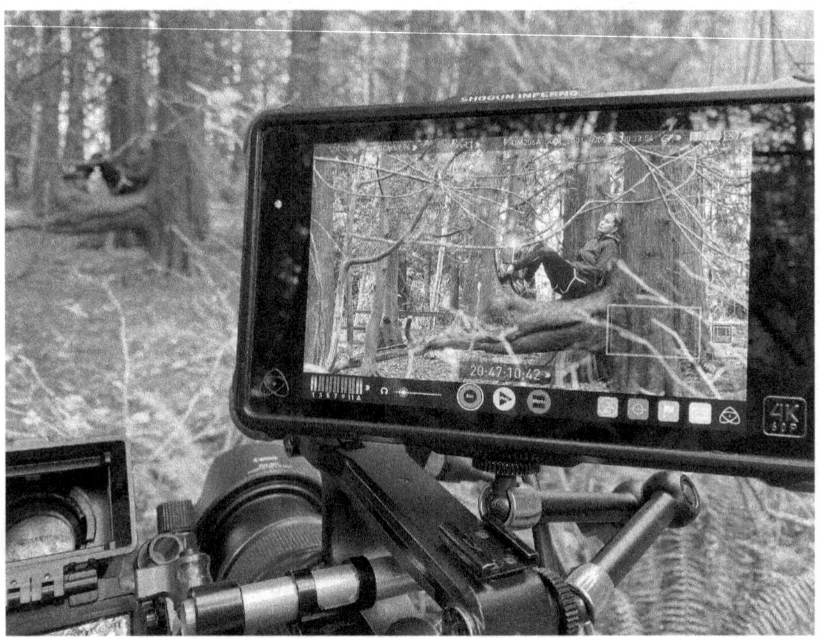

Shooting *KaYaMenTa: Sharing Truths about Menopause* (Jules Koostachin, 2020).

are with me, not taking me away from my work—*they are an integral part of my practice*. My family has been included in all my films thus far, from my first documentary feature, *Remembering Inninimowin* (2010), to other projects such as *PLACEnta* (2012), *Without Words* (2015), *AskiBOYZ* (2016), *NiiSoTeWak* (2017), *Butterfly Monument: A Tribute to Shannen Koostachin* (2017), *OshKiKiShiKaw* (2019), and my recent *KaYaMenTa: Sharing Truths about Menopause* (2020).

The stories we tell offer entirely new responses, doing away with discriminatory colonial ideologies. The stories behind my documentaries are weaved within this chapter to demonstrate that storytelling builds capacity within community, keeps our collective memories alive, shifts ways of thinking, and creates a platform for alter*native* approaches to storytelling. *Remembering Inninimowin* was produced while I was in graduate school,* and during production, I approached the filmic process strategically,

* The documentary was produced as part of the Ryerson University Documentary Media program (2008–10).

essentially as a business. Even though the school steered us away from full-length films, I knew that I needed to challenge myself, and so I did. It was not merely a student film; I understood *Remembering Inninimowin* as an opportunity to further my career. This film was not only my opportunity to highlight issues important to my home community of Attawapiskat First Nation, but also a way to showcase my skills as a documentarian. At the time, I had four young children at home, but I still managed to learn how to write, shoot, and edit—the memories associated with the documentary remind me of my journey that led me to today, and they also assure me that I still have a journey ahead. I am also cognizant of the responsibility I carry as an IsKwew mother-storyteller; at the time resources were limited, and I had to prove myself by working harder than my fellow students, but I stayed focused. After graduating in 2010, I was recognized with an Award of Distinction and a gold medal for my thesis work. Since then, I have gone on to produce more projects, such as a television series, media installations, narratives, and documentaries, all the while pursuing my PhD on Indigenous documentary.

I have learned over the years that our stories purposively counter mainstream notions of Indigeneity as transparent, simplistic, and superficial, replacing that representation with a profoundly complex denotation. As a mother-storyteller, my job in this lifetime is to ensure that our children have hope, and to achieve this, I need to work diligently. Adhering to cultural protocols is also necessary and interwoven within my methodology as a storyteller; I am obligated to honor the *spirit* within, the voices of the living as well as the ones from the *spirit* realm. My hope is that the stories I share honor our relationships, and more significantly, deepen our accountability and responsibility to the story itself. I want to support the storytelling platform for individual and collective (respectful) differences and, more importantly, connection.

In 2015, I produced a short documentary *Without Words*, which weaved together two heartfelt stories of resilience; I interviewed my mother, a residential school warrior, and my dear friend Pinchas Gutter, a Holocaust survivor. This *documemory* was a passion project, a story that needed to be told and remembered now, as they are both aging. For a very low (almost nonexistent) budget film, it has done quite well, and has been screened internationally. I applied the same protocols when sharing Pinchas's story as I did with my own mother's. *Without Words* is a story of cross-cultural healing;

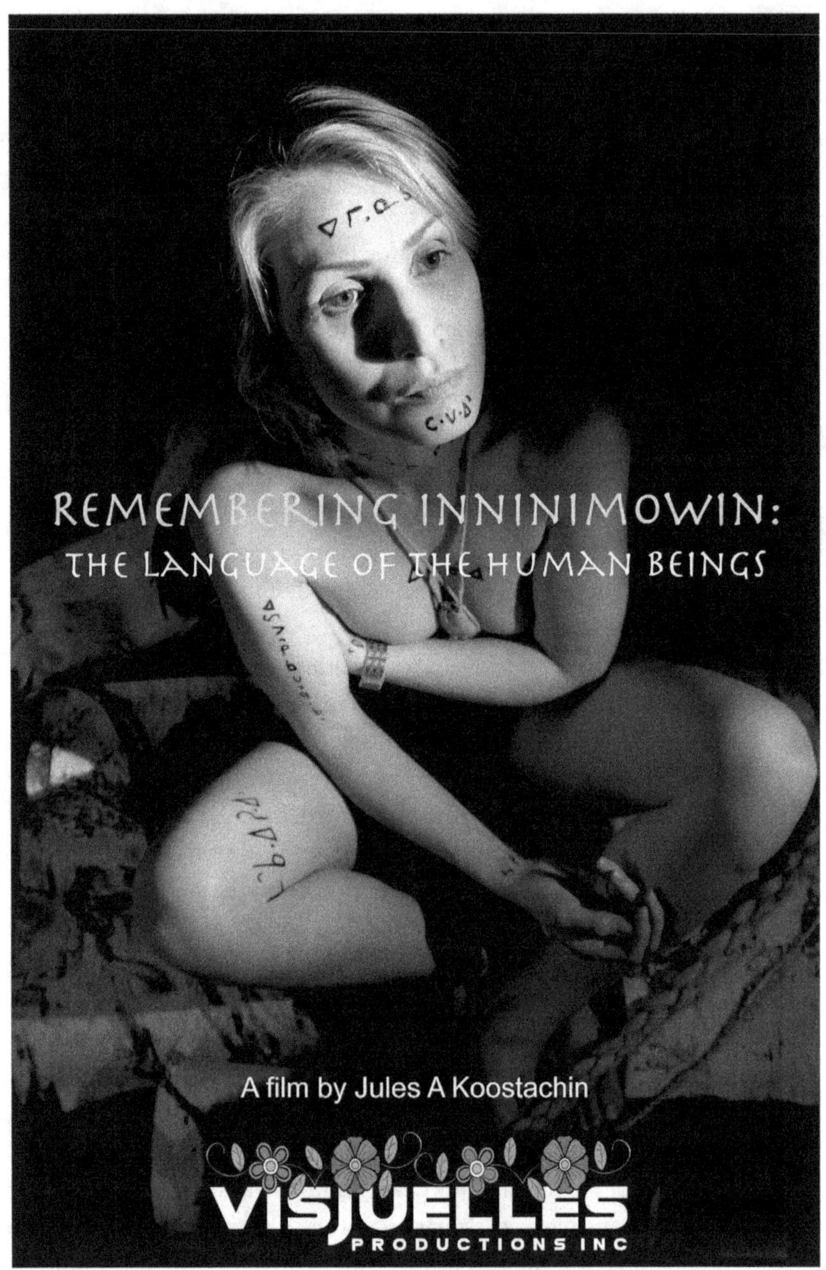

Poster for *Remembering Inninimowin* (Jules Koostachin, 2010).

therefore there are protocols in place to ensure the safeguarding of their stories. If other opportunities present themselves to me in terms of working with non-Indigenous stories, I would continue to follow methodologies and protocols, because my arts practice is an integral part of who I am as an InNiNew.

Based on my experience in the industry, and especially working with Indigenous story, I have witnessed that IsKweWak have had a long-standing herstory as active practitioners, as storytellers. Documentarians play a fundamental role in the creation of space wherein to explore Indigenous lived experience and positionality. Our responsibility is rooted in our relationships, community, and in our connection to all life-forms. Colonial representations of Indigeneity are detrimental; this oversimplified notion of Indigenous life is entrenched in a web of rhetorical colonial untruths, and so *we* continue to assert our narrative sovereignty. Nowadays, documentary is recognized for its varied approaches and methods; it has experienced an extraordinary shift in storytelling practices, as Corinn Columpar has argued.[4] We are transforming the injurious dominant perceptions of Indigenous identity by shedding light on important sociopolitical and cultural issues relevant to us as caregivers and community members. We have been exploring the varied aspects of documentary storytelling and will continue to do so—respectfully finding the best fit for our stories.

The 1960s were an interesting time for IsKweWak documentarians across all diverse forms of artistic, investigative, and observational expression. These filmmakers were integral in advantageously deploying pertinent and contemporary issues in the public sphere. Media scholar Michelle Raheja reminds us that Indigenous identity allows for profoundly different ideas of the self and community conveyed through multiple modes of expressions. She states, "The '60s is recognized as a transformational period in history especially for Indigenous peoples."[5] Overall the '60s were a pivotal time for Indigenous people as a whole, but especially for IsKweWak. Scholarship claims that fourth wave cinema supported the advancement of Indigenous filmmaking; for example, the National Film Board of Canada initiatives have provided opportunities for IsKweWak in documentary.[6] Indigenous documentary is at the core of cinema; Indigenous people moved from in front of the lens to key creative roles. Documentary became a means to reignite generations of viewers, highlighting the importance of self-representation, while moving beyond the figurative story of the alluring *other*.[7] As Edward

Said argues, "It is perfectly natural for the human mind to resist assault on it of untreated strangeness; therefore cultures have always been inclined to impose complete transformations on other cultures, receiving these other cultures not as they are but as, for the benefit of the receiver, the way they ought to be."[8] Perhaps settlers were comforted by these fixated fantasies of us as *other*, but there exists a beautiful mosaic of diversity that make up our Indigenous identities—we are not fixed or static, and never will be.

The '60s were a truly transformational time, as documentary became more available to Indigenous peoples, and it has proven to be a powerful vehicle for IsKweWak to speak out against injustice, gender disparities, and other inequalities.[9] Women reemerged from the margins of colonial society in full force and quickly became recognized as the *activists* and *advocates* for Indigenous rights.[10] As scholar Patricia Demers claims, IsKweWak are not monolithic, but they are influenced by various sociopolitical circumstances. Although IsKweWak are plagued with gender disparities, they are also concerned about the well-being of their whole communities. According to art director Roberta Smith, quoted by Demers, "Native activists [are] concerned with more than just female marginalization . . . fight[ing] for fishing, land, water, and treaty rights, and at the same time . . . [not wanting] to be called inferior because they are women."[11] Demers proposes that Indigenous activism renegotiates roles and values, demanding a response. Story warrior Alanis Obomsawin, working with the National Film Board of Canada, has ingeniously inserted herself into the role of narrator.[12] Documentaries by Obomsawin created a space for Indigenous representation and voice. In addition, scholar Carol Kalafatic pays tribute to the significant contributions made by other IsKweWak in documentary, such as Loretta Todd, Shelly Niro, and Christine Welch. Kalafatic states, "The films of these three women suggests that, unlike the 'primal scream,' our catharsis of expression should be a continuous activity, a way of life that should flow naturally with/from our legacy as storytellers."[13] Kalafatic explains that the *story* acts as a witness, becoming a testimony of truth that reclaims Indigeneity. IsKweWak are part of a continuum of artists who uphold their own distinct voice and who defend communities, land, family, and relationships. The camera became a tool for IsKweWak to carefully *unearth* stories, stories that support community wellness.

My television series *AskiBOYZ* (2016), and my first short, CBC documentary *NiiSoTeWak: Two Bodies, One Heart* (2017), are youth-oriented productions, acting as a form of resistance because I am replacing the colonial narrative with an Indigenous one. I had noticed that children like mine did not see themselves reflected on-screen, or if they did, Indigenous people were seen as a deficit. Therefore, I produced films that would change the mainstream narrative; my family and I were often disappointed by stories told about us, so I took action. As a mother-storyteller, I felt it was my inherent responsibility to create change with story—my stories are about futurity. At a recent screening in my home community, the youth were smiling and laughing while engaging with my work—I knew I was on the right path. If they could forget about their hardships for only a moment, I was doing my part to create meaningful change. Mind you, I also provide space for dialogue—I am open to discussing whatever the youth wish to share and always with support.

Documentary can be a means to restore, heal, and empower the *self*, as well as our collective selves. As feminist scholar Joyce Green stresses, "Colonialism is closely tied to racism and sexism. These twin phenomena exist in the context of colonial society, directed at Indigenous peoples, but they have also been internalized by some Indigenous political cultures in ways that are oppressive to Indigenous women."[14] Documentary by IsKweWak repairs the ruptures in our socio-political fabric, and also calls attention to inequalities. As an IsKwew myself, I work to ensure that those who are deeply impacted, for the most part children and youth in our communities, will be free from discrimination. My projects work to achieve wellness, balance, and narrative sovereignty through the act of documentary—hoping to sustain knowledge, cultural practices, and spiritual beliefs. These principles and values live in our storytelling methodologies, collaborative dialogues where we contribute to the storytelling process.[15] We are redefining ourselves through *documemory* and doing away with the colonial lens by replacing it with our own.[16] By sharing Indigenous narratives we are remaining in our position of *power*, continuing to care for stories and ensuring the roots are healthy.

Through my years of research I have come to appreciate that IsKweWak are instrumental in the creation of a necessary space—be it physical, spiritual, or mental—a space for Indigenous peoples to assemble, and a space to explore the fluidity of our identity. I have done this with my own productions. Scholars Elise Marubbio and Eric Buffalohead posit "both cinema of sovereignty and visual sovereignty as aspects of media sovereignty: the act of controlling the camera and refocusing the lens to promote Indigenous agency in the media process and in their own image construction."[17] Documentaries by IsKweWak not only challenge the *authoritative settler ideologies*, they also address the remnants of disempowerment and attempted erasure. In the act of decolonization, we are putting forth an *ourstory*, one that offers hope. As Raheja states, "Visual sovereignty simultaneously addresses the settler population by creating self-representations that interact with older stereotypes but also, more importantly, connects film production to larger aesthetic practices that work toward strengthening treaty claims and more traditional (although by no means static) modes of cultural understanding."[18] Documentary is the means to bring modes of cultural understanding to the forefront by examining our own collective responsibility inherent in our Indigenous rights. In the case of *Butterfly Monument: A Tribute to Shannen Koostachin* (2017), co-produced/written/directed by Rick Miller, we acknowledge the advocacy of my relation, a young Cree warrior who was only fifteen when she passed away.[19] She is most known for her activism, educating settler Canadians about the inequality and discrimination experienced by Indigenous youth and children. We understood the complexities and high emotions regarding her story, so we made sure the family was part of the decision-making process. We followed protocol by informing Shannen's immediate family of our intentions at every stage, both with the creation of the monument and with the *documemory* itself—we wanted to contribute to her legacy by documenting the story of her memorial. Scholar Kim Anderson writes, "In seeking out and listening to these stories, we engage in an act of decolonization; we engage in a way of imagining a stronger way of life, one which belongs to us because it comes from our peoples and our past."[20] By learning about the power of kinship through our stories, and through ideologies of reciprocity, we come to understand the foundation of our lived lives. Our stories arise from the diversity of our collective memories, which is constant and permanent.

Central to the *fluidity* of Indigenous identity—*being Indigenous*—we birth *ourstories*, and in doing so we speak against untruths. Feminist scholar Elizabeth Kalbfleisch states, "Reconciling a cultural identity bound in so many important ways to land and borders with notions of identity informed by contemporary cultural politics is an assiduous challenge."[21] The course of hegemonic negotiations is evident within documentary; documentaries by IsKweWak demand a response, insisting that viewers take part in a broad critical discourse regarding the impact of the colonial gaze. Anderson

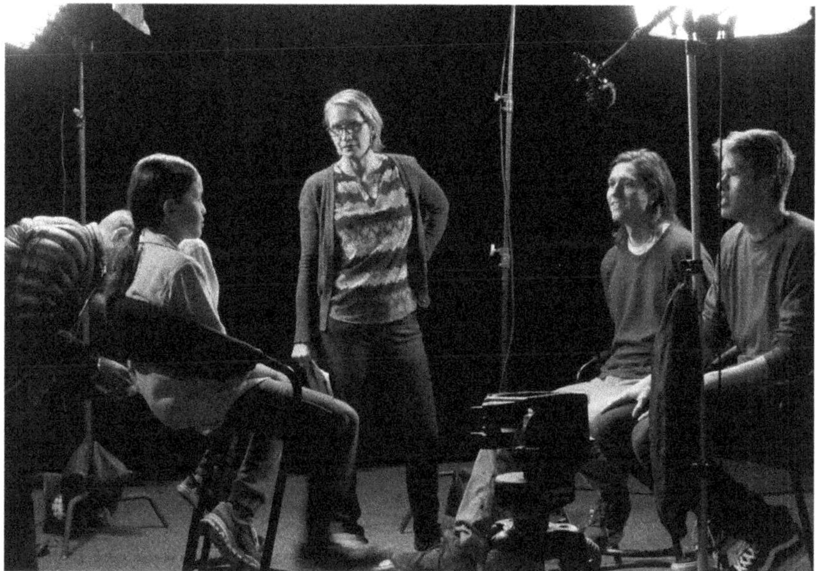

Working with family on *NiiSoTeWak* (Jules Koostachin, 2017).

stresses that creative expression is a means for healing and identity recovery; she argues, "Whether at the individual level or the national level, creative expression is essential for the recovery of our identity."[22] Artistic expression is the heart of survival and renewal; furthermore, it embodies how story can provide a way back to community and perhaps ceremony.

However, this is not to say that there are no documentarians who work in the mainstream or create apolitical narratives. My concern here is in regard to *documemories* that are culturally driven, employing discourse in relation to Indigeneity. I am not so much interested in cataloguing the growing community of documentarians and providing critical summaries of their films; this has already been done in the growing scholarship. I am more concerned with documentaries that inform, challenge, intervene, and entertain—with stories that pose critical questions. Unfortunately, Indigeneity through the colonial lens is often submerged in the language of *otherness*. Said asserts that there are links between culture and history, ones that bind us—*Indigenous and settler*—together. Transformation can occur if there is a real attempt to understand the past and the present; only then will we be able to imagine a future. He states, "We are beginning to learn that de-colonization was not the termination of imperial relationships but merely the extending of a geo-political web, which has been spinning since the Renaissance. The new media have the power to penetrate more deeply into a 'receiving' culture than any previous manifestation of Western technology."[23] Documentarians like myself exemplify this notion. Documentary is for the most part understood as *restorative*, working to mend the ruptures in the socio-political fabric by informing the *receiver of story* of an alter*native* reality. Producing narratives concerning our diverse realities from a place of knowing has created space for dialogue.

With the growth of Indigenous documentary, we are resuming our role as *guardians* of story. The editors of *Indigenous Women and Feminism* acknowledge the implication of culture as a means of intervention: "Culture has gained particular importance as it has confronted the silencing, marginalization, and invisibility of Indigenous women in patriarchal narratives and social practices."[24] Through documentary, there is a fundamental shift in how we actualize the *self*. We are also repositioning the *self*, moving past the narrative of resistance and colonialism. Commencing our narrative from the colonial void weakens our authority; it is imperative to acknowledge the prevailing threads of our own stories—*stories mended by spirit*—yet unfortunately, there are times when our stories are trapped within the colonial snare. According to Marubbio, "The perpetuation of the Indian in American iconography and cinematic representations results in an ambiguous relationship that is deeply connected with issues of race and colonialism."[25] Unearthing our *truths* reveals our ties to the past—*memory*—and the present; unearthing our stories allows for a future full of possibility. We are offering our story on our own terms.

We are dedicated to exposing national histories, such as in the socio-politically driven documentary films of Alanis Obomsawin; her documentaries challenge viewers, delivering and asserting filmic proof of inequality by adapting and changing documentary conventions. Scholar Zuzanna Pick claims Obomsawin inscribes her presence in her documentaries, all the while demystifying notions of the disinterested observer.[26] Obomsawin, in addition to many other Indigenous documentarians, upholds socio-political agendas in order to enact change. As media scholar Maeghan Pirie proposes, "Obomsawin uses film as a recuperative pedagogical force, in which film functions as a didactic intervention that confronts mainstream Canadian education's failure to account for its ongoing marginalization of First

Nations. This confrontation and re-visioning through film is a common theme throughout this filmmaker's repertoire."[27] Obomsawin's interviews become testimony: as Pick writes, "The interview in its testimonial form affectively anchors the relationship between Obomsawin and her social protagonist, between social protagonist and audiences."[28] Documentary engages in activism, strategizing and employing theory, and building upon Indigenous storytelling methodologies. Pick reminds us that Indigenous documentary places the protocol of documentary at the service of unorthodox methods of historical and ethnographic representation. Also, documentary deplores systemic racism and sexism by offering a collective agenda where narrative sovereignty can be achieved.

Storytellers are the *backbone* of community, shaping and defining the kinds of communities we *desire*, drawing upon the *vision* of the collective. Hence, documentary can also play a central role in producing revolutionary methods by doing so from a place of inherent responsibility. IsKweWak are shaping the documentary industry; we have been influential in exposing inequities, making room for Indigenous people to speak for themselves, and underscoring our experiences through *documemories*.

When producing documentary there is an obligation determined by our community to explore ways of expression, ensuring we are conscientious. Morally, collectors of story are obliged to warrant Indigenous methods and practices as part of the translation of oral stories into documentary, which, as Norris expresses, was particularly viewed as women's role.[29] I understand the implication of being left with only remnants of story, but I am still compelled—always with community approval—to mend the severed pieces. As Sto:lo scholar Jo-Ann Archibald claims, "The mystery, magic, and truth/respect/trust relationship between the speaker/storyteller and listener/reader may be brought to life on the printed page if the principles of the oral tradition are used."[30] I concur; the same principles are easily applied to documentary methods in terms of *listener/viewer*, and it is under this scope of communal agency where we as storytellers bring to light, determine, and unearth in order to reveal truthful filmic representation of Indigenous—*spirit*—identity. Thus, when investigating narratives, taking precaution is a necessary means of ensuring we are honoring the root of the story.

Through the practice of documentary, cultural ways of being are sustained through knowledge reciprocity of *storyteller/listener*. This exchange is embedded in the principles of ancient storytelling, especially as it relates to IsKweWak, who often carry the responsibility of storyteller. In this act of *unearthing* story, it is imperative that protocol is part of production. According to Catherine Martin, "This telling of story as a way to begin a healing process is one of the most powerful methods that I know to help begin a dialogue over what many have been silent about. The telling of story, from the perspective of those whose lives it impacted is vital to getting to heart of the story, to the truth."[31] I agree; breaking through the silences to uncover *truths* must be done with the upmost respect and consideration. I am often faced with stories of trauma, as in the case with my documentaries *Remembering Inninimowin* and *Without Words*, and so building trust becomes critical in my approach.

To return to the beginning, our identities as Indigenous peoples have been devastated by colonialism, but in honoring my teachings through the platform of *documemory*, I am exposing the fault lines of these ideologies by unveiling the deceptions. In doing so, a different way of thinking about Indigenous identity materializes. It is in Indigenous documentary that we are able to host dynamic subjects, thereby enabling us to realize different spaces from which we can speak freely. Kristin Dowell writes, "I define visual sovereignty as the articulation of Aboriginal peoples' distinctive cultural traditions, political status, and collective identities through aesthetic and cinematic means."[32] Our stories are not time capsules; they are still with us, providing us with a sense of *spirit* and a collective memory that transcends time and space. The disruptions of story experienced through the generations have undeniably obstructed the transmission of knowledge, yet we continue to assert *ourstories*.

In acknowledging our vast knowledge, we situate ourselves to better understand the impact of colonialism, all the while honoring our lives prior to contact. Narrative sovereignty has been unsettled through incessant acts, be they colonial discourses, gender inequality, systemic violence in the form of the Indian Act, treaties and legislation, or dislocation. Our sovereignty upholds our distinctiveness as Indigenous peoples—*human beings from these Ancestral lands*—and reaffirms our connection to this place. Scholar Jo-Ann Episkenew claims, "Holism also defines Indigenous communities in which a person is never really a singular, isolated individual . . . Indigenous people are part of a complex network of relationships that, when healthy, respect autonomy of the individual within the supportive environment of the group."[33] We have positioned ourselves as authorized creators of Indigenous epistemologies, and we are reclaiming our authority. Indigenous knowledge systems—*living in all of us*—are interwoven within the veins of sovereignty, and this includes the need to ensure the well-being of our emotional, spiritual, mental, and physical beings.

Over the decades, commencing with the work of Nancy Columbia and those of countless other documentarians, IsKweWak have *ourselves* utilized technology to assist in sustaining our fluid identities and, most importantly, our connection to ourstories. We as documentarians have revolutionized the platform by deconstructing mainstream constructs—*MooNaHaTihKaaSiWew*—and we have collectively *unearthed* the *spirits*, breathing life back into our story. We have recovered—*unearthed*—the position of *Knowledge Keeper* within our communities. Through the stories we choose to tell/share, we explore our diverse identities by respecting the strength and resiliency we carry within. We have established a platform to speak many *truths*, and in honoring ourselves, we also pay tribute to the stories that continue to feed our *Ancestors*, *spirits*, and future generations.

Filmography

AskiBOYZ. Directed by Jules Koostachin. Toronto: APTN, 2016.

Butterfly Monument: A Tribute to Shannen Koostachin. Directed by Jules Koostachin and Rick Miller. Toronto: V Tape Distribution. VisJuelles Productions, Inc., and Dragonfly Documentary, 2017.

KaYaMenTa: Sharing Truths about Menopause. Directed by Jules Koostachin. CBC Short Docs: VisJuelles Productions, Inc., 2020.

NiiSoTeWak: Two Bodies, One Heart. Directed by Jules Koostachin. CBC Short Docs: VisJuelles Productions, Inc., 2017.

OChiSkwaCho. Directed by Jules Koostachin. VisJuelles Productions, Inc., 2018.

OshKiKiShiKaw: A New Day. Directed by Jules Koostachin. CBC Short Docs: VisJuelles Productions, Inc., 2019.

PLACEnta. Directed by Jules Koostachin. Toronto: Commonwealth, 2012.

Remembering Inninimowin: The Language of the Human Beings. Directed by Jules Koostachin. Toronto: V Tape Distributions. VisJuelles Productions, Inc., 2010.

Without Words. Directed by Jules Koostachin. Toronto: V Tape Distribution. VisJuelles Productions, Inc. and Sharik Productions, 2015.

Notes

1 Paula Becker, "Miss Columbia Is Declared Queen of the Carnival at the Alaskan-Yukon-Pacific Exposition in Seattle on August 19, 1909," *History Link*, January 1, 2009, historylink.org/File/8881.

2 Kenn Harper, "Nancy Columbia: Inuit Star of Stage, Screen and Camera," *Above & Beyond: Canada's Artic Journal*, July 3, 2014, arcticjournal.ca/featured/nancy-columbia-inuit-star-of-stage-screen-and-camera/.

3 Mary Jane Norris, "The Role of First Nations Women in Language Continuity and Transition," in *Restoring the Balance: First Nations Women, Community, and Culture*, ed. Eric Guimond, Gail Guthrie Valaskakis, and Madeline Dion Stout (Winnipeg: University of Manitoba Press, 2009), 319.

4 Corinn Columpar, *Unsettling Sights: The Fourth World on Film* (Carbondale: Southern Illinois University Press, 2010), 69.

5 Michelle Raheja, *Reservation Reelism: Redfacing, Visual Sovereignty, and Representations of Native Americans in Film* (Lincoln: University of Nebraska Press, 2010), 107–8.

6 Stephen Foster and Mike Evans, "The Prince George Metis Elders Documentary Project: Matching Product with Process in New Forms of Documentary," in *Reverse Shots: Indigenous Film and Media in an International Context*, ed. Wendy Gay Pearson and Susan Knabe (North York: Wilfrid Laurier University Press, 2014), 221–32.

7 Lewis Randolph, *Alanis Obomsawin: The Vision of a Native Filmmaker* (Lincoln: University of Nebraska Press, 2006), 28–31.

8 Edward Said, *Culture and Imperialism* (New York: Knopf, 1993), 67.

9 Kristin Dowell, *Sovereign Screens: Aboriginal Media on the Canadian West Coast* (Lincoln: University of Nebraska Press, 2013), 53.

10 Jennifer Gauthier, "Dismantling the Master's House: The Feminist Fourth Cinema Documentaries of Alanis Obomsawin and Loretta Todd," in *Native Americans on Film: Conversations, Teachings and Theory*, ed. M. Elise Marubbio and Eric L. Buffalohead (Lexington: University Press of Kentucky, 2013), 90; Elise M. Marubbio, *Killing the Indian Maiden: Images of Native American Women in Film* (Lexington: University Press of Kentucky, 2006), 170; Carla Taunton, "Indigenous (Re)memory and Resistance: Video Works by Dana Claxton," in Marubbio and Buffalohead, *Native Americans on Film*, 125.

11 Roberta Smith, quoted in Patricia Demers, "Location, Dislocation, Relocation: Shooting Back with Cameras," in *Indigenous Women and Feminism: Politics, Activism, Culture*, ed. Cheryl Suzack, Shari Huhndorf, Jeanne Perreault, and Jean Barman (Vancouver: University of British Columbia Press, 2010), 301.
12 Randolph, *Alanis Obomsawin*, 108.
13 Carol Kalafatic, "Keepers of the Power: Story as Covenant in the Films of Loretta Todd, Shelley Niro, and Christine Welsh," in *Gendering the Nation: Canadian Women's Cinema*, ed. Kay Armatage, Kass Banning, Brenda Longfellow, and Janine Marchessault (Toronto: University of Toronto Press, 2016), 113.
14 Joyce Green, *Making Space for Indigenous Feminism* (Nova Scotia: Fernwood, 2007), 23.
15 Judy Iseke, "Spirituality as Decolonizing: Elders Albert Desjarlais, George McDermott, and Tom McCallum Share Understandings of Life in Healing Practice," *Decolonization: Indigeneity, Education & Society* 2 (2013): 36.
16 Demers, "Location, Dislocation, Relocation," 299–301.
17 Elise M. Marubbio and Eric Buffalohead, introduction to Marubbio and Buffalohead, *Native American on Film*, 10.
18 Raheja, *Reservation Reelism*, 19.
19 "The Bravery and Tragedy of Shannen Koostachin," *Maclean's*, August 20, 2015, www.macleans.ca/news/canada/were-not-going-to-quit-the-bravery-and-tragedy-of-shannen-koostachin/.
20 Kim Anderson, *Life Stages and Native Women: Memory, Teaching and Story Medicine* (Winnipeg: University of Manitoba Press, 2011), 161–62.
21 Elizabeth Kalbfleisch, "Bordering on Feminism: Space, Solidarity, and Transnationalism in Rebecca Belmore's Vigil," in Suzack et al., *Indigenous Women and Feminism*, 285.
22 Kim Anderson, *A Recognition of Being: Reconstructing Native Womanhood* (Toronto: Women's Press, 2016), 144.
23 Said, *Culture and Imperialism*, 353.
24 Shari M. Huhndorf and Cheryl Suzack, "Introduction: Indigenous Feminism: Theorizing the Issues," in Suzack et al., *Indigenous Women and Feminism*, 9.
25 Marubbio, *Killing the Indian Maiden*, 4.
26 Zuzana Pick, "Storytelling and Resistance: The Documentary Practice of Alanis Obomsawin," in Armatage et al., *Gendering the Nation*, 77.

27 Maeghan Pirie, "Situating Indigenous Knowledges: The Talking Back of Alanis Obomsawin and Shelley Niro," in Pearson and Knabe, *Reverse Shots*, 253.
28 Pick, "Storytelling," 79.
29 Norris, "The Role of First Nations Women," 319.
30 Jo-Ann Archibald, *Indigenous Storywork: Educating the Heart, Mind, Body, and Spirit* (Vancouver: University of British Columbia Press, 2008), 20.
31 Catherine Martin, "The Little Boy Who Lived with Muin'skw (Bear Woman)," in *Aboriginal Oral Traditions: Theory, Practice, Ethics*, ed. Renate Eigenbrod and Renée Hulan (Halifax: Fernwood, 2008), 55.
32 Dowell, *Sovereign Screens*, 2.
33 Jo-Ann Episkenew, *Taking Back Our Spirits: Indigenous Literature, Public Policy, and Healing* (Winnipeg: University of Manitoba Press, 2009), 194.

15

Becoming A(p)parent

New (and Old) Ways of Making A Deal with the Universe

So Mayer

Jason Barker's first-person documentary *A Deal with the Universe* (2018), which follows his (eventually successful) attempts to conceive and carry to term, ends with an unusual logo: its text reads, *This Film Was Made in School Hours*. The words circle three lower-case i's in shades of orange and gold, the ident for Raising Films, a campaign and community by and for parents and carers in the UK film and television industry. Barker and his editor Rachel Meyrick are working parents who time-tabled post-production around childcare, enabling the film to be the first production or organization to receive certification from Raising Films, for the film's premiere at the British Film Institute (BFI)'s Flare festival in 2018.[1] In addition to committing to family-friendly labor practices for the edit, Barker and Meyrick participated in Raising Films' two training programs: the one-day intensive Making it Possible, for parents and carers returning to work in film and television; and CLOSR, which focused on project development via expanding regional filmmaking networks.

Barker commented, "It was so empowering to be amongst a community of parent filmmakers with the same worries and fears and it became apparent to all of us that we had to find new ways of working."[2] In response, I consider *A Deal with the Universe* not only as a cinematic text but as evidence of "new ways of working" that are rooted in but move beyond the practical and affective labor practices highlighted by Raising Films' surveys and reports.[3] Grounded in embodiment, *A Deal* necessarily engages both filmmakers and viewers in affective and spiritual practices, asking what it means to "become a(p)parent" in and through film, and how *A Deal* explores "old ways" of being and becoming in order to find them.

In a roundtable on trans cinema, filmmaker Chase Joynt asks a question he sources in Angela Davis's *Freedom Is a Constant Struggle: Ferguson, Palestine, and the Foundations of a Movement* (2016): "How can theorizing trans cultural production move beyond stable categorization to enable new pathways for creative and critical inquiry about violence and marginalized people?"[4] This question is deeply rooted in trans theory and politics, with Emi Koyama's pathbreaking "The Transfeminist Manifesto," first published in 2000, noting that trans politics historically intersect both with the class struggle and the movement for reproductive justice.[5] The new (old) ways that traverse and connect trans parenting and filmmaking generate an ecology that "enable[s] new pathways," which I describe herein as becoming a(p)parent.

A Baby's Been Born

> *I wake up. It's the middle of the night. I know a baby's been born, but I don't know if I've had the baby or I am the baby.*
>
> —Jason Barker, voice-over, *A Deal with the Universe*

A Deal with the Universe was "made in school hours" only insofar as the film was shaped through five months of post-production. Most of the filming took place before Barker's child was born, during the long and complex process of becoming a(p)parent. The film was woven together from fifteen years of home video footage, detailing Barker's decision to conceive and carry a child after his partner Tracey, the planned gestational parent, was diagnosed with breast cancer. Her treatment meant that Tracey would not be able to conceive, so the couple decided that Barker would stop his testosterone treatment and not follow top surgery with a hysterectomy, in order to undertake IVF. Barker decided to film the process as it unfolded, sometimes self-shooting and sometimes addressing the camera operated by Tracey. The film was thus largely shot before school hours were an issue, yet it asserts retroactively that becoming a(p)parent unfolds not just from birth but throughout more than a decade of medicalized, socialized, and intimate processes of (not) conceiving and carrying to term.

The film opens and closes with two long takes of darkness that bracket the process of becoming a(p)parent. As the film opens, Jason is speaking close to the camera's microphone over the persistent sound of crickets.[6] He calls directly to Tracey to join him, saying, "There's nothing to see but there's everything to hear. . . . Look, that could be a shooting star." There is a brief, blurry flare that suggests Barker is filming the rural night sky with an early digital video camera. At the end of the film, there is similarly a dark, grainy screen with a voice-over conversation, only now there is no verbal reference to the image. Its status is unclear: it could be shooting with the lens cap on or the same footage as the opening. On the soundtrack, we hear:

> JASON: So what I'm going to do, I'm going to make a film about how you ended up to be in your daddy's tummy.
> CHILD: Ohhhhhhhpffffff.
> JASON: Will you help me make it?
> CHILD: Yeah.
> JASON: Okay.
> CHILD: If you want me to.
> JASON: Yeah, definitely. It's the story of you, and it's the story of me, and it's the story of your mummy.

Cut to end credits, soundtracked by "Do Whatever the Heck You Want" by nonbinary singer Rae Spoon, who provided several songs for the film. The film thus ends, in a real sense, with its own conception, in the conversation between Jason and his child, who not only consents to the film being made but agrees to participate. Rather than there being a tension between the song's title (which refers to liberating gender identities and social behaviors) and the negotiation of consent and participatory filmmaking implied in the conversation (which follows a series of short clips of Jason and the child, at various ages, goofing off for the camera), there is a suggestion that the film results from the permission to "do whatever the heck you want" that arises from Jason's openness with his child and the film's openness with the viewer. The film (which begins by saying, "There's nothing to see here") cannot preexist this conversation, and yet it does. Echoing the feeling identified in Jason's voice-over quoted above, which follows his labor, as to whether he *had* the baby or *is* the baby, the film conceives itself retroactively to have always existed in this closing moment.

Embraced by the two scenes, the film is suggestively both a cosmology and a cosmogony: a study of the universe at its largest scale and a study of specific origin theories. Stardust condensing on the one hand, and a conversation about beginning(s), very different from Genesis, on the other. In both, the observer effect is paramount. Like the shooting star that is more palpable (and audible, in description) than visible in the opening, the film becomes a(p)parent through its reflexive awareness of the relations between modern technology, both cinematic and obstetric, and folk beliefs, particularly around sacred waters, that layer the film with elemental imagery. After the shooting star, the grainy dark cuts to a gorgeous sunlit image of a woman, whom we learn to be Tracey, treading water in a wave-dappled sea. "If all goes to plan," says Jason in voice-over, "this will be the last holiday we take as just the two of us." Cinematicity and the elemental are combined in the *idea* of the shooting star, which references, realizes, and makes real the Disney(fied) call to "wish upon a star" (for a child, is the implication). To watch the film is to accept the efficacy of both sets of practices at their intersection: the closing reprisal of the grainy-dark screen entwines the shooting star and the living child as wished-for result. Cinema, like conception, is shifted between the technological and the embodied-spiritual.

In doing so, the film redefines the "apparitional," a term that has moved productively but also problematically between queer literary theory, with particular reference to the "apparitional lesbian," in Terry Castle's resonant phrase, and the concern with "the vanishing lady" in feminist film studies, particularly in early cinema.[7] In reconceiving (pun intended) the apparitional as that which becomes a(p)parent, *A Deal with the Universe* addresses a dual recursive vanishing point: cinema's inability to register experiences associated with the lived experience usually defined by/as femininity, although not limited to or limiting it, including pregnancy and breast cancer, without reflexive concerns relating to the gendered deployment of cinematic technology; and the highly contentious context, contemporaneous to the film's premiere and release, of the UK government's consultation on amending the Gender Recognition Act (GRA) and of vocal transphobia from Britain's so-called radical feminist community.[8] While the film does not address these issues in depth, Jason mentions the transphobic backlash over the headlines concerning Thomas Trace Beatie's pregnancy in 2008, which prompted him to "put the camera away for a bit," leaving IVF attempts 34–57 undocumented.

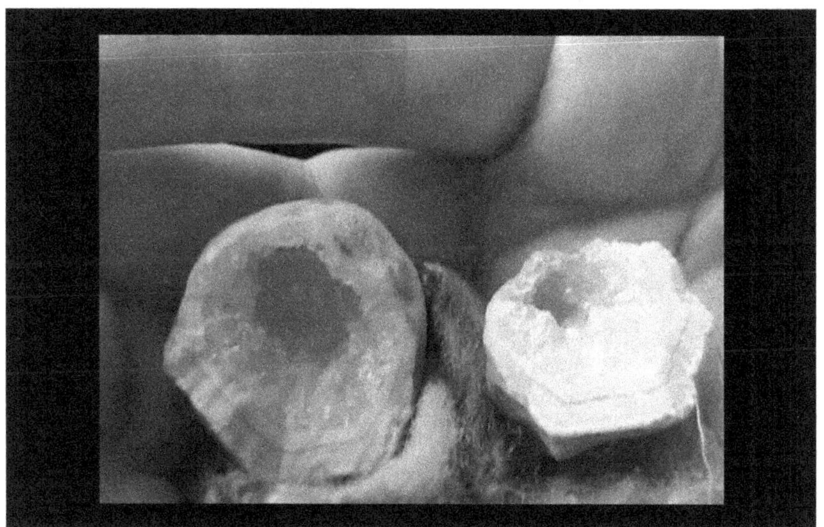

Tracey holds the broken agate, which Jason says is science, not magic, in *A Deal with the Universe* (Jason Barker, 2018).

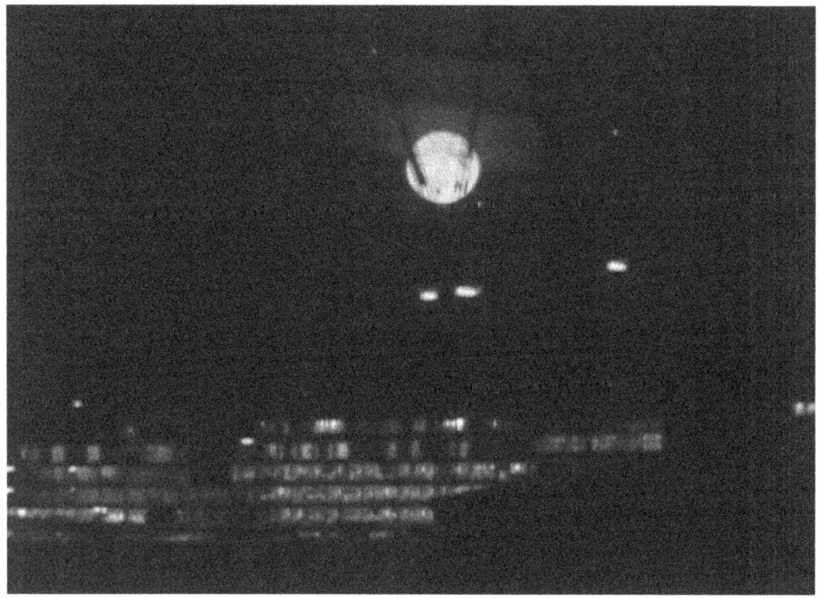

The moon rises over London as Jason makes "a deal with the universe" in *A Deal with the Universe* (Jason Barker, 2018).

The film subsequently includes very few images of Jason's eventual pregnancy, and none of birthing. This refusal wields the apparitional as a counter-strategy. As Jack Halberstam writes of the press photograph of a shirtless, pregnant Beatie, "In this one image, Beatie was the queer family, he was the erotically charged pregnancy, he became the visible transgender man. But in this riot of visibility what price was paid, and by whom?"[9] Visibility has been a key concern for social scientists studying trans parents and families in order to argue for better service provision and to combat transphobia: yet both Halberstam and Barker critique reifying visibility within dominant regimes of representation.[10] *A Deal* navigates the "riot of visibility" through the apparitional, including the extensive use of hushed, intimate voice-over to remind us that this is an authored first-person film, placing us *as if* inside the filmmaker/subject's body, as we are conceived along with the film and child.

Intertitle: MAGIC

Alright, so I know I said we were approaching it scientifically.
This is geology; it's not superstition at all.

—Jason Barker, voice-over, *A Deal with the Universe*

It is not only the shooting star. There is a broken agate, egg-shaped, that has to be fitted back together again and tied in place with a ribbon (much desired by Stig the cat), and a visit to Swallowhead Springs, an ancient British fertility site fringed with willows, where Jason and Tracey clamber over wet rocks to drink from the pool in the typically British pouring rain. They climb gravel steps to Chapelle Notre Dame de Grâce in Normandy, where there is a statue of the Virgin Mary famed for its fertility powers. They try "yogic breathing" close to some English standing stones after the first successful implantation. Tracey searches for a pagan goddess on a caravan trip to Rutland but finds a bird's nest and then a stone column around the back of a church on which breast whorls are still faintly visible—possibly a sheela na gig. Jason worries that Tracey's breast cancer is a curse on them for trying to conceive as a queer couple, but later says, "I thought the universe would *love* this: pregnant man—I'll have some of that."

He decides that filming the process might be the curse and switches the camera off during attempts 26–31 (and again during a later attempt, saying, "I'm not gonna hex this"), but turns the camera back on for attempt 32 in 2006, introduced by a shot of a golden full moon among London construction cranes. He turns the camera on not because the treatment was successful but because his best friend Brixton Brady had just been killed by a lorry while cycling. An artist, performer, filmmaker, and community builder, Brady was described by Barker in an obituary note written for *DIVA* magazine in terms that resonate strongly with *A Deal*'s cosmology:

> Our beloved Brixton Brady never settled for the ordinary. She asked the universe for things—some she got, like a most beautiful love, others she didn't. But she never compromised with life. . . .
>
> To be with Brixton Brady was to enter another, much more magical world than our own. . . .
>
> She believed in the dramatic last minute rescue and, you know what? The day was, more often than not, saved. The life of Brixton Brady was an adventure. Way, way too short but still an epic.[11]

Over the shot of a moonlit night, Jason explains that this was the moment of the titular deal with the universe: would he give up on any attempt at a successful conception in exchange for Brixton once again "being alive and well"? Instead, he tells Brixton, via the spiritual connection of the film's voice-over, that, as he's going ahead, she'll "have to be a ghost parent." Attempt 32 does not result in a pregnancy, but there *is* a dramatic last-minute rescue when, some time later, after all options appear to be exhausted, a friend of Brixton's offers to be a sperm donor, the news cued by the intertitle MAGIC.

Thus Brixton becomes an apparitional parent, disrupting the Euro-Western scientific and religious belief in heteronormative binary parenting and conception. Brixton's ghost parentage reminds us that Jason and Tracey are joined by multiple other a(p)parents, including anonymous and known sperm donors. Through Brixton, there is also a suggestion that the trans and queer arts communities in London are a(p)parents, as Jason and Brixton met through performance and were working together on the Transfabulous film festival in 2006. Before Brixton's (unseen) friend arrives at Jason and Tracey's Hackney flat to make his donation, the couple sets out KY jelly and a plastic cup, then Jason pulls out a copy of *Quim* (1989–95), a London-based indie porn magazine subtitled "For Dykes of All Sexual Persuasions," and quips, "I can see all my exes." It takes a (queer) village to make a child.

What becomes a(p)parent through the film is the queer enmeshment of family and community, where community is constituted both sexually and creatively. The film includes a number of excerpts from Barker's stand-up and cabaret performances, including one routine where he is dressed as a uterus. Dealing with the multiple traumas of prolonged IVF treatment, breast cancer, mourning, and transphobia, *A Deal* fits into the genealogy of lesbian/queer performance and video (and their close interrelation) charted by Ann Cvetkovich in the first chapter of *An Archive of Feelings*. Cvetkovich categorizes this body of work as documenting "the everyday life of queer trauma," an insidious experience that "resists the melodramatic structure of an easily identifiable origin . . . opening up the need to change social structures more broadly rather than just fix individual people."[12] Jules Joanne Gleeson uses the term "social reproduction" to describe the ways in which "transgender lives are not made possible by any one piece of legislation, and instead are allowed for by the winding road Marxist feminists have come to term 'life-making.'"[13] The road to conception, like the Fallopian tubes of Barker's costume, is presented *as* being winding in the film, which refuses to straighten it out: that is part of its magic, part of its trauma, and part of its queerness.

Black feminist scholars of both mothering and trans practices have turned to the New York drag ball scene as a model of what Gleeson calls "social reproduction" and "life-making." Alexis Pauline Gumbs writes that "MotherING is another matter, a possible action, the name for that nurturing work, that survival dance . . . worked by house mothers in ball culture who provide spaces of self-love and expression for/as queer youth of color in the street. What would it mean for us to take the word 'mother' less as a gendered identity and more as a possible action, a technology of transformation?"[14] Reading *Paris Is Burning* (Jennie Livingston, 1990) alongside the Haitian documentary *Of Men and Gods* (Anne Lescot and Laurence Magloire, 2002), about gender-variant practitioners of Vodou, Omise'eke Natasha Tinsley suggests that the way to answer Gumbs's question is through attending to the apparitional: the spiritual and cosmological. Tinsley quotes Barbara Browning's observation that *Paris* housemother Angie Xtravaganza is "Ezili Danto, the solitary, hard-working, sometimes raging mother."[15] As Tinsley argues through the multiple figure/s of Ezili, African diasporic spiritual-material practices of building kinship and community, with traditions reshaped by and resisting dispossession, forced migration, and slavery, offer the grounding of a trans parenting genealogy that non-Black artists, activists, and thinkers are only beginning to practice and formulate.

To change (homophobic, transphobic, classist) social structures, *A Deal* develops a language for "life-making" by situating the effects of and interventions into those structures both in the intimate and, unusually for a Euro-Western film, in the cosmological. Thus human, as well as and through more-than-human/supernatural, communities and ecologies intersect in and through Brixton's performance-presence in the film to become a(p)parents. Early in the film we see a scene of Brixton tap-dancing in Jason and Tracey's kitchen; just before her friend offers to be a sperm donor, there is a similar scene of Jason's mum, Dot, tap-dancing and trying to teach Jason to tap. In the same way that the lesbian apparitional becomes the queer and trans a(p)parent, the "melodramatic [linear] structure" identified by Cvetkovich becomes instead the collective, cumulative, often recursive structure of the cabaret or variety performance. Linking vaudeville, with its English working-class and queer resonances, to the invocatory practice of table-tapping, these lively and lovely dance scenes argue for the music of the universe playing out through living sexual bodies and genealogies. It *is* geology, the palpable logic of standing stones and agates, as well as the science of pregnancy tests, cancer treatments, and IVF, that allows for becoming a(p)parent. The camera, with its power to imagine apparitionality into the darkness, becomes the hinge between the technological and the cosmological. It does so not only as an extension of Jason's and Tracey's bodies, held close to their breath and their bruises, but holding equally close a cosmogony of feminist, queer, and trans film and video production and exhibition born from performance.

Rewind a Few Years

About twenty years ago someone did my tarot cards and said, "You'll have a child," and we just held on to that. That's the truth of how we kept going.

—Jason Barker, Q&A after screening of *A Deal with the Universe*, University of Westminster LGBTQ Staff Network screening, Regent St Cinema, April 17, 2019

After we see Tracey swimming in the sea and the couple visiting the Chapelle de Notre Dame de Grâce, Jason says in voice-over that the narrative will "rewind a few years." Within the film, this returns us to an interview with Jason's mum, Dot, about his adoption of his then new name in the early 2000s. It is suggestive of the need for a cinematic genealogy as well, with the term *rewind* marking the film's self-evident and self-reflexive participation in the genealogy of feminist and LGBTIQ+ filmmaking, particularly the practice of first-person video diaries.

As a first-person film, *A Deal* boldly draws on—and draws together—the modes of address and community politics of both second-wave feminist documentaries, often shot on Super 8, such as Amalie Rothschild's *Nana, Mom and Me* (1974), specifically concerned with narrating feminist genealogy; and queer first-person film and video such as Gregg Bordowitz's *Fast Trip Long Drop* (1993), which—like *A Deal*—situates the individual at the nexus of the medical and ethical, the political, and the personal.[16] As Cathy Brennan points out in her interview with Barker for *Sight & Sound*,

> *A Deal with the Universe* taps into a legacy of intimate video explorations by LGBT+ filmmakers, such as Jonathan Caouette's *Tarnation* (2003) and the recently departed Barbara Hammer's *Super Dyke Meets Madame X* (1976). The latter in particular, in which Hammer and the avant-garde artist Max Almy document their relationship, is echoed in the way Tracey and Jason take turns holding the camera, enabling audiences to view themselves through a lover's gaze. Barker would see many such films at lesbian and gay film festivals in London. "That's something I grew up with, those personal stories told by somebody in the first person."[17]

Barker worked for several years as a programmer for BFI Flare (formerly the London Lesbian and Gay Film Festival), as well as for Transfabulous and other UK film festivals, so that *A Deal* was embedded from its inception in the language of queer film and video.

Films that premiered in the United Kingdom at Flare during Barker's tenure included Chelsea McMullan's *My Prairie Home* (2013), a bio-documentary about *A Deal* contributor Rae Spoon, as well as Sophie Hyde's *52 Tuesdays* (2014). Hyde's directorial debut (after several documentaries as producer) is a formally innovative film made *around* school hours to enable writer/director/producer (and production designer) Hyde and her partner, producer, cinematographer, and editor Bryan Mason, to make the film while raising their then pre-adolescent child Audrey (who appears briefly in the film), and to facilitate the participation of teenage actor Tilda Cobham-Hervey.[18] *52 Tuesdays* was filmed every Tuesday for a year, a production process that echoes the film's fictional narrative, in which Del and his daughter Billie (played by Hervey) meet every Tuesday after Del asks Billie to live with her father for a year.

Played by Del Herbert-Jane, a gender-nonconforming performer who was initially attached to the project as a gender-diversity consultant, Del is transitioning. Both he and Billie use digital video cameras to document and process their year together-apart, with Del's camera trained on his masculinizing body while Billie records a video diary that she intersperses with news footage and documentation of sexual explorations with two school friends. Del also travels to San Francisco—close to where Hammer made her 1970s 16 mm films "out of sex and life," as she titled her autobiography—for a conference, where he records video interviews with trans men and their children to send to Billie.[19] These short documentaries, becoming a(p)parent within the fictional narrative, are partly ghostly/ancestral because they are so strongly reminiscent of the foundational trans documentary *Gendernauts* (Monika Treut, 1999), which also trained its camera on San Francisco as the locus of cutting-edge lived experiments, often intersecting, in both gender and technology.

The 1990s era from which Treut's film derived, and in which Barker began performing in London, is also palpable in his film. The film's most signal transfabulous parent is Sally Potter's *Orlando* (1993), not least because Potter's irreverent use of to-camera address for her protagonist, rooted in her own experience of feminist live performance, aligns her fiction—indeed, fantasy—film with first-person video diaries. *A Deal* and *Orlando* share an eccentric Englishness that is rooted in landscape, oriented toward openness, and resolutely, wryly gender/queer. Barker's documentary includes incidental scenes that wink at *Orlando*, like the scene of Jason and Tracey ice-skating. Alongside the tap-dancing scenes, there is also footage of Barker's stage performances at London's legendary LGBT+ cabaret Club Wotever, one of which features a chamber group very similar to the group that plays at the balls in *The Gold Diggers* (Sally Potter, 1982).

Importantly, *A Deal* retro-activates *Orlando* so that it becomes a(p)parent as a trans parenting film. As Jane Maree Maher has noted, pregnancy and parenthood are critically neglected aspects of *Orlando*; she argues that "Potter's version of *Orlando* suggests rethinking and reworking visual meaning as a strategy to challenge deterministic accounts of pregnancy and the body."[20] Jason confronts determinism and essentialism directly in his dealings with the National Health Service (NHS), for example, struggling to get IVF medication prescriptions made out to Jason Barker and completing clinic forms that demand the identification of the mother and the father. *Orlando*'s fantastical resistance gives permission to *A Deal* to engage with nonrational and nonscientific strategies, what we could call the apparitional, in conceiving itself.

Orlando remains present as a "ghost parent" to the last. *A Deal*'s final exchange between Jason and his child is hauntingly reminiscent of the closing scene of *Orlando*, in which Orlando's daughter (Jessica Swinton), transformed from the son in Virginia Woolf's novel, turns a video camera on her parent and asks, "Why are you sad?" Orlando (Tilda Swinton), seated beneath the same oak tree where they began the film four hundred years previously, responds, "I'm not. I'm happy. Look up there," directing the child's, and the camera's, attention to the gold lamé-clad Angel (Jimmy Somerville) hovering in the oak's crown, a shot echoed melancholically by the golden moon over cranes that marks Brady's last night on earth in *A Deal*.

Subtly paying homage, *A Deal* draws on a key "shimmering image," to use Eliza Steinbock's definitional term for trans cinema's aesthetics of change.[21] As Steinbock argues, Barker's and Potter's films shimmer in the constellation of the cinematographic with the body of the live performer, specifically here the queer vaudeville or cabaret performer. As well as having a cast rich in queer theater luminaries, Potter dedicated *Orlando* to her grandmother Beatrice Quennell, known as "Hunny," who had been a stage performer in interwar London. "She always said yes to the artist in me," Potter told Scott MacDonald, a "yes" that *Orlando* roots in a shimmering theatrical genealogy of presence, one that validates apparitionality.[22]

Karen Beckman locates the dis/apparitional vanishing lady of early cinema in music hall and vaudeville magic acts; in their queer vaudevillian "shimmering," Potter and Barker suggest an alternate and apposite apparitional genealogy for a feminist cinema, particularly one concerned with pregnancy and childrearing: one rooted in the labor practices and material realities of theater rather than in its illusionism. Just as the shooting star blurs the (cinema)technological into the embodied-cosmological, so too the golden moon/angel situates a trans parenting aesthetic within the relation between the knowing, *laboring* queer body—whether performing or birthing—and its transformation into film. "Look, Tracey," begins Jason; "Look up there," ends Orlando, drawing our eyes to the shimmering that is becoming a(p)parent.

In My Window Boxes

> *What prompted Jason to finish* A Deal with the Universe *was the "transgender tipping point," a brief period in 2014 and 2015 he describes as "a golden age" of trans visibility.*
>
> —Cathy Brennan, "Body and Soul," 2019

A Deal is deeply concerned with looking relations, and with the screens and windows that enable the gaze. Throughout, the camera is placed in relation to the windows of the flat and caravan that Jason and Tracey share, particularly watching over the plant and bird life on the flat's balcony. The pigeons are placed in direct relation to Jason's lived experience when we hear him say off-camera, "Please don't lay an egg—what am I going to do with it? . . . I'm full of fucking estrogen; I don't want pigeons' nests in my windowboxes." Thus the window/box is linked to another frequent on-screen presence: the blank window or box of the pregnancy test, with its always-apparitional, wished-for lines. Watching the natural/cultural world thus takes place on camera, but it also takes the place of other kinds of viewing, as Jason's film programming work is never discussed, and neither films nor TV are excerpted.

Yet, as Brennan suggests, the film, edited between 2014–15 and 2018, has a sibling relation to the streaming service shows that, more than anything in big-screen cinema, have marked the transgender tipping point: in particular to two shows with trans creators: *Transparent* (created by Joey Soloway, Amazon Prime, 2014–) and *Sense8* (created by J. Michael Straczynski, Lana Wachowski, and Lilly Wachowski, Netflix, 2015–18). Formally, narratively, and in terms of geographical and class location, *A Deal* is quite distinct from the two American shows, each in their way fantasias. Yet each features a rebirthing scene that, bridging realism and fantasy as *Orlando* does, speaks to Jason's productive confusion between *having* and *being* the baby that is born: that is, to becoming a(p)parent, the ways in which trans narratives of pregnancy and parenting, through their invocation of the apparitional-fantastic, change and challenge techno-deterministic and bio-essentialist theories and practices of both the cinematic and the medical.

In *Transparent*, protagonist Maura Pfefferman (Jeffrey Tambor) and her daughter Ali (Gaby Hoffmann) experience a vision or epigenetic memory in which Maura's absent father arrives to see his wife in hospital, expecting his child to be a daughter, and giving her a girl's name (2.10, "Grey Green Brown & Copper"). This revisioning is connected to Ali's possibly drug-induced visions of her grandmother Rose (also played by Hoffmann) and great-aunt Gittel (Hari Nef) in Weimar Berlin. Gittel, whom we first see as a cabaret performer, refuses to masquerade as her assigned gender in order to get papers to escape to America. Maura is suggestively not only (re)born female, but inherits, embodies, and reincarnates the doubly-lost Gittel. Being trans becomes an epigenetic form of consciousness, a genealogy that blends the cultural, the familial, and the apparitional, as the perceptual status and transmission mechanism of Ali's and Maura's knowledge of the past is never ascertained.

Predominantly realist, and using home video aesthetics to mark its flashbacks of and within Maura's adult life, *Transparent* shares its visionary non-realist aspect with *Sense8*. As Cáel M. Keegan notes, "More than any current popular visual text, *Sense8* seeks to aesthetically translate transgender as a form of consciousness—a way of perceiving or knowing that occurs between and across bodies, cultures, and geographies."[23] Its trans character, Nomi (Jamie Clayton), is a San Francisco-based hacktivist and tech blogger, a character deeply reminiscent of the gendernautical digital artists captured on camera two decades earlier by Treut. Yet Nomi is also part of a "sensate" cluster of eight people around the world who experience one another's feelings and histories. This is highlighted in episode 1.11, "Just Turn the Wheel and the Future Changes," in which the sensate cluster shares an extended experience as one of their number, Riley (Tuppence Middleton), takes Ecstasy while watching her father play a concert in their hometown of Reykjavik. In her heightened state, Riley revisits her double birth trauma: both her own home birth (during which her father was away playing a concert), and the birth of her daughter Lúna in the wreckage of a car crash. The latter scene arrives in delayed fragments amid the cluster's plural recollections of their own births, including Nomi's memory of her mother's hippie 1970s West Coast water birth. Through rapid editing, Nomi's birth is entwined with both Riley's and Lúna's, so that she (re)experiences both being born and giving birth as a woman.

There is no such scene in *A Deal*—at least not explicitly. Yet there is a central image suggestive of birthing and rebirthing. The key promotional image on the film's poster shows a pregnant Jason swimming in an outdoor pool, quoting a late scene in the film. In some stills, Jason is floating prone, starfishing with his hands above the water. In other versions, Jason is floating supine, his knees curled toward his belly. The second version is especially reminiscent of an in utero fetal scan, both displacing and replacing the expected image, which is never shown in the film.

As Maher writes when considering how *Orlando* refuses the dominant logic of visibility for pregnancy, "Informed by ultrasound images, the pregnant belly always signals to the 'fetus/baby' within. Feminist theorists of pregnancy have argued that this visibility is most often used to construct the pregnant woman as the 'carrier' of the fetus. In turn, this has led to the fetus attaining public status, often diminishing the rights of pregnant women."[24] Jason, floating within the frame, in the blue box of the pool that recalls his window and the windows of pregnancy tests, takes the place of the fetus; rebirthing himself. His body, wearing bright board shorts, sporting armpit hair and top surgery scars as well as a very pregnant belly, offers a "shimmering image" that makes both trans and pregnancy a(p)parent in a numinous reality reminiscent of both Maura's and Nomi's more fantastical experiences.

Echoing the shape of the agate egg and the theme of water running from the opening shot of Tracey, this joyous culminating image is reminiscent of the definitional "Blue Marble" image of Earth taken by the crew of Apollo 17 in 1972, an image whose alteration of Euro-Western ideas of the visible (as knowable) is often compared to that of Lennart Nilsson's color photographs of human embryos, published in *Life* magazine in 1965. As Donna Haraway writes: "The fetus and the planet Earth are sibling seed worlds in technoscience. . . . The global fetus and the spherical whole Earth both exist because of, and inside of, technoscientific visual culture. Yet, I think, both signify touch."[25] In Barker's "shimmering" restaging within the film's narrative, neither fetus nor planet nor parent is "free-floating." The viewer is aware that Tracey is operating the camera, and that both the pregnancy and the film are the manifestation of a palpable community, human and other-than-human, alive in and beyond the material present.

Signifying the communitarian and/as cosmological, and the performative (Jason's poppy-splashed board shorts are visual echoes of his uterus costume) and/as parental, this image makes a(p)parent the film's central theme, its dealing with the universe. Resisting dominant culture's insistence on visibility and normative origin stories, it cheekily reconceives Genesis to offer not only a new story of parenting and filmmaking but a new (relation to the) world. Exactly "life-making," *A Deal with the Universe*, brought into being in collaboration with its queer and trans cinematic, televisual, and lived "ghost parents," welcomes us into its space.

Notes

1 Raising Films, accessed July 9, 2020, www.raisingfilms.com/raising-films-ribbon/.

2 Jason Barker, "How to Make a Film during School Hours," *Raising Films*, October 2018, www.raisingfilms.com/how-to-make-a-film-during-school-hours/.

3 See Chapters 1 and 2 in this volume.

4 Chase Joynt, in Jules Rosskam, "Making Trans Cinema: A Roundtable Discussion," *Somatechnics* 8, no. 1 (2018): 18.

5 Emi Koyama, "The Transfeminist Manifesto," in *Catching a Wave: Reclaiming Feminism for the Twenty-First Century*, ed. Rory Dicker and Alison Piepmeier (Boston: Northeastern University Press, 2003), 244–59.

6 I will use Jason to refer to the voice-over speaker and on-screen presence/subject/character, and Barker to refer to the director.

7 See So Mayer, "Uncommon Sensuality: New Queer Feminist Film/Theory," in *Feminisms: Diversity, Difference and Multiplicity in Film Cultures*, ed. Anna Backman Rogers and Laura Mulvey (Amsterdam: Amsterdam University Press, 2015), 86–96; Karen Beckman, *Vanishing Women: Magic, Film, Feminism* (Durham, NC: Duke University Press, 2003).

8 These attitudes are indeed apparent in the *Sight & Sound* review commissioned from a writer who is vocally gender-critical. See Hannah McGill, review of *A Deal with the Universe*, *Sight & Sound* 29, no. 5 (2019): 61.

9 Jack Halberstam, "The Pregnant Man," *Velvet Light Trap* 65 (Spring 2010): 77.

10 Beth A. Haines, Alex A. Ajayi, and Helen Boyd, "Making Trans Parents Visible: Intersectionality of Trans and Parenting Identities," *Feminism and Psychology* 24, no. 2 (2014): 238–47.

11 Barker, republished anonymously on Ghost Bikes from the now-deleted Transfabulous film festival website, accessed June 16, 2020, ghostbikes .org/london/brixton-brady.
12 Ann Cvetkovich, *An Archive of Feelings: Trauma, Sexuality, and Lesbian Public Cultures* (Durham, NC: Duke University Press, 2003), 33.
13 Jules Joanne Gleeson, "On *The Guardian*'s Transphobic Centrism," *New Socialist*, October 21, 2018, newsocialist.org.uk/on-the-guardians -transphobic-centrism/.
14 Alexis Pauline Gumbs, "M/other Ourselves: A Black Queer Feminist Genealogy for Radical Mothering," in *Revolutionary Mothering: Love on the Front Lines*, ed. Alexis Pauline Gumbs, China Martens, and Mai'a Williams (Toronto: Between the Lines, 2016), 22–23.
15 Omise'eke Natasha Tinsley, *Ezili's Mirrors: Imagining Black Queer Genders* (Durham, NC: Duke University Press, 2018), 73.
16 Alisa Lebow, introduction to *The Cinema of Me: The Self and Subjectivity in First Person Documentary*, ed. Alisa Lebow (London: Wallflower/ Columbia University Press, 2012), 10.
17 Cathy Brennan, "Body and Soul," *Sight & Sound* 29, no. 5 (2019): 11.
18 Sophie Hyde [interview], Raising Films, February 2018, www .raisingfilms.com/interview-sophie-hyde/.
19 Barbara Hammer, *Hammer! Making Movies out of Sex and Life* (New York: Feminist Press, 2010).
20 Jane Maree Maher, "Prone to Pregnancy: Orlando, Virginia Woolf and Sally Potter Represent the Gestating Body," *Journal of Medical Humanities* 28 (2007): 20.
21 Eliza Steinbock, *Shimmering Images: Trans Cinema, Embodiment, and the Aesthetics of Change* (Durham, NC: Duke University Press, 2019), 20.
22 Sally Potter, in Scott MacDonald, "Sally Potter," in *A Critical Cinema 3: Interviews with Independent Filmmakers* (Berkeley: University of California Press, 1998), 425.
23 Caél M. Keegan, "Tongues without Bodies: The Wachowskis' *Sense8*," *TSQ: Transgender Studies Quarterly* 3, nos. 3–4 (2016): 606.
24 Maher, "Prone to Pregnancy": 19.
25 Donna Haraway, *Modest_Witness@Second_Millennium. Female_Man©_ Meets_OncoMouse™: Feminism and Technoscience* (New York: Routledge, 1997), 174.

16

On Sharing Films, Learning Care, Keeping Watch, and Finding

Kristi McKim

I like . . . film to capture that which is so fragile.

—Agnès Varda, CinéVardaExpo, 2015

We are here to keep watch, not to keep.

—Kathryn Schulz, "When Things Go Missing," 2017

"Be courageous, Henry, and don't hit your head," Agnès Varda—laughing, clapping, rollicking—advised my then two-year-old as he crawled under the hotel's glass-paneled coffee table. My family and I had traveled to the University of Chicago's CinéVardaExpo (2015); yet, for all of our scheduled plans and appropriate to the whimsy of the subject (Varda and her work), it was at not a formal event but instead at our hotel's continental breakfast that we first, unexpectedly, came upon Varda in person. Overcome with the need to thank her though not wanting to violate her privacy, I nervously rationalized that the breakfast buffet was public; and so it went, right there in front of the grapefruit: I praised her work; she welcomed me with gentle warmth, invited us to sit with her, doted on a mutually enamored Henry, talked lovingly

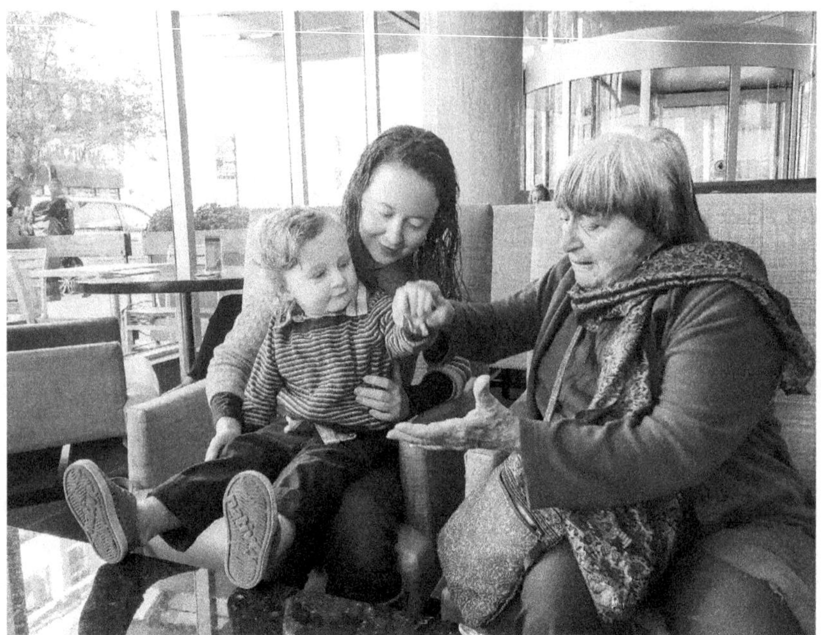

Agnès Varda, my son Henry Robert Barr, and me, October 2015. (Photograph by Mark Barr.)

about family, asked more about teaching, and wondered about how Henry would grow and learn.

She remarked that, because I know her films well, "we see together." At her talk later that afternoon, she described how she tries "to change the connection between people and what they see," how a director and audience can "become friends" through aligned perception. Toward the end of her remarks, she returned to her 1962 film *Cléo from 5 to 7*, "a film about a light meeting, the fragility of moments, how an encounter can change everything. I like the film to capture that which is so fragile." Such has been the subject of her entire oeuvre.

Turning her own body into a cinematic subject, Varda's 1958 *L'Opéra-Mouffe* extends her subjectivity as a pregnant woman into a way of seeing. Even before I became a mother, Varda's film revealed to me how anticipating motherhood heightens sensitivity to passing time. I hardly could have known, though, how films—Varda's and others'—would come to shape my actual *mothering*. Inspired by intimate film-centric experiences and built of hoped-for connection with a reader, this essay aspires to behold the fragile, to keep watch, to find: a way of caring for my children by describing how we learn to "see together," and a way of *learning* care as a kind of attention, a "finding" heightened by the movement and change that a shared experience of film and world can yield.

This essay affords me an opportunity to clarify what I otherwise experience more intuitively: a way of giving form to these film-inspired patterns of care. As most writers can say of their writing, every word of this essay is hard won. As Maggie Nelson offers in her brilliant *The Argonauts*, "I cannot hold my baby at the same time as I write."[1] My computer doesn't cry, giggle, nurse, make eye contact, or reward my attention with coos and squeals, after all; yet it's precisely because these patterns are otherwise invisible that I structure them here.

Sharing Films

Paddington (Paul King, 2014) features one of our family's favorite movie scenes, which we've often replayed to peals of laughter: when the titular bear arrives at the Browns' home and is left to freshen up in their bathroom, he cleans his waxy ears with toothbrushes, overfills a bathtub, and then—after the overflowing bathwater pushes open the closed door—rides the wave down the Browns' winding staircase. With each repetition, our laughter begins earlier as we anticipate what's to come: our wild glee to behold Paddington atop the rushing water is a promise fulfilled.

I teach film studies at Hendrix College. In spring 2017, my son Henry, then three years old, accompanied me to class (it was his preschool's in-service day, and we couldn't find childcare), where he promised to sit quietly. He slinked into the classroom; students greeted him with smiles and a warm welcome. He quickly scanned the room, then whispered to me that he'd like to sit under the table in the back, shyly rendering himself as inconspicuous as possible. I unpacked his bag, set up his space, arranged his peanut butter sandwich and coloring book and crayons on the floor before him, and proceeded to teach. Near the end of class, he began crawling from the back of the room, right down the middle aisle, crawling as if to be discreet while being anything but. "Mommy," he loudly whispered, as if I'd somehow missed this spectacle. "Mommy, Mommy," he continued, then offered that he'd like to show my students the *Paddington* bathtub scene. We were not studying *Paddington* that day, but—with my students' enthusiastic consent—we saved the final minutes of class for Henry's teaching moment.

In striking contrast to his earlier shyness, he introduced the clip, offering or withholding necessary details, as if a perfect storyteller (or teacher). We played the scene (twice!). He beamed with the joy of something beloved becoming shareable. He and I walked from the classroom hand in hand, fulfilled—although for different reasons, I imagine. He'd brought what he loved at home into the classroom and made people laugh, in an experience that we couldn't have anticipated. And maybe he could sense that we needed it (we had been studying the opening of *The Act of Killing* [Joshua Oppenheimer, 2012], after all), or maybe I'm giving him too much credit. But he gave us a moment we'd not expected, a scene we'd not otherwise have encountered, a sensation of childhood delight with an unscripted, spontaneous moment of child-led "teaching." I couldn't have predicted the ways that, like Henry's gaining confidence and finding a voice in the classroom, I also have found my way—not just in teaching but also in my new experience of mothering—thanks to the comfort and familiarity afforded me by sharing films together.

After eighteen years of teaching film and literature, I've grown comfortable presenting complex theory with clarity and confidence, enthusiasm and joy; for what once flummoxed me and felt hard to comprehend, I have—in my way, for better or worse—developed my own pedagogical style, able to place various concepts within a knowable form. As a professor, I feel prepared, experienced, and qualified. As a mother of a child who's discovering his own enchantment with movies, I both accidentally and consciously transform those theories into practice, my conversations with my son inadvertently structured by how I teach narrative expectation, film form, spectatorship, history, and theory. Film studies has given me a mode through which to know myself as a mother, a series of questions and ideas with which to disrupt narrative momentum and introduce a new kind of pleasure. One Sunday afternoon, as I walked to the park with Henry, we talked about the sound of the wind in the trees and the shimmer of sunlight on the sidewalk, details I might well have missed were it not for Christian Keathley's cinephilia or Jean Epstein's celebration of sound cinema ("we will soon hear the grass grow").[2] Parenting has for me included moments like this—much like teaching in a classroom—when what I've learned, read, and studied conveniently seems at my fingertips, a means of discovering in the world beyond my discipline an attention cultivated *by* my discipline, in ways inextricable from mothering and love.

In the summer before your third birthday, during an afternoon repeat screening of Annie *(John Huston, 1982), I taught you how to use the remote control. You'd pause the film periodically, say to me, "Talk about it," and we did, together: costumes, clouds, sky, faces, buildings, gestures. A kind of maternal and cinephilic quest, buoyed by the force of your curiosity to see more in every frame. You hopped down from the couch to belt out "Tomorrow" as you twirled through the living room.*

When talking about films together—or when reading lessons from film theory out into the world—mothering feels most "natural," as it becomes that for which I've been practicing all my life. Four years ago, I wrote an essay about returning to the film classroom after maternity leave.[3] In my son's infancy, theories of cinephilia informed how I *looked at* him, how I indexed and collected moments; I described loving his details, celebrating his possibility, archiving his ephemeral newborn state—aspiring to be an attentive beholder and celebrant of his changes, growth, becoming. Feeling terrific maternal responsibility, I sought to keep hold of, through language, my son's swift early months. And now—as my talkative and curious son becomes an individual with articulable desires, preferences, fears, and hopes—theories of film give me a form through which I can feel most proud of being a mother, most capable and not at a loss. When he hits his head or bites his tongue or suffers a stomach virus, for example, I feel helpless and concerned at his and thus my vulnerability and contingency. Yet when we're talking together about film—or even when we're not talking about *film* but phenomena more generally (as we cook, dance, sing, play music, take walks, read books, practice yoga)— I've far more confidence and ability through a patience and practice I've learned from both studying and teaching film.

When we laugh raucously at Charlie Chaplin's antics in *Modern Times* (1936), I feel both pleasure and relief: *phew, he gets it, a gift, I can never give him more than this laughter*. Something about the laughter clinches his grip on the world in ways I cannot describe except to say that I feel teary and wistful to try. Witnessing and sharing his delight makes me fall in love even more, creates emotions in me that I've learned anew to articulate with Henry, thanks to what we've shared. In *Inside Out* (Pete Docter, 2015), eleven-year-old Riley attempts to run away from her family's new home; homesick and lonely, Riley returns to her parents, and—after a collective expression of feelings, conveying instead of masking sadness—they share a family hug. In the film's logic, a moment of sadness gains a brighter tint of joy; a more mature remembering happens, built not of one emotion but a hybrid of two. Watching *Inside Out* together affirms our status as family, as our sharing a film-invoked sadness yields a new form of joy, built of cinematic intimacy. Thanks to *Inside Out*, we have language and an image (the marbled "memory" ball of blue-yellow) to visualize this complexity.

Learning Care

Films open possibilities for not only my teaching Henry but also his caring for the world. Thanks to *Wall-E* (Andrew Stanton, 2008), Henry enjoys recycling, celebrates plant growth, feels concern for our warming planet, appreciates the pleasures of "earth." Thanks to *E.T.* (Steven Spielberg, 1982), he reads generously the strange and unfamiliar, imagines a shared vulnerability with that at which we look, uses *Inside Out*'s language to describe his rhapsodic happy-sad experience of the ending as he sorts through the film's climactic pain of a simultaneous farewell between friends and reunion with family (we all cry in this moment). Thanks to *Robin Hood* (Wolfgang Reitherman, 1973) and *City Lights* (Charlie Chaplin, 1931), he has visions of building a flourishing community through shared wealth (even if he might not use these terms). He asks about the young boys in *Annie*, those on the doorstep of the orphanage whom the camera pauses to notice, "What's going to happen to them?"; he talks about the kind eyes of the woman kneading dough in *Cameraperson* (Kirsten Johnson, 2016) and offers, "I want to see the person who is filming these people. What does she look like?"; he expresses concern that because Snow White had such fun with the dwarfs, "won't she be lonely in the castle?"; he knows that Miss Piggy and Kermit are falling in love because their clothes match; at a few months old, his infant eyebrows raised in accordance with *Vertigo*'s (Alfred Hitchcock, 1958) orchestral score, perfectly mapping the film through sensory stimuli alone. I proudly celebrate his attention to detail, his tenderness toward characters, his patience in enjoying these and innumerable other films; I'm conscious of swaying him accordingly. I unapologetically want his sense of the world to be inclusive, want him to be sensitive and open, curious and empathetic, humble and caring. I want his laughter to be abundant and warm, his delight in the world to be not at the expense of others but shared with them, a means of exercising care and not disgust or judgment.

Yet when Henry invites our mail carrier into our home, modeling Mister Rogers's warmth toward Mr. McFeely; when he hops onto a lamppost or cries out because *Singin' in the Rain*'s (Gene Kelly and Stanley Donen, 1952) Lina Lamott (Jean Hagen) receives a pie in the face; when he leaps up during joyful scenes (for example, *Tomboy*'s [Céline Sciamma, 2011] "Always," *Swing Time*'s [George Stevens, 1936] "Pick Yourself Up," *Trolls*'s [Mike Mitchell, 2016] "Can't Stop the Feeling," *Monsoon Wedding*'s [Mira Nair, 2001] "Aaj Mera Jee Kardaa," *It's a Wonderful Life*'s [Frank Capra, 1946] "Charleston," *Stormy Weather*'s [Andrew L. Stone, 1943] "Jumpin' Jive," *Take This Waltz*'s [Sarah Polley, 2011] "Video Killed the Radio Star") and asks to replay them (and dance) over and over; when he points to Dorothy's (Judy Garland) bedroom window and announces, "Look, she's watching a movie, like us"; when he laughs with his whole body at physical comedy—not just *Paddington* but *Modern Times, The Gold Rush* (Charlie Chaplin, 1925), *Home Alone* (Chris Columbus, 1990), *Chicken Run* (Nick Park and Peter Lord, 2000); when he asks me to read aloud all the end credits, asks what each title means, says that he wants to talk to these people, to thank them: in all these instances he's more the teacher of me than I of him, collaborating to make these films anew through our shared delight and concern.

You wondered how Mary Poppins (Julie Andrews) could sit on a cloud, asked about how to make a movie, and we demonstrated (lights, camera, action!) while you were the actor: a lilting downward gaze for sadness, your crunched-up nose for anger, your teeth and wide grin for happiness.

I'm now a new mother all over again, to the stunning and inimitable George Oliver, four years younger than Henry. In George's first week, I began describing to him the new rain outside our window. And, full of postpartum hormones that amplify real feelings, I wept with some kind of heartbreak that there weren't more ways of regarding phenomena in the world, the language derivative of my celebrating Henry's first rain, my initially spontaneous utterance with Henry now a script for motherhood that I was reading to George. In retrospect, I realize the exceeding privilege of such a plight, even as it registers the acute emotional strife of those fragile days following

George's birth. But I wanted to honor George in all his uniqueness, even as mothering him inevitably echoes my mothering of Henry, a startling vertigo as if I'm reliving my older son's infancy or imagining my younger son's preschool age. Yet I've also realized that mothering Henry involves its own kind of script, one learned from teaching. Screens offer a means by which to project and reconfigure our new familial dynamics.

In the weeks after George's birth, our family screened *Planet Earth II* (2016) together. The animal world's on-screen pressure—around which the documentary turns—to feed and protect newborn offspring felt both too familiar and validating of my own anxiety. I found comfort in the company of mothers of many species, laboring to keep their children alive. Helping my postpartum self to feel less alone and charging my four-year-old son with a surge of protectiveness, this documentary aligned us in our shared affinity for newborn animals. It's no coincidence that in the following weeks Henry expressed repeated disappointment that he can't birth a baby. The documentary preys upon and thus creates maternal anxiety. I'm rightly suspicious of this connection to a screen animal, am wary of and embarrassed by my identification via such phallocentric conventions (David Attenborough never appears but tells us what to see, as he spins the narrative and exacerbates drama). The film theorist in me knows how these genre-induced affinities work, grows uneasy with the anthropocentric taming of wildness within family narrative, and registers how we're succumbing to a form that prescribes our feelings. But my son and I pause repeatedly, cuddle, consider *how* the film tries to make us feel this way, talk through—in the language of *Peg + Cat* (2013–18)—a "really big problem!"; the screen helps us to appreciate our environment—maternal and cinematic, domestic and wild—built through cameras and screens, and further made through our talking together.

Like our beloved animals of the documentary, I'm a mother who cares for her young, yet I can do so without fear of predation, without hawks or bears threatening to make off with my children, without strangers breaking down my door to mate. The baby elephant (BBC's *Life* series, "Mammals" episode) walked miles on its first day, following the herd as her mother sought water to help her milk come in. I imagined their exhaustion, felt kinship, felt relieved that my work seemed easy by comparison.

Sharing these films with my family while caring for our youngest member makes it possible for us to see life cycles, to imagine companionable species, to gain a zoomed-out perspective on survival. Before and after

George's birth, Henry sang *The Lion King*'s (Rob Minkoff and Roger Allers, 1994) "Circle of Life" through the house and neighborhood. As George grew older, Henry would playact the scene, George as baby Simba, held up to the skies; Henry would invite us and all visitors to the house to don his makeshift costumes and carry stuffed animals for the ceremonial opening (I have taken comfort that Henry emphasizes the celebration of George as a "new king" instead of the movie's far darker strains of fratricide). Though it portrays generational passing, *The Lion King* hardly reflects a natural life cycle, entrenched as it is in human-imposed monarchy and marriage. Yet even to think about life cycles is, after all, to bear witness to a pattern that entails attention to fragility, mortality, and the existential drama that we all share.

I remember sitting in my own kindergarten classroom and watching our weekly Friday movie—this one a nature documentary about seals—and checking the time on my new wristwatch, with curiosity about what my mother was doing right then; that day when I came home from school, I learned that my grandfather had been rushed to the hospital with a heart attack that would prove fatal. I have always marked those days—my first encounter with the death of someone I loved—as framed by sitting in the dark, watching the seals, checking the time, wondering about my mother. I remember the death of shopkeeper Mr. Hooper (Will Lee) on *Sesame Street* in 1983, which prompted my panicked demand to my parents that we take a photo of the screen immediately, lest I never again see his image. I remember *The Electric Grandmother* (1982), in which a grandmother robot (Maureen Stapleton) survives a car accident at the film's end (she's a robot, thus only "broken" and not mortally wounded), prompting me to weep to my parents in preemptive mourning of their deaths (I was five). I think about those kindergarten seals, about Mr. Hooper and the "Electric Grandmother," about my affection for the slowness and patience with which Fred Rogers taught me to feed fish or witness crayon production, about innumerable other examples.

Keeping Watch

I see differently now. I am newly startled by *Battleship Potemkin*'s (Sergei Eisenstein, 1925) Odessa steps sequence—the shrillest and clearest image of mother love. And *Koko: A Talking Gorilla* (Barbet Schroeder, 1978) strikes me as revelatory, less for the fact that a gorilla speaks sign language and more for the picturing (even in its fraught ethics) of on-screen real-time long take unfolding of what it's like to care for another being, to continually revise one's intentions in accordance with that being's cooperation or lack thereof, to incorporate spontaneously that being's desires into one's own.

Though you technically knew that all that lives also dies, Coco *(Adrian Molina and Lee Unkrich, 2017) startled you, compelled us to talk again about death. How celebratory, then, the "day of the dead," you said, "but it's still sad that they can only return for one day."*

During Cinderella *(Kenneth Branagh, 2015), you felt upset at the mother's (Hayley Atwell) death. We paused to talk about it. You stopped weeping, softened your sniffling, caught your breath, as we reminded you that it's a pretend story and a real actress pretending to die. And we all pretended to die, showed how we could pretend and then jump right back up, and we did this repeatedly, until we were laughing.*

During the stage performance of the traveling Broadway Lion King, *you announced to me (and to all seated in our vicinity) after Scar killed Mufasa, "He's not really dead. He's just an actor, pretending to be dead. I hope that he didn't get hurt when he fell down."*

Acknowledging the great losses that accompany aging, operating with full knowledge that "we will lose everything we love in the end," *New Yorker* essayist Kathryn Schulz urges a privileging of finding over losing: "It is *finding* that is astonishing. . . . You have a thought and find the words. You face a crisis and find your courage. All of this is made more precious, not less, by impermanence. No matter what goes missing, the wallet or the father, the lessons are the same. Disappearance reminds us to notice, transience to cherish, fragility to defend. . . . We are here to keep watch, not to keep."[4] Simply writing about how I want to be a keeper of watch doesn't make me one; I've every day new reminders of its challenge. Yet Schulz's phrase gives me something to which to aspire, something I know I should be, or that the world forces regardless. In Adrienne Rich's words, "My heart is moved by all I cannot save."[5]

Both spectatorial and maternal, sharing films entwines my son's and my subjectivities—not because the mother is absorbed in or dissolved by motherhood, but because we're sharing the camaraderie of spectatorship in tandem with the self-making acts of dialogue and reflection. We together grow older and younger, imagine other kinds of embodiment, travel in time and space, appreciate the subjectivities of other species. According to Walter Benjamin, we age when we encounter traces of the other lives or destinies we haven't time or opportunity to live; and I think that movies offer a glimpse of these other lives, therein aging us while also slowing down and mixing up the birth-to-death trajectory of passing time.[6] Using the pause button to sustain a moment defies clock time and challenges conventional forms, as we make the films ours. And literally, too, when we snuggle together on the couch, my always-moving preschooler becomes more still, an existential pause button allowing me to register his growth: his newly broadened shoulders, for example, or his stronger hands. Sharing films allows me to hold more of Henry's ages, to hold more of the love I've felt in its different forms, to remember the versions of care and fear, hope and anxiety, I've known throughout his young life. Screens make strange, make nonlinear, make creative and generative—in ways beyond procreation—an otherwise telos-oriented way of writing personal, familial, and broader histories. As Varda suggests is possible, we see together—mindful of birth and death and celebratory of all the living in between. We keep watch, knowing what we know.

As a writer and teacher acutely inclined toward the phenomenological, I feel keen to loop Henry into these conversations, to encourage him toward becoming a subject who thinks himself always as relational, interested in and with space for reflection. Yet I'm also dramatizing how movies reproduce motherhood at its most conventional, a screen that projects and reflects some family of my dreams, a romantic site of domestic togetherness built of the fantasies we've consumed from the movies themselves. This essay, even in its efforts to individuate our experience, seems dully to celebrate the unremarkable fact that films can reinforce and make a family, how films yield both pleasure and pedagogy, how we're always student and teacher, child and adult, in ways that shift and turn. In Henry's and my reenactment of *The Sound of Music*'s (Robert Wise, 1965) "The Lonely Goatherd," for example, how are we not epitomizing the ways that movies teach us how to play, to reinforce status quo, to project ideological norms, to become the very historical subject that the screen seeks to create? If films inspire our imagination, then so too do they establish the parameters *for* our imagination, shape what we can dream and become, tell us what to do and how to be, give us scripts by which we can discuss life and death, alterity and empathy, history and futures.

Yet it's precisely the *talking* about films, the attention to production, the thoughtfulness about who makes what and for whom, that I hope will help Henry (and later George) to understand these screened worlds not as natural but made, as yielding attention and care but not replacing or supplanting the world. In the spirit of Laura Mulvey's "Visual Pleasure and Narrative Cinema," our talking together about films relocates pleasure in revealing the construction, exchanging conventional modes of looking for a new lineage of care.[7] We love *Mary Poppins* (Robert Stevenson, 1964) all the more after we let ourselves imagine the production of the clouds, after all; each time *The Sound of Music* opens, Henry celebrates both the landscape *and* the helicopter shot. Just as films can both delimit and inspire our imagination, so might we say the same about mothering, after all, or about caregiving more broadly: the recipients, beneficiaries of time and attention yet unwittingly at the mercy of the caregiver.

In this way, caregiving becomes a way of teaching, engendering students who themselves become teachers, a dialectic that moves us through generations and histories. Further, films can teach us how to see them, and people can teach us how to love them.[8] As Henry becomes a brother, I behold how he watches George, assesses his audience, and modulates his language in accordance with what he imagines George to comprehend. When George cries, he soothes him: "Don't worry, George, it's me, Henry, it's your big brother! You're not alone." Henry tries to facilitate a seeing-together, in Varda's sense, a friend-making intimacy through shared perception. Henry teaches George not yet about movies but about things in the world: Q-tips, pencil sharpeners, a stuffed toy dolphin, Sophie the Giraffe, *Dr. Seuss's ABC's*, sweet potatoes. Having learned that babies learn through eye contact, Henry has worked to master the art: "I'm making eye contact, Mommy! George, look, we're making eye contact, what are you learning? George is loving me with his eyes; he's throwing so much love at me; he's making eye contact!" Through teaching about phenomena, Henry finds his own way of being a brother, developing a voice both his own and one that bears traces of how he's been loved. He names, feels, and exercises a benevolent perception, a loving pedagogy: he tells George what to see, wonders about what George learns, incites George's wonderment and discovery, marvels as their relationship becomes more dynamic.

At the end of many films, you leap up as if it's your duty: hands on hips, you dance and strut around the living room, climb on chairs, in a kind of physical celebration of what you've just beheld, the film charging you with an energy that invigorates your limbs, moves through your body, through the house. Leaving the movie theater—or simply ending a film in our living room—is, for you, kinetic, a way of carrying out and carrying on the film, infusing you with a new vigor, as if you're tagging in to a ring not of fighting but of living vigorously.

Finding

I'm writing this account while on maternity leave with George, and this memory-work enmeshes Henry's growth and George's infancy. Roland Barthes calls photographs a "counter-memory," blocking more than giving rise to remembrance.[9] Even as my mothering George recalls my experiences with baby Henry, it also effaces the singularity or precision of those years—my arms conforming to George's body, or George's growing into Henry's old clothes—in ways that blur and forget exactly how it was with Henry. I'm remembering Henry's early years while I'm experiencing George's, variations on beholding that help me to keep finding. Henry recently called me a "good finder" after we held a relievedly-successful "finding party" for his little orange forklift. Would that it were always so easy.

I have approached this essay as if a record of conversations and impressions of my son's growth, a fossil made by what films *meant* to him at a given time, a catalogue of what we've together found. In all of this, I have wanted to add more details, as if somehow the fuller portrait would make it truer, would make me a better mother, a more vigilant keeper of watch. I have wanted to quote from more essays and books to honor ideas that enrich my perception. Yet such a bursting-full account—I try to assuage my concerns—betrays a desire to cling more than behold. Henry once asked me to "catch," with my camera, his playing. Less possessive than "capture," more temporary than "keep," "catch" implies a reciprocity of receiving and giving back, an arc of coming toward and moving away. It lends a structure to this writing as well, moved as I am to make a form that honors the fragile and fleeting—youth, cinema, ephemera—as something to be loved through attention.

This essay also becomes my way of beholding Henry's own subjectivity, his own coming into being. I register how he's caring for me, making his own memories, developing an interiority not because his mother chronicled his impressions but because experiences marked his senses. For me—for any mother—to "keep watch" and not futilely try to keep, I have to learn to watch my child become someone who can keep watch on his own. How I love the shared watching; how I cherish the talking together, the reenacting, the dancing, and even the crying that we do; but mothering also means watching him go. Though my nearing-five-year-old isn't exactly leaving home soon, his memory and emotions increasingly shape instead of are shaped by mine: a gift, marvel, miracle, and delight, the way it should be. In Sarah Manguso's words, "I'm watching my little son change . . . from day to day and minute to minute. Watching him learn things is like watching a machine become intelligent, or an animal become a different animal. It's terrifying and beautiful, and this has all been said before."[10] As Henry and I have learned together, there's no place like home; home is where you want to leave and return; emotions are never just one thing. Sharing films shapes how we move through the world: attentive to the fragile yet courageous all the while; ever contingent, ever beholden, ever keeping watch, ever delighting, ever bearing witness, ever prepared to leap from the couch in a dance, or to sit together in tears because it's hard.

Somewhere and somehow my children have grown. I see the shape of these changes, though the changing itself exceeds my perception. I feel sometimes overwhelmed at the keeping watch, as I photograph and write and make albums as a way of loving these boys better, so it would seem. I try futilely every day to name and show and give the force of this love.

And I'm unsure of the difference between—am myself regularly confusing—the keeping with the keeping watch. Yet it's also very simple, what I want to say: that I have an affinity for studying film because it lends a structure to what we lose and keep; that sharing films with my son helps me not only to feel more comfortable as a mother but also to buoy my sensitivity—supercharged in the experience of mothering—to the ephemeral; that all of this becomes a case study in Schulz's elegiac paean to the virtues of finding: finding myself a mother, overwhelmed and bewildered in perpetual astonishment and sometimes exhaustion at this new responsibility and privilege; finding ways to make my education and profession have newfound urgency; finding a form to anchor my son's first four years, as they disappear to memory, and a shape for how I'll keep learning from and with both of my children. I write to reconcile the unproductive and tiresome age-old binary that pits family and home against work and profession. I write from a position of both confidence and insecurity, wanting to share what I've experienced as if—here, in writing—to make it more true and permanent. I write for validation during this volatile time in which I've felt equal parts more inadequate and sure than ever I have in my life. Because writing about what I can't keep is also a way of keeping. I write because I love fiercely this time, and I don't trust our memories to hold onto this ritual that we've shared, and I want to keep it, not as something that stagnates or doesn't change, but as an index to what I've held, a marker for what we've seen, a gift for who I love.

At the film's end, your little lips turn down, your eyes well with tears, as it seems that Eva's lost Wall-E. Eva looks into Wall-E's face but he shows no recognition. You climb into my lap, hold my face and hands, whisper softly and breathlessly, "Mommy, this is so sad," and you answer me, nodding, when I ask, "Do you remember what happens?" but you insist, "I remember what happens but right now it's too sad because she loves him but he can't see her." And then Wall-E remembers with his "hands," and I think about Vivian Sobchack's "What My Fingers Knew," how this robotic yet tactile knowing ushers in the happy ending.[11] *And we describe—a chorus of all that's good—the change, the memory, the "camera" that soars over the newly leafing Earth, the friends together again and life restored to the planet. You whisper again, breathlessly, evoking your prior sadness but with a desperate relief, "And they will stay together forever and the friends will never be apart, Wall-E and Eva will never again be apart because now they're together." I nod and smile and realize that you will someday have to bear loss that's not restored, but may you find—oh, may you find, always—something to keep. May you keep finding. May we all.*

Acknowledgments

Special thanks to Rashna Wadia Richards and Robin Clarke, not only for feedback on this essay but also for the friendship that makes possible my voice here (and so much more). I write also in memory of Agnès Varda (May 30, 1928–March 29, 2019), who passed away as I was making my final edits. Her death makes all the more urgent the meaning I try to find here. I dedicate this essay to George Oliver Barr, in his becoming, for all he's yet to see, and for all we've yet to find together.

Notes

1 Maggie Nelson, *The Argonauts* (Minneapolis: Graywolf, 2015), 37.
2 Christian Keathley, *Cinephilia and History; or, The Wind in the Trees* (Bloomington: Indiana University Press, 2005); Jean Epstein, "The Slow

Motion of Sound," trans. Franck Le Gac, in *Jean Epstein: Critical Essays and New Translations*, ed. Sarah Keller and Jason N. Paul (Amsterdam: Amsterdam University Press, 2012), 382.

3 "Teaching Film Nonfictionally: The Reciprocity of Pedagogy, Cinephilia, and Maternity," in *For the Love of Cinema: Teaching Our Passion in and outside the Classroom*, ed. Rashna Wadia Richards and David T. Johnson (Bloomington: Indiana University Press, 2017), 125–42.

4 Kathryn Schulz, "When Things Go Missing," *New Yorker*, February 13 and February 20, 2017, www.newyorker.com/magazine/2017/02/13/when-things-go-missing.

5 Adrienne Rich, "Natural Resources," in *Dream of a Common Language* (New York: Norton, 1978), 67.

6 Walter Benjamin, "The Image of Proust," in *Illuminations*, trans. Harry Zohn, ed. Hannah Arendt (New York: Schocken Books, 1968), 201–16.

7 Laura Mulvey, "Visual Pleasure and Narrative Cinema," *Screen* 3 (1975): 6–18.

8 Stanley Cavell, *Pursuits of Happiness: The Hollywood Comedy of Remarriage* (CambriAdge, M: Harvard University Press, 1981), 131.

9 Roland Barthes, *Camera Lucida*, trans. Richard Howard (New York: Hill & Wang, 1980), 91.

10 Sarah Manguso, *Ongoingness: The End of a Diary* (Minneapolis: Graywolf, 2015), 70.

11 Vivian Sobchack, "What My Fingers Knew: The Cinesthetic Subject, or Vision in the Flesh," *Senses of Cinema* 5 (2000), sensesofcinema.com/2000/conference-special-effects-special-affects/fingers/.

Contributors

Susan Berridge is lecturer in film and media at the University of Stirling. Her research has explored the gendered impact of caring responsibilities on experiences of working in film and television. She has published on this theme in *Feminist Media Studies* and the *European Journal of Cultural Studies*. Previous research has explored representations of gender, age, sexuality, and sexual violence in teen film and television, and in popular culture more widely. She is currently working on a project on intimacy coordination and cultures of consent in the television industry.

Maria Cabrera is a film programmer and doula-in-training dedicated to celebrating the stories of Black and Latin American people, using film as a tool for creating spaces of discussion and unearthing personal identities and histories. Maria is the co-founder of Reel Good Film Club (no longer active), has coordinated programming and filmmaking initiatives with the Barbican, Creative Skillset, and LAWRS, and has delivered talks and hosted discussions at the Whitechapel Gallery, the British Film Institute, Queen Mary University, and ICA London.

Elinor Cleghorn has a background in feminist visual culture and history, and her critical writing has been published in several academic journals, including *Screen*. After receiving her PhD in in 2012, Elinor spent three years as a postdoctoral researcher at the Ruskin School, University of Oxford, working on an interdisciplinary medical humanities project. She has given talks and lectures at the British Film Institute, where she has been a regular contributor to the education program, Tate Modern, and ICA London, and she has appeared on the BBC Radio 4 discussion show *The Forum*. In 2017, she was short-listed for the Fitzcarraldo Editions essay prize. She now works as a freelance writer and researcher, and lives in Sussex. Her first book, *Unwell Women: A Journey through Medicine and Myth in a Man-Made World*, was published by W&N (United Kingdom) and Dutton (United States) in 2021.

Corinn Columpar is associate professor of cinema studies at the University of Toronto. She is the author of *Unsettling Sights: The Fourth World on Film* (Southern Illinois University Press, 2010) and co-editor, with So Mayer, of *There She Goes: Feminist Filmmaking and Beyond* (Wayne State University Press, 2009). Additionally, she has published articles in numerous journals, such as *Camera Obscura*, *Quarterly Review of Film and Video*, and *Women Studies Quarterly*, and many anthologies, including *Indie Reframed: Women's Filmmaking and Contemporary American Independent Cinema* (Edinburgh University Press, 2016), edited by Linda Badley, Claire Perkins, and Michelle Schreiber, and *A Companion to Australian Cinema* (Wiley Blackwell, 2019), edited by Felicity Collins, Jane Landman, and Susan Bye.

Kristy Guevara-Flanagan is an associate professor at UCLA's School of Theater, Film, and Television, where she heads the MFA Directing Documentary concentration. She has been making documentary and experimental films that focus on gender, death, and the Latinx community for nearly two decades. Kristy's work has been screened at the Sundance, Tribeca, SXSW, and Rotterdam film festivals as well as the Getty and Los Angeles County Museums. These films can be seen online at the *New Yorker* and *Kanopy* and have been broadcast on PBS's Independent Lens and the Sundance Channel. Many of her films are currently in distribution with Women Make Movies. She lives in Los Angeles with her daughter, pup, and two stray kitties. You can learn more at www.chuparosafilms.com/.

Alice Haylett Bryan is a visiting researcher in film studies at King's College London. Her publications include "Inhospitable Landscapes: Contemporary French Horror Cinema, Immigration and Identity," in *French Screen Studies* 21, no. 3 (2021), "'I Only Like Seeing Myself in Small Bits': Catherine Breillat's Reflections of the Female Body" *Cine-Excess*, no. 2 (2016), and "Surgery, Blood and Patriarchal Sex: Excision and *American Mary*," in *Transgression in Anglo-American Cinema: Gender, Sex and the Deviant Body*, edited by Joel Robert Gwynne (Columbia University Press, 2016). She is currently writing a monograph on the womb phantasy in international horror cinema.

Jules Arita Koostachin was raised by her Cree-speaking grandparents in northern Ontario, and she is a band member of Attawapiskat First Nation. She completed her PhD at the University of British Columbia with a focus on Indigenous documentary. In 2010, she completed her master's degree at Ryerson University in documentary media, winning the Award of Distinction and Graduate Ryerson Gold Medal. Among her productions are the documentary films *Remembering Inninimowin* (2010) and *KaYaMenTa* (2020), and the television series *AskiBOYZ* (2016). In 2018, her poetry book *Unearthing Secrets, Gathering Truths* was published by Kegedonce Press, and she is currently writing her first novel, *Moccasin Souls*. Jules's feature script *Broken Angel* was selected for Women in the Director's Chair, the TIFF Filmmaker Lab (2018), and the Whistler Screenwriters Lab (2019). Jules has extensive knowledge of working in the Indigenous community and these experiences continue to feed her arts practice.

Irene Lusztig is a feminist filmmaker, visual artist, archival researcher, and mother. Often beginning with rigorous research in archives, her work brings historical materials into conversation with the present day, inviting viewers to contemplate questions of politics, ideology, and the production of personal, collective, and national memories. Much of her work is centered on public feminism, language, and histories of women and women's bodies, including her debut feature *Reconstruction* (2001), the feature-length archival film essay *The Motherhood Archives* (2013), the ongoing web-based *Worry Box Project* (2011), and the performative documentary feature *Yours in Sisterhood* (2018). She teaches filmmaking at the University of California, Santa Cruz, where she is professor of film and digital media.

So Mayer is a writer, film curator, and activist. Their books include *The Cinema of Sally Potter: A Politics of Love* (Wallflower, 2009), *Political Animals: The New Feminist Cinema* (I. B. Tauris, 2015), and *A Nazi Word for a Nazi Thing* (Peninsula, 2020); their BFI Film Classics on *Orlando* is forthcoming in 2023. So is the co-editor (with Corinn Columpar) of *There She Goes: Feminist Filmmaking and Beyond* (Wayne State University Press, 2009) and (with Elena Oroz) *Lo personal es politico: Feminismo y documental* (INAAC, 2011). They are a member of the queer feminist film curation collective Club Des Femmes, sharing feminist film and discourse around the United Kingdom and beyond; a co-founder of Raising Films, a campaign and community for parents and carers in the film and TV industry; a board member of LUX, the artists' film organization; and a regular contributor to *Sight & Sound*, *Film Quarterly*, *Literal*, BFI DVD, and Criterion.

Kristi McKim is professor of English/film and media studies at Hendrix College, where she was honored as the 2014–15 United Methodist Exemplary Professor, nominated for the CASE U.S. Professors of the Year Award, and recognized with the 2019–20 Carole Herrick Award for Excellence in Advising. Online editor of *Film Matters*, she has published the books *Love in the Time of Cinema* (Palgrave Macmillan, 2011) and *Cinema as Weather: Stylistic Screens and Atmospheric Change* (Routledge, 2013), and is writing a forthcoming BFI Film Classic that approaches *Rushmore* through a phenomenological, ecocritical, and feminist framework. Her published essays range from scholarly to personal in journals such as *ISLE* (forthcoming), *Camera Obscura*, *Studies in French Cinema*, *Senses of Cinema*, *Bennington Review*, *New England Review*, *Bright Lights Film Journal*, and the collection *For the Love of Cinema* (Indiana University Press, 2017), edited by Rashna Wadia Richards and David T. Johnson.

Missy Molloy is senior lecturer in the film program at Victoria University of Wellington in New Zealand. She is co-editor of *ReFocus: The Films of Susanne Bier* (Edinburgh University Press, 2018) and co-author of *Screening the Posthuman* (forthcoming from Oxford University Press), and her work has featured in journals, including *Jump Cut: A Review of Contemporary Media*, *Studies in Spanish & Latin American Cinemas*, and *Journal of Popular Television*. Her current research focuses on women's, alternative, and activist cinemas.

Tessa Ashlin Nunn received a PhD in romance studies from Duke University. Her publications include include "The Screaming Mother and Silent Maid in Ousmane Sembene's *La noire de . . .*," in *Women in French Studies* (2019), "Meghan Markle's Healthy Lifestyle in the Media: Multiracial Exceptionalism and the Cult of Slimness," in *Women's Studies International Forum* (2021), "Music Video Images of Ballet," in *Race/Gender/Class/Media 4.0* (Routledge, 2019), "The Collector as Flâneur in Georges Rodenbach's Bruges-la-Morte," in *New Directions in Flânerie: Redefining Genius, Geography, Gender, and Genre*, edited by Marylaura Papalas and Kelly Comfort

(Routledge, forthcoming), "Hailing Divine Women in Godard's *Hail Mary* and Miéville's *The Book of Mary*," in *A Sharing of Speech: Works on or Inspired by the Work of Luce Irigaray*, edited by Ruthanne Crapo, Yvette Russel, and Brenda Sharp (State University of New York Press, forthcoming), and "Vivre dans un corps féminin: La lutte contre la violence et pour la liberté," in *La France contemporaine: Unité et diversités, polarisation et solidarités*, edited by Michel Gueldry and Armelle Crouzières-Ingenthron (French Review Book Series, 2020). She teaches in Lyon, France.

Claire Perkins is head of film and screen studies at Monash University, Melbourne. She researches primarily on independent and indie media culture and contemporary "quality" television, with a focus on the gendered discourses of each. She is the author of *American Smart Cinema* (Edinburgh University Press, 2012) and co-editor of six collections, including *Independent Women: From Film to Television* (Routledge, 2021), *Indie Reframed: Women's Filmmaking and Contemporary American Independent Cinema* (Edinburgh University Press, 2016), *Transnational Television Remakes* (Routledge, 2016), and *US Independent Film After 1989: Possible Films* (Edinburgh University Press, 2015). Her writing has also appeared in journals, including *Feminist Media Studies, Camera Obscura, Continuum: Journal of Media and Cultural Studies*, the *Velvet Light Trap*, *Celebrity Studies*, and *Critical Studies in Television*.

Raising Films Research Collective comprises Herval Almenoar-Webster, Mounira Almenoar, Tamsyn Dent, Cat Forward, Laura Giles, So Mayer, and Sarah Louise Smyth, who collaborated variously on Raising Films UK's three reports from 2015 to 2019. Special mention goes to lead researcher and writer Dr. Tamsyn Dent, currently a postdoctoral fellow in the Department for Culture, Media and Creative Industries (CMCI) at King's College London. She is currently working on a European Commission-funded project titled "Developing Inclusive and Sustainable Creative Economies" (DISCE). Her research interests are in the cultures, structures, and spaces that inform creative practice, with a particular interest in systemic inequalities. She is a fellow of the Higher Education Authority and has held previous teaching roles at Bournemouth University and Oxford Brookes University. Tamsyn has provided consultancy for a number of European and British organizations, including B&S Europe, Birds Eye View, Screen Skills (formerly

Creative Skillset), Women in Film and TV, Raising Films, and The Offsite, and has recently collaborated on a research report for the British Government's All Party Parliamentary Group (APPG) on creative diversity.

Elissa Rashkin is a research professor in cultural and communication studies at the Universidad Veracruzana, Mexico. She is author of the books *Women Filmmakers in Mexico: The Country of Which We Dream* (University of Texas Press, 2001) and *The Stridentist Movement in Mexico: The Avant-Garde and Cultural Change in the 1920s* (Lexington Books, 2009), as well as other books and articles on Mexican and international film, photography, literature, and cultural history. She is currently writing a biography of the early U.S. birth control activist and filmmaker Juliet Barrett Rublee.

Rashna Wadia Richards is dean of faculty reviews and assessment and professor of media studies at Rhodes College. Her first book, *Cinematic Flashes: Cinephilia and Classical Hollywood* (Indiana University Press, 2013), offers a cinephiliac history of the studio system. Her second book, a co-edited collection titled *For the Love of Cinema: Teaching Our Passion in and outside the Classroom* (Indiana University Press, 2017), explores the role of love, of cinema, and of cinema studies in teaching film. Her most recent monograph, *Cinematic TV: Serial Drama Goes to the Movies* (Oxford University Press, 2021), explores how contemporary serial dramas copy, quote, and appropriate American cinema.

Sara Saljoughi is assistant professor of English and cinema studies at the University of Toronto. She is co-editor of the volume *1968 and Global Cinema* (Wayne State University Press, 2018) and a co-editor of the journal *Discourse*. Her essays have appeared in *Camera Obscura*, *Feminist Media Histories*, *Iranian Studies*, *Film International*, *Jadaliyya*, *Film Criticism*, and *Iran Namag*. She is currently writing a book on the aesthetics and politics of Iranian art cinema during the 1960s and 1970s.

Index

CPSIA information can be obtained
at www.ICGtesting.com
Printed in the USA
JSHW030848200222
23057JS00005B/19